Women's Education in the Third World: Comparative Perspectives

Women's Education in the Third World
Comparative Perspectives

Edited by
Gail P. Kelly
State University of New York at Buffalo
and
Carolyn M. Elliott
Ford Foundation, New Delhi

State University of New York Press
Albany

Published by State University of New York Press, Albany

© 1982 State University of New York

For information, address State University of New York Press, State University Plaza, Albany, N.Y., 12246

Library of Congress Cataloging in Publication Data

Main entry under title:
Women's education in the Third World

    Bibliography: p. 345
    Includes index.
    1. Underdeveloped areas—Education—Addresses, essays, lectures. 2. Education of women—Addresses, essays, lectures. I. Kelly, Gail Paradise. II. Elliott, Carolyn M.
LC 2607.W65   370'.9172'4   82-789
ISBN 0-87395-619-2   AACR2
ISBN 0-87395-620-6 (pbk.)

Cover photo courtesy Conservative Baptist Foreign Mission Society

Contents

Acknowledgments

This volume would not have come into being without the encouragement and support of the Ford Foundation and the *Comparative Education Review*. Four essays in this volume — Mary Jean Bowman and C. Arnold Anderson's "The Participation of Women in Education in the Third World;" Jeremy Finn, Janet Reis, and Loretta Dulberg's "Sex Differences in Educational Attainment: The Process"; Rati Ram's "Sex Differences in the Labor Market Outcomes of Education"; and Robert A. LeVine's "Influences of Women's Schooling on Maternal Behavior in the Third World" — were commissioned by the Ford Foundation and presented at a foundation conference in the winter of 1979. Elinor Barber of the Ford Foundation played a major role in shaping these papers and making funding available to the *Comparative Education Review* to publish a special issue in June 1980 on the education of women in the Third World. The present volume added to the foundation-initiated papers a number of empirical case studies selected after the Ford meeting, in partial response to the issues identified there. Most of the following articles were written independently of the Ford Foundation and several did not appear in the *Comparative Education Review* special issue of June 1980. While the Ford Foundation exercised no control in the selection of chapters for this book, most would not have been generated had it not been for the foundation's support for the special issue of the journal.

We wish to thank a number of individuals — Robert Arnove, Ximena Bunster, Remi Clignet, Susan Cochrane, Julie DaVanzo, Erwin Epstein, Robert Evenson, Samira Harfoush, Kathleen Howard-Merriam, Robert Klitgaard, Thomas LaBelle, Karen Leonerd, Kristin Mann, Vandra Masemann, Barbara Metcalf, Hanna Papanek, Helen I. Safa, Joseph Szyliowicz, Lois Weis, Ann Williams, and Matthew Zachariah for their comments on earlier drafts of various chapters.

Finally, we wish to acknowledge the support and encouragement of Philip Altbach, Editor of the *Comparative Education Review*, at all stages in the preparation of this book.

Carolyn M. Elliott
Ford Foundation, New Delhi, India

Gail P. Kelly
State University of New York at Buffalo

1. Orientations Toward the Study of Women's Education in the Third World

GAIL P. KELLY AND CAROLYN M. ELLIOTT

The number of women being educated in the Third World nations of Africa, Asia, Latin America, and the Middle East and the amount of education women receive have both expanded markedly since the 1960s. Female enrollment in primary school has more than doubled, and at the secondary and tertiary levels the increases have been as dramatic.[1] Despite these gains, women remain under-represented at all levels of education relative to men. Fewer females than males enter educational programs, be they formal or nonformal; fewer receive technical and vocational training; and women account for a very small proportion of enrollment in postsecondary education.

The undereducation of women—its causes, the changes in female education patterns, and their significance both to societies and to women's lives—is the focus of this volume. Our goal is to stimulate further scholarship on the education of women in the Third World and develop research that will serve as a basis for educational reform to enhance women's participation in schooling, improve women's lives, and ultimately promote social well-being. The underlying premises of this book are that women ought to be educated, that education can have beneficial effects on women, and that the current pattern of female undereducation in the Third World can and should be changed.

The study of women's education is our major concern and we take it very seriously. The past decade has witnessed a proliferation of excellent research studies on very important topics concerning women—their roles and relative status, their participation in the work force and in politics, their contribution to economic development, and so forth. This scholarship is rich and highly relevant for understanding the significance of education to women's lives. However, most of it does not directly consider education. We learn little from this body of knowledge about why women attend school, what they learn in school, how education affects them, or whether education makes a contribution to improving their lives apart from class, ethnicity, and other social background factors. These are among the issues that we hope to illuminate in the following pages.

There is a considerable research literature on the education of women in Western industrialized societies. Most studies have focused on women's education in the United States and Canada, but there is a

[1] Isabelle Deblé, *The School Education of Girls* (Paris: UNESCO, 1981).

1

growing body of scholarship on Britain, Australia, the Soviet Union, and Western Europe. This literature identifies a number of trends that provide a useful basis for asking questions about educational patterns in the Third World. Such studies can only be suggestive for Africa, Asia, Latin America, and the Middle East since cultural values, family structures, sex-role divisions of labor in the family, economies, and so forth differ so markedly in the Third World. These differences distinguish Third World countries from one another as much as they distinguish them from Western nations. Therefore, we have chosen to concentrate this book on studies of the Third World. We present research that is sensitive to the cultural/historical context of each society and provides sufficient information to enable comparisons among countries.

We have decided to concentrate on the Third World despite an all too vivid sense of the problems of women's education in the United States. We have both taught in American colleges and universities and participate actively in efforts to remedy the discrimination and sexism that pervade American education. Our decision to focus on the Third World arises, not from a sense that our own house is in order, but from our desire to learn about Third World countries without making assumptions about the relevance of American problems to these societies.

Our claims for this book are both modest and very ambitious. We are modest about how much knowledge we are able to provide about women's education and its significance. There is a host of questions for which we have data on one country at best, and many on which no research has been conducted. Much of the research that does exist follows models established in the United States and may be inappropriate for studies of women's education in other cultures. Studies of career aspirations, for example, cannot use occupational status scales developed in the United States. Nor can studies of linkages between education and women's labor force participation rest on the assumption that paid work is a nontraditional activity for women.

An important theme throughout these essays is how research on women differs from research on men. Understanding the patterns of women's education requires more than simply re-analyzing old data to detect sex differences along the standard dimensions of analysis. It requires asking new questions that are generated by looking at the world from the perspective of women's lives. Research on the outcomes of women's education, for example, cannot be allowed to conclude that, because educated women respond to the labor force in ways different from men (labor force participation for women does not always rise as a result of education as it does for men), education has little or no effect on women. Nor is attention to the impact of education on the private sphere of marriage, reproduction, and child rearing sufficient. This is to assume a bifurcation between private and public spheres that does not adequately describe most women's lives in the Third World, or elsewhere. What is needed is study of the ways in which private and public spheres interact and how education mediates this interaction. The following chapters attempt to show the fruitfulness of such a perspective for studying women.

Perspectives on the Study of Women's Education in the Third World

A volume on women's education in the Third World might address many questions. One might, for example, structure a volume around the question of whether education functions in the same way for women as for men, focusing exclusively on female educational achievement and attainment and the social, political, and economic outcomes of schooling for women relative to men. Or, we could ask whether expanding female educational opportunity and the years of schooling women receive contributes to national development in the same way as has been presumed to be the case with men. We do not deny the importance of these questions. However, we have chosen not to focus exclusively on them for several reasons.

First, the answer to such questions are self-evident. Past research on women's education in the Third World, sparse as it is, has demonstrated that education does not have the same social and economic outcomes for women as it has for men. Nor does schooling have the same relationship to women's work force participation and status as it has for men;[2] the individual rates of return for women's investment in education are lower, although there is substantial variance both within and among Third World nations.[3] In short, to focus this volume on whether education has the same social and economic outcomes for males and females would be tantamount to asking old questions and would not significantly advance our knowledge of the meaning of women's education.

Much previous research on women's education and its outcomes has ignored sex-gender systems that limit women to narrowly defined roles, consigning them to political and economic inferiority. Such studies have merely charted the differences in educational outcomes for men and women; they have been at a loss to explain whether these differences are socially generated, and if so how. They assume that the dif-

---

[2] See, for example, Audrey Chapman Smock, *Women's Education in Developing Countries: Opportunities and Outcomes* (New York: Praeger, 1981); Guy Standing and Glen Sheehan, eds., *Labor Force Participation in Low-Income Countries* (Geneva: International Labor Organization, 1978).

[3] Maureen Woodhall, "Investment in Women: A Reappraisal of the Concept of Human Capital," *International Review of Education* 19, no. 1 (1973): 9–29.

ferences are natured and immutable, and that schooling has little power to change them. Scholarship of this sort can provide little basis for reforming schools; nor can it tell us what impact education has on women, even if that impact is different from that on men.

In this volume we take the perspective that the social and economic outcomes of women's education are shaped by sex-gender systems that place women in subordination to men. These systems influence the very ability of women to obtain an education as well as the type of education schools distribute to women who attend. We ask how schools contribute to sex-gender systems either by denial of access to schools or by the kind of education provided to women who attend. The extent to which education equal in quality, quantity, and content is made available to males and females, and whether policies are enforced to ensure that women who receive education can use it, may well predict whether the educational, social, and economic outcomes of schooling will be the same for females as for males. Research has shown that few, if any, nations have done more than attempt to provide more access to schools for girls. No country has dealt adequately with the quality of education girls receive, the content of that education, or the structural barriers to women's full participation in social and economic life.[4] Rather than ask whether education has the same outcomes for males and females, therefore, in this volume we ask how different provisions for schooling in Third World nations either reduce or exacerbate the unequal outcomes previous research has detected. Our goal in so doing is to provide policy guidelines for reform.

We do not presume that girls who are educated accept passively the roles to which such institutions as schools assign them. Quite the opposite, we take the stance that women respond to institutions in ways that meet the needs women perceive, given the circumstances of their daily lives. This is so in the Third World as well as in all societies. Whether women will receive education may well depend on a host of factors other than the availability of educational opportunity. Women's education is also affected by whether girls and their families believe schools will better their lives, regardless of the complicity of schools in maintaining women in subservience to men. How ethnicity, social class, and rural/urban factors interact to predict females' responses to schooling—either in the form of their school attendance, their retention rates in school, their acceptance of school-legitimated knowledge, or the uses to which women who get an education put their schooling, both as a result of, and despite, sex-gender systems—is a concern of this volume.

In order to understand how education affects women, one must

[4] Deblé.

begin with women's day-to-day realities and the ways in which education changes women's lives as mothers, wives, citizens, and workers. The nature of these roles varies considerably in the Third World, adding complexity to questions about the impact of schooling. Nonetheless, we need to ask whether education changes women's lives for the better despite sex-gender systems that oppress them. Does education, for example, give women greater control within the household? Does it have any effect on their role as mothers? Does education enable women to widen their roles beyond the household, mitigating the impact of marriage, childbearing, and child rearing on women's participation and status in social, economic, and political life? To what extent does education's effect on the conditions of women's lives vary among and between Third World nations, and why? If we begin with women, in short, we can better understand what schooling does and does not do for women and how schools might be reformed to meet women's needs.

The perspective of this book, in sum, is to ask how education affects women and can be made to improve women's lives, recognizing that schooling throughout the Third World functions in the context of social systems that oppress women. We maintain that schools need not merely reflect or reinforce such systems, as they do today, but rather that schools can be made into instruments to transform those very systems. The task of transformation is one for educational and social policy makers. It extends beyond providing the opportunity to be schooled to the provision of equal quality, quantity, and content of education, and to the development of conditions that will allow women to use education to improve their lot.

The Organization of this Book

We have organized this book around sets of closely related issues. We begin with a discussion of factors that affect women's access to education. While admitedly women's access to education, like that of males, relates to socioeconomic background, ethnicity, and urban versus rural locale, there are distinctive factors that predict whether women will or will not attend school. Identifying them is no easy task, and the chapters in Part I of this volume underscore their complexity. These ask whether in countries that practice sex-seclusion there are substantially lower female educational enrollments than in countries in which such practices are nonexistent. They also inquire whether the level of a nation's economic development predicts female educational enrollments, or whether other factors are more significant. Those factors explored are the nature of and consistency of government policies directed at encouraging female enrollments, the types of schools made available to women — and their quality and status within the educational system relative to the schools males attend, and the articulation between schools girls attend and the job market. In short, in Part I we ask how ethnicity, class, the sex-role division of labor within the family and society, and educational policy and school availability affect women's access to education and their survival rates in school.

Part II focuses on the kind of education girls receive, once in school. The chapters do not presume the school as the proverbial "black box," but rather analyze sex differentiation in the formal and hidden curriculums of the schools, which too often have been presumed to be gender-neutral institutions. The essays in Part II ask: To what extent do schools encourage girls to succeed in their academic life? Do they prepare girls the same way as they do boys for society, once schooling is completed? Does sex differentiation in the content of schooling vary significantly across Third World countries, and do these practices shape the educational and social outcomes of schooling for girls? In short, in Part II we ask how meaningful equality in access to education between the sexes can be without changes in the content of education, the ways in which that content is transmitted and the structure of everyday life in the schools.

In Parts III and IV, our focus is on the outcomes of female education. We ask whether education enables women to mediate the impact of the family on their economic and social roles, and whether education substantially affects women's lives in the family. Part III focuses on the work force, Part IV on women as mothers. While the research presented in these two sections by no means provides definitive answers, these sections do suggest quite clearly the fruitfulness of studying the educational outcomes of women's schooling from a perspective centric to the female, rather than the male, in the context of male-dominated societies.

Limitations

While the research brought together here comes as close as possible in a single volume to representing the current state of knowledge about the education of women in the Third World, this book has obvious limitations. It has been oriented around the question of how education changes women's lives in the gamut of roles women assume. Although we have attempted to investigate the impact of education on women's lives in the family, we have not inquired into all its aspects. For example, while several essays focus on education's relation to childbearing and child rearing, no attention is paid to education's relation to marriage choice or changes in power relations and decision making in the family. These are important issues, issues we would like to have treated. The lack of such studies in this book reflects a general void in scholarship on these issues as they pertain to the Third World.

Not only is this book constrained in its treatment of the effect of education on all aspects of women's lives in the domestic sphere, it also lacks comprehensiveness on the relation of education to women's participation and power in all aspects of public life. While several essays address the effect of education on women's entering the work force, none investigates whether education changes women's patterns of political participation and roles in public policy formation, their patterns of social life, or their social status. Research has yet to address these issues.

Most of the studies we present derive their data from a single nation; few are comparative. While the scholarship covers a broad spectrum of geographic regions in the Third World, not all Third World nations are included. This limits the kind of generalizations that can be derived from this book. However, it is our hope that the research presented and the questions raised will generate comparative studies and provide a basis for further generalizations.

While we do cover a wide range of Third World nations, the studies that follow do not consider whether there is variance in the patterns of educational access, processes, attainment, and outcome by the very nature of the political system in which schools are situated. Solid research on women's education in Cuba, Nicaragua, China, Mozambique, and other self-proclaimed revolutionary societies was simply unavailable.

Above all, this book may fail to convey the passionate dedication to education that historically has motivated many men and women all over the world. To individual women, as well as men, education represents a possibility of escaping the drudgery of poverty and domestic routines. Agnes Smedley's fictional autobiography, *Daughter of the Earth*, provides a particularly moving example of such a quest for education. To social and political reformers, women's education has represented a route to national dignity and independence by countering such obscurentic social practices as child marriage and burning of the widow. Roden Adjeng Kartini's *Letters of a Javanese Princess* gives eloquent testimony of her belief in education to free her nation. Tribute to the power of women's education is also paid by its impassioned opponents over the years. Although outright opposition is decreasing, criticism of women's studies for pressing women to assume nontraditional roles draws from this same heritage.

It is difficult for such social science analysis as is presented here to capture the great hopes education has aroused in the lives of women, yet perhaps this volume can contribute to the formulation of policies which will ensure that such hopes are not belied.

PART I
Factors Affecting Women's Access to Education

2. The Participation of Women in Education in the Third World

MARY JEAN BOWMAN AND C. ARNOLD ANDERSON

> Once upon a time, statisticians only explored. Then they learned to confirm exactly —to confirm a few things, each under specific circumstances. As they emphasized exact confirmation, their techniques inevitably became less flexible. The connection of the most used techniques with past insights was weakened. Anything to which a confirmatory procedure was not explicitly attached was decried as "mere descriptive statistics," no matter how much we had learned from it. [John Tukey]

This discussion is descriptive and exploratory, for which we make no apology. Until research provides a panorama of common and diverse elements of women's education at various levels and in different lines of study, the finer-grained analyses of econometricians and other disciplines will float in unmapped space. It is particularly essential to clear away the many fallacies that pervade the literature on "access." to education for females, as they pervade discussions about opportunities for other "minorities." There are few sterile approaches: The problem is to fit perspectives together. This article is excerpted from a monograph that relies heavily on what Tukey calls "confirmatory models" for identifying the key determinants of girls' education; however, little of the tabular or cartographic material is brought into the present version.[1]

Orientation to Methods and Viewpoints

We shall discuss only participation in schools and shall make some comments about literacy. We do so knowing that schooling is not an exclusive preparation for adult activities anywhere and that the boundaries between spheres of education are especially vague in "less developed countries" (LDCs). In some places, especially among Muslim families, women of the elite receive much or all of their schooling at home. Nor have girls everywhere been excluded from monastery and temple schools. Thus the significance of any single index of girls' participation in schools can be appreciated only in the context of the whole array of educational agencies.

The index we shall use is years of schooling for each sex. It provides measures of utilization (for this, not access, is what most statistics mea-

[1] Mary Jean Bowman and C. Arnold Anderson, "The Participation of Women in Education in the Third World" mimeographed (New York: Ford Foundation, 1978); John W. Tukey, *Exploratory Data Analysis* (Reading, Mass.: Addison-Wesley, 1977).

Reprinted from the *Comparative Education Review* 24, no. 2 (part 2)(June 1980): S13–32.

sure). Our question is, How far do girls go in school, compared with boys, and what do they study? Increasingly, sex differences in utilization pertain to secondary and tertiary levels. Data about dropouts, repeating, and other forms of "wastage" give additional information about sex differences. Throughout our presentation, we shall ask why these differences in provision of schools and participation in them occur.

Participation versus Access

The availability of educational options does not ensure their utilization. This distinction between provision and utilization is basic for policy, especially in the LDCs. Reluctance or refusal of families to make use of available schools can be illustrated by the Masai in Kenya, by district variations within India, and also by the history of education in Appalachia. Many societies have their counterparts to those British working-class mothers who discouraged postcompulsory schooling as "not for the likes of us." More often today the injunction is "not for girls."

Children have little to say about whether they avail themselves of opportunities for education; it is not the child but parent, kinfolk, or neighbors who decide about primary schools. For whom, then, do we measure accessibility? From a collective or public policy viewpoint, primary schooling is available to the family for daughters as well as for sons. But for a girl whose parents dread the classroom give-and-take with boys, the free school across the road can be inaccessible. Such barriers against accessibility are deeper than "social disadvantage." There are also outlays for fees and "incidentals," and there are forgone economic contributions to the household or in other work that could yield cash. If schools are to be costless to families there must be complete subsidization. To go still further, to construe accessibility in terms of individual children whatever their parents' attitudes would lead us into a conceptual maze, discussion of which would unduly extend this paper. Therefore, we will focus on the least common denominator of worldwide statistics, the rate of participation of girls. We can then explore sex differentials in financial constraints and distortions of opportunity by examination of differences between boys and girls who do go to school.

The Scope of the "Why?" Questions

Why girls' participation in primary schools differs from that of boys cannot be answered without looking at ensuing school participation and the sequels to education in the postschool years. Whether schooling of a daughter is deemed worthwhile will be influenced by perceptions (or expectations) of the effects of schooling on jobs, on acquisition of a "better" husband, on quality of domestic life, on the daughter's personality development, and on the well-being of her children. Parental perceptions vary on many dimensions, requiring complex sets of data to disentangle their major determinants. In this article, however, we can include no direct examination of how parental perceptions or motivation affect access of the child to education.

How girls perform in school compared with boys is affected by the same factors that determine initial access and by other factors as well. If girls more often are kept at home to help with chores, and if they must do housework after school while brothers are allowed time for homework, girls actually have less access to education. Repetition of a grade or becoming an "early leaver" are crude indices to these more subtle components of access.

Another question is, How do changes in the provision of schooling affect girls compared with boys? The availability of schools (for boys, girls, or both) may reflect community *demand* for schools, even though to each family the availability of places is a *supply* or cost factor in its decision about schooling.

Finally, we should point out the usefulness of studying educational patterns for understanding social change. The link between educational participation and prospective effects of schooling means that sex differences in educational participation can be used as indicators of changing attitudes and expectations about life patterns of each sex, often signaling deep societal changes.

Literacy and Primary Schooling across the Generations

Despite herculean efforts by Unesco statisticians for 30 years, the data about enrollments for most of the Third World provide direct information only on short-term trends. However, literacy rates for age categories serve as useful proxies for time series.[2] Four contrasting types of situations are illustrated in table 1. For each country the literacy rates by age of females are compared with those of males within rural and urban populations. Many of the patterns of sex differences in primary school utilization that have been found by demographers and social scientists are reflected in these four national histories.

We make two broad generalizations based on these and similar data for other countries. First, males are more often literate than females, irrespective of place of residence. (More males attended school, which is the best indication of literacy, for literacy obtained outside of school is rare and is found primarily among older persons in a few societies.) Literacy is higher among urban residents, whether males or females.

---

[2] These sorts of statistics are, of course, affected by migration. However, for a whole nation this error would not be great, though it does exaggerate the urban-rural differences. Similar data for subnational units could have larger errors. The fact that in El Salvador even young rural boys were largely illiterate suggests that the urban-rural contrasts cannot be attributed mainly to biases due to migration.

TABLE 1

LITERACY ACROSS THE GENERATIONS IN FOUR COUNTRIES (% Literate)

Country and Year	Age						
	55–64	45–54	35–44	25–34	20–24	15–19	10–14
Morocco, 1971:							
Urban:							
Males	29	31	41	59	77	84	85
Females	8	8	8	18	42	56	62
Rural:							
Males	12	13	16	21	34	37	34
Females	1	1	1	1	3	4	5
Chile, 1970:							
Urban:							
Males	89	91	94	96	96	97	96
Females	84	88	92	94	96	98	96
Rural:							
Males	62	65	72	79	86	90	86
Females	53	60	67	75	85	90	88
El Salvador, 1961:							
Urban:							
Males	69	73	77	82	85	89	84
Females	48	58	59	68	76	82	83
Rural:							
Males	31	32	35	39	46	47	44
Females	15	18	22	28	38	44	44
Thailand, 1970:							
Urban:							
Males	81	89	94	97	98	98	98
Females	43	64	83	90	96	96	97
Rural:							
Males	67	78	87	91	94	95	96
Females	17	39	72	82	90	92	94

However, societies differ in the relative literacy of urban females and rural males, and in any given society these relative positions may alter over time.

Second, literacy rates for women tend to converge with those for men. However, the timing and speed of convergence depend on cultural heritage and on stages in the spread of schooling. How much convergence we estimate to have occurred will depend on how we measure disparities or changes in them. These four countries illustrate four distinctive patterns of change.

1. In rural Morocco the absolute difference in literacy between men and women increased substantially from the older adults to present-day children. Rural women remained almost wholly illiterate until recently; rural males made slow but marked progress. Even today, however, only a minority of young rural men can read and write. The male/female differential cannot be explained by social patterns associated with Islam, for

literacy has been spreading rapidly among urban females in Morocco. Urban women do, however, continue to lag behind urban men, and the gap has scarcely narrowed.

2. In some countries (especially in Latin America) sex differentials in literacy are small at all ages and in both rural and urban communities. In Chile a majority of even the oldest rural females are literate, and younger females have overtaken the males —just the opposite of Morocco.

3. A relatively common pattern that appears where primary schooling has spread rapidly is a shift from marked disparity between males and females to virtual parity in urban places, but with a continuing large gap between urban and rural youth of each sex. This pattern (illustrated by El Salvador) implies that educational development is just beginning and reflects a different configuration of forces than those in either Chile or Morocco.

4. The pattern exemplified by Thailand is unusual. Sex contrasts are large among older people in both urban and rural communities, but females have become literate at a rapid pace and match the males in younger age groups.

When one narrows the age span to consider only children and younger adults, data are available for many countries. They show that lags in schooling for girls can be very persistent. Comparing ages 25–34 with 15–19 (or 10–14), male literacy has spread so widely in many African countries that sex contrasts have widened absolutely despite substantial gains among females. Our knowledge of how diffusion proceeds should lead us to expect just such patterns. Perhaps more surprising, among many Muslim countries of Asia and the Middle East (generally in contrast to North Africa) young women are beginning to catch up with men. Viewed against the history of Western education since the early nineteenth century, we find that females are approaching parity with males in pretertiary schooling in an astonishing number of LDC countries. In parts of Latin America (and in three African societies with unusual livelihood patterns) young adult women seem to be literate more often than their male contemporaries.

Enrollment Rates and Wastage around the World

Enrollment data entail more difficulties than those for literacy. Countries differ greatly, for example, in proportions of overage pupils and in whether overage is due mainly to late entry or to repetition of grades. These latter variations are associated in diverse ways with dropout rates by sex and level of school. Although societies display much individuality in these patterns, we begin with comments on highly aggregated data, always with an eye to female representation.

Overview of Enrollment Rates

Across the world regions, sex differentials among children aged 6–11 are negligible in "European" countries and in Latin America (although rates in the latter are lower). In these regions only small differentials occur for ages 12–17. Even at tertiary ages (18–23) sex contrasts are moderate: males 51 percent and females 45 percent in North America; 29 and 22 percent, respectively, in Europe; and 22 and 18 percent in Latin America.

The situation in the Third World is different. Asian rates (excluding Japan) for 6–11-year-olds are 71 and 50 percent, respectively, and for Africa 59 and 43 percent; at ages 12–17, in Asia 38 and 22 percent, and in Africa 39 and 24 percent. For ages 18–23, Unesco estimates male and female enrollments to be 10 percent and 4 percent in Asia, and 3 percent in Africa. Everywhere outside the most developed regions, intercountry variations in enrollment rates are very large for both sexes, as are sex disparities in those rates.

Instead of expressing rates by age categories without regard to school level, rates are frequently estimated by relating enrollments at a given level of school to the population of the "normal" age range for this level. In many of the LDCs these rates, especially for boys, exceed 100 percent, sometimes by a wide margin. This occurs mainly where the true rates are relatively high and there is much repetition (whether in initial grades or when sitting for examinations). Excess enrollments by overage boys combined with low rates for girls occur especially in Africa and in Muslim countries; in Latin America overage girls are not uncommon.

Data for secondary schools may also have distortions, but these seem to be less severe and less systematic than for primary schools. In most of Latin America and in non-Muslim Asian countries, girls match (sometimes even surpass) boys in secondary attendance. However, for most LDCs (in contrast to the "developed" world) the absolute gap in secondary enrollment rates between boys and girls is greater. One can ask, To what extent are we observing a dramatic drive to more schooling among boys, with girls soon to catch up? Alternatively, do we see behind these figures more persistent restraints on continuation of girls at school during their adolescent years? The answer surely varies among countries and among ethnic or regional subpopulations within countries.

Some of the contamination of enrollment rates by overage pupils can be circumvented by using the age with the highest rate in most countries —for primary schools, age 8. In most of Latin America there is parity between the sexes at this age or even a preponderance of girls. High rates for both sexes occur in a number of Asian countries. For Africa we can identify two categories: (*a*) a cluster of countries that are early in the spread of primary schools (with male rates ranging from 15 to 40 percent and girls from 10 to 20 percent), and (b) countries with boys' rates ranging 55 to 100 percent and girls', 33 to 95 percent.

When we look at pupils of the comparatively advanced age of 16, LDCs usually show low enrollments for both sexes. Within Africa the range for boys extends from zero to beyond 50 percent, but in only one case is the rate for females over 25 percent. Asian countries are highly disparate, whether Muslim or not.

Wastage, Promotion, and Retardation

Crude figures do not distinguish between (a) high enrollments for 1 or 2 years with few pupils continuing and (b) more modest rates of entry to school but with relatively few dropouts. These two situations have quite different implications, but there is no easy way to distinguish between them without detailed figures. To compute survival rates for elementary pupils by taking the ratio of grade 6 to grade 1 pupils in the same year will yield exaggerated dropout rates when any of three conditions prevail (only for the first of which are sex disparities unlikely): (a) The numbers entering grade 1 may be rising rapidly due to population growth (or immigration) without any rise in enrollment rates for the age group, (b) rates of beginning school may be (usually are) higher in successive cohorts, and (c) the proportion of repeaters may be distinctively high in grade 1. The most reliable data would come from following successive cohorts of pupils through a school, but such data are unusual.

Cohort estimates of 5- and 6-year survival rates for nine countries are shown in table 2.[3] Even though in each of the last six countries fewer than a tenth of entrants survived to the sixth grade, in none was the outcome for girls much worse than for boys. The figures for Iran are hard to believe, though a pattern like this could occur where few children begin

TABLE 2

SURVIVAL RATES PER THOUSAND ENTRANTS TO PRIMARY SCHOOL IN NINE COUNTRIES, BY SEX

	Male	Female
After 5 years:		
India	475	407
Iran	789	756
After 6 years:		
Cambodia	439	226
Libya	90	86
Syria	80	68
Panama	73	76
Costa Rica	67	72
Benin	51	42
Rwanda	30	27

[3] M. A. Brimmer and L. Pauli, *Wastage in Education: A World Problem* (Paris: Unesco, 1971), pp. 48–49.

school and few drop out. Persistence in India is moderately high, and sex differentials are modest. Cambodia is similar to India for boys, prospects for continuation of girls are poorer.

These summaries cannot tell us about the amount of repetition, the grades in which it is concentrated, or its relation to dropping out. Does dropping out closely follow nonpromotion or arise mainly from conditions outside the school? Different school systems seem to have developed distinctive norms for one or another cause of wastage, sometimes varying by sex. For Algeria we can separate the repetition and dropout components of wastage for each sex. Aggregate pupil years over the span of six grades ("inputs") greatly exceed the number of completers ("outputs"). For the years 1963–69, boys averaged 530 repetitions and 606 dropouts per 1,000 entrants to grade 1; for girls the numbers were 408 and 702. Before dropping out or completing primary school the grades repeated by girls were: none, 24 percent; one grade, 32 percent; two grades, 26 percent; and three grades, 17 percent (no one repeated more than three). The percentages for boys were within one or two points of those for girls.

We must often make do with quasi-cohort enrollments and grade-by-grade transitions for a single year; these comparisons are often dramatic. For rural India, ratios of grade 6 to grade 1 enrollments so estimated vary among states from 27 to 70 percent for boys and from 10 to 60 percent for girls. Dispersion would be even greater if districts were used as units. One investigator estimated the components of total cost per grade 7 completer for states in India.[4] "Excess" costs due, respectively, to dropouts and repetition varied quite dissimilarly for the two sexes. The proportion of excess cost assignable to dropouts averaged two-thirds for boys and three-fourths for girls—suggesting that boys showed more persistence, even with repeating. But the percentage of wastage costs attributable to dropouts varied among states from 45 to 98 percent for boys and from 33 to 97 percent for girls.

Proportions of Pupils Who Are Girls

Since the population of potential pupils is almost evenly divided by sex, girls would be expected to comprise half of enrollments if there were no sex differences in use of schools. There is virtual parity at the primary level among the developed countries and in most of Latin America. Shortfall of girls typically is largest at the tertiary level, but since 1960 there have been remarkable gains in the female share of these enrollments everywhere including within the developing countries.

A country can rank quite differently at each level of school for the proportion of girls, and countries vary greatly in female shares of pupils. For the rural sector alone in 1960, among countries girls ranged from 20

[4] K. Venkatasubramanian, *Economic Aspects of Growth of Primary Education in Tamil Nadu* (Baroda, 1977), p. 170.

to 50 percent of primary and from 6 to 63 percent of secondary pupils. In no African country were girls half of secondary pupils, and in four they were less than a sixth.

The school systems of Francophone Africa are based on one model and have been administered largely by Frenchmen. Nevertheless, among 14 countries Deblé found a range in female proportions of secondary enrollments from 40 percent in Madagascar to 7 percent in Chad.[5] One might interpret the Dahomey figure (30 percent) or those for Mali and Upper Volta (24 percent) as depicting either favorable opportunities for women or the opposite —what has been called the "fully/only" choice of interpretations of given facts. However, no one would characterize Chad as "fully" 7 percent or Mauretania as "fully" 9 percent.

The distribution of 128 countries in female share of tertiary students around 1970 was as follows: under 10 percent, 13 countries; 10–19 percent, 28; 20–29 percent, 30; 30–39 percent, 24; 40–49 percent, 28; 50–59 percent, 4; and over 60 percent, one country.[6]

Early Marriage and Schooling

It is a byword that in traditional societies early marriage is a major impediment to expansion of schooling among girls, especially at upper-primary or secondary years. A graphic comparison of countries reveals that where girls are married at ages 15–19, their enrollments at those ages are lower. However, there is no simple trade-off between marriage and schooling, for in most countries the proportions married plus those in school add up to much less than 100 percent. Rather, it appears that there are common causes for both early marriage and low school attendance.

Associations between resistance to schooling for girls and their early marriage take many forms. Rarely is it simply incompatibility between two concrete activities, attending school and wifely duties. In some places, girls who are already married remain in school several years before their marriage is consummated. While more schooling usually improves chances for a superior husband, it can also have the opposite effect, and fear of moral corruption of adolescent girls by school attendance is not directed solely to sexual matters. Thus, Yates writes that, in the Leopoldian Congo, parents feared girls residing at a mission would refuse to marry the man who already had paid the bride price.[7] Mothers sometimes asked payment for girls to be in school, and there were rumors that mission pupils became barren.

[5] Isabelle Deblé, "De quelques indicateurs du fonctionnement des systèmes scolaires," *Bulletin de l'association francophone*, dedo comparée no. 2 (December 1973), p. 37.

[6] Elise Boulding et al., *Handbook of International Data on Women* (New York: Halsted Press, 1976), p. 157, table 54.

[7] Barbara A. Yates, "Sex Differences in Career Opportunities and Education in the Belgian Congo" (paper presented at the meetings of the American Educational Research Association, New Orleans, 1978).

Similar anxiety is still widespread. Trevor reports that the Wazir who taught the Koran in a British boarding school in the Sudan feared that girls' "scholastic ambitions might tempt them not to give their full attention to their proper role as wives and mothers."[8] And for graduates, "the moral threats of working outside the home were too much for a sensitive woman, and threatened the peace of the home." This suggests that anxiety about moral danger for girls arising from Western education may be less a fear of Western knowledge than of attitudes accompanying the new schooling.

Ambiguities of Coeducation

Just as the alternatives of school and marriage are linked only tenuously, so one must be uncertain about the correlates of coeducation. One might expect that in societies where there is the strongest resistance to education of girls, those who attend, especially during adolescence, would be placed in segregated schools. Yet Muslim societies occur nearly everywhere on a graph relating proportion among total pupils who are girls to proportion of female students who are in coeducational facilities. Clearly, segregated education has been the way in which education for women was most easily accommodated in Muslim societies (especially for adolescents) but it is not only Muslims who have wanted to keep their young girls in protective environments. Nor does coeducation ensure parity of treatment in instruction or in choice of curricula.

In all aspects of girls' schooling, the availability of women teachers is salient as both an instrument and a product. Insistence that girls have women teachers (especially in secondary schools) can speed up formation of a cadre of female teachers, but until there is a generous flow of girls through postprimary grades, this supply of acceptable teachers will remain scanty. Once this knot is untied, girls' schooling can advance rapidly —though it need not do so.

The supply of women for secondary teaching and their willingness to accept such employment are affected strongly by practices about tertiary schooling for women (especially among elite families) and about acceptability of different employments for women. In some countries (perhaps especially in Muslim Asia) it may be secondary rather than tertiary schooling that is critical; in these countries proportions of secondary teachers who are female parallel the proportions of females among secondary pupils. In Muslim Africa, however, girls make up a larger proportion of secondary pupils than of teachers. This may reflect an early phase in a recent spread of secondary schooling among girls, but it means that adolescent girls are being taught by men nonetheless.

[8] Jean Trevor, "Western Education and Muslim Fulani/Hausa Women in Sokota, Northern Nigeria," in *Conflict and Harmony in Education in Tropical Africa*, ed. G. N. Brown and M. Hiskett (1975), pp. 247–70.

Women's Schooling in Muslim and in Latin American Countries

Some Muslim societies do present a sort of ideal type of female seclusion with a large shortfall in girl pupils. Perhaps these societies are experiencing more severe strains arising from adaptation to new feminine roles. The advantage surrendered by women in "modernizing" their lives may be most visible in these societies.

Youssef compared Muslim with Latin American societies.[9] She concluded that in the Middle East, normative expectations about roles for women were usually fulfilled, while in Latin America a similar ideal for differentiation of sex roles was weakly implemented. She sees Latin America as "distinctive," arguing that Latin American women could diverge from the norm "because the machinery of control over women is not institutionally strong, nor is it tightly integrated." But does this make Latin America "distinctive" in a world perspective?

More important is Youssef's emphasis on contrasts between women of the populace and of the elite in Latin America. At the same time, she observed that tertiary enrollments (for 20–24-year-olds) in three of the six Middle East countries she studied exceeded those in five of her six countries in Latin America, although in the Middle East girls made up a smaller proportion of school enrollments at secondary and lower levels. The contrast between elite and populace would seem to be large in the Middle East as well —or are we involved here in who are elite?

Goode contends that it is not the daughters of the elite but of middle-class men (possessing advanced schooling and/or high incomes) who have led the way to educational opportunities for women in Muslim societies.[10] In collating these opposing viewpoints it is difficult to weigh the handicaps of purdah within elite or would-be elite families against opportunities of women for schooling and for responsible roles within segregated structures. It may be that it is the segregation of opportunities for school and work rather than the magnitude of those opportunities that most characterizes orthodox Muslim societies.

One does develop reservations about the prevalence of a distinctive Muslim pattern for exclusion of women from opportunities for schooling. Perhaps it is the strength of tradition where poverty is endemic that most discourages schooling of Muslim girls. As has been said with respect to the Sudan and Northern Nigeria, girls' handicaps may be due less to conflict between Western and Muslim schooling than to situations "inherent in any confrontation between conservative and radical functions of education."[11]

[9] Nadia H. Youssef, *Women and Work in Developing Societies*, Population Monograph Series no. 15 (Berkeley: University of California Press, 1974), chap. 8.
[10] William J. Goode, *World Revolution and Family Patterns* (London: Free Press, 1970).
[11] G. N. Brown and M. Hiskett, "Islamic Education in Tropical Africa," in Brown and Hiskett, eds., p. 94. A full array of attitudes for and against schooling of girls in Muslim sub-Saharan Africa

21

Forgone Earning and Forgone Learning

The decision to send a girl to school flows from a diverse set of expectations about the effect of schooling upon her adult life. Only under certain conditions will these expectations lead to substantial schooling for girls, even where boys attend in large numbers. With ongoing development the positive elements in both marriage and job markets usually come to outweigh the negative ones. But even when these circumstances are favorable, the time children spend in school entails costs in terms of activities forgone. New investigations are raising our estimates of how much time and labor children contribute to the economy of the household. Often the burdens placed on girls exceed those for boys. Child care and household tasks do not exhaust girls' contributions to the family economy; they may work in garden or field, fetching and carrying, or help in trade and do home processing of products for sale. Time spent by girls in these activities can be especially important in poorer families where perceptions of benefits from the schooling of girls are dimmer. Econometric estimates of forgone productive activities resulting from school attendance tend to pick up boys' activities more successfully than girls', unless the analyst has detailed local knowledge.

Too often we ignore that when girls (or boys) go to school there may also be substantial forgone learning. Traditional ways of life must be learned, and time spent in (Western) school takes time away from this learning. For instance, in some societies (most often cited are those in West Africa) women have traditionally been independent and have encountered a high risk of divorce. Their means to independence is in subsistence farming and petty trade learned at the mother's side. When they try to combine schooling with home apprenticeship, the choice between work time and study time may lead to family tensions, poor lessons, and dropouts. One could not imagine a sharper contrast than that between the cultures of seclusion in many Muslim societies and the lives of trading women in West Africa. Yet in each case valuable time of young people in working and in traditional learning is forgone while they attend school.

Intracountry Variations in Schooling of Girls

Excepting casual mention of ethnographic reports, we have referred mainly to statistics aggregated to the national level. Perhaps the richest findings will come, however, by examining the large differentials in schooling of girls (or in disparities between girls and boys) between re-

---

can be found in Alan Peshkin, "Social Change in Northern Nigeria: The Acceptance of Western Education," in *Social Change and Economic Development in Nigeria*, U. G. Damachi and H. D. Seibel (New York: Praeger, 1978).

gions within countries —and among ethnic and socioeconomic subpopulations.

Spatial Diffusion of Schooling

The proportion of girls who are in school can vary more among provinces than among countries taken as wholes. In Sierra Leone, primary rates for girls range from 11 percent in northern and 29 percent in southern to 77 percent in eastern provinces. In one hinterland province of Morocco, only 6 percent of primary pupils were girls, in contrast to over 40 percent in Rabat and Casablanca. Writers on education and development often observe that literacy is highest in coastal zones or along major waterways where the first contact with the Western world occurred. Even where competition between Christian missions generated more attention to the hinterland, the diversities were similar. In Africa especially, localized evangelization produced almost helter-skelter spatial patterns, partly because missions held divergent views about the importance of literacy, especially for girls. Cities of the interior tend also to be advanced in schooling because patrons for schools emerge with urbanization and a more complex economy in which the rewards to formal schooling are visible. But even in countries that remained independent (as Ethiopia and Thailand), inauguration of modern schools elicited uneven responses in accordance with levels of development of districts. These historic patterns tend to persist even now. Boys and girls display similarly high (or low) propensities to attend school in the same districts, with attendance among boys leading that of girls until a late stage in the diffusion of schooling.

Location of secondary schools (especially those for girls) was more erratic than location of primary schools, and the influence of outside agencies, such as missions or colonial administrators, played an even larger part. The catchment areas for girls' secondary schools (especially if boarding) were typically as large as for boys, but fewer girls than boys attended from the remoter areas. Schooled mothers everywhere are key influences on the spread of girls' schooling, and such mothers also are role models. But since schooled women are often few, the better-schooled fathers may have the greater influence in spurning traditional resistance to allowing girls to begin or continue in school. Considering the mosaic of inducements and resistances, the stricter social selection among girls in relation to distance from school is not surprising.

Some years ago Fattahipour-Fard used data from a special 1956 census of Iran to explore associations between schooling and other characteristics of the 119 census districts of that country.[12] Most of his findings

---

[12] Ahmad Fattahipour-Fard, "Educational Diffusion and the Modernization of an Ancient Civilization: Iran" (Ph.D. diss., University of Chicago, 1963).

came from the study of a zero-order correlation matrix of many variables. The following, drawn from his more detailed findings, may serve as useful hypotheses for futher study:

1. In districts where teachers are predominantly male, literacy and enrollments were relatively low, especially for girls.

2. Where fertility was low, enrollments were slightly higher for each sex within rural sectors.

3. Districts in which a large proportion of villages possessed a mosque had lower literacy for each sex, and where many non-Muslims resided enrollments were higher.

4. As one would expect, districts in which many villages lacked a school had lower literacy and enrollments; this relationship was closer for boys, perhaps because girls more often were kept at home, even receiving instruction there. We may be observing mainly an index of village isolation; thus, in districts where few villages had a radio, educational advancement from older to younger cohorts was retarded for both sexes. Higher enrollments went along with village possession of bath and clinic.

5. The more urbanized districts and those with larger proportions of immigrants had more literacy, but this relationship was weak for girls.

6. Nonagricultural employment stimulated education, even for daughters. Proportions working at professional and technical jobs had even more positive influence, especially on schooling of girls.

7. Literacy of rural adult males seemed to foster schooling of boys more than of girls, whereas literacy of rural adult women benefited each sex equally. Within urban communities, the effects of adult literacy were stronger for girls.

These data for Iran and similar data for other countries could be incorporated in more sophisticated analyses; a discussion of analytical models and their applications for such work is included in the monograph from which this article is drawn.[13]

Sex and Social Selection for Schooling

Members of particular social categories may be given privileges or suffer restricted opportunities in various formal ways or simply by custom. Unequal opportunity alone does not constitute discrimination, nor does one experience discrimination solely because others have the intent to restrict. Both elements are required. We have emphasized that "difference in educational attainment" need not be the result of "unequal access to education." What a disinterested observer deems to be opportunity

[13] The models we discussed in the monograph are diverse, including examples from path analysis, simultaneous equation models dealing jointly with determinants of fertility and the education of children, and models related to that used by Goldblatt (Phyllis Goldblatt, "Education in Relation to Social and Economic Change in Mexico" [Ph.D. diss., University of Chicago, 1968]; see also Susan H. Cochrane, *Fertility and Education*, World Bank Staff Occasional Papers, no. 26 [Baltimore: Johns Hopkins University Press, 1979]).

often is not matched by its utilization. Sexual inequalities of opportunities for education are especially difficult to specify because of the pervasiveness of differentiated sex roles in human societies and the relationship of associated customs with utilization of opportunity for education. Among the most problematic factors for girls are the costs of travel to school (in time or hazards), a matter of both logistics and cultural norms. Furthermore, teachers may discourage all but the determined girls by condescending attitudes; by virtue of their own humble rank, pretertiary teachers usually can make only modest aspirations vivid for girls in their classrooms. Interiorized norms may be only vestigial feelings of timidity, as in the proverbial reticence of girls in mathematics. Outright educational discrimination weighs relatively lightly in the total configuration of disparities in opportunity, however measured.

The factors affecting educational opportunities are numerous and crosscutting. Urban girls of a depressed ethnic group can obtain more schooling than rural boys of a superordinate group. Girls from well-placed homes may enjoy greater opportunities than boys from a lower stratum. Distance from a school handicaps lower-status individuals of either sex more than those from higher-placed homes. Rising aspirations for schooling normally diffuse down the status scale and along the networks of the ecological structure. On the other hand, families aspiring to a better status may tacitly reaffirm traditional practices such as female seclusion.

Amid this complexity, we can mention only a few salient patterns of social selectivity in education of girls. This must be done cautiously, for too often simplistic generalizations take on a life of their own. Perhaps the firmest generalization is that socioeconomic status of parents has more influence on the schooling of girls than of boys. This influence often is greater in rural localities or among disadvantaged ethnic groups than it is in favored segments of the population. However, whichever instance of selectivity we focus on, countries range widely.

There are three ways of portraying selectivity: (a) the percentage distribution (profile) of parental status among categories of occupations or schooling for different samples of pupils, (b) the "selectivity index" or the ratios for each parental-status category of percentage of pupils to percentage of adults in the population at large, and (c) the enrollment rates of pupils from each parental-status category. (Indices b and c are arithmetically convertible, and a is most conducive to misinterpretation.) Writers often do not make clear which of the three indices they are using, and comparison with other societies is virtually always omitted as it is difficult to put these findings in perspective. More important is the common disregard of the fact that while a small decline in percentage of students who come from upper-class families will markedly diminish their selectivity index, a considerable rise in the proportion who have lower-status parents will bring only a slight rise in their selectivity index, because the latter families make up so large a part of the base population.

If one wishes to delineate the social milieu of schools, the profile of parental status (index *a*) is appropriate. That index is appropriate also if one wishes to estimate how soon low-status families could replenish the elite, given impartiality of employment, but for that purpose index *c* also is required. Comparisons of these status profiles can tell us a lot about sex differences in social selectivity for the special reason that the status distribution of the adult population is the same for boys and girls. But for assessing equality of opportunity, normally the selectivity index (see *b*) is more appropriate.

Weeks gives a graphic picture of status opportunities for girls in Papua New Guinea where prestige is indicated by the title of "big man."[14] Of high school girls, 75 percent had fathers who were "big men" in contrast to only 25 percent of the boys; at the tertiary level these proportions were 100 and 50 percent. Here are status patterns in a nutshell: Girls come from higher-status homes than do boys, and tertiary students are more selected socially than are secondary pupils.

Parental schooling may be a more sensitive predictor of children's schooling than paternal occupation, though many writers would contend that the latter has a broader explanatory power. Over much of the Third World, secondary and even higher students come from humbler homes than do those in advanced countries; yet in the latter, elementary (and sometimes secondary) pupils may be close to a cross-section of families. For the Third World as elsewhere, pupils with poorly schooled or illiterate parents are underrepresented, even in primary schools; yet in the Third World they make up a large proportion of all enrollments. Data for Muslim Tunisia and non-Muslim Senegal (both within Francophone Africa) illustrate different patterns of parental schooling among secondary pupils, distinguishing sex of parent as well as of pupils.[15] Both parents of girls have more schooling than do parents of boys, fathers of girls being distinctively well schooled. (Only index *a* is available for these data.) Tunisia is at a later stage in the diffusion of schooling, and more parents possessed above minimal schooling; these contrasts with Senegal were considerably greater for girls (table 3). Data for the Philippines would portray a society in which girls were quite close to parity of opportunity. In both Senegal and Tunisia, partly as a result of assortative mat-

[14] Sheldon G. Weeks, "The Social Background of Tertiary Students in Papua New Guinea" Research Report no. 22 (University of Papua New Guinea, Educational Research Unit, 1976).

[15] There is more dissimilarity in profile of schooling between parents of boys than of girls in Tunisia, while there is a weak opposite tendency in Senegal. (Because the index of dissimilarity is altered when two distributions have different numbers of categories, here comparisons can be made only within each country.)

26

TABLE 3

PERCENTAGE DISTRIBUTION OF PARENTAL SCHOOLING OF SECONDARY PUPILS IN SENEGAL AND TUNISIA,
BY SEX (1967)

Parental Schooling	Boys		Girls	
	Father	Mother	Father	Mother
		Senegal		
None	63	90	37	77
Primary	22	7	34	15
Secondary	11	2	20	6
Tertiary	4	1	9	2
	100	100	100	100
Illiterate	42	81	2	24
Rudiments	13	7	12	22
Primary	24	8	27	32
Secondary	19	3	40	18
Superior	2	...*	19	5
	100	99	100	101

SOURCES. —Senegal: Marie Eliou, "Scolarité primaire et acces au second degré au Niger et Sénégal, 1967," *Tiers monde* 9, no. 44 (October 1970): 745–46; Tunisia: Lilia Ben Salem, "Democratisation et l'enseignement en Tunisia: Essai d'analyse du milieu d'origine des étudiants tunisiens," *Revue tunisienne de sciences sociales* 6 (1969): 109.

NOTE. —In Senegal the index of dissimilarity between parents was 27 for boys (cols. 1 and 2) and 40 for girls (cols. 3 and 4); in Tunisia the respective indexes were 39 and 37. In Senegal the index of dissimilarity between fathers of boys and of girls (cols. 1 and 3) was 26 and that between mothers of boys and of girls (cols. 2 and 4) was 13; the respective indexes for Tunisia were 41 and 58.

* Under 0.5%

ing for education, for each category of maternal (paternal) schooling, girls' fathers (mothers) were better schooled than were boys'. The relatively higher social status of girls (which also indicates the lag in opportunities among girls in less privileged families) is an indicator of where a country is on the scale of aspirations for schooling and for utilization of opportunities. It shows where in a society we will observe the strongest resistance to schooling of girls. These status patterns, of course, have been affected by how long schools have been present in a society.

The Assessment of Progress

From several angles we have pointed out how early and current "exposure" to new ways of life and to imported values enlarges girls' opportunities for schooling. The concepts of exposure and resistance (of "tellings" and "resistances" in Hägerstrand's terminology) are fruitful in explaining how schooling spreads.[16]

[16] Torsten Hägerstrand, *Innovation Diffusion as a Spatial Process* (Chicago: University of Chicago Press, 1967).

Hägerstrand delineated and explained diffusion of innovations in spatial terms. His concepts become useful by adapting them to a notion of "social space." Hägerstrand focused on "information fields" (networks of tellings) —rather neglecting "resistances" —and he concluded that person-to-person tellings outweighed nonpersonal communication in facilitating diffusion. Messages flow out from nodes in communication networks and jump between nodes, leaving intermediate "deficit troughs." The tellings may be mainly information or mainly valuations: The balance between these and their content affect the acceptance of innovations.

Rather than resistances, we can speak of "readiness" to adopt innovations as individuals and groups become aware of potentialities. Here is where the economist brings to bear his analyses of benefit/cost and similar criteria of decision. Resistance to schooling of girls may be less an expression of tradition than lack of economic or other tangible benefits expected from training girls; it may also be an index of their contribution to the household economy. Forgone learnings as well as forgone earnings are among the resistances in educational decisions.

We should expect that exposure to the urban environment would alter life styles and increase propensities to send girls as well as boys to school. Schooling represents both a response to new options and a manifestation of changing ideas and attitudes. But not all urban people respond in the same way or to the same degree; pockets of people in even the most dynamic society are insulated from change, and in both town and country men and women can experience quite different mixtures of exposures to the modern and the traditional. However often this process recurs in history, it always has some poignant accompaniments. People are always deciding whether a prospective change in style of life that would follow acceptance of an innovation (in this case more or different education) is worthwhile. Moreover, education distinctively sets the conditions for its own further diffusion.

One would expect the spread of schooling normally to follow some variant of the S-curve: changes in proportions attaining any given level would be slow at first (expressed in absolute percentage increments), rise substantially in the middle range, and then slow as some ceiling on the diffusion is approached. Some curves may be steeper (more rapid diffusion); some may approach a plateau at a lower fraction of the population than others. Diffusion of education can be called "epidemiological"; at first there are few tellings; then the process accelerates until only the most resistant to the novelty remain, when spread fades away. There are also developments outside of education that alter the benefits and costs of schooling, speeding up or slowing down the pace of change.

It must be evident that neither the absolute percentage comparisons nor ratios of percentages are satisfactory for comparing gaps in educational participation, for assessing progress in the diffusion of schooling, or for showing the relative gains of females as compared with males. For such analyses it is most appropriate to think in probabilistic terms (whether in a probit or a logistic formulation). We may ask either or two questions: (a) What is the likelihood that an individual with given characteristics (e.g., the daughter of a peasant) will attend secondary school? Or (b) cumulating the individual likelihoods for a group with specified distributions of traits, what proportions of boys and girls would we expect to enroll in secondary schools? Applied to data for a group, the logit is the natural logarithm of the bettor's odds, or $\ln [p/(1-p)]$, where p is the proportion adopting a practice. This formulation is similar to the expression of normal distributions in cumulative form as probits, but on grouped data it is easier to work with the logistic formulation. The logit provides a dependent variable in a simple linear transform of the logistic curve.

Probit and logit models are coming into wide use in many different kinds of studies of educational participation. One or the other of these methods (which yield similar results) are used in econometric studies of decisions relating to numbers of children and their schooling. The first education-related application of this model seems to have been in the study of Mexico by Goldblatt.[17] Anderson used logit analysis to reassess Swedish progress in the democratization of university attendance.[18] Devindra Sharma is completing a study in which he applies logistic analysis in two ways: (a) examining variations in schooling among boys and girls in 150 districts of India and (b) portraying the spread of schooling over more than 50 years for each of the states of India, with particular attention to changes after independence.

Conclusions

A quarter of a century has passed since the rush to change the world by educating everyone began to accelerate, with its short-term combination of recklessness and optimism. We are searching now for more realistic and longer-term frameworks.

This paper has summarized part of a study of schooling of girls and the spread of that practice among various populations. Girls rarely have more schooling than boys, although, of course, schooling of girls in some subpopulations exceeds that of boys in others. Sex disparities are more pronounced at higher levels of the system, and virtually without exception social selectivity into schools tends to be greater among girls. But perhaps most impressive is the diversity in patterns of sex differentiation.

[17] Goldblatt.
[18] C. Arnold Anderson, "Expanding Educational Opportunities: Conceptualization and Measurement," *Higher Education* 4 (1975): 393–408.

There are also some patterns that have received less attention: for example, the relative sex equality in education over much of Latin America and the uneven Muslim resistance to education of girls.

Analysis of the spread of education among females must be closely tied to evidence concerning how education affects their subsequent roles and behavior. Parental expectations of these effects along with parental estimates of forgone production and forgone learning of schooled girls are crucial, not only in initial access of a daughter to schooling but also in the performance of girls in school. This, in turn, affects their progress through school and what they learn.

Despite a proliferation of studies pertaining to education of girls, many people find it difficult to understand these matters in a time perspective and in a context of change. The next step in our understanding will require more penetrating studies of the factors that hasten or retard change, and that give it one shape or another.

3. Educating Girls in Tunisia: Issues Generated by the Drive for Universal Enrollment

MARIE THOURSON JONES

Official commitment to the universal education of girls is a dramatic innovation in Middle Eastern nations. Though a departure from centuries of practice, it was a relatively simple decision for government officials to make. In the late 1950s when the newly independent Tunisian government first voiced such a commitment, officials' faith in the attractiveness of schooling and in the power of education to transform society facilitated their choice. But, despite substantial growth in enrollments over the past 20 years, Tunisia, like other nations, has found universal schooling an elusive goal.

Rapid but incomplete expansion has generated serious, second-order policy problems that are neither so clearly perceived nor so simply solved as the earlier task: how to close persistent gaps in enrollment and what sort of job-related training to provide. Demand for education and an increased supply of schooling have varied across time and space; their interaction lies at the heart of each of the issues examined here. Popular demand is affected by cultural and socioeconomic factors, as well as by previous experience. Governmental supply of services is constrained by costs, competing pressures, and incomplete information.

Two policies are examined in this chapter because, in important ways, they compete for the attention of policy makers and the resources of the government. More important, taken together they yield a more nuanced understanding of official Tunisian policy toward women, both equal access to schooling and outlets for children as they leave school and enter the job market. In the following pages, I will examine the political issues and the government's response, similarities and differences in policy for boys and girls, and implications for understanding the effects of public policies on women.

Expansion of Enrollments

In the mid-fifties, leaders of newly independent Tunisia viewed education as one of the most important means to effect fundamental social change. The 1958 Educational Reform established a timetable for the enrollment of all 6-year-olds by 1966–67, and full enrollment

This article is based on field research on policy making in Tunisia, conducted in 1975–76. I am indebted to the Social Science Research Council for their generous support of my study. Additional materials were collected in 1980 during a research trip, funded by the Spencer Foundation.

31

of all primary school-aged children by 1971–72.[1] The official rationale for heavy expenditures of money and energy on public education rested on human-capital arguments, the goal of national unity, and the view that literacy was a basic requirement for social development. Widespread education of girls was also depicted as a corollary and complement to earlier legal reforms on the status of women.

Compared to other Arabo-Muslim nations, the Tunisian government had taken an exceptionally strong stand in favor of women's rights. Despite the reticence or opposition of prominent jurists, President Habib Bourguiba promulgated a new Personal Status Code shortly after independence in 1956. This new law granted women rights of divorce equal to those of men, abolished polygamy, set minimum ages for marriage, and required the consent of the woman for marriage. Although it was cast in Islamic justifications, the code was a revolutionary break from custom and practice, which had accorded men the prerogatives in family life.[2] Enforcement and compliance did not follow automatically, especially in the countryside, but the law represented a strong official commitment to support changes in women's personal lives through a variety of measures, including education.

During the 1960s, demand for entrance into school greatly exceeded capacity, obscuring the fact that demand was not universal. Officials assumed that demand for schooling already existed, could be mobilized easily by Destourian Party campaigns and presidential speeches, or would follow quickly from social and economic development efforts. Accordingly, planners were preoccupied with how to stretch available resources to expand capacity as quickly as possible. The Ministry of Education's share of the national budget grew from about 18% in 1959 to a peak of 34.5% in 1971.[3] A severe shortage of teachers, which confronted officials in 1958, led the ministry to relax minimum qualifications for instructors, shorten the school day in primary school, and eliminate one year from secondary school, even though these measures risked lowering the quality of schooling. When it became apparent in the early 1960s that universal enrollment could not be achieved on schedule, officials blamed faulty demographic projections and insuf-

---

[1] Republic of Tunisia, Ministry of Education, *Nouvelle conception de l'enseignement en Tunisie* (Tunis: Ministry of Education, 1958), pp. 32 ff. (hereafter cited as *Nouvelle conception*).
[2] For a general treatment of differences in women's status in Middle Eastern nations, see E. H. White, "Legal Reform as an Indicator of Women's Status in Muslim Nations," in *Women in the Muslim World*, ed. Lois Beck and Nikki Keddie (Cambridge, Mass: Harvard University Press, 1978), pp. 52–68. On the Tunisian code, see M. Borrmans, "Codes de statut personnel et évolution sociale en certains pays musulmans," *IBLA* 26 (1963): 205–59; and N. Lakehal-Ayat, *La femme tunisienne et sa place dans le droit positif* (Tunis: Dar el amal, 1978).
[3] *Nouvelle conception*, p. 18; and Republic of Tunisia, Ministry of Education, "Rapport préliminaire sur l'éducation et la formation" (unpublished report, Tunis, 1975), p. 3 (hereafter cited as "Rapport préliminaire").

ficient resources; at the time, demand still exceeded capacity. As late as 1968, the minister of education reported that 35,000 children were still on a waiting list to enter first grade.[4]

Up to 1969 or 1970, total enrollment grew substantially every year, and the percentage of seats filled by girls increased annually. This impressive growth in the enrollment of girls came despite widespread coeducation, to which, in some regions, both parents and teachers objected.[5] In spite of the customary practice of secluding women and the illiteracy of most adults, many parents were confident enough in the benefits of schooling to send their daughters to class, at least for a few years.

Slackening of Growth

By the early 1970s, however, visions of universal primary schooling were belied by the stagnation of new registrations and by persistently high dropout rates. Both trends left the rate of girls' registration well below that of boys. Table 1 reflects the stagnation of total enrollments from 1970/71 through 1975/76. Between 1970/71 and 1974/75, the proportion of children aged 6–14 enrolled in primary school apparently declined: For girls the participation rates were 54% and 51% respectively, and for boys 85% and 77%.[6] The sharp drop in total enrollment in 1972/73 resulted partially from a massive expulsion of over-age repeaters. Likewise, the recovery of total enrollment after 1973/74 in part reflected growth in the number of repeaters. Accustomed to the steady growth of the previous decade, those responsible for the Fourth Plan (1972/76) had confidently extrapolated rates of expansion without considering whether saturation might be near and whether special measures might be required to achieve the new targets. But, whereas boys' enrollments in 1976 exceeded projections by 2%, enrollments of girls fell short of targets by 12.5%.[7]

A more troubling sign was the failure of new registrations to continue expanding toward universal entry into the first grade. After

---

[4] A. Ben Salah, "Discours à la réunion élargi des cadres de l'enseignement," in *Discours sur l'éducation* (Tunis: Ministry of Education, 1969).

[5] On the history of and reactions to coeducation, see Halima Chabouni, "L'enseignement mixte en Tunisie" mimeographed (Paris: UNESCO; ED/WS 263, 1971).

[6] Republic of Tunisia, National Institute of Statistics, *Annuaire statistique de la Tunisie* 23 (1976–77): 104. Similar, though not identical figures appear in *Evolution de l'enseignement en Tunisie* (Tunis: Ministry of Education, 1980), p. 10. The May 1975 census enumerated children not in school; calculations from these figures yield comparable enrollment rates. Republic of Tunisia, Ministry of Planning, National Institute of Statistics, *Recensement général de la population et des logements, 8 mai 1975*, 4 vols. (Tunis: Ministry of Planning, n.d.), vol. 3: 157–58, 167–68; vol. 4: 201 (hereafter cited as *Recensement*).

[7] Republic of Tunisia, Ministry of Planning, *Quatrième plan de développement économique et social, 1973–76*, 2 vols. (Tunis, Ministry of Planning, 1973), vol. 2, table VIII–8 (hereafter cited as *Quatrième plan*); and *Cinquième plan de développement économique et social, 1977–1981* (Tunis: Ministry of Planning, 1977) (hereafter cited as *Cinquième plan*).

TABLE 1

PRIMARY SCHOOL ENROLLMENTS, 1958–80

Year	Total Boys	Total Girls	Annual Growth Rate* Boys	Annual Growth Rate* Girls	Girls as Percentage of All Pupils
1958/59	218,135	102,227			31.9
1960/61	278,528	130,230	13.0	12.9	31.8
1963/64	396,687	196,372	12.6	14.2	33.1
1966/67	500,133	277,553	8.0	12.2	35.7
1969/70	551,942	348,577	3.4	7.9	38.7
1970/71	563,131	359,730	2.0	3.2	39.0
1971/72	572,870	361,957	1.7	0.6	38.7
1972/73	541,574	341,980	− 5.4	− 5.5	38.7
1973/74	532,822	332,964	− 1.6	− 2.6	38.5
1974/75	551,730	346,734	3.5	4.1	38.6
1975/76	562,182	358,742	1.9	3.5	39.0
1976/77	581,276	375,831	3.4	4.8	39.3
1977/78	591,272	389,983	1.7	3.8	39.7
1978/79	593,005	401,185	0.3	2.9	40.4
1979/80	605,995	418,542	2.2	4.3	40.9

SOURCES: Republic of Tunisia, National Institute of Statistics, *Annuaire statistique de la Tunisie* 20 (1970–71): 96, 113; 23 (1976–77): 95; Republic of Tunisia, Ministry of Education, *L'enseignement primaire en chiffres, 1979–80* (Tunis: Ministry of Education, 1980), p II.

*Figures for 1960/61 through 1969/70 are average annual growth rates for the immediately preceding years.

1968/69, new registrations hovered between 130,000 and 140,000 leaving an estimated 11,600 boys and 32,400 girls 6 years old not enrolled in school.[8] The ratio of girls to all first graders fluctuated uncertainly from 1966/67 to 1975/76 (see table 2).

High attrition rates likewise depressed enrollment. As does its French counterpart, the highly selective Tunisian school system generates large numbers of repeaters and dropouts at all levels. Students are forced out of school if they fail the end-of-cycle exams repeatedly or if they reach the age limit. Alternatively, parents may withdraw their children from school at any time. Of 1,000 children who start the first grade, only 370 will enter secondary school, 65 will receive the high school baccalaureat, and 38 will receive a college degree. Sixty-two others will get one of the terminal high school degrees.[9]

Girls are somewhat more likely than boys to drop out of school at all levels, with the greatest difference in attrition rates occurring during primary school. Accordingly, as a group of children progresses through the schools, the proportion of girls falls. The cohort that was 32% female in primary school in the early 1960s was one-quarter female by the time it reached the university in 1974 (see table 3). It is not unusual to find

[8] "Rapport préliminaire," pp. 16–17. The *Cinquième plan* estimated that in 1976 roughly 91.0% of 6-year-old boys and 71.5% of girls entered the first grade (p. 19.16).

[9] *Cinquième plan*, p. 19.3. On the selectivity of Tunisian schools, see C. Tarifa, "L'Enseignement du premier et du second degré en Tunisie," *Population* 26 (March 1971): 149–80.

TABLE 2

TUNISIAN FIRST-GRADERS

Year	Total New Pupils	Girls as Percentage of All First-Graders (New and Repeaters)
1958/59		36.5
1960/61	73,003	34.3
1963/64	106,767	37.6
1965/66	119,840	39.7
1966/67	127,600	40.9
1967/68	117,078	41.3
1968/69	144,390	41.9
1969/70	137,927	43.2
1970/71	130,587	41.8
1971/72	140,377	40.8
1972/73	138,140	40.5
1973/74	129,654	40.3
1974/75	135,760	40.6
1975/76	140,796	41.5
1976/77	141,879	42.7
1977/78	144,470	43.3
1978/79	156,106	43.8
1979/80	160,753	43.9

SOURCES: Republic of Tunisia, National Institute of Statistics, *Annuaire statistique de la Tunisie* 20 (1970–71): 96, 105; 22 (1974–75): 91, 102; 23 (1976–77): 90, 98; Republic of Tunisia, Ministry of Education, *L'enseignement primaire en chiffres, 1978–79* (Tunis: Ministry of Education, 1979), pp. 3, 7; *1979–80* (Tunis, 1980), p. III; Republic of Tunisia, Ministry of Education, *Evolution de l'enseignement en Tunisie* (Tunis: Ministry of Education, 1980).

parents who allow their daughters to attend school only until puberty, or who are less tolerant of a girl's failure than of a boy's. Official statistics indicate, for example, that female dropouts are usually younger than males, and that a higher proportion of girls than boys have never repeated a grade.[10] Some families may send their sons away to a boarding high school but not allow their daughters to live away from home. Because high schools are located in towns, rural students must live with a relative or board at school. In 1975–76, girls made up 32.4% of total secondary school enrollment but they were only 17.2% of all boarding students. Without figures on waiting lists and vacancies, it is impossible to determine the degree to which this gap is due to parental reticence or to shortage of places.[11]

Evidence from Tunisia and from more conservative Islamic societies suggests that parents do not necessarily see a conflict between some schooling for girls and other cultural restraints on women. But this does not mean that under identical conditions they will support equal

[10] Republic of Tunisia, Office of Tunisian Workers Abroad, Employment, and Vocational Training, *Abandons scolaires* (Tunis, 1974), p. 13; and Republic of Tunisia, Ministry of Education, *L'Enseignement secondaire en chiffres, 1975–76* (Tunis: Ministry of Education, 1976), p. 25 (hereafter cited as *L'Enseignement secondaire*).

[11] *L'Enseignement secondaire*, pp. 4, 6.

35

schooling for boys and girls. We now turn to the relationship between the characteristics of demand and the conditions of supply of schooling to explain why growth in enrollment slackened well short of full enrollment.

TABLE 3

SECONDARY AND UNIVERSITY ENROLLMENTS

	1956/57	1964/65	1970/71	1974/75	1979/80
Secondary					
Male	26,108	50,281	130,506	122,736	153,479
Female	6,816	17,512	50,016	56,251	84,838
Percentage Female	20.7	25.8	27.7	31.4	35.6
University					
Male	1,777	3,728	7,993	10,295	17,551
Female	363	859	2,136	3,428	8,051
Percentage Female	17.0	18.7	21.1	25.0	31.4

SOURCES: Ministry of Education figures cited in T. Cheikh-Rouhou, "La Femme Tunisienne et l'Emploi,' *El Mar'a* no. 12 (March 1976), p. 17; Republic of Tunisia, Ministry of Education, *Note de synthèse sur l'enseignement secondaire, technique et professional* (Tunis: Ministry of Education, 1980), p. 15; Republic of Tunisia, Ministry of Higher Education, "Données statistiques pour l'élaboration du bilan du V Plan 1977/81," mimeographed (Tunis: Ministry of Higher Education, n.d.).

Demand and Supply

After the rapid growth of the sixties, slackening of growth, especially of new registrations, perplexed and embarrassed officials. One reason for stagnation was that existing demand was sufficient to propel most but not all children into school. Whereas evident demand could be relied upon to fuel growth in the 1960s, full enrollment would require more official attention to stimulating demand and improving the supply of schools. The reason for this is linked to the characteristics of those not yet in school and to the timing of this stagnation. But instead of increased effort, the early seventies were marked by a weaker commitment to the measures required for full enrollment. This trend, in turn, has apparently been reversed since 1974.

Enrollments of girls have been particularly depressed in rural areas of interior provinces where the population is poor, dispersed, and relatively less exposed to new ideas about women's roles in society. In 1975/76, girls made up 22.4% of all pupils in the arid, south-central province of Sidi Bou Zid, but 47.2% in Tunis Nord immediately around the capital. On the district level, only 15.0% of primary school pupils were female in south-central Souassi (Mahdia province), while one section of Tunis claimed 48.8%. For the most part this discrepancy was more related to urbanization than to region; there tends to be greater variation among districts within provinces than among major cities. Of the districts encompassing the 15 towns with populations over 20,000 (1975), all but two had female participation rates exceeding the national average. Only one such urban district had a rate below the provincial average.[12] The effect of urbanization often does not penetrate far into the surrounding countryside. Some districts within 30 or 40 miles of Tunis had very low participation of girls in primary school. Trends in enrollments have been mixed. From 1971/72 to 1975/76, the proportion of girls to all pupils grew in the north and much of the south but actually fell in parts of the coastal Sahel region, the political heartland of Tunisia's ruling elite.[13]

Because thinly populated rural areas also had lower rates of boys' enrollments, the number of girls in primary school was doubly depressed.[14] That is, girls suffered from the same hindrances as boys (distance from school, low value placed on modern education, nomadism), compounded by barriers that apply particularly to girls (concern for preserving a daughter's reputation). Several specific explanations, however, could fit the geographical variation in the enrollment patterns equally well: "traditional mentality" (seclusion of girls at puberty since familial honor depends on the chaste behavior of females); perceived irrelevance of schooling for girls, objections to coeducational classes,[15] distance from schools,[16] need for child labor at home, or lower quality of schooling in

---

[12] *Annuaire statistique de la Tunisie* 22 (1974–75): 92–93, 99–101; 23 (1976–77): 99–100. *Recensement* 3: 50. Enrollment figures by zone of population density indicate that urban areas tend to look more like other urban areas than like rural areas within provincial borders. There are some consistent variations among provinces nonetheless. Republic of Tunisia, Ministry of Education, *Les aspects démographiques et physiques de l'enseignement primaire, 1978–79* (Tunis: Ministry of Education, 1979), p. 6 (hereafter cited as *Aspects démographiques*).

[13] Compare the 1975/76 statistics above with those in *Annuaire statistique de la Tunisie* 20 (1970–71): 103–4.

[14] The proportion of children aged 6–12 in school in 1972–73 varied by province from 66.5% (Kasserine) to 100.0% (Nabeul) for boys and from 28.7% (Kasserine) to 76.6% (Nabeul) for girls (T. Cheikh-Rouhou, "La femme tunisienne et l'emploi," *El Mar'a* 12 [March 1976]: 16). A correlation of provincial scores for boys and girls yielded an R of .776. These figures are probably overestimates of the true proportions. I calculated provincial scores from the 1975 census data on children not currently in school and found that enrollment rates varied from 56.6% (Kairouan) to 92.3% (Tunis) for boys and from 23.6% (Sidi Bou Zid) to 86.2% (Tunis) for girls. (*Recensement* 3: 157–58, 167–68; 4: 201.)

[15] All public primary schools are now coeducational. Even in 1968, the remaining hundred single-sex schools (of 2,151 schools total) were all located in large cities. As of 1978–79, 80 percent of secondary schools were coeducational. Republic of Tunisia, Ministry of Education, "Evolution de la mixité en Tunisie" (Tunis: Ministry of Education, n.d. [1979?]), pp. 2, 5. Officials have denied that this is a source of serious resistance to primary schooling. But newspaper accounts of meetings between the minister of education and local citizens' or teachers' groups report that coeducation does trouble Tunisians in some parts of the country. For example, A. Ben Salah, "Discours au séminaire des cadres de l'enseignement primaire," in *Discours sur l'éducation*; reports in *L'Action* (September 2, 6, and 9, 1970; July 20, 1971); and Chabouni, *L'enseignement mixte*.

[16] The average radius of school attendance zones is 1.6 kilometers in areas with populations exceeding 50,000 and 5.5 kilometers in areas with fewer than 200 people, *Aspects démographiques*, p. VIII.

rural areas.[17] Data currently available fit any one of these explanations and therefore do not shed much light on what remedial action to take. This is a significant problem, since each explanation for depressed enrollments calls for a different response: Persuasion campaigns might alter families' perceptions of the importance of schooling for girls, but where distance to school is the main problem, special transport or more schools will be necessary. Alternatively, where coeducation is not well received, separate schools might increase the registration of girls, though in areas of dispersed housing, this procedure might conflict with bringing schools closer to homes. To understand patterns of growth and stagnation, it is necessary to see that demand cannot be divorced from the conditions of supply. People react to the specific schools offered them, not just to the abstract idea of education. Therefore, evaluation of supply is central to understanding trends in enrollment.

For the government, uncertainty about what to do has been complicated by cost. Members of the 1976 planning subcommittees on education suggested three types of measures to diminish the gap between boys' and girls' enrollments: information campaigns, school improvements (more schools, provision of transportation, more financial aid for poor families), and social changes (regrouping dispersed population).[18] It would be politically unthinkable for the government to abandon its public commitment to universal primary education. Even in private meetings, officials preparing the Fifth Plan (1977–81) called increases in enrollment both desirable and amenable to political action. They did not simply dismiss it as an achievement that would have to await the evolution of "peasants' attitudes." Members of the Fifth Plan education subcommittee asserted the importance of schooling for girls, noting especially that literacy was crucial to the success of such social programs as family planning and hygiene.[19] The plan itself, like its predecessors, projected large increases in the proportion of girls in school, although the projected rise in total enrollment was not expected

---

[17] Variations in the distribution of fully accredited teachers, for example, followed roughly the same pattern as provincial differences in the percentages of 6- to 12-year-olds in school (R = .707) (Raw data is from Cheikh-Rouhou, p. 16, and from *Annuaire statistique de la Tunisie* 20 [1970–71]: 93). In part, these figures reflect the reluctance of many teachers to work in outlying areas. The government committed itself to providing more housing for teachers in rural areas, with the result that in 1978–79 teachers in the least densely populated zones were four times more likely to have housing provided than were teachers in the most densely populated zones. Nevertheless, in the former areas, 39% of the schools were without running water and 87% lacked electricity (*Aspects démographiques*, p. 5) See also Souad Chater, *La femme tunisienne* (Tunis: Maison tunisienne de l'édition, n.d. [1978?]), pp. 126–33).

[18] Many of these measures were discussed in preparatory planning documents, but were not detailed in the Fifth Plan itself.

[19] "Rapport préliminaire," p. 49.

to be much greater than the growth of the school-aged population.[20] Expression of such goals is no guarantee of action, however. The Fourth Plan, after all, fell short of its optimistic projections of girls' enrollments, and saw the completion of only one-half the classrooms planned. As will be discussed later, results during the Fifth Plan have been more encouraging.

Policy makers have been constrained by a combination of economic factors: diminishing marginal returns, political unwillingness to let education's share of the budget continue to grow,[21] and increasing demands for expenditure of the education budget on activities other than the expansion of primary school. First, it is possible that getting the unschooled into schools will be more expensive per pupil than was the original spurt in enrollment. Stimulating demand through campaigns is itself costly. More important, demand is rarely absolute; it is to some degree contingent on the quality and conditions of supply. The enthusiasm of early growth in enrollments masked the fact that growth came on terms that parents found acceptable. For the as yet unschooled, those conditions may be more expensive to meet, whether they are equal to or more stringent than those of parents who responded earlier. Extraordinary programs like meals and buses are costly, as is the spread of schools, teachers, and basic utilities to areas less and less thickly populated and farther from all-weather roads.

In the first years after the 1958 reform, expenditures could be concentrated on expanding primary schooling at relatively low cost per pupil. But rapid growth in the number of pupils created pressures to expand more expensive secondary and university facilities, and to improve the quality of education.[22] Programs to make all schools more "relevant to employment" and to expand technical and vocational training put further claims on budget, time, and personnel. Moreover, the most articulate citizens were more likely to have already found places for their children in primary school and therefore to be concerned with

[20] The girls' proportion of total elementary pupils was projected to rise from 39.3% in 1976 to 42.1% in 1981, and among first-graders it was to rise from 42.9% to 45.2%. By 1981, 96% of all boys and 83% of all girls were supposed to enter first grade, compared to 91% and 71.5%, respectively, in 1976 (*Cinquième plan*, pp. 19.15–19.16).

[21] The portion allocated to the Ministry of Education in the total government budget for current expenditures peaked at 34.5% in 1971, and fell to 26.3% by 1974 ("Rapport préliminaire," p. 3). In 1979, the Ministries of Education and of Higher Education received 28.8% of the total, and in 1980, 28.6%. (Republic of Tunisia, Ministry of Finances, *Le Budget Tunisien, 1980* [Tunis: Dar el Amal, 1980], p. 22).

[22] Published accounts of official deliberations on education in the 1970s reflect the government's preoccupation with measures that would raise the quality of schools: increasing the number of hours, upgrading teachers, reforming the curriculum (see the minister of education's annual press conference in October, or accounts of the National Assembly's annual December budgetary debate).

upgrading and with expanding access to postprimary schools. In political dialogue on education, primary school expansion fell into the background. Indeed, a dramatic shift in the ideological orientation of the government in late 1969 was followed by concentration on controlling the cost of education. This new emphasis was marked by a series of measures that had the apparent aim of limiting demand; pass rates fell, older children were expelled in large numbers, and there was a clear slowdown in the opening of new classrooms.

Some students of Tunisian affairs perceived a decline in official commitment to equality for women in the early 1970s.[23] Certain evidence suggests that this issue did decline in salience to the government and to ordinary citizens. But as an explanation for recent trends in educational policy, it is far less satisfactory than economic and political considerations. Declining interest in equality may help explain why, in a few exceptional districts enrollments of girls actually fell, while enrollments of boys increased. But this argument is less useful in explaining the supply of schooling, since stagnating enrollments affected boys as well as, or more than, girls. Also, during this period postprimary programs for schooling and training girls continued or expanded, as will be discussed in the next section. Analysis of economic and political constraints suggests that even more vocal commitment to women's rights would not be sufficient to resolve the difficult choices at hand.

After 1975/76, total enrollment and new registrations rose anew as did the proportion of 6- to 14-year-olds in school.[24] The overall gain from 64% to 68% reflects a larger percentage of girls in school, while growth in the enrollment of boys is not much larger than increases in the size of the age group. Accordingly, the proportion of girls per hundred pupils increased nationwide, with the greatest gains coming in some of the provinces that had the lowest bases. In Sidi Bou Zid, girls comprised 22.4% of all pupils in 1975/76 and 31.9% in 1979/80.[25] Surprisingly, the absolute number of girls increased more than the number of boys in all provinces but one (Kairouan), even in provinces where there were still large numbers of boys not in school. Despite trends indicating narrower disparities in schooling for boys and girls, the attrition rates

[23] M. Tessler, J. Rogers, and D. Schneider, "Tunisian Attitudes toward Women and Child Raising," in *Women's Status and Fertility in the Muslim World*, ed. J. Allman (New York: Praeger, 1978), pp. 289–311.

[24] According to one set of official statistics, the percentage of 6- to 14-year-old girls has risen from 50% in 1974/75 to 56.6% in 1979/80, while the enrollment of boys has hovered around 78%. For boys this is below the high of 85% in 1970 (*Evolution de l'enseignement*, p. 10). See also Younes Zoughlami, "L'Enseignement en Tunisie vingt ans après la réforme de 1958," *Maghreb-Machrek*, no. 78 (October–December 1977), pp. 48–52.

[25] *Annuaire statistique de la Tunisie* 23 (1976–77): 96–97; and Republic of Tunisia, Ministry of Education, *L'Enseignement primaire en chiffres, 1979–80* (Tunis: Ministry of Education, 1980), pp. 34–51 (hereafter cited as *L'Enseignement primaire*).

within a cohort in the late seventies were still far greater for girls than for boys. While in Tunis itself such differences were minimal, they were large in several provinces with the lowest entry rates for girls.[26] That differences in attrition were also sizeable in two provinces with above average entry rates for girls (Gabes and Medenine) suggests that, in some regions, parental decisions to send girls to school and to keep them there may still be quite independent.

Notwithstanding the optimism conveyed by these incomplete figures for the Fifth Plan, universal enrollment is not yet in sight. Over the past 10 years the proportion of boys in school has increased little if at all. What official statistics suggest is not that universal enrollment is close but that enrollments of girls have not yet reached their apparent ceiling. How to attain full enrollment still awaits an answer.

Because Tunisia reached a plateau in primary school enrollment in the early seventies, its experience suggests dilemmas that other nations will face. Tunisian officials defend their selective school system on the grounds that everyone has an equal chance at the beginning. But there, as elsewhere, the provision of equal opportunity may require vastly unequal efforts. Initial expansion of enrollment is fueled largely by demand from parts of the population willing to accept existing conditions of school supply. This initial surge of interest is likely to be insufficient to reach universal enrollment in countries with great variations in the population's attitudes and characteristics (especially degree of isolation and dispersion). Girls are not the only group at a disadvantage; rural children as a whole lag behind their urban fellows. These groups are especially vulnerable to shifts in political priorities in education.

Questions of equal opportunities and equal facilities for boys and girls do not stop at school entry. Full equality among young children is less complex than equality of chances among adolescents on the threshold of adulthood. At that point questions about the role of the sexes in society impinge directly on school policy.

Schools and Employment

Commitment to universal enrollment generates one set of problems around those children who never enter school. It creates a second set of problems for those who do enter: What will happen to them upon their departure from school? Ironically, if predictably, these two problems compete for the attention and resources of the central government. If policy makers were once preoccupied with getting children into schools, one might say that they are now worried about getting them out — in proper numbers, at proper levels, with proper skills. Generally stated,

---

[26] Compare *Annuaire statistique de la Tunisie* 22 (1974–75): 94–95; with *L'Enseignement primaire, 1979–80*, pp. 9, 11.

the problem is how to anticipate and guide the effects of education on individuals' adult lives. In Tunisia the government has been particularly concerned with links between schooling and employment; mismatches between instruction (training) and work have been blamed for a variety of social and economic ills.[27]

Employment and training issues affect both boys and girls, but they affect them in different ways, with substantially different ramifications for policy. Whereas the government can assume that nearly all men will work and that they will be employed in nearly all fields, the same assumptions cannot be and are not made for women. Not only is the size of demand for female employment uncertain, but there are also fundamental cultural issues influencing the types of professions that women enter or that the government chooses to encourage them to enter. But because large numbers of girls are now attending school, their later fate cannot be ignored. The issues involved have no simple answers; choices must be made to allocate resources between boys and girls, and the approaches chosen will shape the future division of labor in the society.[28]

Employment

Until recently, few Tunisian women worked outside the family.[29] But industrialization of textiles, encouragement of tourism, and expansion of schooling have all greatly increased female demand for employment and have made training of girls imperative. The nonagricultural, active female population (including the unemployed) rose from an estimated 58,000 in 1966 to 233,000 in 1975, largely through the growth of employment in textile industries and the encouragement (and better enumeration) of women engaged as artisans at home (see table 4). Unemployment figures for women are low, but much potential demand—women who would work if acceptable jobs were available—is not counted as unemployment. There is undoubtedly far greater interest in work than is indicated by official statistics.[30] The Fifth Plan expected

[27] Although the need to prepare children for work has been singled out for special attention by the government, it is part of a more general problem of the transition from school to adult life. Tunisian schools have been faulted for failing to stimulate creativity and problem-solving ability, prepare children psychologically for the adult world, and create well-rounded individuals. For a more detailed treatment of Tunisian educational policy, see M. T. Jones, "Public Influence on Government Policy: Family Planning and Manpower Development in Tunisia" (Ph.D. diss., Princeton University, 1979).

[28] Saida Mahfoudh addresses some aspects of other policies on boys and girls not treated here. ("Scolarisation et emploi feminins," *Revue Tunisienne des Sciences de l'Education* 4 [June 1977]: 89–128.)

[29] On low activity rates among Middle Eastern women, see Nadia Youssef, *Women and Work in Developing Societies*, Population Monograph Series, no. 15 (Berkeley: University of California Press, 1974).

[30] At times official documents have simply equated demand with the number of positions available (*Quatrième plan*, 1: 108).

42

that the rate at which women entered the labor force would stabilize at 1975 levels, with about 21% of the additional women in the 18–59 age group seeking work.[31] Finally, planners assumed that the better educated a girl was, the more likely she was to seek work.[32] There is some evidence to support this assumption; a 1972 study in Tunis found that 75% of 15- to 19-year-old girls who had reached secondary school before dropping out were looking for work.[33]

TABLE 4

NONAGRICULTURAL EMPLOYMENT OF WOMEN

	1966	1972	1976
Adult female population (ages 15–64)	1,203,441	1,406,000	1,523,600
Total employed	50,000	90,300	199,380
Textiles		41,000	125,640
	24,231		
Other manufacturing		6,100	10,740
Administration and teaching		12,000	26,550
Transport, communications		1,200	1,600
Tourism	24,033	2,000	2,800
Commerce, banks, insurance		8,000	6,850
Other services, including household workers		20,000	25,200

SOURCES: 1966–1976 census figures reported in Taoufik Cheikh-Rouhou, "La Femme Tunisienne et l'Emploi," *El-Mar'a* 12 (March 1976): 9–10, 1972–Republic of Tunisia, Ministry of Planning, *Quatrième Plan, 1973–1976*, 2: 293, 295; 1976–Derived from 1975 census data. Republic of Tunisia, Ministry of Planning, *Cinquième Plan, 1977–1981*, p. 98 and table VII-3.

The depth of interest in employment may surprise the outside observer. For most women, the reason for seeking work is economic need — often when no male is available to support a family. Even among some middle-class families, there is a feeling that both spouses must work in order to maintain a desirable standard of living. Only some well-educated women have the luxury of working for self-fulfillment as

[31] Estimates of the number of men and women who will enter the labor force were based on current age-specific activity rates, though authors of the plan were not confident about the accuracy of extrapolating present rates for women (*Cinquième plan*, pp. 10.5–10.9).
[32] The Third Plan (1969–72) projected that all women who attained at least their junior year in high school, along with half of those dropping out after their freshman or sophomore year, would seek work. (Republic of Tunisia, Ministry of Planning, *Plan de développement économique et social* [Tunis: Ministry of Planning, 1969], p. 55). The Fourth Plan assumed that all women receiving a university education or special training would seek employment, but indicated uncertainty about those with less schooling (*Quatrième plan*, 1: 108–111).
[33] Republic of Tunisia, National Institute of Statistics, *Enquête migration-emploi*, cited in Cheikh-Rouhou, p. 13.

well.[34] Parents do not always view employment as the reason to educate their daughters, but they are aware of the connection. There are more girls than boys enrolled in private, fee-paying vocational schools in Tunisia.[35]

Although expanding employment marks a substantial change on the surface, the degree to which it represents deeper changes in family authority may well vary by class and education. The economic attraction of jobs has helped overcome customary reservations about women's status, or at least allowed people to accommodate the idea of women working outside the home without becoming personally hostile to the women involved. So, while one must temper interpretations of employment as an indication of broadly changing attitudes toward women, employment may also increase where there has not been much general progress on women's rights.

Vocational Training and Academic Tracking

Initially, vocational training programs were overwhelmingly directed at boys. The imbalance was greater in Ministry of Labor programs (pre-apprenticeship, apprenticeship, specialized training) than in Ministry of Education schools (vocational and technical education). Openings for skilled labor and for cadres, created by the departure of Europeans after independence, were perceived to be mainly in "male occupations." In addition, there was evidently more public demand for, and receptivity to, programs to help boys. In absolute numbers, more boys than girls were coming out of the schools, and more of them were seeking work. Finally, officials saw males' unemployment as more disruptive than females' unemployment.

In recent years, however, the amount and variety of training offered girls has greatly increased. This expansion reflects both alterations in the economy and changing beliefs about the importance and acceptability of women working outside the home. Furthermore, as the number of female school leavers rose, increasing numbers were both available for, and interested in vocational training. The growing realization that girls want training may be an outcome of the effort that the Tunisian Women's Union invested in training rural girls in home

[34] N. Karoui, "Famille et travail: Les Ouvrières de Menzel Bourguiba," *Revue tunisienne de sciences sociales*, no. 45 (1976), pp. 75–98; L. H. Durrani, "Employment of Women and Social Change," in *Change in Tunisia*, ed. R. Stone and J. Simmons (Albany: State University of New York Press, 1976), esp. pp. 64–65; A. Hochschild, "Women at Work in Modernizing Tunisia: Attitudes of Urban Adolescent Schoolgirls," *Berkeley Journal of Sociology* 11 (1966): 32–53.

[35] In 1975 there were 6,216 girls and 1,690 boys in private vocational schools (Republic of Tunisia, Office of Tunisian Workers Abroad, Employment, and Vocational Training, *L'Enseignement et la formation professionnelle en dehors de l'éducation national - 1975*, 2 vols. [Tunis, 1976], 2: 70).

crafts.[36] In some ways it is easier to give women skills that allow them to earn supplementary incomes than it is to give men skills that—in the absence of sufficient growth in the supply of real jobs—will allow them to earn primary-support wages. Training offered by the Rural Development Program is overwhelmingly directed at teaching women marketable crafts, while agricultural training for boys has rarely been considered very satisfactory.[37]

Examination of training offered to both educated and uneducated girls reveals implicit definitions of what work is appropriate for women, or at least an estimate of what jobs the public (parents, employers, husbands, and women themselves) will accept. Until a few decades ago, few Tunisian women worked in public—that is, in contact with strangers—so any switch has been both recent and at least partly conscious. With a few notable exceptions, there is a definite separation of male and female occupations, reflected also in training opportunities (see table 5).

TABLE 5

GRADUATES OF NONSCHOOL TRAINING PROGRAMS, 1972–74

	Three-year Totals	
	Boys	Girls
General mechanics	2658	0
Metal construction	2036	0
Wood and Furniture	2064	0
Building trades	9867	3
Textiles and shoes	1842	24832
Auto and diesel mechanics	1277	0
Electricity	918	50
Administrative jobs	2676	4407
Miscellaneous	10229	2755
Services	4916	1421
Agriculture	7509	469
Crafts	834	14125
	46826	48062

SOURCES: Republic of Tunisia, Office of Tunisian Workers Abroad, Vocational Training, and Employment, *L'Enseignement et la formation professionnelle en dehors de l'education nationale–1975*, vol. 2:13.

Government policies must be understood as both responding to demand for work and influencing the form and amount of demand that appears. Policy makers may try to guess what choices individuals will

[36] From 1972–75, the Women's Union trained 3,000–5,000 girls per year, mostly in sewing and crafts (Ibid., 2: 37, 69).

[37] In 1973 the Program in Rural Development trained about equal numbers of boys and girls. In 1974, it reached 7,302 girls and 2,725 boys, and in 1975, about 7,000 girls and 3,000 boys (Ibid., 2: 41).

make in order that public policy will increase social benefits of private actions. That is, if girls wish to work anyhow, they should be provided with marketable skills for jobs that will be open to them. But mere provision of schooling and training will influence the proportion of women aspiring to jobs and the types of jobs to which they aspire. Because government bodies regulate or operate almost all vocational training programs, official choices on which facilities to make available to women have broad repercussions on emerging patterns of employment.

For girls with minimal schooling, employment has meant either production at home or labor in textile factories and centers for artisans. While the cultural ideal used to hold that a woman would remain at home until marriage and be secluded in her husband's house thereafter, rural women in particular and poor women in general have never been able to afford the luxury of idleness or seclusion. To some degree, the wage employment of barely educated and uneducated girls reflects a shift from field labor. Large numbers of women (including many who are young and unmarried) have been attracted to factory work with the approval of their families, drawn by the promise of steady cash wages.

Training opportunities for girls with a primary school education or less mirror their opportunities in textiles or as artisans.[38] There is definitely a link between job opportunities and the training provided by the government. While provision of such training may be "realistic" in its responsiveness to current job openings, it also establishes and perpetuates a given division of labor. In addition to cultural restraints on the mixing of sexes at work, the male unemployment rate of 15%[39] may pose an insurmountable barrier to extending the variety of training offered women at this level.

For individuals with more education, however, there is a greater overlap in male and female jobs, particularly in teaching and administration.[40] At this level, the designation of certain professions as appropriate to women does not reflect a long, customary division of public labor, although it does mirror Tunisian and foreign assumptions about

[38] Training programs open to girls with a primary school education or less include textile crafts, gardening, homemaking, sewing, and needle trades. Courses open to girls at vocational junior high schools are sewing, needle trades, weaving, and hairdressing. In 1978/79, 3% of all girls in vocational junior high school were studying electricity, metals, general mechanics, leather working, and bookbinding, all of which had traditionally been open to boys only. That year there were 484 girls out of 38,639 pupils studying such ostensibly male subjects. (Republic of Tunisia, Commission for reflection on the development of technical education for girls, "L'Enseignement technique et professionnel féminin" [Tunis: Ministry of Education, 1979?]).

[39] *Cinquième plan*, p. 10.2. Includes the unemployed for the first time.

[40] Girls who reach the last three years of secondary school can receive training as midwives, medical secretaries, hotel receptionists, and hotel housekeepers. While many technicians' and mechanics' courses enroll no girls, both boys and girls may study to become radiologists, nurses, social workers, nutritionists, physical education instructors, primary school teachers, laboratory or pharmaceutical technicians, statistical clerks, bookkeepers, and government clerks.

the nature of male and female. Job patterns reflect, first, those occupations that people feel are modest or otherwise appropriate, and second, those skills women actually have. The latter is determined somewhat independently of demand by the agencies that provide training. For women with at least some secondary schooling, jobs and training are encouraged in those fields that seem to grow naturally out of women's tasks of child rearing and family nurture, such as teaching and medicine.[41] Encouragement of female medical and paramedical training also stems from the need to serve women who are still reticent about consulting male health cadres. In addition, Tunisians have emulated certain European employment patterns. They were exposed to French divisions of occupations during the 75-year Protectorate; since independence, international funding agencies have influenced the content of vocational training institutions. For example, feminization of secretarial positions does not find roots in traditional cultural patterns. Until recently in fact, literacy itself was virtually a male monopoly, and the idea that a woman should be in frequent face-to-face contact with nonkin males was unacceptable. But today most secretarial training is aimed exclusively at girls. This pattern does fit assumptions that women should be subordinate to men. Finally, in the university, girls are disproportionately represented in letters and teaching; they are represented in proportion to their numbers in the sciences, medicine, and journalism; and they are underrepresented in economics, law, theology, management studies, technical teaching, and engineering.[42] Their representation is low in some of the fields with the greatest opportunities for employment.

A student's choice of fields at the university is limited by the track he or she followed in high school. School officials make tracking decisions on the basis of students' test scores, class work, and expressed preferences. National targets for the number of students in each track have become tools the central government uses to try to determine the supply of different sorts of cadres. Like many other Third World nations, Tunisia faces the threat of increased unemployment among those leaving secondary school and university, especially in those fields for which the main job outlet is teaching: humanities and natural sciences. To avoid or delay this problem, in recent years the government has tried to direct more and more high school students to terminal technical schools and to the applied science track leading to the university. Because technical tracks are divided largely by sex, increasing emphasis on technical education primarily involves shifting boys. The Fifth Plan

[41] This is also true elsewhere in the Middle East. See A. I. Meleis, N. Sanabary, and D. Benson, "Women, Modernization, and Education in Kuwait," *Comparative Education Review* 23 (February 1979): 115–24.

[42] Dordana Masmoudi, "L'Etudiante tunisienne de 1975," *El Mar'a*, no. 12 (March 1976), p. 21.

predicted that in coming years a higher proportion of girls than boys would be sent to the university tracks of letters and basic sciences (see table 6).[43]

TABLE 6

DISTRIBUTION OF BOYS AND GIRLS AMONG SECONDARY SCHOOL TRACKS

| | (Percentage) | | | | | |
| | 1976 | | 1981 (projected) | | 1979/80 | |
	Boys	Girls	Boys	Girls	Boys	Girls
Baccalaureat tracks (Lead to university)	72.3	76.0	65	74	74.1	84.2
Letters	15.5	29.1	10	30	18.9	38.8
Basic sciences	44.2	46.4	37	40	42.9	44.5
Applied sciences	12.6	0.5	18	4	12.3	0.9
Technical tracks (generally do not lead to university)	27.7	24.0	35	26	25.9	15.8
Industrial	22.5	0.1*	30	3	23.5	3.5
Secretarial	0	16.2	0	15	0	8.0
Bookkeeping	5.2	7.7	5	8	2.4	4.3
	100	100	100	100	100	100

SOURCES: Republic of Tunisia, Ministry of Planning, *Cinquième plan de développement écononique et social, 1977–1981* (Tunis: Ministry of Planning, 1977), 19.19; Republic of Tunisia, Ministry of Education, *Note de synthèse sur l'enseignement secondaire, technique, et professionnel* (Tunis: Ministry of Education, 1980), p. 16.
    *All studying needle trades.

Comparisons with 1979 enrollments indicate that these targets are far from fulfilled, even among students just entering one of the tracks. The deficit is concentrated in secretarial studies and bookkeeping rather than in industrial subjects and may reflect a decision to decrease the Ministry of Education's role in such training. In view of the continued expressed commitment to technical training, it would not be surprising if the Sixth Plan re-endorsed stress on industrial subjects.

Parents and other adults would need time to adjust to this shift in orientation. Historically, the best students have gone to the university tracks, and high school technical tracks have taken on some of the stigma of manual labor. Technical school does lead to the university for a small and rising proportion of students, but even at the tertiary level these fields seem to enjoy less prestige than the more academic fields. The fact that there has been confusion in the public mind and in some official documents about the difference between vocational schooling (junior high level, aimed at training skilled workers) and technical

---

[43] A similar shift outlined in the Fourth Plan was carried out as projected at the secondary level, but not at the university ("Rapport preliminaire," pp. 12–13).

education (high school level or higher, aimed at training highly skilled workers and technicians) has not helped matters.

It is too early to know the effects of this policy. If technical schools fail to acquire prestige in the minds of parents and employers, a higher proportion of girls than boys will have escaped its effects. If, however, unemployment does increasingly single out letters and natural science students, then women will bear this burden out of proportion to their numbers. To the degree that women feel, and express, less pressure for life-long careers, this policy may render unemployment among the educated less explosive for the regime. Even if the shift of students creates a better allaround balance between students and jobs, a new pattern of employment will represent a shift in the gender composition of professions and could impart new sex typing to modern jobs.

A small but potentially important countertrend also appears in table 6. More girls have been directed to the study of industrial subjects; whereas most are still specializing in the needle trades, one-fifth are in subjects previously restricted to boys. This innovation may begin to break down the nearly total exclusion of women from engineering and electronics. The current tracking policy demonstrates two sides of the government's intervention into the labor market via education and training: The government may simply reflect and respond to current divisions of labor, but it can also offer women training that will break down current divisions of work. In providing instruction for girls, a Middle Eastern government cannot escape taking a position on the proper activities of women in society, the acceptability of mixing the sexes on the job, and the relative importance of women's public roles to the nation.

Conclusion

Tunisia has registered substantial growth in enrollments of girls over the past 20 years. That growth has presented the government with a number of difficult spin-off policy problems compared to which the original decision to seek universal enrollment looks clear and unambiguous. When levels of enrollment were low nationwide, commitment of resources to rapid expansion had little competition. But as the level of enrollment rose, so did demands—from the population, from within the educational bureaucracy, from other ministries—for longer and better education. The Tunisian experience suggests that plateaus between automatic gains in enrollment and the need for extra effort is likely to be reached just when a major commitment is becoming harder to muster.

Policies often are designed for those in the population who have already expressed demand for services or who are experiencing sufficiently rapid social change to respond quickly to services offered. But assumptions about, and measures for, early acceptors may be inappropriate later in the program's development when demand is weaker and must be stimulated from outside the group. Ironically, the very success of a policy in its early stages is likely to sustain its reputation for effectiveness over an artificially long period and therefore delay reexamination of basic assumptions. At that point, policy makers must gain a fresh understanding of why people act as they do and reconsider how to create incentives and minimize hindrances to public acceptance of social programs. Because the gap between boys' and girls' enrollments has persisted even where diminished, any slackening of effort toward full enrollment affects girls more than boys, just as it affects rural more than urban children. If the uneduated have less access to techniques to help cope with a changing world, then any systematic bias in attendance or dropping out may have long-term repercussions on social or cultural divisions.

Demand has affected manpower policy in other ways. In job training and school tracking, content is as much an issue as is simple expansion: What sorts of training should be offered to women? Whereas the number of places open to girls has greatly expanded in the past 15 years, the options effectively open to girls have been limited. Officials' guesses as to what the public will accept, reigning cultural definitions of female roles, and the level of males' unemployment have all served to define the range of programs for girls. It is easier to endorse equal rights for men and women than it is to pursue programs aimed at promoting such equality. In Tunisia the goal of increasing job training for women — important as that is — has been implicitly divorced from equal opportunity for the sexes. While the reasons for this are understandable, current official choices will shape employment patterns for years to come. Even in a country where commitment to improving the status of women is high, the government finds itself pulled between stimulating social change or merely following it.

4. Social Origins and Sex-differential Schooling in the Philippines

PETER C. SMITH AND PAUL P. L. CHEUNG

Economic change involves transformations at both the individual and societal levels. Notable among these are changes in the process of social stratification and in the distribution of the most important status characteristics—education, occupations, and income. As central elements of the social hierarchy and means to success in other respects, both the process of educational attainment and the resulting distribution of schooling undergo change as economic development takes place. Economies experience increased demand for specific kinds of skilled labor, and to meet this demand societies sponsor systems of essentially universal and often free education. At the same time, alternate claims on the time of children diminish with industrialization and urbanization, further accelerating the trend toward longer exposures to schooling.

These are the aggregate trends in virtually all developing societies, though tempo and configuration of change vary with social setting. Among the most important aspects of this educational transformation are how increases in years of schooling are allocated across the population and how that pattern of allocation contributes either to educational equality or to increased variance in its distribution. Ultimately, policymakers need to understand the contribution of the educational system to the prevailing pattern of access to material well-being.

Much of the available research on the matter of distribution focuses on inheritance of status or opportunity from parents. Data from a number of countries suggest that with industrialization several systematic changes occur:[1] (1) occupational inheritance diminishes; (2) educational attainment grows in importance as a factor in the allocation of occupational roles; (3) the occupational persistence that remains is achieved indirectly, through the education of offspring; and (4) at the same time, the influence of parental characteristics on educational attainment diminishes. The last change is said to occur because in industrial societies a substantial amount

Hagen Koo, Linda Martin, and Andrew Mason commented on an earlier draft. Diana Chapon and Fred Montenegro provided statistical support.

[1] Donald J. Treiman, "Industrialization and Social Stratification," in *Social Stratification: Research and Theory for the 1970s*, ed. Edward O. Laumann (New York: Bobbs-Merrill, 1970), pp. 207–34; and Donald J. Treiman, *Occupational Prestige in Comparative Perspective* (New York: Academic Press, 1977), chap. 5. This is the widely accepted view. For another perspective, see Samuel Bowles, "Schooling and Inequality from Generation to Generation," *Journal of Political Economy* 80 (May–June 1972): S219–S251, and "Unequal Education and the Reproduction of the Social Division of Labor," in *Social Mobility*, ed. A. P. M. Coxon and C. L. Jones (Baltimore: Penguin, 1975), pp. 258–82.

Reprinted from the *Comparative Education Review* 25, no. 1 (February 1981): 28–44.

of free education is available, provided by the society at large. Moreover, it is in the interest of the society as a whole that educational advances be predicated on personal performance and not on extraneous attributes or resources, parental or otherwise.

This is of course a rather rose-colored view of what has occurred or is now occurring across the globe. Notably, it ignores the persistence of ascriptive, primordial mechanisms of allocation (race, color, sex), as well as the many means that can be employed by high-status parents to all but insure the success of their offspring. The existence of race-based allocation has not been ignored altogether by researchers either in the developed or the developing countries.[2] But until recently the sex-based allocation of educational and occupational attainment has been given little attention, and even the most thorough research has been based upon exclusively male samples.[3]

If educational attainment is increasingly to determine the way that jobs are distributed within generations, as well as the pattern of status transmission across generations, then it is important that we understand how schooling itself is distributed in a variety of cultural and economic settings undergoing change. In this article we examine one developing society, the Philippines, which exhibits a particular pattern of culture and social organization. We look at Philippine data describing the upward course of educational attainment during a period of especially rapid economic change. Our main interest is in the distributional features of schooling as a status characteristic; we relate the distribution of education to some important personal characteristics, including sex and aspects of social origin.

The Philippines is a paramount example of the contemporary drive for universal education as a component of national development. The modern system of education in the Philippines began even before the colonial era had ended. The Spanish regime (1565–1898) did little to encourage the schooling of the *indio*, or native, population,[4] but American colonial policy (1898–1946) placed considerable stock in the power of education. The impact of this colonial investment in formal schooling, and of the educational system which has evolved since Philippine independence in 1946, is unmistakable in even the crudest of comparisons over time. When the first American census was conducted in 1903 only 20 percent of the adult popu-

[2] For a discussion of developed countries, see Otis Dudley Duncan, "Inheritance of Poverty or Inheritance of Race?" in *On Understanding Poverty: Perspectives from the Social Sciences*, ed. Daniel P. Moynihan (New York: Basic, 1969), pp. 85–110; for a study of race-based allocation in a developing country, see Charles Hirschman, *Ethnic and Social Stratification in Peninsular Malaysia*, ASA Rose Monograph Series (Washington, D.C.: American Sociological Association, 1975).

[3] The best known is Peter M. Blau and Otis Dudley Duncan, *The American Occupational Structure* (New York: Wiley, 1967).

[4] On Philippine education in the Spanish period, see Henry F. Fox, "Primary Education in the Philippines, 1565–1863," *Philippine Studies* 13, no. 2 (April 1965): 207–31; John J. Carroll, *Changing Patterns of Social Structure in the Philippines, 1896–1963: An Outline Survey* (Quezon City: Ateneo de Manila University Press, 1968), pp. 45–53; and Karl Schwartz, "Filipino Education and Spanish Colonialism: Toward an Autonomous Perspective," *Comparative Education Review* 15 (June 1971): 202–18.

lation claimed any exposure to formal education, and the Spanish language, necessary for most dealings in commerce and government, was spoken by very few.

Yet even at this very low overall level of schooling and literacy, socioeconomic differentials were substantial. Variations by social class cannot be documented directly, but the available data do permit us to outline geographic and sex differentials. The percentage literate in 1903 varied widely across provinces, from near half in the advanced areas near Manila to little more than 10 percent in some of the more remote provinces.[5] In each, male literacy exceeded female literacy by a substantial margin. Colonywide, only one in 10 females was literate compared with three in 10 males.[6]

By the 1970s several remarkable changes had occurred. The American regime made a substantial investment in *barrio* schools, mainly out of a concern for inculcating loyalty to the new government and a sense of American-style citizenship.[7] The result was that by 1918 virtually all of the colony's 800 municipalities had at least an elementary school and, even more remarkably, one in four of the more than 16,000 *barrios* had some kind of school in operation.[8] The impact of this program for universal schooling was felt quickly—in rising literacy and in longer durations of exposure to formal education. The commitment has been extended since independence with continued good results.

This paper provides documentation and analysis of this twentieth-century revolution in educational attainment. But, with this picture of progress as a backdrop, we focus on two less sanguine but equally important features of Philippine education: its unequal distribution across social groups, and the dependence of years of schooling on social background. As we will show, the equity situation has improved in some respects but has remained stagnant in other ways. One very positive development is the virtual disappearance of the sex differential in schooling that existed to the benefit of males at the turn of the century. In contrast, differentials by birthplace, father's schooling, and father's occupation have persisted. We show that the elimination of the sex bias in schooling is a socially delimited rather than a society-wide phenomenon; in the large, generally poor,

[5] U.S. Bureau of the Census, *Census de las Filipinas* (Washington, D.C.: Government Printing Office, 1905), 2:83–93.

[6] Elizabeth Eviota and Peter C. Smith, "The Migration of Women in the Philippines" (paper prepared for the Working Group on Women in the Cities, East-West Population Institute, East-West Center, Honolulu, March 5–23, 1979), and *Population of the Philippines*, Country Monograph Series no. 5 (Bangkok: Economic and Social Commission for Asia and the Pacific, 1978), chap. 12.

[7] Chester L. Hunt and Thomas R. McHale, "Education and Philippine Economic Development," *Comparative Education Review* 9 (February 1965): 63–73. For a contemporary statement, see David P. Barrows, "What May Be Expected from Philippine Education?" *Journal of Race Development* (October 1910), pp. 156–68.

[8] Census Office of the Philippine Islands, *Census of the Philippine Islands* (Manila: Bureau of Printing, 1921), pt. 2, 4:128.

and more traditional sectors of the society, wherever the educational attainment of fathers is still low, significant sex differentials in the schooling of their offspring persist.

Data Sources and Pattern of Analysis

The cross-sectional information available in the censuses provides a valuable but analytically limiting view of our topic. Although a long series of censuses is available, enumerations were conducted irregularly, few questions on education were asked, and the resulting tabulations are not extensive. By turning to retrospective information gathered recently in household surveys, we are able to examine the changes that have occurred from a cohort perspective. We can also tabulate microlevel data to examine the influence of social background on schooling. The data that we employ derive from two recent national surveys. The National Demographic Survey of May 1968 was the first nationally representative demographic survey of households conducted in the Philippines. It yielded an important baseline of information on socioeconomic characteristics and demographic behavior.[9] A similar survey was conducted in May 1973 to provide an opportunity for comparison and assessment of change. Extensive fertility analysis has been conducted with both surveys, but other important socioeconomic information has not been utilized as fully.[10]

Each of the samples is based upon a stratified, two-stage, clustered sampling design distinguishing urban and rural sectors. The first-stage sampling unit was the enumeration district in urban areas and the *barrio*, or village, in rural areas. The 1968 survey includes information from 7,237 households and 44,960 persons aged 10 or over, upon which information the present analysis is based. The 1973 survey includes interviews of 9,412 households and 28,482 persons aged 15 and over from whom socioeconomic information was collected.[11]

In the 1968 survey, years of schooling were reported for all persons aged 10 and over. Present educational attainment data were supplemented by similar information for November 1965 (the date of the most recent national election) and February 1960 (when the last census was conducted). Other background information included father's educational attainment

[9] The results of the 1968 survey are reported in Wilhelm Flieger and Peter C. Smith, eds., *A Demographic Path to Modernity* (Quezon City: University of the Philippines Press, 1975). Appendix C is a brief methodological evaluation.

[10] The 1973 survey has been the basis for numerous studies. For an assessment of data quality, see Josefina Cabigon, "The Validity of Measuring Philippine Fertility Change through Birth History Analysis" (M.A. thesis, University of the Philippines, 1976); see also Luisa Engracia, Robert D. Retherford, Peter C. Smith, and Lee-Jay Cho, *Estimates of Fertility in the Philippines Derived by the Own-Children Method: 1960–1968*, Monograph Series, no. 9 (Manila: Republic of the Philippines, National Census and Statistics Office, 1977).

[11] The sample designs are described in greater detail in *The BCS Survey of Households Bulletin*, Series no. 27 (Manila: Republic of the Philippines, May 1968), and Series no. 32 (Manila: Republic of the Philippines, May 1973).

when he was age 40 (if alive then), father's occupation, and residence information including place of birth (urban or rural). The 1973 survey provided essentially the same information (with reference dates of May 1970, another census date, and November 1965). But in this survey information on fathers was asked only of ever-married respondents and no information was collected from persons under the age of 15.

In the present analysis we make use of information from both these surveys on current educational attainment, father's educational attainment at age 40, father's occupation, and place of birth. Because in both surveys years of schooling were coded in detailed categories, recoding into equivalent years of schooling was straightforward.

A Cohort Perspective on Progress in Education

The historical trend in years of schooling is depicted in table 1, where information is given separately by period of birth (cohort), place of birth (urban or rural), and sex. In this way we introduce the variables of interest and juxtapose similar data from the two surveys. Mean number of years of schooling is supplemented by two indicators of dispersion on educational attainment within each subgroup of the population: the standard deviation, and the coefficient of variation.

The length of exposure to formal schooling has risen dramatically and quite steadily across the cohorts and the residence groups shown, and it has done so for each of the sexes.[12] But there is no systematic trend in the amount of variation within each subgroup, save perhaps among females of rural origin, for whom standard deviations were constrained in the early cohorts by especially low mean attainment levels. Nevertheless, in all the subgroups shown the coefficient of variation declines systematically across cohorts, suggesting that a process of homogenization has accompanied the overall upward trend.[13]

[12] In comparisons over very long periods of time, years of schooling is an imperfect indicator of classroom exposure. Very early in the century, students spent varying amounts of time in school during a school year, and the average student was in school for less time than at present (U.S. Bureau of the Census, *Censo de las Islas Filipinas* [Washington, D.C.: Government Printing Office, 1905], 2:table 34). On the other hand, changes in the quality of education are not reflected either, and the quality of Philippine education may have declined in the postwar period; see World Bank, *The Philippines: Priorities and Prospects for Development* (Washington, D.C.: World Bank, 1976), chap. 12.

[13] Two final points should be clarified before we proceed further. First, there is an indication in table 1 of fewer years of schooling in the most recent cohorts. We do not interpret this as a genuine pattern, but merely as a reflection of the fact that most recent cohorts had incomplete educational histories at the time of the surveys. In particular, higher education tends to be excluded and will certainly increase the ultimate mean levels of schooling of recent cohorts above the levels for preceding ones. Second, it should be noted that mean values from the 1973 survey (which found each cohort 5 years older than in the previous survey) generally are slightly lower than those for 1968. This pattern contradicts the general expectation that older persons will have a greater tendency to exaggerate their schooling (Robert M. Hauser and David L. Featherman, "Equality of Schooling: Trends and Prospects," *Sociology of Education* 49 [April 1976]: 99–120). The differences between the surveys are small, however, and they probably can be attributed to differences in survey procedures and perhaps to somewhat poorer survey coverage among the poorly educated in 1968. Nonresponse was more prevalent in the 1968 than in the 1973 survey. In addition, the 1973 survey benefited from a renovation of the sampling frame and design which took place after the 1970 census.

TABLE 1

MEAN YEARS OF SCHOOLING OF THE HOUSEHOLD POPULATION IN MAY 1968 AND MAY 1973,
BY BIRTHPLACE, SEX, AND PERIOD OF BIRTH

Birthplace, Sex, and Period of Birth	Mean Years of Schooling		Standard Deviation		Coefficient of Variation (SD/Mean)	
	1968	1973	1968	1973	1968	1973
Urban:						
Female:						
1954–58	*	9.49	*	2.88	*	.30
1949–53	9.03	10.80	3.22	3.80	.37	.35
1944–48	9.96	9.95	4.28	4.22	.43	.47
1939–43	9.72	8.93	4.22	4.45	.43	.50
1934–38	8.56	8.81	4.35	4.55	.51	.52
1929–33	8.05	7.86	4.54	4.50	.56	.57
1924–28	7.20	7.06	4.57	4.37	.63	.62
1919–23	6.68	6.43	4.70	4.61	.70	.72
1914–18	6.06	5.80	4.57	4.21	.75	.73
1913 or earlier	5.11	4.35	4.75	4.51	.93	1.04
Male:						
1954–58	*	9.20	*	2.92	*	.32
1949–53	8.86	10.15	3.03	3.67	.34	.36
1944–48	9.72	9.80	3.98	4.04	.41	.41
1939–43	9.62	9.68	4.24	4.38	.44	.45
1934–38	8.89	9.12	4.14	4.37	.47	.48
1929–33	9.43	8.92	4.37	4.47	.46	.50
1924–28	8.47	8.17	4.69	4.47	.55	.55
1919–23	7.99	7.65	4.47	4.56	.56	.60
1914–18	7.17	7.26	4.92	4.67	.69	.64
1913 or earlier	7.16	5.87	4.75	4.90	.66	.83
Rural:						
Female:						
1954–58	*	7.68	*	3.15	*	.41
1949–53	7.40	8.09	3.25	4.04	.44	.50
1944–48	8.06	7.26	4.24	4.27	.53	.59
1939–43	6.88	6.39	4.37	4.01	.64	.63
1934–38	6.39	5.71	4.32	3.90	.68	.68
1929–33	5.92	5.45	4.35	4.17	.73	.77
1924–28	5.48	4.44	4.36	4.05	.80	.91
1919–23	4.79	3.87	3.96	3.90	.83	1.01
1914–18	4.15	3.40	3.90	3.42	.94	1.01
1913 or earlier	3.20	2.75	3.70	3.49	1.15	1.27
Male:						
1954–58	*	7.30	*	3.26	*	.45
1949–53	7.19	7.74	3.15	3.92	.44	.51
1944–48	8.20	7.28	4.04	4.13	.49	.57
1939–43	7.58	7.01	4.20	4.12	.55	.59
1934–38	7.05	6.46	4.38	4.26	.62	.66
1929–33	6.62	6.19	4.49	4.40	.68	.71
1924–28	6.57	5.57	4.40	4.45	.67	.80
1919–23	5.40	4.76	4.23	3.99	.78	.84
1914–18	5.92	4.55	4.62	4.00	.78	.88
1913 or earlier	4.52	3.73	4.30	4.00	.95	.93

SOURCE.—National Demographic Surveys, 1968 and 1973.
*Not computed.

Comparisons across Cohorts

It is apparent from table 1 that increases in years of schooling are persistent if somewhat uneven from one cohort to another. Some of the fluctuation undoubtedly represents only the vagaries of sampling, but some may also be due to specific historical events—for example, the Second World War and its aftermath. These fluctuations in the tempo of change notwithstanding, substantial long-term increases in cohort educational attainment are indicated. The increases between the earliest cohort shown and the cohort of 1949–53 (aged 15–19 in 1973) range from 3.3 years among males of urban origin to 6.4 years among females of urban origin. The average schooling differential between adjacent cohorts ranges from 0.8 years among urban females to 0.4 years among males of urban origin.

It is noteworthy that urban-born females advanced farther than rural-born females, whereas among males it was the rural-origin group that experienced the greatest progress. As a result of this difference between the sexes, the urban-rural schooling differential has expanded somewhat among females, whereas among the males the place-of-origin differential has diminished. An urban-rural differential of 2.5 years or so persists across cohorts of females and even increases until the most recent cohort, while the male urban-rural differential (somewhat higher initially) has declined slightly but steadily. On the other hand, relative differences between the urban born and the rural born diminished considerably for both sexes, from around 60 percent to well under 40 percent of the respective rural levels.

The Demise of the Sex Differential

The implication of these patterns for sex differentials in schooling is clearly indicated. There has been a steady convergence of the sexes in absolute as well as in relative terms. The sex differential among persons of urban origin was about 1.5 years (more than 25 percent of the prevailing level) in the oldest cohorts, but it dropped below 1 year by the cohort of 1929–33 and declined sharply thereafter. The rural sex differential was not so great initially (though it was even larger in relative terms), but it declined rapidly. The convergence of the sexes occurred earliest in the urban sector, but by the early 1950s (the cohort of 1944–48 and thereafter) young people of both origin groups were receiving essentially equal education regardless of sex. Most remarkable in light of the sex-bias pattern characteristic of the past is the recent educational superiority of females over males. It is not clear from the data available whether this recent differential favoring females is likely to increase or if an essentially stable equality of the sexes has now been attained.

Generations of Change

The survey information on father's educational attainment allows us to consider the educational transformation from the perspective of intergenerational comparisons—a useful supplement to our discussion of the trend across cohorts. Indeed, when change is as substantial and rapid as it has been in the Philippines, much of the social import is felt in generational terms. Children have substantially higher educational attainments than their parents, and they are therefore in a position to contribute heavily to family income. They often have central roles in family strategies for survival and social mobility. At the same time, intergenerational gaps in educational attainment may be the cause of a variety of conflicts within families as well as in the larger society. Most important, we demonstrate subsequently that parental (father's) characteristics are of central importance in explaining both the upward trend in schooling and the persistence or elimination of socioeconomic differences in schooling.

The 1968 data on the schooling of fathers are shown in table 2; they provide a century-long view of the progress that has been achieved.[14] The oldest cohorts of respondents had fathers who were born near the end of the nineteenth century. Those men had, on average, fewer than 2 years of formal schooling—less than 1.5 years for fathers of rural-origin respondents and about 3 years for fathers of the urban born. As low as these schooling levels are, they may well be overestimates of true years of schooling many decades ago. Given the much higher levels of schooling prevalent more recently, there is likely to be some tendency for contemporary respondents to overstate parental educational attainment when it was quite low. In addition, since survivorship both of respondents and of their fathers is correlated with socioeconomic status and education is an important component of socioeconomic status, the oldest cohorts of respondents and their fathers must underrepresent the low-SES (low-education) population somewhat.

Rural fathers whose offspring were born in the period just preceding World War II had fewer than 4 years of schooling, compared with less than half as much education among fathers during the century's first 2 decades (we do not have direct evidence, but we must infer that the educational attainment of mothers in these times was meager indeed). By the immediate postwar period the mean education of fathers had exceeded 4 years, and the most recent rural-origin cohorts had fathers with nearly 5 years of schooling, while in the urban-origin cohorts this level had reached 7 years or more.

Further Analysis

We have now introduced some significant patterns of variation and change in educational attainment. In this section we look more closely at

[14] We base this part of our analysis on the 1968 survey, which provides information for the fathers of all adult respondents. The analogous questions in the 1973 survey were asked only of those who had ever been married.

TABLE 2

Advances beyond Father's Mean Years of Schooling: Household Population in May 1968 by Period of Birth, Sex, and Birthplace

Period of Birth	Female					Male				
	Urban		Rural		Total	Urban		Rural		Total
	Father's Schooling	Respondent's Advance beyond Father	Father's Schooling	Respondent's Advance beyond Father	Father's Schooling	Father's Schooling	Respondent's Advance beyond Father	Father's Schooling	Respondent's Advance beyond Father	Father's Schooling
1949–53	7.71	1.32	4.72	2.68	5.62	8.07	.79	4.96	2.23	5.78
1944–48	7.34	2.62	4.72	3.34	5.44	7.15	2.56	5.16	3.04	5.59
1939–43	6.92	2.80	3.85	3.03	4.59	6.83	2.79	4.25	3.33	4.71
1934–38	6.40	2.17	3.40	2.99	4.02	5.52	3.37	3.77	3.28	4.09
1929–33	5.68	2.37	3.09	2.83	3.70	6.02	3.41	3.02	3.60	3.65
1924–28	4.84	2.36	2.96	2.52	3.34	4.84	3.62	3.14	3.43	3.45
1919–23	4.61	2.07	2.48	2.31	2.91	4.35	3.63	2.52	2.88	2.90
1914–18	4.42	1.64	2.29	1.86	2.70	3.46	3.71	2.65	3.27	2.77
1909–13	4.32	2.03	1.86	2.08	2.30	3.97	3.58	2.36	2.93	2.50
1908 or earlier	2.56	1.31	1.29	1.18	1.50	3.25	3.52	1.43	2.32	1.60

SOURCE.—National Demographic Survey, 1968.

some of the separate and shared influences of social background characteristics that may be implied in these patterns. We pay particular attention to
the important intergenerational influence of father's schooling on the
overall upward trend in education and on the observed convergence of the
sexes.

Our first step is to consider the relative importance of these sources of
variation in a multivariate framework. We find that some influences maintain their importance, while others, notably the sex factor, diminish in
importance. Two of the factors under investigation are inherently classificatory in nature (place of birth and sex), and the remainder can be considered in classificatory terms. Therefore, multiple classification analysis is
employed to obtain an assessment of the various effects.[15]

The first two rows of table 3 summarize the effects of sex, birthplace,
and father's schooling across the entire sample. This is followed by separate analyses by cohort. Three coefficients are shown: eta, or η, which
measures the total effect of each variable on years of schooling; the
partial standardized regression coefficient, or β, which indicates the effect
of each net of the others; and R^2, indicating the proportion of variation
accounted for by the combination of variables.

The influences of two background characteristics, birthplace and father's education, are substantial and remain, undiminished, over the cohorts represented. In contrast, the importance of respondent's sex diminishes from a high level in the early cohorts to a very low level by the cohort
of 1934–38 and remains low thereafter. The β's and η's for respondent's sex
are very similar in magnitude, reflecting the fact that the sex distribution
of respondents is virtually random in relation to birthplace and father's
education. But the latter variables are associated (table 2), and the slightly
diminished β's for these variables reflect their shared influence on respondent's years of schooling. In the analysis for all cohorts combined we have
included cohort membership as a predictor. It is noteworthy that despite
the evident upward trend in years of schooling across cohorts, father's
schooling remains the most important predictor of respondent's education.

The variation in respondent's schooling accounted for by all these
predictor variables taken together ranges from 20 to 31 percent. A substantial proportion of variance is accounted for, yet much variation remains
unexplained. On balance, these results are similar to those reported in
other studies employing roughly analogous sets of explanatory variables.[16]

[15] Multiple classification analysis (MCA) is an application of the general linear model in which a
continuous dependent variable is regressed on a combination of categorical and continuous predictors,
subject to the constraint of no statistical interaction between any two categorical predictors in respect
of their effects on the dependent variable. See Frank Andrews, James Morgan, and John Sunquist,
Multiple Classification Analysis (Ann Arbor, Mich.: Institute for Social Research, 1969).

[16] In a study of U.S. male samples, R^2 was about .31 when the predictor variables were father's
education, father's occupation (scaled as prestige scores), number of siblings, and whether parents'
marriage was intact. The coefficient of determination reached .36 when region of birth, race, and

TABLE 3

RELATIVE IMPORTANCE OF SOCIODEMOGRAPHIC FACTORS
ASSOCIATED WITH RESPONDENT'S EDUCATIONAL ATTAINMENT (May 1968)

Period of Birth	Sex	Birthplace	Father's Education	Cohort	R^2	N
All cohorts:						
η	.05	.19	.45	.20		
β	.05	.09	.42	.17	.24	15,974
1949-53:						
η	.05	.22	.45	*		
β	.05	.10	.43	*	.22	4,463
1944-48:						
η	.00	.16	.49	*		
β	.01	.07	.48	*	.24	2,973
1939-43:						
η	.04	.22	.54	*		
β	.03	.11	.52	*	.31	2,079
1934-38:						
η	.07	.15	.50	*		
β	.05	.07	.49	*	.26	1,746
1929-33:						
η	.13	.19	.41	*		
β	.13	.11	.39	*	.20	1,441
1924-28:						
η	.15	.19	.45	*		
β	.14	.12	.42	*	.23	1,077
1919-23:						
η	.06	.19	.46	*		
β	.07	.10	.44	*	.23	800
1914-18:						
η	.22	.18	.46	*		
β	.20	.10	.43	*	.26	581
1909-13:						
η	.19	.24	.41	*		
β	.19	.12	.37	*	.22	445
1908 or earlier:						
η	.24	.15	.39	*		
β	.22	.12	.36	*	.21	369

SOURCE.—National Demographic Survey, 1968.
*Not included.

The persistence of father's schooling as an important influence on the educational attainment of respondents can be a double-edged sword from the standpoint of educational progress and improvements in educational equality. We have shown that an advance in schooling in one generation is the foundation for further progress in the next, a fact which has worked to

cohort were added. See Robert M. Hauser and David L. Featherman, "Equality of Schooling: Trends and Prospects," Sociology of Education 49 (April 1976): 99–120. In another study of U.S. males, R^2 was .43 when psychological measures were introduced as well; see Kenneth L. Wilson and Alejandro Portes, "The Educational Attainment Process: Results from a National Sample," American Journal of Sociology 81, no. 2 (1975): 343–63. Duncan reported R^2 values within cohorts ranging from .15 to .18 when father's education was the only predictor (Beverly Duncan, "Education and Social Background," American Journal of Sociology 72 [January 1967]: 363–72). In the Monterrey study of Mexican males, R^2 was .29 when father's occupation, size of community of origin, and cohort were employed (George Balan, Harley L. Browning, and Elizabeth Jelin, Men in a Developing Society: Geographic and Social Mobility in Monterrey, Mexico, Latin American Monograph Series, no. 30 [Austin: University of Texas Press, 1973]).

the educational benefit of nearly everyone. Yet it is the precise form of the relationship between father's and offspring's schooling that determines whether the distribution of education will improve or worsen over time.

Thus far we have considered individual-level variation in cross-sectional, synchronic terms. Now we look at the role of background characteristics on changing patterns over time. We disaggregate the influence of father's schooling by adding a broad classification of father's occupation to the variables already considered and by presenting data for respondents within categories of father's education. The information on father's occupation adds an important dimension to our understanding of intergenerational influences because it assesses, at least in a general fashion, the social milieu of upbringing apart from that indexed by father's schooling. We find that the influence of father's education has changed over time and that it varies with social background. Most significantly, we show that the demise of the sex differential in schooling is a phenomenon that is confined to certain categories of the population. Some of our conclusions are drawn directly from the pattern of respondents' schooling (table 4); others we base on a standardization procedure (table 5).[17]

The variables under examination have been part of a twentieth-century social transformation, and their changing distributions across cohorts of respondents reflect the processes at work. An overview of several decades of change is provided by table 4, which presents the background composition of fathers from two cohorts representing schooling in the first 2 decades of this century and in the early 1950s. In the time period shown, the proportion urban (both sexes) rose slightly, from .20 to .25, and the nonfarm share of the rural population rose from .30 to .40, while in the urban sector fathers in blue- and white-collar occupations maintained their respective shares. Urban growth over the period was widely distributed in these broad occupational categories, while in rural areas nonfarm occupations expanded disproportionately.

As the standardization results in table 5 indicate, the small shifts in the proportion urban account for very little of the observed increase in schooling for either sex. An analogous kind of standardization for father's occupation in the urban sector likewise has little or no effect. On the other hand, the shift in father's occupation among the rural born does account for one-sixth or so of the increase in the schooling of male respondents. Overall, between 18.2 and 45.3 percent of the observed changes are accounted for, with most of the change that we can account for with this standardization procedure reflecting shifts in father's schooling within

[17] Standardization is a technique for adjusting the overall means (e.g., mean years of schooling) of groups undergoing comparison for their differences in composition and differences in their means for component subgroups. The adjustment consists of obtaining "standardized" overall means which reflect a presumed common or "standard" composition; see Evelyn M. Kitagawa, "Standardized Comparisons in Population Research," *Demography* 1, no. 1 (1964): 296–315.

TABLE 4

MEAN YEARS OF SCHOOLING OF THE HOUSEHOLD POPULATION IN MAY 1968, BY PERIOD OF BIRTH, SEX, BIRTHPLACE, FATHER'S OCCUPATION, AND FATHER'S EDUCATION

Birthplace, Father's Occupation, and Father's Education	Male					Female				
	Period of Birth				Gain over Cohorts*	Period of Birth				Gain over Cohorts*
	1939–48	1929–38	1919–28	1918 or Earlier		1939–48	1929–38	1919–28	1918 or Earlier	
Rural:										
Farm	6.57	5.85	5.21	4.29	2.28	6.42	5.21	4.23	2.95	3.47
0–3	5.31	4.71	4.26	3.23	2.48	5.10	4.20	3.35	2.38	2.72
4–6	7.42	7.57	6.74	7.67	−.25	7.15	6.80	6.23	4.89	2.26
7–11	9.69	9.54	9.94	9.27	.42	10.26	8.55	8.02	8.76	1.50
12+	9.38	6.62	7.07	5.26	4.12	9.30	5.79	5.03	3.17	6.13
Nonfarm:										
0–3	9.81	8.93	7.99	6.90	2.91	9.38	8.19	7.28	4.56	4.82
4–6	6.91	5.99	5.51	4.36	2.55	5.94	5.34	5.53	3.05	2.89
7–11	9.21	8.90	8.15	8.47	.74	8.81	8.38	7.39	6.60	2.21
12+	11.05	11.42	11.18	10.82	.23	11.66	11.02	9.85	7.30	4.36
	12.04	10.92	9.84	9.53	2.51	11.50	10.51	9.60	5.99	5.51
Urban:										
Blue collar:										
0–3	8.81	8.03	7.20	6.42	2.39	9.03	7.32	6.13	4.51	4.52
4–6	6.40	5.96	5.47	4.23	2.17	6.26	4.78	4.12	2.38	3.88
7–11	8.83	8.72	8.66	7.18	1.65	8.63	7.71	7.47	7.27	1.36
12+	10.49	10.62	11.14	11.35	−.86	11.28	9.88	9.44	9.11	2.17
	11.64	10.31	8.11	9.57	2.07	12.50	10.70	8.89	5.08	7.42
White collar:										
0–3	11.38	11.59	10.87	8.73	2.65	11.59	10.59	8.84	7.08	4.51
4–6	8.17	9.95	7.42	6.18	1.99	6.09	7.32	4.16	5.74	.35
7–11	9.85	9.39	10.48	9.83	.02	8.93	8.80	8.21	7.57†	1.36
12+	11.38	12.36	12.39	11.76	−.38	12.16	11.39	10.89	9.61	2.55
	12.91	12.46	10.85	10.22	2.69	13.61	12.08	10.12	7.14	6.47

SOURCE.—National Demographic Survey, 1968.
*Cohort of 1939–48 vs. cohort of 1918 or earlier.
†Fewer than 10 cases.

63

TABLE 5

STANDARDIZATION RESULTS INDICATING THE EFFECTS OF INTERCOHORT SHIFTS
IN BIRTHPLACE, FATHER'S EDUCATION, AND FATHER'S OCCUPATION

Sex, Birthplace, and Father's Occupation	Distribution		Percentage of Intercohort Change accounted for by Standardization			
	Cohort of 1918 and Earlier	Cohort of 1939–48	Father's Occupation	Birthplace	Father's Education	All Variables
Female	1.00	1.00	⋯	⋯	⋯	27.1
Rural	.81	.75	4.7	3.5*	⋯	⋯
Farm	.56	.47	⋯	⋯	18.2	⋯
Nonfarm	.25	.28	⋯	⋯	29.3	⋯
Urban	.19	.25	0.0†	⋯	⋯	⋯
Blue collar	.13	.17	⋯	⋯	19.0	⋯
White collar	.06	.08	⋯	⋯	33.5	⋯
Male	1.00	1.00	⋯	⋯	⋯	39.2
Rural	.79	.74	14.6	3.1*	⋯	⋯
Farm	.56	.43	⋯	⋯	22.8	⋯
Nonfarm	.23	.31	⋯	⋯	34.4	⋯
Urban	.21	.26	.0	⋯	⋯	⋯
Blue collar	.14	.17	⋯	⋯	35.6	⋯
White collar	.07	.09	⋯	⋯	45.3	⋯

SOURCE.—National Demographic Survey, 1968.
NOTE.—Totals are italicized.
*This result is for blue- versus white-collar fathers among the urban born and farm versus nonfarm fathers among the rural born.
†Standardization increases the difference slightly.

each of the other social background categories. Notably, father's education is a more powerful explanatory variable for male than for female respondents, and the background variables in the model are together more effective in accounting for the male than for the female trend.

Nevertheless, much of the observed difference between the two cohorts is not explained by the variables under consideration. This is readily seen by returning to table 4, where we find increases in the mean years of schooling within categories of the cross-classification reflecting all our background variables. Substantial gains are indicated for nearly every social-background category, even when father's schooling is held constant. These unexplained increases in cohort years of schooling must remain an inducement to further investigation.

It is also apparent from table 4 that the impact of father's schooling is pervasive. Within most social-background categories additions to father's schooling are associated with substantial additions to the educational attainment of respondents. There is only one exception to this pattern, one that we cannot explain. Throughout the social-origin categories, fathers with the highest level of schooling (12 years or more) do not pass on to their offspring as much education as do fathers with 7–11 years of schooling. Whatever the source of this anomaly, it characterizes rural-origin fathers more than those of urban origin, and it disappears in the recent urban cohorts, where fathers with high education do have children with very high educational attainments.

Although the impact of father's education is widespread, the strength and form of that impact is variable. This is especially evident when we consider the influence of father's education on sex differentials in schooling within categories of father's education and other background variables. Among urban categories of father's occupation and father's schooling, the female advantage is found to be substantial only when father's education is relatively high. In fact, at lower levels of father's schooling, regardless of type of father's occupation, fathers provide more education to sons than to daughters. That is, within any social-background category daughters benefit more than do sons from advances in father's schooling. This result moves us a step closer to understanding the observed convergence of the sexes on years of schooling by locating it more precisely within the social structure. Apparently, the long-term progress in father's schooling within each of the social background categories has shifted recent sibling sets into the categories of father's schooling wherein daughters can benefit most.

The data suggest one further observation: equal allocation (or even an advantage for daughters) characterizes high-education families in both the blue- and white-collar urban milieu but among neither farm or nonfarm families in the rural sector. Thus, equal treatment of daughters and sons must be described as a recent phenomenon found among relatively well-educated urban-background families. Moreover, this is the case regardless of type of father's occupation. The phenomenon is absent among nonfarm families of rural origin, even when father's education is high. Nor does it occur among urban families (regardless of type of occupation) when father's education is low.

Discussion

We conclude with some observations on how patterns in the Philippines might be interpreted against the theoretical background described at the outset of this paper and in relation to other important changes in the structure of opportunity in the Philippines, especially opportunities for women.

There is no question that the overall rise in schooling that comes with industrialization has characterized the Philippines as much as it has other developing societies. The Philippines may even stand as an extreme case in this regard, with even rural, farm parents now placing their offspring in the schools for an average of more than 6 years and urban parents bettering this by 2 years. Similarly, the observed homogenization of educational attainment meets our general expectation, as does the slight convergence of urban-rural educational differentials. Finally, the convergence in the educational exposure of males and females is certainly an example of the demise of a primordial allocative mechanism.

On the other hand, our data demonstrate the persistence of father's schooling and father's occupation as determinants of educational attainment. As industrialization occurs, this dependence on father's characteristics ought to diminish. There is, apparently, a persisting rigidity in Philippine society despite all the change that has occurred and despite the government's efforts to open up the system of educational allocation. The mechanisms supporting the persistence are many; most notably, it remains possible in the Philippines, as in all market-oriented societies, to purchase education (or at least certification) for one's offspring of sufficient quality and reputation to ensure status maintenance and even some status attainment.

The convergence of the sexes on educational attainment is certainly of great practical and human importance, but it is also theoretically intriguing, for it introduces the issue of changing allocative mechanisms within families. Thus, we find that educational allocation by sex differs sharply with high versus low education of fathers, and it differs somewhat with rural versus urban upbringing. Why do families with highly educated fathers of urban background allocate their educational resources between sons and daughters differently (more equitably) than families with fathers of rural origin or less education? At this point we can do no more than suggest some further avenues for investigation of this and other issues.

First, our analysis has been limited to a few background, parental characteristics, and these variables are about as successful in explaining variance in educational attainment as they have been in other settings. The empirical literature suggests three additional classes of variables that we have not been able to examine: (1) personal characteristics, such as intelligence and salient aspects of personality; (2) sibling-set attributes (including respondent's location within the sibling set), which might illuminate that portion of the variance in educational attainment that is *intra*family and therefore not a product of differences among parents or family backgrounds; and (3) characteristics of the economy that may be operating to shift the parental calculus of returns to the schooling of offspring.

With regard to our findings on sex differentials in schooling, for example, the examination of sibling-set features and changes in the structure of the economy and labor force may be especially fruitful. The underlying bilateral structure of Philippine kinship raises the possibility that under modern conditions of land scarcity daughters increasingly are taking their share of patrimony in the form of schooling, while their brothers continue to receive the diminishing family parcels of land. Similarly, the recent penetration of females into heretofore male-dominated sectors of the occupational structure, and the recent surge of female-dominated migration to towns and cities,[18] may all be elements in the same process of parental reasoning. Investigation is continuing in the hope of untangling some of these possibilities.

[18] Wilhelm Flieger, Brigida Koppin, and Carmencita Lim, *Geographical Patterns of Internal Migration in the Philippines: 1960–1970*, Monograph no. 5 (Manila: National Census and Statistics Office, 1976); and Elizabeth Eviota and Peter C. Smith, "The Migration of Women in the Philippines" (prepared for the Working Group on Women in Cities, East-West Population Institute, East-West Center, Honolulu, March 5–23, 1979), and *Population of the Philippines*, Country Monograph Series no. 5 (Bangkok: Economic and Social Commission for Asia and the Pacific, 1978), chap. 12.

5. Sex and Ethnic Differences in Educational Investment in Malaysia: The Effect of Reward Structures

BEE-LAN CHAN WANG

Around the world, the lower propensity of women to continue their education much beyond high school has been attributed to the fact that higher education enhances men's abilities to fulfill their future roles as breadwinners but is of much less utility to women in this regard.[1] It has also been argued that the attitudes and behaviors necessary for completing higher education —such as amibition, drive, and competitiveness — are in conflict with general social expectations of the feminine character. Educational and occupational success by women can result in social rejection, dislike, and prejudice.[2] Therefore, concern with marriageability and the feminine image is probably partly responsible for the lower educational intentions of girls and their severely limited occupational choices.[3]

While the women's movement may have moderated the effects of these factors, women still earn less than men with comparable social origins, educational attainments, occupational status, and other economically relevant characteristics.[4] Part of the difference in incomes may be attributed to the institutional constraints on the married woman because of her family role, but part is probably due to discriminatory policies based on sex.[5] It is also generally true that the occupational options of working women are very limited —at the higher levels, to teaching and government jobs; at the middle levels, to nursing, secretarial, and clerical jobs.[6] Top-level jobs in any occupation are usually dominated by men. Even in the Soviet Union, where women are very active in the economy, they are confined to the lower rungs in fields in which they predominate.[7]

[1] Tove Thagaard Sem, "Kjonnsroller og studiemotivering" [Sex roles and motivation for higher education] Norges Almenvitenskapelige Forskningerad (Oslo: Utredningsaudelningen, 1967); abstracted in Helen S. Astin, Allison Parelman, and Anne Fisher, Sex Roles: A Research Bibliography (Washington, D.C.: National Institute of Mental Health, 1975).

[2] Matina S. Horner, "Toward an Understanding of Achievement-related Conflicts in Women," Journal of Social Issues 28 (Spring 1972): 157–75.

[3] Alan E. Bayer, "Marriage Plans and Educational Aspirations," American Journal of Sociology 75 (February 1969): 239–44.

[4] Larry E. Sater and Herman P. Miller, "Income Differences between Men and Career Women," American Journal of Sociology 78 (January 1973): 962–74.

[5] H. Sanborn, "Pay Differences between Men and Women," Industrial and Labor Relations Review 91 (July 1964): 534–50.

[6] E.g., Catherine Bodard Silver, "Salon, Foyer, Bureau: Women and the Professions in France," in Changing Women in a Changing Society, ed. Joan Huber (Chicago: University of Chicago Press, 1973).

[7] Norton T. Dodge, "Women in Economic Development: A Review Essay," International Review of Education 19, no. 1 (1973): 161–66.

Reprinted from the Comparative Education Review 24, no. 2 (part 2)(June 1980): S140–59.

"Sexual stratification" as a concept has only recently become part of sociological thinking. Stratification theories and research fall largely into one of two major perspectives. Recent studies have tended to use path models of the status-attainment process, accelerating a trend that was started by Blau and Duncan's *The American Occupational Structure* in 1967.[8] Emphasizing the role of home and school inputs and individual characteristics of ability and ambition, these studies have added to our understanding of the *distributive* aspects of social class.[9] However, some scholars believe that the *relational* aspects have been relatively neglected.[10] These include questions regarding the institutional mechanisms by which the political and economic structure influences the relative life chances of different social groups. For example, critics of the cultural-deprivation hypothesis emphasize power and control relationships which serve to maintain the status quo. This article investigates the application of both perspectives to understanding sexual and ethnic stratification in Malaysia.

In most societies, the group occupying the highest economic position is the one with political and social power, and therefore it is difficult for researchers to separate the effects of socialization or disadvantaged family backgrounds from those of social and economic powerlessness or lack of opportunity. In Malaysia, however, a unique situation exists in which political control is exercised by the least economically and educationally advanced ethnic group. Therefore, a study of Malaysia can shed light on some of the institutional mechanisms through which social power and control can enhance the upward mobility of groups which have suffered past or background disadvantage.

This study examines the effect of the external structure of rewards on the life chances of individuals irrespective of background characteristics. In particular, the following hypothesis is examined: Insofar as members of sex and ethnic groups are influenced by perceived returns to further education, then those groups perceiving greater benefits from further education will have greater tendencies to continue in school than those perceiving lower benefits, other relevant variables being the same.[11]

[8] Peter M. Blau and Otis Dudley Duncan, *The American Occupational Structure* (New York: Wiley, 1967); see, e.g., Karl L. Alexander and Bruce K. Eckland, "Sex Differences in the Educational Attainment Process," *American Sociological Review* 39 (October 1974): 668–82.

[9] John H. Goldthorpe, "Class, Status and Party in Modern Britain," *European Journal of Sociology* 13 (1972): 342–72.

[10] Lewis A. Coser, "Presidential Address: Two Methods in Search of a Substance," *American Sociological Review* 40 (December 1975): 691–700.

[11] Here I refer not to percentage increments in earnings but to marginal rates of return. For instance, group X high school graduates may earn so much less than their group Y counterparts that going to college may fetch a greater marginal rate of return for group X high school graduates despite lower absolute after-college earnings when compared with group Y (see Mark Blaug, *An Introduction to the Economics of Education* [Harmondsworth, Middlesex: Penguin, 1970]). For a discussion of sex differences in earnings as they relate to the profitability of investment in education for

The Malaysian Case: Ethnic and Sex Differences

The multiethnic society of Malaysia is especially suitable for distinguishing the effects of control of reward structures from background disadvantage or "deprivation" in the usual sense. Malays, constituting 45 percent of the population, have historically been the least economically and educationally developed group. However, special constitutional provisions for them as the indigenous people and the fact that they hold political power mean that the reward structure for educated persons is greatly skewed in their favor. Non-Malays, particularly the Chinese, are generally from higher socioeconomic backgrounds than Malays but, as the data below will confirm, expect poorer job and educational opportunities. The Chinese and Indians, who make up about 35 and 9 percent of the population, respectively, immigrated to Malaysia as laborers, petty merchants, craftsmen, and the like, in the first 4 decades of this century. These non-Malays, most of whom are now Malaysian born, are heavily involved at all levels of the country's occupational structure and dominate the modern industrial, commercial, and professional sectors of the economy. The large majority of the Malays work as poor, rural peasants engaged mainly in rice farming, fishing, and other small-scale agriculture.

This situation is rapidly changing as a result of the government's aggressive policies and programs designed to promote Malay economic and educational development and to "restructure the economy . . . so as to eliminate the identification of race with economic function."[12] The educational system is the major institution through which this is to be accomplished. The government has reserved about 80 percent of government scholarships for Malays; it has used ethnic quotas in educational selection, especially at the tertiary level; and it has lowered entry requirements for Malays into scientific and technical courses of study. These policies have specific constitutional sanction. In addition, recruitment into and promotion within government and quasi-government services, which together employ most of the educated manpower in the country,[13] are done with the primary goal of ethnic restructuring in mind. Private companies are also under pressure to employ Malays.

The main point in this article is that even though the Malays as a group were, until recently, less mobile into the modern sectors of the

---

women, see Maureen Woodhall, "Investment in Women: A Reappraisal of the Concept of Human Capital," *International Review of Education* 19, no. 1 (1973): 9–28.

[12] Tan Sir Ghazali bin Shafie, then minister with special functions and minister of information and broadcasting; speech in Parliament, Kuala Lumpur, on March 5, 1971.

[13] This is typical of less developed countries, where government is the main agent for promoting economic growth as well as for providing social and educational services.

economy,[14] had fewer members with secondary education, enjoyed lower incomes, and were more rural in origin than the non-Malays, particularly the Chinese, the changes of the last 10 years in occupational opportunities for educated Malays have caused Malays to be more eager to undertake postsecondary education than non-Malays. This is true because Malays, as well as non-Malays, respond to the perceived benefits of further education.

It is necessary to examine ethnic differences among males separately from females, because the motivational bases of educational behavior for the two sexes are likely to be different.[15] This article also examines sex differences in educational decision making to probe the role of external reward structures versus internalized cultural norms. If women with the same educational qualifications as men expect lower earnings than men, the position of women relative to men is comparable to that of non-Malays relative to Malays. This is particularly true of high school seniors in Malaysia, since it has been shown that girls in the last year of high school are generally from higher-status family backgrounds than are the boys.[16]

Therefore, to return to the general hypothesis, these are the sex and ethnic comparisons examined in this study: (*a*) Malay/non-Malay differences among males in perceived benefits of and propensities to further education; (*b*) the same, among females; (*c*) male-female differences among Malays; and (*d*) the same, among non-Malays.

Data and Methods

Form 5 is the last year of secondary schooling in Malaysia, and form 6 consists of 2 years of preuniversity education. About 21 percent and 5 percent of the appropriate age groups in the population were enrolled in form 5 and form 6 in 1972, when this study was conducted. After form 5, students who pass the final Malaysian certificate of education examinations have three alternatives: (*a*) enter the labor market, (*b*) go to form 6, or (*c*) enter a teaching or technical college or nursing school, if one is accepted. Only a small minority are offered the opportunity for *c*. The vast majority of Malaysian students wish to go to form 6 and then university if they can, and the students in our sample evidenced the same

[14] Charles Hirschman, *Ethnic and Social Stratification in Pennisular Malaysia* (Washington, D.C.: American Sociological Association, 1975).

[15] Ralph H. Turner, "Some Aspects of Women's Ambition," *American Journal of Sociology* 70 (November 1964): 271–85.

[16] Bee-Lan Chan Wang, "Sex Differences in Career Goals and Orientations toward Higher Education in West Malaysia" (paper presented at the 21st Annual Meeting of the Comparative and International Education Society, New Orleans, February 16–19, 1977) (hereafter cited as "Sex Differences").

aspiration.[17] In addition to being the necessary transition to university, form 6 improves one's prospects in the job market after successful completion of the higher school certificate examinations.

A stratified sample of form 5 students with unequal numbers of respondents from each stratum was obtained by the following method. All government and fully aided,[18] upper-secondary schools in the state of Penang and province Wellesley were classified into 10 categories on the basis of locality, language medium of instruction (Malay, English, and formerly Chinese but now English-medium schools), sex (boys, girls, and coeducational), and type of school (academic, technical, and vocational).[19] A random sample of one, two, or three schools was then drawn from each category. This gave a total sample of 17 out of 42 upper-secondary schools in the state in 1972.

All the schools in the sample were visited between January 5 and 15, 1972. In most of these schools, all the form 5 students present on the day of the researcher's visit were given the questionnaire to answer. In the large schools, the questionnaire was administered to a random sample of half of the form 5 classes. Thus a total of 1,728 out of a universe of 6,073 form 5 students in the state responded to the questionnaire.

The sampling method resulted in certain of the 10 categories of schools being more highly sampled than others. Therefore, the final sample of students was weighted as follows:

$$\begin{matrix}\text{Weight for each student} \\ \text{in a category A school}\end{matrix} = \frac{\begin{matrix}\text{Total form 5 students in} \\ \text{category A in the state}\end{matrix}}{6{,}073} \times \frac{1{,}728}{\begin{matrix}N \text{ of students of} \\ \text{category A in sample}\end{matrix}}$$

The weighted sample was used for the analysis reported in this paper after vocational school students were eliminated (since vocational schools are terminal institutions whose students have no option of going to form 6). This resulted in a smaller sample of 1,517 students. Form 5 enrollment data for the state for 1972, obtained from the Department of Edu-

[17] Bee-Lan Chan Wang, "An Inter-Ethnic Comparison of Educational Selection, Achievement, and Decision Making among Fifth-Form Students in West Malaysia," (Ph.D. diss., University of Chicago, 1975) (hereafter cited as "Inter-Ethnic Comparison"); Yoshimitsu Takei, John C. Bock, and Rex H. Warland, "Aspirations and Expectations of West Malaysian Youth: Two Models of Social Class Values," *Comparative Education Review* 17 (June 1973): 216–30.

[18] The vast majority of all schools fit this description. The exceptions are private schools which are composed mostly of students who have either failed the government selective examinations or are too old to qualify for a place in a regular school.

[19] These variables were chosen because the social characteristics of students tend to vary according to these categories. There were only 10 categories because some types of schools were not divisible by sex (e.g., all rural, Malay-medium schools were coeducational) or locality (e.g., there was only one technical school, and all formerly Chinese-medium girls' schools were urban). Schools located in communities of 10,000 or more were considered urban, others rural.

cation, showed that, after weighting, our sample of students was representative in ethnicity and sex of the form 5 population.

Model

The model used in this study is based on the economic theory of private decision making, although this study is not a cost-benefit analysis in the usual sense.[20] A form 5 student's decision whether to go to form 6 is expected to be affected by the following factors:

1. Costs of a sixth-form education: These include both the direct outlays for fees and purchase of books and supplies and the indirect or opportunity costs in forgoing what would be earned by taking up a job instead of going to form 6. The direct costs of form 6 are the same for all students and are minimal compared with forgone earnings.

2. The ability to afford both the direct and indirect costs, measured by the student's family's total income. Income included earnings of both parents, contributions of elder brothers and sisters, plus income from other sources, such as renting rooms.

3. Expected benefits of a sixth-form education: These include the perceived salary of a sixth-form graduate, the perceived ease with which a sixth-form graduate could find a desired type of job (such as a white-collar as opposed to a blue-collar job), and the "option value" of the opportunity that a sixth-form graduate would have to enter university, perhaps even with a scholarship.

4. The perceived probability that one will indeed pass the certifying examination (for the higher school certificate) at the end of 2 years of sixth form. As Malaysian students typically predict their future performances from their past performance, this factor is measured by the lower certificate of education examination scores, the most recent standardized examination taken by the respondents.[21]

The dependent variable consisted of responses to the following set of questions:

> You are given a choice between taking a job and going to Form Six next year. The following are the possible decisions you can make:
> 1. Go to Form Six and do not take the job.
> 2. Take the job and do not go to Form Six.
> Let us say you are offered a place in Form Six next year (without a scholarship) and also a job. . . . If the job has a starting salary of $300 per month, which would

[20] For detailed discussions of the theory of cost-benefit analysis in education, see Blaug, chaps. 2 and 6.
[21] Students also indicated their detailed scores on individual subjects offered on the lower certificate of education examinations. In this article, the mean score for the four core academic subjects taken by all students is used as a measure for academic ability; these subjects are general mathematics, general science, history, and geography.

you choose? If the job has a starting salary of $200 per month, which would you choose? If the job has a starting salary of $100 per month, which would you choose?

Worded this way, these questions posed hypothetical but specific opportunity costs of form 6.[22] Since direct costs are minor and constant for all students, the questions asked students if they were willing to invest in form 6 at each of three levels of total costs. Their answers constitute factor 1 in the model above, providing the dependent variable in this study.

The effects of factors 2, 3, and 4 on the dependent variable will be examined separately for each sex-ethnic group in the first part of the presentation, followed by an exploration of the explanations for observed interethnic and intersex differences in responses to the questions above. The aim of this article is not to discover the relative strengths of the effects of the independent variables in a path-analysis approach but to identify the sources of group differences in educational decision-making behavior.[23] For purposes of clarity, however, the full model for each sex-ethnic group is shown in figure 1, which includes theoretically probable indirect effects of income and ability as well as their direct effects on decision making.

Findings

Individual-Level Analysis

First, it is necessary to confirm that the model is true of individual behavior in each sex and ethnic group. The data in the first part of table 1 show that expected pay after form 6 has a positive though moderate effect on male students' choices of form 6 over a $200-per-month job. The τ_c values indicate that the desire to continue schooling beyond form 5 is enhanced by expectations of high post–form 6 pay in all groups except Chinese girls, among whom the correlation is close to zero. Chinese girls are also the only group in which the majority does not wish to attend form 6 if it could find a $200 job.

Table 2 shows that, independent of ability, family income has a significant, direct effect on the decision for form 6 in most sex and ethnic groups, with the exception of Malay boys.

Table 3, part A, shows the correlations between ability and the desire to continue into form 6 when family income is held constant. Among Chinese students, ability has a strong and significant effect on the desire

[22] The salaries of the vast majority of jobs available to form 5 graduates in Malaysia in 1972 were $100, $200, or $300 per month (Malaysian dollars, here and throughout).

[23] The dependent variable is a dichotomy (form 6 or job), while the independent variables are coded on ordinal scales. The nature of the data and size of the sample when broken down into ethnic and sex categories posed limitations on possible statistical analyses.

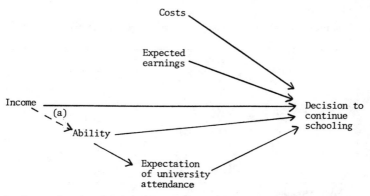

FIG. 1. —Factors in educational decision making. Broken line indicates that family socioeconomic status is often correlated with grades, but in this study the relationship was nonexistent among Malay boys and nonlinear among Malay girls and Chinese boys.

TABLE 1

EFFECT OF EXPECTED PAY AFTER FORM 6 ON CHOICES BETWEEN FURTHER SCHOOLING AND WORKING

	Preferred Form 6 over $200 Job (%)						
Expected Pay after Form 6 ($)	Male Students				Female Students		
	Malays		Chinese		Malays		Chinese	
149 or less			56	(36)			35	(60)
150–199	62	(45)	52	(77)	69	(45)	25	(96)
200–249			52	(128)			34	(92)
250–299	73	(41)	54	(61)	38	(21)	34	(44)
300–349	83	(64)	64	(61)	74	(68)	29	(70)
350–399	81	(52)	65	(34)	63	(30)	45	(33)
400 +	80	(82)	80	(40)	81	(36)	27	(30)
Total preferring form 6 (%)	87.1	(284)	57.9	(439)	68.0	(200)	31.4	(446)

Correlation between choice of form 6 over $200 job and expected pay after form 6:

Kendall's τ_c	.13	.14	.11	.03
P	<.05	<.01	<.10	N.S.

Correlation between strength of desire to continue into form 6* and expected pay after form 6:

Kendall's τ_c	.13	.10	.11	.07
P	<.005	<.01	<.05	<.05

NOTE. — N's in parentheses.

* Defined as follows: 0 when response to the question, "If you are given a choice between taking a $100-a-month job and going to form 6, which would you choose?" is "Take the job"; 1 when the respondent chooses a $200 job (but not a $100 job) over form 6; 2 when a $300 (but not a $200 or $100) job is chosen over form 6; 3 when a $300 job is rejected in favor of continuing into form 6. The questionnaire did not pose choices between form 6 and any job over $300, as it is highly unlikely for a form 5 graduate to start with a salary of over $250.

TABLE 2

EFFECT OF INCOME ON STRENGTH OF DESIRE TO CONTINUE INTO FORM 6,[a] ABILITY HELD CONSTANT
(τ_c)

Average LCE Grade[b]	Malays				Chinese			
	Males		Females		Males		Females	
2.49 or better					.38***	(65)	.44***	(37)
	.17	(29)	.58	(7)				
2.50–3.49					.30***	(57)	.28***	(57)
3.50–4.49	.02	(52)	.48**	(16)	.34***	(78)	.28***	(52)
4.50–5.59	−.11	(45)	−.08	(33)	.40***	(79)	.35***	(78)
5.50–6.49	.01	(69)	.19**	(48)	.14*	(88)	.04	(86)
6.50–7.49	.19**	(82)	.28***	(59)	.11	(60)	.23***	(74)
7.50 or worse	.21	(25)	.02	(33)	.48**	(15)	.02	(63)

NOTE. —N's in parentheses.
[a] See asterisked note to table 1.
[b] The mean score for the four core academic subjects taken by nearly all students in the national lower certificate of education (LCE) examination at the end of form 3: general mathematics, general science, history, and geography.
* $P < .10$.
** $P < .05$.
*** $P < .01$; no asterisk indicates lack of statistical significance at $P = .10$.

for further schooling, whereas the effect is moderate or statistically insignificant among Malays. Table 3, part B, holds constant the expectation of qualifying for university admission after form 6. Two observations may be made from it: (1) ability has a *direct* effect on desire to continue independent of its contribution to the "option value" of form 6 (as a necessary stepping-stone to university) in all ethnic or sex groups, although again the effect is more pronounced among Chinese; (2) the N values indicate that close to 100 percent of Malay students expected to qualify for university admission, reflecting heightened optimism as a result of favorable admission quotas for Malays.

Table 4 shows the effect of expectation of university admission on the tendency to invest in form 6, with ability held constant. Again, this effect is significant and positive among Chinese, but observable only among low-ability Malay students. The primary reason for the nonsignificance of the τ_c values among moderate and high-ability Malays is that close to 100 percent of them expect to qualify for university admission after 2 years of form 6.

The preceding data confirm that the model is by and large true of each sex-ethnic group. In particular, it is clear that the expected salary level after form 6 (with the exception of Chinese girls) and the expectation that form 6 will lead to university entrance have positive effects on the strength of students' desires to continue their schooling beyond form 5. Family income and academic ability are also significant influences, particularly among Chinese students.

TABLE 3

EFFECT OF ABILITY ON STRENGTH OF DESIRE TO CONTINUE INTO FORM 6[a] (τ_c)

Monthly Family Income ($)	Malays				Chinese			
	Males		Females		Males		Females	
	Income Held Constant							
< 100	.19**	(80)	−.06	(38)	−.06	(24)	−.10	(31)
100−199	.15**	(83)	.21**	(48)	.18**	(99)	.28***	(99)
200−299	−.07	(59)	.29**	(26)	.20***	(40)	.21**	(76)
300−399	.18	(25)	.25*	(24)	.20***	(89)	.12	(63)
400−499	} .01	(32)	} .05	(28)	.10	(32)	.42***	(51)
500−599					.41**	(22)	.42***	(35)
600−799	} .19	(16)	} −.13	(14)	.63***	(24)	.55***	(36)
800−1,199					.53***	(26)	.24*	(28)
1,200 +	.32	(6)	.11	(32)	.33**	(32)	.07	(32)
	Expectation of Qualifying for University[b] Held Constant							
Expect to qualify	.10**	(268)	.12**	(186)	.28***	(314)	.29***	(249)
Do not expect to qualify	.39**	(21)	.02	(20)	.16**	(109)	.21***	(182)

NOTE. —N's in parentheses.

[a] See asterisked note to table 1.

[b] Response to the question, "If you go to form 6 next year, do you think you will get accepted into a university 2 years later if you apply?"

  * $P <.10$.

 ** $P <.05$.

*** $P <.01$; no asterisk indicates lack of statistical significance at $P = .10$.

TABLE 4

EFFECT OF EXPECTATION OF UNIVERSITY ADMISSION ON STRENGTH OF DESIRE TO CONTINUE INTO FORM 6, HOLDING ABILITY CONSTANT (τ_c)

Average LCE Grade	Malays				Chinese			
	Males		Females		Males		Females	
2.49 or better	} −.10	(29)	} ...	[a]	.12	(72)	.20	(31)
2.50−3.49					.27**	(53)	.30***	(55)
3.50−4.49	} −.04	(89)	} −.05	(47)	.40***	(74)	.11	(52)
4.50−5.49					.17**	(82)	.27***	(76)
5.50−6.49	−.08	(69)	.41***	(48)	.28***	(84)	.33***	(87)
6.50−7.49	.19**	(81)	.32***	(63)	.32***	(62)	.37***	(74)
7.50 or worse	.19	(28)	.26**	(40)	.04	(19)	−.11	(65)

NOTE. —N's in parentheses; for further explanations, see all footnotes to table 2.

[a] The τ_c cannot be completed because *all* eight Malay girls with average LCE scores of 3.49 or better expected to qualify for university after 2 years of form 6; that is, there were no negative responses.

Group Differences

How do the various groups compare with one another in their choices between further education and stipulated job alternatives? Among Malay males, 46 percent, 76 percent, and 93 percent preferred form 6 over $300, $200, and $100 jobs, respectively, compared with 31 percent, 58 percent, and 86 percent of Chinese males faced with the same choices. Among females, too, Malays were more likely than Chinese to prefer to attend form 6 than to accept a job with any of the given salaries; the corresponding percentages were 36 percent, 67 percent, and 87 percent for Malay girls; and 14 percent, 31 percent, and 64 percent for Chinese girls. The figures above also show that, within each ethnic group, males were more likely than females to prefer form 6 over specified job alternatives. In summary, these data show that Malays and males are willing to incur greater indirect or opportunity costs (earnings forgone) in order to attend form 6 than are Chinese and females, respectively.[24] As a group, Chinese females are by far the least willing to invest in form 6.

The reasons for these group differences are suggested by the model presented above. The wording of the questions eliciting responses on the dependent variable had the effect of holding total costs of form 6 constant for all respondents. Therefore, the independent variables that remain are family income, expected benefits of a sixth-form education (including the expectation of qualifying for university admission, the expected salary of a sixth-form graduate, and the difficulty or ease of finding a job after form 6), and the likelihood of success in the higher school certificate examinations after form 6 as indicated by past examination performance.

Taking each of these factors in turn, we observe, first, that the Malays in the sample (and in the population) were from lower-income families than the Chinese in each sex, and the boys were lower in family income than the girls in each ethnic group.[25] Therefore we would expect Chinese

[24] If a graph is drawn with salary on the horizontal axis and percentage who will accept the job (rather than attend form 6) on the vertical axis, the approximate minimum salary above which more than half the students of any particular sex-ethnic group become more likely to accept the job than to attend form 6 can be determined: It is the salary at which the plot for that group intersects the 50 percent line. (This procedure assumes that the proportion of students taking the job increases linearly from one measured salary level to the next. The data do not enable one to determine the exact shape curve, but it seems reasonable to assume that it would not be very different from the straight line.) By probability theory, this is the minimum salary at which any particular individual in the group is more likely to accept a job than go to form 6. The figures thus obtained for each of the groups are: Malay males $287, Malay females $254, Chinese males $230, and Chinese females $143. These figures show that the minimum salary at which a Malay, or a male, is more likely to accept a job than go to form 6 is considerably higher than the corresponding figure for a Chinese, or a female, respectively.
[25] Percentages of each sex-ethnic group in the low-income category ($200 or less per month) were: Malay boys, 57 percent; Malay girls, 47 percent; Chinese boys and girls, 30 percent. Percentages in the high income category ($400 or more per month) were: Malay boys, 16 percent; Malay girls, 25 percent; Chinese boys, 29 percent; Chinese girls, 38 percent.

and girls to be more likely than Malays and boys, respectively, to choose further education over entering the labor force. However, the observed group differences in propensity to continue into form 6 were the opposite of these predictions.

Group differences between Chinese and Malays in examination performance would also lead one to expect Chinese of each sex to be more likely than their Malay counterparts to desire further education, as Chinese scored significantly better than Malays (two-tailed t-test significant at .001 among both boys and girls). However, again the opposite was observed.

Comparing boys and girls of each ethnic group, the males in the sample reported significantly better examination scores than did the females (two-tailed t-test significant at .01 among both Chinese and Malays). Therefore one would predict boys to be more likely than girls to desire further education, as is borne out by the data. However, it cannot be concluded that sex differences in academic ability explain the observed differences in propensities to continue into form 6, because propensity differences do not disappear when ability is held constant. Table 5 shows that, controlling for ability, the observed sex differences in desire to continue into form 6 remain in the case of Chinese students and do not disappear entirely among Malays. The fact that girls come from higher-

TABLE 5

DIFFERENCES BETWEEN SEXES IN STRENGTH OF DESIRE TO CONTINUE INTO FORM 6* HOLDING ABILITY CONSTANT

Average LCE Grade†	Male Students			Female Students			One-tailed t-test
	M	SD	N	M	SD	N	
				Malays			
3.49 or better	2.68	.69	29	2.69	.78	7	N.S.
3.50−4.49	2.19	1.04	50	2.23	.58	17	N.S.
4.50−5.49	1.94	.92	43	1.92	1.20	32	N.S.
5.50−6.49	2.21	.85	66	2.03	.90	46	N.S.
6.50−7.49	2.13	.91	77	1.89	1.13	62	<.10
7.50 or worse	1.84	1.07	27	1.50	.96	35	<.10
				Chinese			
2.49 or better	2.47	.84	74	1.83	1.25	39	<.001
2.50−3.49	1.95	.93	55	1.70	1.11	50	N.S.
3.50−4.49	1.66	1.12	74	1.22	.89	50	<.01
4.50−5.49	1.63	.99	78	1.15	.99	77	<.005
5.50−6.49	1.54	.95	86	.91	.87	90	<.001
6.50−7.49	1.45	1.05	64	.80	.94	87	<.001
7.50 or worse	1.07	.88	12	.61	.85	57	<.05

* See asterisked footnote to table 1.
† See footnote b to table 2.

income families than boys would lead one to expect that when ability is held constant girls would be found more anxious than boys to further education; however, this was observed *not* to be the case.

The only variables left in the model that could explain the interethnic and sex differences in desire for further education are the expected benefits of a form 6 education, which are summarized in table 6. There are marked differences between Malays and non-Malays of each sex in expected salaries after form 6 and, likewise, in perceived ease with which form 6 graduates can get jobs, Malays being much more optimistic than non-Malays. This is not surprising, in light of government efforts to increase Malay participation in the modern sector. Table 6 also shows that Malays are much more optimistic than non-Malays in expectations regarding university admission after form 6, despite their lower examination scores.

The preceding findings leave us with the clear conclusion that the major —indeed, the only —reason for Malays to be so much more likely than non-Malays to pursue education beyond form 5 is the greater perceived benefits that a form 6 education will bring.

Table 6 shows that in each ethnic group girls expect to receive lower salaries than boys do, although they do not differ significantly in their

TABLE 6

ETHNIC AND SEX DIFFERENCES IN EXPECTED BENEFITS OF FORM 6

	Male Students			Female Students			Difference-of-Means Test P^*
	M	SD	N	M	SD	N	
	Perceived Starting Salary of a Sixth-Form Graduate (\$)						
Malays	362	127	287	339	112	203	<.05
Chinese	270	110	439	252	95	450	<.01
Difference-of-means test P^*		<.001			<.001		
	Perceived Number of Months to Find a Job after Form 6						
Malays	6.9	6.2	305	7.8	7.8	207	>.10
Chinese	9.8	9.2	441	9.7	7.3	441	>.10
Difference-of-means test P^*		<.001			<.01		
	Expectation of University Admission†						
Malays	1.98	.47	304	1.95	.58	211	>.10
Chinese	2.20	.64	444	2.42	.63	446	<.001
Difference-of-means test P^*		<.001			<.001		

* Two-tailed significance level.

† Respondents chose one of the following four responses to the question, "If you go to form 6 next year, do you think you will get accepted into a university 2 years later if you apply?": 1 = definitely yes, 2 = probably yes, 3 = probably no, and 4 = definitely no.

perceptions regarding ease or difficulty of finding a job after form 6. Furthermore, Chinese girls are also less optimistic regarding university admission than are their male counterparts. While differences between the sexes in these variables are not as marked as interethnic differences, it may also be concluded that boys in each group are more likely than girls to pursue education beyond high school because they expect greater rewards from further schooling.

However, expectations of higher wages are not the only reason for boys' greater propensities to continue schooling. The data in table 1 show that when expected post–form 6 wages are held constant, the differences in percentages of boys and girls who would reject a $200 job in favor of form 6 are reduced (but do not disappear) in the case of Malays but not in the case of Chinese. In the latter group, sex differences in expectation of university admission are also important. As demonstrated below, the reason for this is that both Malay and Chinese girls are constrained by social norms regarding female roles. That is, noneconomic factors are also important in shaping girls' versus boys' desires to obtain further schooling.

The Job Market, Discrimination, and Sex Roles

It is not immediately apparent why boys in general perceived salaries of sixth-form graduates to be higher than girls did. A probable reason is that girls earn less than boys with the same educational qualifications. This could be because females in the same job are paid less and/or females tend to get less well-paying jobs than do males. The first reason —that females are paid less for the same job—is true in Malaysia. In developing countries, the government is usually the major employer of educated manpower, and Malaysia is no exception. The Malaysian government pays the same basic salaries to men and women according to certification and seniority, but fringe benefits, such as cost-of-living and housing allowances —which can amount to a considerable sum—are much higher for men than women.

The second plausible reason for differences between the sexes in perceived earnings is that boys perceive that a wider range of jobs, and better-paying ones, are open to them. There are two explanations for this. First, there is considerable and open discrimination against women in hiring for jobs that offer greater opportunities for promotion and also pay higher initial salaries, as evidenced by, for example, positions-vacant advertisements in the papers which blatantly state that males are invited to apply. In our sample of form 5 students, 18 percent of the boys interviewed expected to get professional, high technical, administrative, or managerial jobs,[26] if they completed form 6, compared with only 7 per-

[26] E.g., surveyor, architect, draftsman, managers, assistant superintendent of police, or captain or higher officer levels in armed forces.

cent of the girls. The large majority of the girls expected to get teaching or clerical jobs.

Another explanation for girls perceiving fewer and less lucrative job options may be that they are more constrained by societal role expectations, less aggressive than boys in seeking out rewarding jobs, and/or less aware of new opportunities in private industry and commerce. Malaysian fifth-form girls tend not to accept technical, blue-collar, or nonsedentary jobs, even though such jobs are perceived to pay better than clerical jobs. Table 7 shows that both male and female form 5 students perceive that some blue-collar or technical workers earn more money than do white-collar workers below the administrative or professional level. In particular, clerks are perceived to earn very poor salaries compared with persons in the other jobs listed, including factory work.[27] Technicians are perceived to earn the most, while mechanics and customs officers are in between. However, in each ethnic group, more girls are willing to accept the white-collar jobs (clerk, customs officer) than higher-paying blue-collar or technical jobs (technician, factory worker, mechanic) against the alternative of going to form 6. This is brought out most clearly by figure 2, which plots the jobs on a vertical scale indicating the percentage of students of each sex-ethnic group who would accept the job, against a horizontal scale of the average salary of the job as perceived by the same group of students. These findings indicate that the job preferences of educated girls conform to socially accepted sex-role images in Malaysia.

Summary and Discussion

Reasons for differences in educational attainment between sex or ethnic groups may be classified into two categories. The first is "socialization," or internalized norms and values resulting from one's home, school, and general social environment. General academic ability is also often influenced by one's background experience. In the United States, both educational aspirations and attainment have been shown to be affected by socioeconomic status and school grades or ability, as well as a list of other school-related, psychological, and family variables. However, at least one study has shown that after inclusion of these variables there still remains a considerable unexplained difference between the sexes in educational attainment.[28]

The second category of reasons emphasizes control of reward and incentive structures by socially powerful groups. In most societies, the

[27] This may seem surprising in view of the situation in many developing countries, where clerical or administrative jobs pay very well. In Malaysia, however, there is an oversupply of form 5 graduates qualified to become clerks, while the new and growing industries are in need of technical personnel.
[28] Alexander and Eckland (n. 8 above).

TABLE 7

ACCEPTANCE RATES AND MEAN PERCEIVED SALARIES FOR FIVE DIFFERENT JOBS (by Ethnicity and Sex)

Type of Job	Will Accept Job* (%)		Mean Perceived Pay† ($)		SE of Perceived Pay		Respondents (N)	
	Male	Female	Male	Female	Male	Female	Male	Female
Technician	41.7	35.1	435	395	10.8	13.3	283	192
	52.1	35.4	387	371	8.9	8.3	432	430
Clerk	20.6	21.2	268	231	5.6	7.0	291	197
	26.9	55.0	254	223	4.6	4.1	434	443
Customs officer	40.0	35.6	342	315	6.9	8.5	291	196
	42.5	43.2	306	289	5.7	5.3	428	431
Skilled factory worker	13.0	7.9	302	232	8.4	8.8	286	197
	28.3	20.4	289	243	6.5	5.2	433	435
Motor mechanic	26.9	16.2	365	358	9.5	12.9	288	194
	29.9	10.8	301	289	7.0	6.3	431	431

NOTE. —First number in each cell = Malays, second = Chinese.
* Respondents who said they will accept the job of technician, clerk, etc. immediately if offered same after form 5, rather than go to form 6.
† Mean of responses to the question, "What do you think is the average salary of a technician [clerk, etc.]?"

group occupying the highest economic position is the one that exercises such control. Therefore, if discrimination exists or if rewards and opportunities are unevenly distributed, the lower economic groups (be they sex, ethnic, or status groups) are shortchanged. Among the ethnic groups in Malaysia, however, the situation is the reverse. The Malays, who exercise political control, have historically occupied lower economic positions than

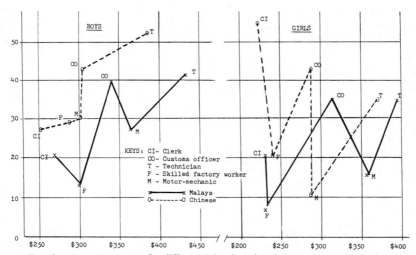

FIG. 2. —Acceptance rates for different jobs plotted against mean perceived salary

the Chinese. This permitted the researcher to separate the effects of differential rewards on educational attainment from those of socialization.

There has been a continuing controversy over whether success values are class differentiated in American society,[29] and this debate has been extended to the Malaysian context.[30] Presumably, aspirations affect the level of motivation, which in turn influences educational and occupational attainment. Indeed, a popular notion among observers of the Malaysian scene was that a primary reason for the relatively low socioeconomic status of the Malays was their lack of desire to achieve worldly success.[31] However, recent studies have shown that educational and occupational aspirations are uniformly high among all social classes of both Chinese and Malays in Malaysia.[32] Even occupational "expectations"[33] do not vary with social class among the Malays, while they do among the Chinese.[34] Earlier ethnographic studies which concluded that Malays did not value success failed to foresee that extensive government efforts to promote higher educational and occupational opportunities for Malays would act as great incentives for Malays to pursue high educational attainment, and that they would be even more willing than the presumably ambitious Chinese to invest in further education.

While success values or aspirations do not differ among ethnic groups or social classes in Malaysia, previously reported research indicates that they do differ between the sexes.[35] Job and earnings prospects were much more salient influences on Chinese boys' than on Chinese girls' choices of field of study in higher education.[36] Personal aptitudes and interests were more frequently quoted by Chinese girls as reasons for their choices. Finally, among both Malays and Chinese, girls were much more inclined toward the less competitive courses of study, such as arts and economics, both of which generally lead to teaching or office jobs. The highly technical and competitive field of engineering was by far the favorite choice of boys because of the lucrative jobs available in private industry. In contrast, preparation for a career or the desire for high earnings is not the

[29] L. Richard Della Fave, "Success Values: Are They Universal or Class-differentiated?" *American Journal of Sociology* 80 (January 1974): 153–69.

[30] Takei et al.

[31] E.g., Peter Wilson, *A Malay Village and Malaysia* (New Haven, Conn.: Human Relations Area File, 1967). Malaysian political leaders themselves also often make this assumption about the Malays and frequently exhort them to be ambitious and work hard.

[32] Wang, "Inter-Ethnic Comparison"; Takei et al.

[33] Realistic assessments; distinguish from "aspirations." The level of expectations is, of course, generally lower than that of aspirations.

[34] Takei et al.

[35] Wang "Sex Differences" and "Inter-Ethnic Comparison."

[36] Since all Malays faced equally good job and earnings prospects because of preferential government treatment, other considerations were most salient influences on their choice of field of study, and no differences between sexes in this motivational factor were observed among Malays.

predominant concern of Malaysian girls. This conclusion is consistent with the data reported above, which show that girls are more likely to accept sedentary or white-collar jobs than technical or blue-collar jobs even though the latter were perceived to pay more.

What are the concerns of Malaysian girls in thinking about their future? Most observers would agree that marriage is high on the list.[37] Most girls are concerned, first, that they should get married and, second, that after marriage they should enjoy comfortable economic circumstances. The accepted model of the family in Malaysia, as in most other parts of the world, is that the husband has the primary financial responsibility. Therefore, an important function of higher education for girls is exposure to eligible men in the social life of the university. Girls enrolled in highly competitive technical fields of study violate conventional norms of femininity and also put men on the defensive by being in direct competition with them. Likewise, for girls who do not go on to higher education, the kinds of jobs they may accept, if given the opportunity, are limited by societal sex-role images, irrespective of the financial rewards associated with them. Thus socialization is an important reason behind the lower educational and economic attainment of Malaysian girls.

However, this article suggests that differences between the sexes in propensities to undertake postsecondary schooling may also be explained by perceived unequal rewards. The data here show that groups higher in socioeconomic status and exhibiting higher academic performance can nevertheless be less likely to invest in further education than groups which are lower in these characteristics but which expect the rewards of further education to be greater. Malays and boys expected greater post–form 6 benefits and were therefore more willing to invest in further education than Chinese and girls, respectively, even though the latter were generally from higher socioeconomic backgrounds and even though the Chinese had better examination scores than the Malays.[38] Because women are often paid less than men for the same job and fewer administrative, technical, or professional jobs are open to women than men in Malaysia, lower salaries and types of jobs are expected by the girls in this study as compared with the boys. This article therefore concludes that actual discrimination and socialization combine to lower the earnings women expect from educational investment and to discourage their attainment of higher education.

[37] E.g., see Michael Swift, "Men and Women in Malay Society," in *Women in the New Asia: The Changing Social Roles of Men and Women in South and South-East Asia*, ed. Barbara E. Ward (Paris: Unesco, 1963): 268–86; Hashimah Roose, "Changes in the Position of Malay Women," in ibid., pp. 287–95.

[38] Indeed, the expected benefits of sixth form in terms of salaries and in terms of the probability of university attendance were so much higher in the case of Malays that income and ability were of little or no influence on individual Malay students' decisions to invest in sixth form.

Bernard points out that research focusing on socialization processes implicitly assumes that women's own attitudes and behavior are primary in explaining sex differences in occupational and educational attainment.[39] In emphasizing individual attributes, this is similar to the cultural deprivation hypothesis advanced to explain the lack of upward mobility by individuals from economically depressed groups. Critics of this approach would rather shift the focus to external power or instructional factors instead of internalized norms, the point being that even if socialization did not operate to influence both men and women, the institutional biases in society still favor men. What are these institutional biases and how do they operate?

Estler, in examining the poor representation of women in professional leadership positions, postulated three explanatory models.[40] The "woman's place" model lays the blame on culturally prescribed norms and the acceptance by women themselves of sex typing in occupations. The discrimination model places the blame on the opportunity structure. The meritocracy model says that women are not found in high-level jobs because they lack the capability and formal qualifications. Estler concluded that the first two models applied in the case of women in the field of public education in the United States, and that in all likelihood cultural norms and institutional discrimination reinforced one another in a self-fulfilling-prophecy situation. The meritocracy model did not apply because there was found to be no lack of formally qualified women.

This study suggests a combined model of cultural and institutional causes and effects related to women's educational attainment, as illustrated in figure 3. Job and pay discrimination against women often exist, causing women to expect lower returns from educational investment. Therefore, as a result of rational choice in weighting the benefits and costs, female students are not as likely to invest in further education as are males. The lack of highly educated women relative to men reinforces cultural norms and prejudices regarding women's abilities and also continues men's numerical superiority in positions of power. Thus discrimination continues, completing the self-reinforcing cycle of causes and effects. In addition, many women have been socialized into regarding only a narrow range of occupations as being suitable for them, thus limiting their options and lowering the earnings they can expect; this constitutes yet another self-reinforcing cycle.

[39] Jessie Bernard, *Women, Wives, Mothers: Values and Options* (Chicago: Aldine, 1975).
[40] Suzanne E. Estler, "Women as Leaders in Public Education," *Signs: Journal of Women in Culture and Society* 1 (Winter 1975): 363–83.

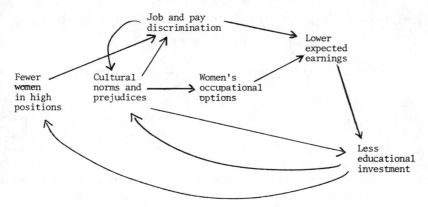

FIG. 3. —Mechanisms explaining women's lower educational attainment

Conclusion

This study demonstrates that even if other relevant factors were equal among the various groups of society, if one group perceives postsecondary education to lead to a greater certainty of university attendance and/or better job prospects, that group is more likely to continue its schooling than other groups which perceive the benefits to be less attractive. Differential opportunities in occupational and higher educational structures thus have repercussions on representation in secondary levels of schooling. Regardless of background factors, groups lacking incentives to continue schooling will fail to obtain the necessary achievement criteria for their own advancement. Therefore, the effect of perceived economic returns in private decisions regarding educational investment is an important factor in explaining group differences in educational attainment, particularly in cases of clear, external institutional constraints on the occupational and earnings prospects of one group versus another. This is one way in which groups in control of the reward structures of society maintain or advance their position. Strictly economically rational considerations merit much more attention as a determinant of sex and ethnic differences in educational attainment than has so far been the case.

6. Lack of Time as an Obstacle to Women's Education: The Case of Upper Volta

BRENDA GAEL MCSWEENEY AND MARION FREEDMAN

The neglected and disadvantaged position of rural girls and women has frequently been noted by scholars. The situation in Upper Volta is similar to that in the rest of sub-Saharan Africa. In 1974 only 10 percent of the eligible age group attended school at the primary level, 7.0 percent of the girls and 11.2 percent of the boys.[1] A great disparity existed between rural and urban areas, with 70 percent of the children in urban areas attending school in contrast to 9 percent of those in rural areas.

Governments of many Third World nations are concerned about inequalities in access to education similar to those noted above. In some cases the disparities have existed despite the absence of any articulated policy of discrimination against females. However, the formal education programs introduced with development have often failed to involve rural women in significant numbers. Thus, in recent years, increasing attention has been given to nonformal education programs which are tailored to address the practical needs of rural populations and to surmount the obstacles which prevent them from acquiring necessary skills.

In Upper Volta a major nonformal education program, the Project for the Equal Access of Women and Girls to Education (hereafter referred to as the project), was initiated in 1967. Its objectives, as stated in the plan of operations, included gathering data on impediments to the full access of girls and women to education and initiating experimental programs to overcome the identified obstacles.[2] The project addressed the issues of extensive work loads of women, poor health conditions, and low standards of living, which preliminary sociological studies had pinpointed as fundamental problems. Thus, the labor-saving technologies of mechanical grain mills, easily accessible water wells, and carts were introduced with the idea that the time saved by the use of these technologies could be devoted to literacy classes, training in the use of modern agricul-

The primary source of data for this article is Brenda Gael McSweeney, "The Negative Impact of Development on Women Reconsidered: A Study of the Women's Education Project in Upper Volta" (Ph.D. diss., Fletcher School of Law and Diplomacy, 1979). This research was made possible with backing from the United Nations Development Programme and the full support of the Voltaic authorities, notably, Ali Lankoandé, Scholastique Kompoaré, and Marcel Poussi. The valuable suggestions of Arpad von Lazar and Robert L. West are gratefully acknowledged.

[1] Data in this paragraph drawn from République de Haute-Volta, Ministère de l'éducation nationale et de la culture, Réforme de l'éducation: Dossier initial (Ouagadougou: Ministère de l'éducation nationale et de la culture, ca. 1975), p. 11.

[2] République de Haute-Volta, "Plan d'opération: Projet expérimental pour l'égalité d'accès des femmes à l'éducation," mimeographed (Paris: Unesco, 1968), pp. 1–2.

Reprinted from the Comparative Education Review 24, no. 2 (part 2)(June 1980): S124–39.

tural methods, health and civic education, and income-generating activities such as collective fields. The villagers themselves were requested to select women leaders from the village, who were then sent to special courses to enable them to be the disseminators of knowledge and agents of change at the local level.

The project was one of the three major experimental programs to increase the access of women and girls to education undertaken in three continents with the assistance of the United Nations Educational, Scientific, and Cultural Organization (Unesco) during the decade 1965–75. The Upper Volta Project was exceptional in that its activities were multifaceted and planned from the outset to last for 10 years. As early as 1968, the United Nations Development Programme (UNDP) participated in the financing of the project, and many other donors were later to cooperate with the government in its extension. The plan of operations indicated that data were to be gathered in order to permit eventual utilization of the results by other countries.[3]

From 1976 to 1979 an evaluation of the project was undertaken. Given that the principle objective of the project was equalizing educational opportunities for women, the research purpose was to obtain maximum information on women's attitudes and time patterns with a view to determining whether time in fact constitutes a significant barrier to educational activities, whether the available technologies are effective in diminishing the time barrier, and whether the project increased the participation of women and girls in education programs. This article will discuss the findings about rural women's time use and analyze the impact of the various labor-saving technologies on rural women's work loads. Participation in the educational activities introduced by the project will be assessed, including the women's perception of benefits. Suggestions will be presented as to the types of interventions and methods of approach which might best enhance the access of women and girls to education and to the benefits of participation in rural development.

Data Collection: Strategy and Sample

Research resources for the evaluation of the project were allocated to a combination of overview and intensive survey techniques. Four project and comparable control villages were selected in each of the three geographical zones reached by the project, regions which differed in their level of economic prosperity, climatic conditions, and ethnic composition. In all, 12 villages were included in the survey, eight of which were project villages. Information was gathered from all women in each of these 12 survey villages, and more detailed data was sought from a random sam-

---

[3] Ibid.

ple in each village of 30 women and their husbands and from women leaders. The questions focused on daily activities, time utilization, impact of technologies, and women's participation in and attitudes toward project-sponsored activities (project villages) or eventual interest in such activities (control villages).

Time budgets were used to obtain more precise time-allocation information. Three cross-seasonal time budgets were prepared for all of the women in the random sample and for women leaders based on observation of their daily activities for 14 waking hours, from the time they arose until evening. These women were then questioned about activities conducted after nightfall when they were no longer observed. Data gathered in this way were recorded without time values. The time budgets recorded the time the activity began and ended and described each activity, the technique or technology used, and any assistance the woman had in carrying it out. To compare the work loads of men and women, three time budgets were prepared for five men from each of the four survey villages in the Kongoussi zone. Five boys and five girls from each Kongoussi zone village were each observed once to furnish indications of the significance of the work contribution made by children.

This article will present material based on advanced processing of data gathered from the sample of 30 women in one project village, Zimtenga, and the sample in one control village, Bayend-Foulgo, in the Kongoussi zone of Upper Volta. The data on women's work loads are derived from time budgets for a minisample of five women and five men from the project village of Zimtenga. The time-budget data on children's work loads are based on an age-stratified sample of 20 children, five from each of the four survey villages in the Kongoussi zone in north-central Upper Volta. The Kongoussi zone is populated by the Mossi, the major ethnic group, and thus may afford the most generalizable data.

Women's Work Loads

The women in Zimtenga spent many more hours working than their husbands did, as evidenced in the analysis of time budgets for the minisample of five women and their husbands. Table 1 indicates the average time allocated to each category/activity in minutes.[4] Figure 1 summarizes the comparative work loads of men and women according to categories.

[4] Table adapted from Brenda Gael McSweeney, "Collection and Analysis of Rural Women's Time Use," *Studies in Family Planning* 10, nos. 11–12 (November–December 1979): 379–83. It is based on an expansion of a framework of informal employment indicators designed by the African Training and Research Centre for Women of the UN Economic Commission for Africa to quantify the sexual division of labor in rural areas (see UN Economic Commission for Africa, *The New International Economic Order: What Roles for Women?* E/CN.14/ATRCW/77/WD3 [August 31, 1977]).

TABLE 1

RURAL ACTIVITIES, KONGOUSSI ZONE: COMPARISON OF TIME ALLOCATIONS BY SEX

	Average Time per Category or Activity (Min)	
	Women	Men
A. Production, supply, and distribution:	367	202
Food and cash crop production:	178	186
Sowing	69	4
Weeding, tilling	35	108
Harvesting	39	6
Travel between fields	30	19
Gathering wild crops	4	2
Other crop production activities	1	47
Domestic food storage	4	1
Food processing:	132	10
Grinding, pounding grain	108	0
Winnowing	8	0
Threshing	4	0
Other processing activities	12	10
Animal husbandry	4	3
Marketing	4	0
Brewing	1	0
Water supply	38	0
Fuel supply	6	2
B. Crafts and other professions:	45	156
Straw work	0	111
Spinning cotton	2	10
Sewing	2	10
Midwifery	41	0
Other crafts/professions (e.g., metal work, pottery, weaving cloth, bee keeping)	0	35
C. Community:	27	91
Community projects	27	0
Other community obligations	0	91
D. Household:	148	4
Rearing, initial care of children	18	0
Cooking, cleaning, washing	130	1
House building	0	0
House repair	0	3
E. Personal needs:	158	269
Rest, relaxing	117	233
Meals	21	29
Personal hygiene and other personal needs (including medical)	20	7
F. Free time:	77	118
Religion	2	6
Educational activities (learning to read, attend-a Unesco meeting or class)	17	4
Media (radio, reading a book)	0	14
Conversation	14	69
Going visiting (including such social obligations as funerals)	43	19
Errands (including going to purchase personal consumption goods, such as kola, next door)	1	6
G. Not specified*	18	0
Total work (A, B, C, D)	587	453
Total personal needs and free time (E, F)	235	387

* When observation did not last the full 14 hours.

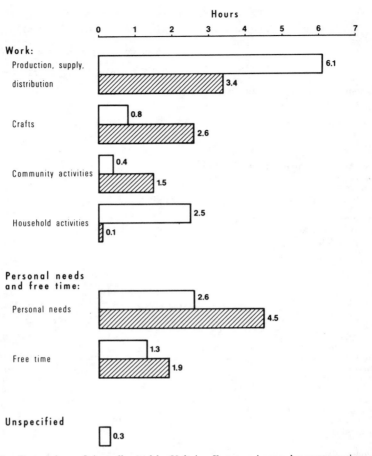

FIG. 1.—Comparison of time allocated by Voltaics, Kongoussi zone, by sex to various types of activities in the first 14 waking hours of the day. Open bar = women, striped bar = men. "Unspecified" = when observation did not last the full 14 hours.

Examination of the data reveals that this sample of women averaged over twice as much time on the production-supply-distribution (including food-processing) tasks as did men, and twice as much time on these activities as on the household tasks of cooking, cleaning, and washing, in addition to child care. The two women with small infants averaged only 45 min per day on child care, although society did seem to make certain allowances for new mothers, as their overall work loads were the lightest and they were the only women with *any* time for conversation and visiting as a primary activity. The free time for women in this sample averages only 1.3 hours per observation, and it is unlikely that increasing the length of the observation would uncover substantial amounts of additional free time, given the meal-preparation tasks which remain. Szalai, based on the findings of the Multinational Time-Budget Project, notes that women dispose of between 2.5 (employed women) and 4 (housewives) hours of free time during the week, 6 hours on days off (employed women), and 6.3 hours on Sundays (housewives). He states that "the inordinately small amount of free time at the disposal of employed women and the constraints put on housewives are two factors that bear a heavy responsibility for women's reduced participation in civic life, professional training, and education."[5] Should the processing of the larger data set corroborate the findings of the minisample that Mossi women dispose of only 1.3 hours of free time in the first 14 waking hours, it is little wonder that the sociologists and other members of the project team put an accent on the introduction of work-load-lightening technologies affecting the processing and portage tasks in an attempt to create time in which women might benefit from the educational opportunities sponsored by the project and so they might be more disposed to allow their young female helpers to attend school.

Technologies and Time Use

The three major technologies introduced by the project were mechanical mills for grinding grain, accessible water wells, and carts. Of the food-processing activities, the grinding-pounding activity absorbs the greatest portion of time —84 percent of total food-processing time, an average of more than 1¾ hours a day. Thus the choice of the introduction of mechanical mills by the project is understandable. Of the women in the minisample, three indicated that they used the mechanical mill (although they do not have the means to go regularly) and did so for the following reasons: to have more time, to diminish suffering, and for ease. Two never used the mill owing to lack of money. Questionnaire response from the full sample of 30 women in Zimtenga indicated that 14 of the 30 used a mill to grind grain. Of the mill users, seven gave as an explanation reasons relating to saving energy, and three women spoke of gaining time. Lack of money was the most frequent reason for not using a mill.

The project team also identified water portage as a time-absorbing activity, particularly in the dry season. Women then had to travel up to 4 km to fetch a jug of muddy swamp water. In the rainy season, pits near the compound retained rain runoffs.[6] Women in the minisample accorded only about 40 min per observation (in the period June to De-

[5] Alexander Szalai, *The Situation of Women in the Light of Contemporary Time-Budget Research* E/CONF.66/BP/6 (New York: United Nations, April 15, 1975), pp. 8, 10.
[6] Oulimata Fall-Bâ, *Projet expérimental d'égalité d'accés des femmes et des jeunes filles à l'éducation: Juillet 1967 –Juillet 1971* (Paris: Unesco, 1972), p. 39; and Suzanne Lallemand, *Projet d'accès des femmes à l'éducation* (Paris: Unesco, 1971), p. 8.

93

cember) to water portage; this figure could be expected to increase substantially as the dry season progressed. The head of the women's group pointed out in an interview during the dry season that in Zimtenga, the cemented well was so crowded that it was almost dry, and the swamp lacked water. She continued, "Water has its priority, especially in our surroundings. Lack of money, and of food, come after the need for water. Water is the first element of life."[7] The well-digging program sponsored by the project aimed both at saving time and at furnishing more potable water. Wells yielded water from 1 to 7 or 8 months a year.

In certain villages, the period just before the rains was reserved for stocking wood for fuel for the duration of the rainy season. Fuel portage absorbed little of the time, on the average, of the women in the minisample. Three women who were never observed fetching wood stated in questionnaire responses that they used a cart. Of the two who were observed fetching wood, one stated that she had no money to pay for the use of technologies, and the other was from a quarter without a cart. More than one-half of the women in the full Zimtenga sample use a cart. Most often the women spoke of its energy-saving advantages, stating that it was easier or they suffered less. Four respondents focused on the time-saving aspects: The cart was faster and held a larger supply. The nonusers usually mentioned lack of money.

When the technology users in the Zimtenga sample were asked about the uses of time saved, one-half of them indicated that time saved was devoted to other household activities (one specifically mentioned water portage). About one-quarter of the women utilized the time saved to spin cotton, which could be for household consumption or for sale. Two women used the newfound time to rest.

Szalai and his colleagues, concerned with the unequal burden placed on women by household responsibilities, have rejected the argument that technological development will "soon liberate women from household chores." Their findings show that time devoted to housework does not seem to depend on the level of the available technology.[8] It seems that clothes may be washed more often or meals prepared with more variety, but the overall burdens of housework have not been lowered.

Overall inspection of the Upper Volta data suggests that a similar phenomenon may appear. A song composed by blind minstrels from a project village concerning a mill acquired by the women on credit from the project serves to illustrate this: "The women of Magniassin have understood that Unity is Strength. They now have their collective field.

[7] Habibou Ouédraogo, head of the women's group of the village of Zimtenga, interview, March 1, 1978 (translated from Mooré to French by Jean-Christophe Bunkungu, Voltaic Scientific Research Center).
[8] Szalai, p. 12.

94

And they now have their millet mill. So that when we come late from the fields, we can now eat. And even the bachelors no longer have to beg the women to grind their flour."[9] The frequency with which women indicated that they used the mill when tired or sick leads one to believe that the minstrel's point —that the mill permits meals which otherwise would have been forgone —represents a pattern. If the women had intended to prepare a meal in the evening in any case, their work loads were thus lightened; if not, their tasks were in fact increased, as cooking time will still be 1–2 hours. Thus, the eventual impact of the mill would have to be sought, not in time savings but, rather, in improved nutrition, increased productivity of the work force, and the like, reflecting Szalai's findings that with the development of household technologies come rising "popular demands on the quality and quantity of household services."[10]

A similar pattern may be discerned with regard to the proximity of water. If the woman has access to a nearby well, she may spend the same amount of time to fetch extra water for personal hygiene or laundry. Accessible water may also facilitate use of a water filter, a specific health education activity introduced by the project. The link between the availability of water and filtering was implied by one old man from Zimtenga in a group interview: "I've been digging a well, you can see that my hands are wounded, it was in trying to reach water. The advice of the project could be carried out if we had a good number of wells. The women would filter water correctly."[11]

Technologies improved the quality and quantity of services, but a definitive judgment about their impact on reducing women's work loads is difficult to make. The introduction of carts was clearly an aid; they saved time and energy. Observations in other villages indicated that the carts may also have led to a redistribution of tasks which were formerly carried out only by women. A man, who, owing to tradition, could not typically carry water, wood, or the harvest on his head, is not adverse to transporting these commodities by bike or cart. The mills seem to have reduced the time spent in pounding and grinding activities, although the time thus freed was used in other household tasks which presumably improved the quality of life. The effect of the wells in reducing work loads is not so clear, given that they were often low during the dry season when women would have had to travel farthest to fetch water. Nonetheless, wells encouraged the adoption of health-related advice.

[9] Minstrels from the village of Magniassin (translated from Kassena to French by Gérard Adouabou, Pô regional director of the Women's Education Project).
[10] Szalai, p. 12.
[11] Interview, population of the village of Zimtenga, January 5, 1978 (translated from Mooré to French by Jean-Christophe Bunkungu).

Technologies and the Work Loads of Girls

Children, and particularly girls, provide important assistance in daily tasks. In order to increase the willingness of parents to send the children to school, and to send girls in equal numbers to boys, it is vital to reduce the work loads of the women who are the main beneficiaries of the assistance of children. It is also important to examine the work loads of girls to evaluate the opportunity costs to mothers of sending the girls to school. The assumption is that if the time it takes to perform those tasks usually carried out or assisted by girls can be significantly reduced, parents would be more willing to assume the tasks themselves and to grant the girls time for schooling.

Children begin working at an early age. Data on children's work loads collected from a single observation of an age-stratified sample of girls and boys ages 7–15 in four Kongoussi zone villages is presented in table 2. Observations were undertaken during the dry season, which the school year totally encompasses, but neither girls nor boys in the sample attended primary school. In one village, two boys were observed reading the Koran.

The data suggest that from ages 7 to 11, girls contribute several hours of work a day, and their contribution is more than twice that of their male counterparts. At age 13, the work load almost evens out, but by age 15 girls are again working twice as many hours as boys. Depending on the age group observed, from 25 percent to 55 percent of a girl's time may be spent in the activities of hauling water, grinding grain, and transport. Other work activities include spinning cotton, doing laundry and dishes, cooking, and fishing. In terms of their capacity to reduce the number of hours needed to accomplish the girls' tasks, the technologies of carts, wells, and mills introduced by the project reflect judicious choices.

TABLE 2

COMPARISON OF PHASING INTO WORK LOADS, KONGOUSSI ZONE, BY SEX

| | Average Hours of Work Daily | |
Age	Girls	Boys
7	5.3 (2.0)	.7
9	7.4 (3.3)	2.8
11	8.5 (2.1)	3.2
13	6.0 (3.3)	5.2
15	8.8 (3.8)	4.4

NOTE.—Numbers in parentheses indicate hours girls spent hauling water, grinding grain, and transporting.

Participation in Educational Activities

Labor-saving technologies were intended to increase the time available for education. The hypothesis being tested is that the project had a positive impact and that measurable differences would be noted between project and control villages in attitudes and behavior toward sending girls to school and the participation of women in nonformal education programs. The education programs introduced by the project were functional literacy classes, a radio program offering advice to the villagers about daily living, and health-education activities, such as instruction about water filtering and latrine use.

The data analysis in this section concentrates on survey results from the sample of 30 women in two villages in the Kongoussi zone — Zimtenga, a village reached by the project, and Bayend-Foulgo, a neighboring control village. The two villages are ethnically homogeneous, all of the women in the sample being Mossi. In Zimtenga, however, there is more Moslem influence than in Bayend-Foulgo.

Schooling for Girls

The women in both the project and control villages were asked if they sent their girls to school and if not, why not; they were then asked the same questions about their boys. In Zimtenga, of the 22 women with girls, 15 sent them to the administration's primary school, and six sent the girls to Koranic school. One woman stated that she could not afford schooling. In the control village, of the 23 women with girls, 19 sent the girls to primary school, and 3 sent them to Koranic school. One woman stated that "the girls have to help with the work." With regard to the education of boys, the statistics were similar to those for girls, and the same reasons were given for not sending the boys to school. Interviews with the husbands yielded comparable results.

In both villages, virtually all of the children were sent to school. These particularly high attendance rates are not surprising in view of the location of a three-grade school in Zimtenga, which is only 6 km from the control village. The respondents in both villages commented on the necessity for education in this world.

To furnish additional information on obstacles to children's education as viewed by their parents, data were examined from the Banfora zone in southwestern Upper Volta, which has lower attendance rates. In the project village of Fabédougou, only one-fifth of the children are sent to school. The reason most commonly furnished for not sending girls to school was "farm work," followed by "not for me to decide," "too young," and "household work." The main reason for not sending boys was "too young," followed by "farm work," "not for me to decide," "only child," and "household work." In the control village of Mallon, more children are in fact sent to school than in the project village. For both of the villages under examination, the primary school to which the children are sent is not located in the village itself.

The hypothesis that more children, and particularly girls, would be sent to school in the project village than in the control village did not hold. An overview of the data indicates, however, that after the age factor, the fact that children helped with the work was cited as the most important obstacle to schooling, and it was cited more frequently with reference to girls than to boys. The work load factor can be expected to influence not only initial enrollment but also achievement for those sent to school.[12] Explanation of the variations between zones, controlling for the factor of school proximity, should be sought in the social and cultural impact of education, including its perceived effect on the marriageability of daughters and the future employment of sons.

Functional Literacy

Functional literacy classes had been organized in 19 of the 24 project villages. In the Zimtenga sample, 15 of the 30 women indicated that they had some education or training. One woman had been to school for one year, while 14 women had attended literacy classes, six of them for up to 3 years and the other eight for more than 3 years. Of the women who had no education or training, 12 lived in outlying areas. In Bayend-Foulgo, the control village, only two of the women had received any training, namely, over three years of literacy training. Comparing the education of the men with that of their wives, four husbands in the project sample had some formal schooling, while only two husbands of women in the control group had been to school.

In a questionnaire response, 12 women from Zimtenga said that they were currently attending literacy courses, while 18 said that they were not. The 12 who attended said that they did so to learn to read and write. Both women nonattenders and their husbands were asked the reasons why they, the women, did not attend the courses. Their responses are summarized in table 3. After the reason of distance, or not introduced, which reflects the fact that the site of the classes was distant from some quarters and thus sometimes seen as not available, the factor most frequently cited by women and men was the lack of time. Two men indicated that a lack of understanding by the male village leaders hindered enrollment, and one said that he thought the classes were not beneficial so he would not let his wife enroll. However, other women insisted that the men supported their participation, even to the point of taking on some of the women's tasks. Thus the perceptions of both men and women of the

[12] See John Simmons, *Towards a Technology of Education: Predicting School Achievement in Rural Africa*, Economic Development Report no. 212 (Cambridge, Mass.: Development Resources Group, Center for International Affairs, Harvard University, April 1972).

TABLE 3

FUNCTIONAL LITERACY: REASONS WOMEN DO NOT ATTEND COURSES (Project Village) OR ARE NOT
INTERESTED IN ATTENDING (Control Village)

| | Project Village: Zimtenga | | Control Village: Bayend-Foulgo | |
| | Women's Responses (N) | Husband's Responses (N) | Women's Responses (N) | Husband's Responses (N) |
Reason Given				
Distance/not introduced	9	3	...	...
Lack time	5	3	4	3
Age (too old)	3	2	4	1
Not beneficial	1	1	...	...
Attitudes of the village men	...	2	...	...
Not enrolled	...	1	...	...

attitudes of husbands toward the participation of their wives in project activities varied.

Radio Programs

Sponsorship of radio programs and listening groups is another major component of the adult education program of the Women's Education Project. According to interview response in the village of Zimtenga, five-sixths of the women in the sample listen, either with the group or at home, to the program, "The Woman Is the Home," which gives advice on issues of concern to rural populations. Of the five nonlisteners, four said that they had no radio, although they all reside in neighborhoods where some of their neighbors do listen to the program. One woman stated that she had too much work to listen to the program. Three-quarters of those women who listened to the program stated that they did so for the advice. The others specified that they listened to be informed, for knowledge, because "it is of great interest," to aid the village, to create a good household, and "to know one's role in the household and the nation."

In the control village, 17 women listened to the program while 13 did not. Of the nonlisteners, most gave as the reason not having a radio. Reasons for listening were similar to those noted above.

Health Education

The health education component of the project focused on environmental sanitation and preventive health measures. Specific themes included water purification and sanitary waste disposal. Of the 30 women in Zimtenga, one-half filter water during the rainy season and two-thirds filter during the dry season. Reasons given for filtering revealed the health-improvement message: to avoid sickness and microbes, to have good health ("clean water gives good health"), to remove the impurities from the water, "because the rains bring many diseases," and to have clean or potable water. The predominant reason for not filtering was no time (six respondents), followed by a lack of means (four respondents) and not knowing how to filter (three respondents). An additional respondent had no place for a filter, and another could no longer see due to age. The increase in water filtering in the dry season in comparison with the rainy season was attributed principally to the time factor: Women had less work and so had more time to filter water.

None of the women in the control village filtered water. Five-sixths of the women in the sample gave as a reason not knowing how to filter. Two stated that they had no filter, and two others that they had no money to pay for the materials. One woman stated that the water from the well in her village was clean.

The latrine program met with less success; only five women, one-sixth of the women in the project village sample, indicated latrine use. Four women gave health-related reasons for use of a latrine, namely, to avoid diseases. One respondent stated that the bush was far away. Of the 25 nonusers, 14 stated that the bush was nearby. Other reasons were lack of means, the husband had no strength to build a latrine, and it was up to the men to construct a latrine and was "not women's work." In the control village, no one used a latrine. Four-fifths of the women stated that the bush was nearby. Twelve project monitors stated that latrine building had only been adopted in four of the 22 villages they reached in the Kongoussi zone. An elder from the village of Loulouka offered an explanation in the form of a proverb: "If the head that you have in the pot is not well boiled, do not attempt to add the feet into this pot."[13] This proverb was cited to indicate that the villagers do not have the financial means to possess latrines, for they do not even manage to resolve more pressing problems.

Assessments of Nonformal Education Activities

With regard to nonformal adult education, the proposition that the project would increase women's levels of training and alter their behavior was upheld. Significant differences were observed between project and control villages, as shown in figure 2. The radio program attracted the highest number of participants in both the project and control villages. There may be several explanations for this, including the fact that it was a passive activity and women could do other tasks, such as spinning cotton or processing condiments, while listening. Also, the program dealt with a broad range of subjects and thus offered something to interest everyone.

An attempt was made in the survey to determine how the villagers felt about the relative usefulness or effectiveness of the various activities introduced by the project. In Zimtenga, 11 stated that they could not single

[13] Interview, population of Loulouka, January 6, 1978 (translated from Mooré to French by Jean-Christophe Bunkungu).

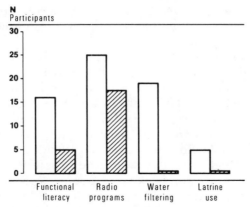

FIG. 2.—Comparison of participation, Kongoussi zone, in nonformal education. Open bar = project village, striped bar = control village. Total N in sample = 30.

out one activity as most beneficial because all were beneficial. Eight women, however, designated water filtering, and three, hygiene. Overall, 15 of the 16 indicated activities were in the area of health education, while one was an income-generating activity. Women leaders concurred in the designation of filtering and hygiene as most helpful.

When queried as to the least beneficial activity, 21 women said that they could not choose one, since all were good. Of the six who did single out activities, four named functional literacy, explaining that they did not understand its importance or benefit. Yet the testimony of those who have succeeded in the functional literacy courses seems somewhat different. In the words of one woman leader, "We are receiving an education (reading and writing), if among us several distinguish themselves, they will continue to teach the others, and so on."[14]

Conclusions and Implications for Planners

The analysis of time budgets indicates that rural women do have very little free time. This situation makes the introduction of labor-saving technologies a precondition for a broader education program. The technologies selected for introduction by the Women's Education Project did address themselves to the most time-consuming activities and did reduce the time needed to perform these tasks. However, rather than create free time, the time saved was used for other household tasks, such as the preparation of meals or spinning of cotton—activities which improved the nutrition of the family and upgraded the standard of living.

[14] Interview, Mrs. Tidébamba, head of the women's group of the village of Douré, March 22, 1978 (independent translations from Mooré to French by Brother Jean-Baptiste Bonkongou and Jean-Christophe Bunkungu).

To the extent that some of the newfound time was used for activities such as water filtering, one can say that the time was also used for functional education.

Despite the fact that women did not gain in free time, women in the the project villages did participate in the educational activities in significantly greater numbers than did the women in the control villages. Activities directly relevant to daily life attracted the greatest participation. Health-related activities were deemed the most beneficial, since the reduction in disease which followed from practices like the use of clean water was demonstrable. For the activity to gain adherents, the benefit to be gained from it had to be clear, and the program had to be easy to follow. Thus latrine use rarely became popular, particularly since the perception of its value derives from an understanding of the ecological chain, and the latrine required construction which some women could not or would not do themselves. Overall, the data show that although time is an obstacle, women will find the time for those activities which visibly improve their lives. To the extent that functional literacy is increasingly seen as a requisite for upgrading one's life and becoming part of the modern world, it, too, is valued,

The one area in which the project did not seem to make a difference was in increasing girls' formal school attendance. There were striking differences in attendance between two zones of the country but little difference between project and control villages within the same zone. Only tentative explanations for this finding can be offered at this time. One factor to be explored is school proximity since, in addition to reducing traveling time and thus reducing the time taken from work for education, the location of a school in or near a village may have a psychological impact on the community. Differences between zones in economic and social conditions, in the work loads of women and children, and in social and cultural mores need to be analyzed in order to determine why one zone where children are an important part of the work force chooses, nonetheless, to send virtually all of its children to school.

This study has several implications for policymakers and program planners. It supports the idea that educational programs should be presented as a package. The value of the reading and writing component of functional literacy courses is less easily perceived at first than the value of practical experience with health or income-related activities afforded by these same courses. Thus literacy classes should be integrated in a plan which introduces appropriate technologies, a dynamic functional learning program, and literacy as the means to improve one's life.

While the introduction of technologies was a sound policy and a key to change, the technologies also introduced problems. Planners must be certain that the technologies are simple, appropriate, adaptable to the conditions of the country, and easily repairable. Planners must ascertain that management questions regarding who is to own the technologies, who is to be responsible for them on a daily basis, who is to repair them, and on what terms others will be allowed to use them are addressed before the technologies are introduced into a village. In order to create a greater proprietary sense, some project staff felt that the villagers themselves should request the technologies and make a monetary contribution toward them.

The commitment of the participants to the program is the key to its acceptance in a broader sense as well. Prior to inauguration of the Women's Education Project, missions were undertaken throughout the country to provide information on the project to local authorities and to study the situation of women in various regions of the country. Villages were kept abreast of project plans on an ongoing basis. Voltaics were trained for the management functions at the central administrative level and for the conduct of the project's multidisciplinary operations at the local level. Villagers chose the women whom they wanted to be trained as change agents. In conclusion, the success of the project in increasing participation in educational activities and access to the benefits of development is attributable to the commitment on the national level, to the sense of involvement by women and men in the participating villages, and to the careful choice of activities which addressed felt needs to such extent that women with virtually no free time nonetheless found the time to participate.

PART II

**Educational Practices and
Differential Male/Female Outcomes**

7. Sex Differences in Educational Attainment: The Process

JEREMY D. FINN, JANET REIS, AND LORETTA DULBERG

Differential patterns for educational attainment for men and women are ubiquitous. No matter how attainment is conceived, the one-sidedness of the issue is clear. Worldwide, females do not enter schools, are not afforded the instructional opportunities, and do not reap the benefits of education that males do. In an attempt to explain the bias, Tinker and Bramsen[1] have identified three classes of "obstacles to women's education": the cultural attitudes which mediate against women's full participation in educational institutions, the lack of relevance of girls' education to the local or national economy, and the teaching methods utilized within schools.

The focus of this paper is on the third set of obstacles. To the extent that attainments are realized differentially as a result of formal education, the process of schooling may be examined for its role in creating or exacerbating sex differences. A model is proposed for viewing the process dimensions which are particularly germane to the problem, and available documentation is summarized. Much of the related research is conducted in Western countries; it is here that social scientists have been able to explore both the advantageous and disadvantageous aspects of formal schooling. However, the same processes, though perhaps in different form, operate in many parts of the world and require careful examination.

Educational attainment is viewed here in a relatively narrow sense as encompassing literacy and numeracy skills, learning in well-defined subject areas, and the concomitant attitudes toward school subjects which develop. Sex differences in these attainments are well documented, and a summary of available figures is given in Finn, Dulberg, and Reis.[2] Unesco reported that in 1970, roughly 34.2 percent of the world's population was illiterate.[3] This total was comprised of 28 percent of the world's

This paper represents the cooperative efforts of all three authors, who are grateful also to Elinor Barber for helpful suggestions and reactions to an earlier version, to Elaine Davis and Nanci Monaco for important references to add to the presentation, and to Mildred Young for assistance with the manuscript.

[1] I. Tinker and B. M. Bramsen, "Proceedings of the Seminar on Women in Development," in *Women and World Development*, ed. I. Tinker and B. M. Bramsen (Washington, D.C.: American Association for the Advancement of Science, 1975), pp. 138–218.

[2] Jeremy D. Finn, Loretta Dulberg, and Janet Reis, "Sex Differences in Educational Attainment: A Cross-national Perspective," *Harvard Educational Review* 49 (November 1979): 477–503.

[3] Unesco, Commission on the Status of Women, *Study on the Equality of Access of Girls and Women to Education in the Context of Rural Development* (Paris: Unesco, 1972).

Reprinted from the *Comparative Education Review* 24, no. 2 (part 2)(June 1980): S33–52.

males and 40.3 percent of females. Likewise, illiteracy was reported to be higher among females in every part of the globe.

The International Association for the Evaluation of Educational Achievement (IEA) conducted an empirical investigation of schooling outcomes in both developed as well as some developing nations. The sex differences reported by IEA are typical of those found within countries in other investigations. For example, boys were found to exceed girls in mathematics achievement at all ages in most parts of the world.[4] The difference was pronounced even in problems presented verbally, and extended to attitudes toward mathematics. Boys of all ages exceeded girls in science performance and attitudes, with the smallest differences in biology. In biology, girls in some parts of the world, notably England and New Zealand, outperform their male peers. In literature and in French as a foreign language, however, girls outperformed boys in most parts of the world. The sex differences in civics appeared to be age related. Ten-year-old girls and boys performed about equally; by 14 years of age, boys outperformed girls in most parts of the world; the male superiority was still larger and more universal by 17 years of age.

These differences arise as a function of all three of Tinker and Bramsen's "obstacles," which do not occur independently of one another. In some instances, cultural and religious values effectively limit or block girls' attendance at school—for example, in the Arab states, India, and parts of Africa.[5] In these areas, and elsewhere, teaching methods reinforce social attitudes by reminding girls who do attend regularly that their objectives are to prepare for marriage and childrearing. The lessons are conveyed in both subtle and obvious manners. Tinker and Bramsen, writing of students who attend Moslem schools in Nigeria, note that "many girls keep their mouths shut in class. They do not ask the teachers any questions. Neither do the teachers ask them. In fact most village school teachers keep the girls at the back of the class away from the boys in order not to incur the displeasure of the mothers."[6] The attitudes exhibited at school reflect those prevalent in the society generally, and cultural press for women to marry and raise families is mirrored even in the schools of countries with higher attendance rates—for example, the emphasis on home economics for American girls and shop crafts for boys.

The second "obstacle" to women's participation is mediated through formal education to the extent that schools prepare girls for limited voca-

[4] The IEA findings with regard to sex are given in greater detail in Finn et al.
[5] See Mary Jean Bowman and C. Arnold Anderson, "The Participation of Women in Education in the Third World" (this issue). Also M. Kalakdina, "The Upbringing of a Girl," in *Indian Women*, ed. D. Jain (New Delhi: Publications Division, Ministry of Education and Broadcasting, Government of India, 1975), pp. 87–98.
[6] Tinker and Bramsen, p. 163.

tional possibilities, if any. As an example, Labarca[7] noted that for boys in parts of Latin America, course choices included mechanical drawing, joinery, carpentry, tapestry, electricity, radio, mechanics, watchmaking, printing, leatherwork, bookbinding, pottery, tailoring, commerce, and agriculture. For girls there was domestic economy, dress designing and making, embroidery, weaving, and agriculture. The pattern is repeated elsewhere. In Sweden and Eastern Europe, with high female employment figures, girls continue to choose characteristically feminine courses, for example, health and beauty care, shorthand, and typing as vocational courses, and boys choose technological, safety, electrical, and mechanical work.[8] While the role of the economy in determining youngsters' educational programs and expectations cannot be minimized, school practices may be examined for the ways in which they direct females away from courses which lead to wage employment. One of the most pervasive enrollment trends—boys' attraction to science courses and girls' to languages—may reflect school tradition and policy as much as pupils' ability or interests.

The basic proposition is made and tested here that formal schooling is itself a significant agent in teaching and reinforcing cultural expectations for males and females. Since much of school process is accessible, and many aspects policy manipulable, schooling may also be an agent in challenging and modifying the effects of those same expectancies. Three dimensions of the school environment are examined: (1) the modeling of sex-appropriate behavior, (2) the exposure of students to specific curricular contents, and (3) the academic support provided to the students. All three are emphasized in instructional theory as significant antecedents of learning for both sexes alike. When provided differentially to male and female students, they are potential causes of differences in attainment.

The following sections summarize current research on these dimensions as they relate to sex differences in school attainment, and suggest further research priorities. Often material reviewed was not addressed specifically to the issue of gender; most of the studies were conducted in Western nations alone. Yet they exemplify how these three aspects of schooling operate and the influence they are likely to have on students' behavior. While the forms that modeling, exposure, and academic sup-

[7] Amanda H. Labarca, "Women and Education in Chile," in *Problems in Education V: Women and Education* (Paris: United Nations Economic and Social Council, 1953).

[8] M. Darling, *The Role of Women in the Economy* (Paris: Organisation for Economic Cooperation and Development, 1975); Ingrid Frederiksson, "Sex Roles and Education in Sweden," *New York University Quarterly* (Fall 1972), pp. 17–24; Margareta Vestin, "School Instruction, and Sex Role Questions," *Western European Education* 4 (Winter 1972–73): 285–307; S. C. Dube, "Men's and Women's Roles in India: A Sociological Rule," in *Women in the New Asia*, ed. B. E. Ward (The Hague: Unesco, 1963), pp. 174–203; United Nations Department of Economic and Social Affairs, *Statistical Yearbook*, 28th issue (New York: United Nations, 1977).

port take may vary from one setting to another, all three dimensions are likely to be in operation everywhere.

Behavior Models in School

Several years ago research attention was directed at the feminine environment of elementary school classrooms; more recent concern is with the diminution of women. Levy writes, "appropriate sex role learning for girls, while functional to the maintenance of male-dominated society, is detrimental to girls' psychological development . . . this fact has been overlooked in the overriding concern that schools might be emasculating our boys."[9] Regarding school performance, Berger adds, "achievement, with its concomitant values of mastery, competence, and success have become part of the stereotype for males and the presence of these manifestations diminishes the feminine image."[10]

Two questions must be addressed: (1) What aspects of school provide models for developing youth which are restrictive in nature? and (2) How do these characteristics affect the students' views? A partial answer to both questions is provided by Saario, Jacklin, and Tittle, who suggest that the images of males and females in elementary school basal readers and in achievement tests present one-sided views of sex roles.[11] In addition, teachers and classmates who are successful/unsuccessful students model sex-appropriate behavior for children from the earliest school years. By providing repeated examples of conformity to traditional sex roles, these factors model the range and limits for male and female achievement expectations and behavior.

A vivid example of the effects of sex-role modeling on performance was provided by Johnson, who compared reading levels of boys and girls in the United States, Canada, England, and Nigeria.[12] While American and Canadian children conformed to the common female-superiority rule in several aspects of reading, the pattern was reversed in England and Nigeria: boys were clearly superior. Both countries, unlike much of the world, have significant numbers of male elementary school and reading teachers. In West Germany, where most elementary schoolteachers are also male, boys also excel.[13] It is possible that male elementary

[9] Betty Levy, "The School's Role in the Sex-Role Stereotyping of Girls: A Feminist Review of the Literature," *Feminist Studies* 1 (Summer 1972): 5–23, quote on p. 19.

[10] Gertrude Berger, "The Socialization of American Females as a Dysfunctional Process: Selected Research," *Journal of Research and Development in Education* 10 (Summer 1977): 3–11, quote on p. 7.

[11] Terry N. Saario, Carol N. Jacklin, and Carol K. Tittle, "Sex Role Stereotyping in the Public Schools," *Harvard Educational Review* 43 (August 1973): 386–416.

[12] Dale D. Johnson, "Sex Differences in Reading across Cultures," *Reading Research Quarterly* 9, no. 1 (1973–74): 67–86.

[13] John A. Downing, *Comparative Reading: Cross-national Studies of Behavior and Processes in Reading and Writing* (New York: Macmillan, 1973); Carol A. Dwyer, "Sex Differences in Reading: An Evaluation and a Critique of Current Methods," *Review of Educational Research* 43 (Fall 1973): 455–67.

teachers provide the models for boys to realize at an early age that reading and learning are male appropriate and subsequently take more active roles in learning.

The effects of sex-role modeling can be seen also when the models do not hold traditional roles. Wolf found that when boys watch a male model play with typically female toys, the children increase their own play with those toys.[14] Likewise, girls played with trucks more often after observing a female model play with a truck. Tibbetts noted that children in the first 4 years of school listed bus driver among the occupations appropriate for men or women.[15] The author found that these children had the experience—unusual at that time in the United States—of having seen women drive school buses.

While many countries have significant numbers of female elementary teachers, elsewhere most teachers are male. In India, women make up only 22 percent of the total teaching force; they are 19.1 percent of primary, 26.7 percent of middle school, and 23.1 percent of the secondary schoolteachers.[16] Everywhere, the preponderance of high school teachers, especially in science and mathematics, is male. Females are often mother-tongue and foreign-language teachers. The IEA studies noted this trend for teachers of French in eight countries, a factor which may affect achievement as well as girls' plans to enter foreign-language instruction as a career.

During adolescence, identification of a student with his/her teacher is extremely common, and may even have a more powerful impact on the individual than instructional methods.[17] According to Bandura and Walters, teachers who become role models may have three types of effects on students' behavior.[18] The "modeling effect" is the direct imitation of the model's behavior, such as that observed in the studies of young children. The "inhibitory or disinhibitory effect" is based on the consequences of the models' experiences; if the student decides that the consequences are undesirable, the result may be behavior in opposition to that observed. For example, when female faculty members are held in low esteem by their male colleagues, or are not treated with equal recognition by the school administration, the effect may be to inhibit females' aspirations toward that profession.[19]

[14] Thomas M. Wolf, "Effects of a Live Modeled Sex-inappropriate Play Behavior in a Naturalistic Setting," *Developmental Psychology* 9 (July 1973): 120–23.

[15] Sylvia-Lee Tibbetts, "Sex Role Stereotyping in the Lower Grades: Part of the Solution," *Journal of Vocational Behavior* 6 (April 1975): 255–61.

[16] A. Harry Passow, Harold J. Noah, Max A. Eckstein, and John R. Mallea, *The National Case Study: An Empirical Comparative Study of Twenty-one Educational Systems*, International Studies in Evaluation, vol. 7 (New York: Halsted, 1976).

[17] Rolf E. Muuss, *Theories of Adolescence* (New York: Random House, 1975).

[18] Albert Bandura and Richard H. Walters, *Social Learning and Personality Development* (New York: Holt, Rinehart & Winston, 1963).

[19] See C. J. Lucas, R. P. Kelvin, and A. B. Ojha, "The Psychological Health of the Preclinical

Third, the "eliciting effect" is the increased susceptibility of a student to be influenced by the model. For example, a female teacher who holds high expectations for girls' performance may have an increased probability of influencing the students' performance through cues which she elicits. Academic support provided by a model of the same sex as the student may be particularly encouraging.

Same-sex modeling is particularly common in one-sex schools, but may limit the range of possibilities or extend achievements to some that are more difficult to attain in coeducational settings. The first extreme is displayed in Australia's schools of domestic science, which present the students with "little alternative to the role of happy homemaking."[20] The more positive effect is seen in England's prestigious all-girls schools. Here, Finn found that 14-year-old girls were superior readers compared with their male peers, while reading comprehension means were about equal in coeducational schools.[21] Further, the girls in one-sex schools performed better in biology and chemistry than boys in all-male institutions, while boys in coeducational schools outperformed girls. The effect may be partially due to the relative selectivity of all-boys and all-girls schools; however, the data showed the students in all-boys and all-girls schools had equal average verbal aptitudes.

Proponents of one-sex schooling point to the importance of women faculty members as successful, competent role models; these women are more likely to provide encouragement for female students to succeed.[22] While the effect has been demonstrated empirically for the college-age years, research on this issue is still needed at younger ages.[23] Psychologists note that adolescent women in the United States display more concern about being liked and respected by their teachers than do males, are more dependent on teachers for emotional support, and more subject to suggestibility.[24] According to Block, the institution may be "more implicative" for males than females: "The effects of single-sex education may not be parallel for the two sexes." In particular, "for males, there is the opportunity in both single-sex and coeducational institutions to identify

---

Medical Student," *British Journal of Psychiatry* 3 (May 1965): 473–78; Kay Deaux, *The Behavior of Women and Men* (Monterey, Calif.: Brooks/Cole, 1976).

[20] Bob Bessant, "Domestic Science Schools and Woman's Place," *Australian Journal of Education* 20 (March 1976): 1–9.

[21] Jeremy D. Finn, "Sex Differences in Educational Outcomes: A Cross-national Study," *Sex Roles* 6 (February 1980): 9–26.

[22] Jeanne H. Block, "Sex Differences in Cognitive Functioning, Personality Characteristics and Socialization Experiences: Implications for Educational Policy" (unpublished paper, University of California, Berkeley, n.d.).

[23] M. Elizabeth Tidball, "Perspective on Academic Women and Affirmative Action," *Educational Record* 54 (Spring 1973): 130–35.

[24] Eleanor E. Maccoby and Carol N. Jacklin, *The Psychology of Sex Differences* (Stanford, Calif.: Stanford University Press, 1974); Leona E. Tyler, *The Psychology of Human Differences* (New York: Appleton-Century-Crofts, 1965).

with role models who are (*a*) of the same sex *and* (*b*) successful."[25] It may also be important for students to see success attained among their peers. This is possible for girls taking science and mathematics, for example, only in all-girls schools.

Some research has been conducted into the behavior of boys and girls in one-sex and mixed-sex settings. Ellis and Peterson studied the effects of sex-segregated class organization on the achievement and attitudes of seventh- and eighth-grade students.[26] The subjects of the study spent about five-sixths of one academic year in same-sex classes. No significant differences were found which were attributable to the same-sex grouping, although no attention was given to the sex of the teachers. Girls in the study received higher marks and standardized achievement scores but responded more negatively to the sex-segregated class than did boys.

The Ellis-Peterson study highlights an important principle about single-sex grouping. Namely, the effects of observing models of sex-appropriate behavior are cumulative over time and settings. In the long run—say, 6 or more years—students' behavior may be significantly shaped by observing adult models. This is especially so if the same values are encountered in most or all of the teachers and reinforced by peers and others outside of school. Although it is not clear precisely what differences Ellis and Peterson expected to find, the "strength of treatment" in the experiment was insufficient.

Lockheed studied the task-oriented behavior of male and female students in single-sex and mixed groups.[27] Although the experiment involved a short-term game-playing task, important differences in participation were observed, presumably reflecting earlier socialization patterns. In particular, all-female groups showed as much task-oriented activity as all-male groups. Mixed-sex groups were dominated by males when the subjects were naive, that is, had no previous experience with the task. On the other hand, mixed-sex groups composed of individuals who had first experienced the game in a single-sex condition showed a more equal distribution of activity between males and females. Zander and Van Egmond found that a boy's "social power" in the classroom determines his behavior more than intelligence does, whereas the power of a girl has little effect on her behavior.[28] Providing females with experience and successful female peers is most easily accomplished in an all-female set-

[25] Block, pp. 57–60.

[26] Joseph R. Ellis and Joan L. Peterson, "Effects of Some Sex Class Organization on Junior High School Students' Academic Achievement, Self-Discipline, Self-Concept, Sex Role Identification and Attitude toward School," *Journal of Educational Research* 64 (July–August 1971): 455–64.

[27] Marlaine B. Lockheed, *The Modification of Female Leadership Behavior in the Presence of Males* (PR 76-28) (Princeton, N.J.: Educational Testing Service, 1976).

[28] Alvin Zander and Elmer Van Egmond, "Relationship of Intelligence and Social Power to the Interpersonal Behavior of Children," *Journal of Educational Psychology* 49 (October 1958): 257–68.

ting and may be one way to counteract the effects of boys' social power. This setting is particularly deserving of further research effort.

Not only do teachers and other pupils model sex-appropriate behavior, but so do communication media and instructional materials, including texts, films, work sheets, and tests. The content of books used in school from the earliest grades presents one-sided views of the roles of men and women which may be particularly salient in the socialization of 4–7-year-olds. Weitzman et al. examined the content of American award-winning picture books for preschool children and found that women were greatly underrepresented in the titles, central roles, and illustrations.[29] Boys were portrayed as active leaders and girls as passive followers and servers; men were portrayed in a variety of occupations and women only as wives and mothers.

This analysis of preschool books characterizes repeated findings from readers and texts used at all levels of schooling and in several parts of the world. Several analyses of primary-grade reading texts revealed that females were portrayed in occupations significantly less than men, and in very limited positions in any case (e.g., teacher, nurse, governess, dressmaker, telephone operator). Women were shown as more often needing help and protection than men, lacking competence, and always more quiet and passive.[30] Pottker, in addition to verifying some of the same results, found that 57 percent of women portrayed in reading textbooks were housewives, while in reality 39 percent of women are homemakers, 54 percent are in the labor force, and 17 percent are students.[31] Forty-two percent of women's occupations were shown in the texts as schoolteacher, while the actual number is only 6.1 percent. Since 75 percent of children's classroom time and 95 percent of homework time is spent with textbooks, the effects of this continual viewing may be inescapable. The author notes also that working-class homes are served least well by the texts, since virtually all of the portrayals are of middle-class homes and occupations. The same biases have also been documented in Australia for both textbooks and films, and in India.[32] In

[29] Lenore J. Weitzman, Deborah Eifler, Elizabeth Hodaka, and Catherine Ross, "Sex-Role Socialization in Picture Books for Preschool Children," *American Journal of Sociology* 77 (May 1972): 1125–50.

[30] NOW, Central New Jersey National Organization of Women, *Dick and Jane as Victims: Sex Stereotyping in Children's Readers* (Princeton, N.J.: NOW, 1972); Ramona Frasher and Annabelle Walker, "Sex Roles in Early Reading Textbooks," *Reading Teacher* 25 (May 1972): 741–49.

[31] J. Pottker, "Psychological and Occupational Sex Stereotypes in Elementary-School Readers," in *Sex Bias in the Schools*, ed. J. Pottker and A. Fishel (Teaneck, N.J.: Fairleigh Dickinson University Press, 1977), pp. 111–25.

[32] June Anstee, "Sex Discrimination in Our System," *Teacher's Journal* (Australia) 2 (September 1976): 3, 7; Victorian Committee on Equal Opportunity in Schools, *Report to the Premier of Victoria* (Melbourne, July 1977); Kamlesh Nischol, *The Invisible Woman: Women and Girls as Portrayed in English-Language Textbooks* (New Delhi: Central Institute of English, Hyderabad, 1976); Narenda Nath Kalia, "Must Men Make History and Women Wash Dishes: How Sexism Rules in Indian School Textbooks of 1978–79" (unpublished paper, Department of Sociology, State University College, Buffalo, N.Y., n.d.).

addition, Skertchly noted strong stereotyping trends in games and toys that are provided in school.[33]

Elementary mathematics texts were analyzed by Jay and by Jay and Schminke.[34] Selecting four publishers' books for grades 2, 4, and 6, the investigators asked parents and students to judge whether the content was masculine, feminine, or neutral. Parents found one-fourth of the grade 4 and one-eighth of the grade 6 material to be decidedly masculine; little was classified as distinctly feminine. These findings were supported by very high rates of agreement among parents and children in their classifications. The settings depicted in the texts appeared neutral, while the portrayal of individuals and work roles was largely biased in favor of males. Among the specific results, 46 of 49 famous people portrayed in over 400 pages of material were male; the females included Queen Elizabeth and the fictional Alice-in-Wonderland.

DeCrow examined kindergarten through grade 3 social studies texts. No women were portrayed outside the home except as a teacher or nurse; no man was shown as doing anything except going to full-time work outside the home. The effect of mandatory school attendance for many years of exposure to such material leads the author to assert, "Textbooks represent an almost incredible conspiracy of conditioning. . . . The general image of the female ranges from dull to degrading to invisible."[35]

Secondary school texts continue to confront students with sex-role stereotyping in specific subject areas. Men are portrayed as active and having greater participation in sports, while women are seen as passive and spectators in sports and in the broader "arena of achievement." In social studies, women are rarely mentioned in historical accounts. Trecker notes that in the United States, areas organized and dominated by women are often ignored, for example, dance, film, and theater.[36] There is little information about colonial women; the suffrage movement and women's attempts to be admitted to college are given little coverage; women's roles in the two World Wars are given brief note; the development of birth control is not mentioned. American black history, recently appearing with greater coverage, is often presented as the history of accomplishments by men.

[33] A. Skertchly, "Women and Education and the Future," *Unicorn* (Australia) 1 (December 1975): 35–50.

[34] Winifred T. Jay, "Sex Stereotyping in Elementary-School Math Textbooks," in *Sex Bias in the Schools*, ed. J. Pottker and A. Fishel (Teaneck, N.J.: Fairleigh Dickenson University Press, 1977), pp. 126–45; Winifred T. Jay and Clarence W. Schminke, "Sex Bias in Elementary School Mathematics Texts," *Arithmetic Teacher* 22 (March 1975): 242–46.

[35] K. DeCrow, "Look, Jane, Look! See Dick Run and Jump! Admire Him!" in *Sex Differences and Discrimination in Education*, ed. S. B. Anderson (Ohio: Jones, 1972), pp. 44–49.

[36] Janice L. Trecker, "Women in United States History of High School Textbooks," *International Review of Education* 19 (1973): 133–39.

Research is needed in all parts of the world into the effects of presenting students with biased portrayals of males and females for 6 or more years of schooling. The connection between the models provided by teachers and learning materials and the personalities or achievements of the students is not well understood or documented. However, the argument is intuitively convincing: stereotypes are at least reinforced if not taught by the continual depiction of (a) women as unimportant in history and politics; (b) women as having negatively viewed personality traits, such as docility, passivity, dullness, and lack of confidence; and (c) women as unable to participate in the broad variety of masculine disciplines of study and occupations. The latter in particular may be seen as the function of schools to remedy rather than to reinforce.

Several authors have suggested ways to improve materials, and in recent years there is some evidence of change. Kelly suggests that girls need to be portrayed as scientists, and also that science instruction needs to be modified to simpler forms of presentation.[37] It may be possible to make mathematics material more attractive to boys or girls by setting problems in familiar and interesting experiences. Kepner and Koehn report shifts in the tenor of recent elementary mathematics texts.[38] Women are cited in more occupations than previously, including doctors and construction workers. Males are not depicted in traditionally female roles, or in joint male-female activities; it seems that these changes may be slower to come. Kuhnke depicts even more dramatic responses from publishers to the critics of sex-role stereotyping.[39] In the texts reviewed, boys and girls were frequently involved in joint tasks and problems requiring the competencies of both sexes. Both were also featured in nonstereotypical roles, for example, men doing domestic work, while females were depicted as having responsibility, initiative, and high activity levels.

Analyses have been conducted of several aptitude, achievement, and interest tests. Tittle reports an extensive review of standardized educational measures in which it was found that males were referred to more often than females.[40] Further analysis revealed a significant sex-role stereotyping of women. A different approach was taken by Strassberg-Rosenberg and Donlon, who conducted item-by-item inspection of re-

[37] Alison Kelly, "Women in Physics and Physics Education" (paper presented at the Conference on Girls and Science Education, Chelsea College, England, March 1975).

[38] Henry S. Kepner, Jr., and Lilane R. Koehn, "Sex Roles in Mathematics: A Study of the Status of Sex Stereotypes in Elementary Mathematics Texts," *Arithmetic Teacher* 24 (May 1977): 379–85.

[39] Helen F. Kuhnke, "Update on Sex-Role Stereotyping on Elementary Mathematics Textbooks," *Arithmetic Teacher* 24 (May 1977): 373–76.

[40] Carol K. Tittle, "Sex Bias in Educational Measurement: Fact or Fiction," *Measurement and Evaluation in Guidance* 6 (January 1974): 219–27.

sponses to the Scholastic Aptitude Test.[41] They found the performance of men and women on the verbal section to be equal, while males exceeded females in mathematics. The significance of their approach lies in the recognition that individual items and item types have different difficulties by specific skills and different content appeal.

Tests serve a special function which lends significance to the study of sex differences. In general they are only some of the plethora of printed materials that routinely confront the student; it is doubtful that either male/female ratios in the content or sex stereotyping are sufficient to mask or create real differences in aptitude or achievement. But the validity of test results for screening and selecting students must be carefully examined. For example, Tittle noted that both the Strong Vocational Interest Blank and Kuder Occupational Interest Inventory show restricted ranges of occupations for women.[42] If these are used for school or career counseling, then the norms which are provided are both inadequate and misleading for women, and perhaps for men as well. Likewise, if students are selected for a task by achievement or aptitude levels, careful consideration must be given to whether the prerequisites for success are—or ought to be—the same for both males and females. Too little attention has been given to these questions.

Exposure to Schooling

Other school practices reward different learning patterns for males and females more directly; in general, these practices provide different amounts and types of curricular exposure to male and female students. Of the many investigations into the components of achievement for boys and girls alike, the extent of students' access to course content is identified repeatedly as a potent antecedent of school learning. One of the most consistent findings of the IEA international studies is that "opportunity to learn" is one of the significant correlates of science and mathematics achievement; opportunity, as used in these studies, connotes student exposure to specifically defined course contents. Further, as noted by Postlethwaite, in countries "where learning conditions were similar, the differences in achievement in mathematics between boys and girls were markedly reduced."[43] These findings underscore the importance of

[41] Barbara Strassberg-Rosenberg and Thomas F. Donlon, "Content Influences on Sex Differences in Performance on Aptitude Tests" (paper presented at the Annual Meeting of the National Council for Measurement in Education, Washington, D.C., March 1975).

[42] Tittle.

[43] T. N. Postlethwaite, "The Surveys of the International Association for the Evaluation of Educational Achievement (IEA)," in *Educational Policy and International Assessment*, ed. A. C. Purves and D. U. Levine (Berkeley, Calif.: McCutchan, 1975).

117

understanding what pupils learn by examining what is taught—to all pupils alike, or more to some than others.[44]

Several major theories of instruction incorporate these ideas. Carroll has postulated a "Model of School Learning" which depicts individual performance in school as a function of the amount of time needed by a student to learn and the amount of time provided.[45] Bloom, in a multicomponent model of instruction, emphasizes the extent of student participation as well as the extension of learning time through study periods, homework, and additional resources.[46] These models depict curricular exposure in terms of the amount of *time* used for learning. From this perspective, additional results were reported by IEA. For example, time for homework was found to be a consistent correlate of student performance. In the study of French as a foreign language, "the national mean scores were in general highly correlated with the average number of years that French had been studied and . . . negatively to the average grade in which the study of French began."[47] In reviewing research from developing countries, Simmons and Alexander found that in general kindergarten attendance has a significant impact on performance in later years, while homework is also generally important.[48]

An analysis of the ways in which school time may be utilized is helpful in identifying how exposure differences for males and females arise. First, the *potential allocated time* is determined jointly by the school through its policy decisions concerning length of the school day and year and by the pupil and his/her family through days and years of attendance. At the extreme, exposure differences are created when access to school is restricted or when males and females do not complete equal years of schooling.

The time allowed for learning a particular topic in a given setting is *actual allocated time*. Sex differences arise in actual allocations when one sex group or the other is discouraged from enrolling in particular courses. In all parts of the world, boys are directed into mathematics and science curricula more actively, while girls—when their education is encouraged—are guided toward languages and the liberal arts.[49] It is not a coincidence that the former subject areas lead to more possibilities for wage-earning employment. In regions where vocational preparation for

[44] See Gaea Leinhardt, Andrea M. Seewald, and Mary Engel, "Learning What's Taught: Sex Differences in Instruction," *Journal of Educational Psychology* 71 (August 1979): 432–39.

[45] John B. Carroll, "A Model of School Learning," *Teachers College Record* 64 (May 1963): 723–33.

[46] Benjamin S. Bloom, *Human Characteristics and School Learning* (New York: McGraw-Hill, 1976).

[47] Postlethwaite, p. 16.

[48] John Simmons and Leigh Alexander, "The Determinants of School Achievement in Developing Countries: A Review of the Research," *Economic Development and Cultural Change* 26 (January 1978): 341–57.

[49] Finn et al. (n. 2 above).

women is possible or even common, the courses, and thus the career possibilities, are narrowly prescribed. While the sources of these differences may lie in cultural values learned at home, school practices also perpetuate and reinforce many of the same attitudes.

In some countries, certain course options are simply not available to members of one sex group or the other; elsewhere, social pressure is so pervasive that a girl enrolling in a typically male course is subject to ridicule from all. Even in Eastern Europe and the Soviet Union, where sex distinctions in careers are purportedly smaller, differences in course enrollment persist. Fogarty, Rapoport, and Rapoport argue that the failure of women to enter nontraditional fields in larger numbers there is due to the failure of educators to present the alternatives effectively, rather than to social or personal resistance on the students' part. Nevertheless, the reported course choices are consistent with well-established achievement patterns—boys higher in mathematics, girls in verbal areas. In Western countries, women "tend more than men and more than women in Eastern Europe to concentrate their interest in a few subjects and to aim for a limited range of occupations."[50] Here, course advisement is often the function of school guidance counselors; scholars have recommended that counselors take strong roles in directing female students, in supporting students in their aspirations for nontraditional goals, and in exposing both sexes to a range of course and career opportunities by speaking to classes, inviting speakers, publicizing and recommending printed literature, and so on.[51]

While these goals are commendable, counselors themselves do not always hold liberal or egalitarian attitudes toward the aspirations of male and female students. In England, Shafer notes the failure of schools to counsel females to study science or mathematics.[52] Oliver and Fox each reviewed studies of career and course counseling practices in the United States, and both concluded that there is often a negative bias toward females who consider entering nontraditional occupations.[53] Also, male counselors tend to be more nondirective with woman clients, perhaps reflecting less concern with the consequences of their decisions. The

[50] Michael P. Fogarty, Rhona Rapoport, and Robert N. Rapoport, *Sex, Career and Family: Including an International Review of Women's Roles* (London: Allen & Unwin, 1971).
[51] P. Z. Boring, "Sex Stereotyping in Educational Guidance," in *Sex Role Stereotyping in the Schools* (Washington, D.C.: National Education Association, 1973), pp. 14–22; Mary E. Verheyden-Hilliard, "Counseling Potential Superbomb against Sexism," *American Education* 13 (April 1977): 12–15; Iris Tiedt, "Realistic Counseling for High-School Girls," *School Counselor* 19 (May 1972): 354–59.
[52] Susanne Shafer, "The Socialization of Girls in Secondary Schools of England and the Two Germanies," *International Review of Education* 22, no. 1 (1976): 5–25.
[53] Laurel W. Oliver, "Counseling Implications of Recent Research on Women," *Personnel and Guidance Journal* 53 (February 1975): 430–37; L. H. Fox, "The Effects of Sex Role Socialization on Mathematics Participation and Achievement," in *Women and Mathematics: Research Perspectives for Change*, ed. L. H. Fox, E. Fennema, and J. Sherman (Washington, D.C.: National Institute of Education, 1977).

former point was demonstrated by Pietrofesa and Schlossberg, who taped interviews between counselor trainees and a coached female counselee.[54] The supposed client would say that she was trying to decide between engineering and education as a profession. Both male and female counselors displayed significant bias against engineering (81.7 percent vs. 18.7 percent), while their verbal statements placed major stress on the masculinity of the occupation.

There is an important sex difference among the counselors themselves. Thomas and Stewart found that female counselors are more liberal toward nonstereotypical goals for high-school students than male counselors.[55] Bingham and House surveyed high-school counselors and found men to agree more often than women that (a) all women's roles are secondary to motherhood, and (b) training women for high-level jobs 's wasteful.[56] To the extent that counselors play a role in creating sex differences in exposure to course material, female counselors sensitive to the issue may be preferable for students of both sexes.

Differences in allocated time may be accentuated in schools which serve only one sex group. For example, while coeducational schools in England require pupils to take science through grades 11 or 12, all-male schools require a higher proportion of boys to continue this far, and all-female schools terminate mandatory science at grade 10.[57] However, there may also be advantages to the single-sex setting. It appears, for example, that women in all-girls schools choose nontraditional majors and take mathematics and science courses more often.[58] According to the IEA survey, some of the largest sex differences in English coeducational schools —namely, boys' superiority in ninth-grade physics, practical science, and science attitudes —are notably smaller between students in sex-segregated institutions. Likewise, sex differences in attitudes toward mathematics are generally smaller in single-sex instititions. These and other developmental trends are at least partially explained by differences in requirements and students' exposure to course content.

A third way of viewing exposure to schooling is the time an individual student actually spends working with materials or participating in learning activities, that is, *engaged time*. While allocated time may form the

[54] J. J. Pietrofesa and N. K. Schlossberg, "Counselor Bias and the Female Occupational Role," in *Sex Bias in the Schools*, ed. J. Pottker and A. Fishel (Teaneck, N.J.: Fairleigh Dickinson University Press, 1977), pp. 221–29.

[55] Arthur Thomas and Norman Stewart, "Counselors' Response to Female Clients with Deviate and Conforming Career Goals," *Journal of Counseling Psychology* 18 (July 1971): 352–57.

[56] W. C. Bingham and E. W. House, "Counselor's Attitudes toward Women and Work," in *Sex Bias in the Schools*, ed. J. Pottker and A. Fishel (Teaneck, N.J.: Fairleigh Dickinson University Press, 1977), pp. 247–55.

[57] Finn (n. 21 above).

[58] Alexander Astin and Robert J. Panos, *The Educational and Vocational Development of College Students* (Washington, D.C.: American Council on Education, 1969); Carnegie Commission on Higher Education, *Opportunities for Women in Higher Education* (New York: McGraw-Hill, 1973).

boundary conditions within which students and school staff interact, engaged time, in particular, has been found to correlate with individual achievement levels. Affected by students and teachers alike, engaged time can also become the basis of different achievement levels for male and female pupils. At an extreme, girls attending a poor-quality all-girls school simply are not spending adequate time in productive learning activities. Even in a coeducational setting, assignments may be given primarily to one sex group or the other, and the participation in class activities encouraged or discouraged for males or females. More often, sex differences in engaged time are created subtly, through teachers' continued differential behavior toward boys and girls.

Many studies have identified teacher-student interactions that differ systematically by sex. Meyer and Thompson[59] observed sixth-grade teachers and recorded instances when approval or disapproval was given to the pupils. Boys received significantly more disapproval than girls and, when queried, both male and female students were aware of this difference. These findings are supported by Levy, who adds that boys receive generally more intense stimuli, while girls may be ignored or rewarded just for following directions.[60] Brophy and Good, in an extensive literature review, note that these differences are characteristic of both male and female teachers.[61]

An important contribution was made in the finer analysis performed by Seewald, Leinhardt, and Engel.[62] Observing second-grade teachers, these researchers noted that more academic contacts were made to girls in reading and more to boys in mathematics. While there were no differences in initial abilities, sex differences were found in end-of-year achievement. Also, it was noted that the teachers had spent the same amount of total time with boys and girls in both subjects and made the usual "more managerial contacts with boys." McNeil tested this effect by providing programmed material to girls and boys for initial reading instruction.[63] Through this instructional mode boys and girls were given equal opportunity to respond, as well as equal amounts of praise and reinforcement. Teachers identified more boys than girls as having little motivation or readiness to read. However, boys did not become inferior

[59] William J. Meyer and George G. Thompson, "Sex Differences in the Distribution of Teacher Approval and Disapproval among Sixth-Grade Children," *Journal of Educational Psychology* 47 (November 1956): 385–96.

[60] B. Levy, "Sex Role Socialization in Schools," in *Sex Role Stereotyping in the Schools* (Washington, D.C.: National Education Association, 1973), pp. 1–7.

[61] Jere E. Brophy and Thomas L. Good, *Teacher-Student Relationship: Causes and Consequences* (New York: Holt, Rinehart & Winston, 1974).

[62] Andrea M. Seewald, Gaea Leinhardt, and Mary Engel, *Learning What's Taught: Sex Differences in Instruction* (Pittsburgh: University of Pittsburgh, Learning Research and Development Center, 1977).

[63] John D. McNeil, "Programmed Instruction versus Usual Classroom Procedure in Teaching Boys to Read," *American Educational Research Journal* 1 (March 1964): 113–19.

readers to the girls, unlike their peers in a teacher-managed control class. Additional experiments are needed with means to provide equal exposure to male and female students, especially at the secondary level, through equating time engaged in learning.

These effects cannot be divorced from the teachers' own attitudes and expectations. While teachers may view young girls' more docile behavior as preferable, by high school, boys' aggression and achievement orientation come to be seen as related to traditional adult roles.[64] For example, Gaite presented high-school teachers with identical profiles of outstanding male and female students.[65] The teachers were asked how they perceived the students' careers at age 21 and 31. Without exception, males were predicted to be engaged in further education at 21 and successful in a career at 31. Female students were predicted to be married with a family at 31. Those females who were predicted to take a career were attributed the usual narrow range —nurse, teacher, secretary. A study done in India documented the prevalence of the same cultural attitudes found in interviews with parents and content analyses of textbooks: " . . . generally they [teachers] tend to accept the traditional sexist role differentiations. This is particularly true in regard to what one might term the 'legacy of motherhood,' since 11 out of 12 teachers believe that women are better qualified than men to respond to the needs of children."[66] The researchers also noted that the teachers view education as preparation for marriage; neither financial independence nor self-development were mentioned as possible educational benefits for girls. These views are all the more revealing since they were delivered after the teachers had participated in an experimental orientation course on sexism in the classroom.

That teachers' attitudes are translated into achievement differences was demonstrated elegantly by Palardy.[67] First-grade teachers were identified who believed that boys could learn to read as well as girls, and other teachers who believed that boys would be inferior readers. At the end of a year's instruction, there was a significant interaction of belief with pupil sex. There were no noteworthy differences between boys' and girls' reading scores for the first group of teachers; for those holding differential expectations, there were large reading differences in favor of the girls.

[64] Teresa A. Levitin and J. D. Chananie, "Response of Female Primary School Teachers to Sex-typed Behaviors in Male and Female Children," *Child Development* 43 (December 1972): 1309–16.
[65] A. J. H. Gaite, "Teachers' Perceptions of Ideal Male and Female Students: Male Chauvinism in the School," in *Sex Bias in the Schools*, ed. J. Pottker and A. Fishel (Teaneck, N.J.: Fairleigh Dickinson University Press, 1977), pp. 105–7.
[66] Kamlesh Nischol and Mary Haney, *Report on the Teacher Orientation Course on Sexism in the Classroom: Pilot Project* (New Delhi: Report to UNICEF, June 1, 1977), p. 9.
[67] J. Michael Palardy, "What Teachers Believe—What Children Achieve," *Elementary School Journal* 69 (April 1969): 370–74.

Differences in curricular exposure for males and females may occur subtly, yet in some geographic areas they create significantly different environments for the two sex groups —especially as effects accrue over many years of schooling. Masemann noted the "hidden curriculum" for girls in some African schools.[68] While the formal curriculum appears the same for the sexes, instructional emphasis is often placed on girls' learning to manage a home and marriage. Smock reports that the school curriculum in the Philippines likewise stresses women's traditional roles as wife and mother.[69] Here women have very high rates of modern employment so that instruction to which they are exposed may be at odds with their occupational needs. The exposure of males and females to curricular content as an antecedent of learning constitutes a major issue for further research in the study of differential attainment.

Academic Support

Exposure to curricular material alone is not sufficient to assure acceptable achievement levels. The academic support and encouragement provided by teachers, peers, and others may be especially important to female students who face social pressure not to excel in school or career-oriented subjects. The undervaluing of women's education is a worldwide phenomenon, expressed both in school and out, and its effects on girls' attainments are profound. As an example, Eliou has noted that academic expectations for African girls are generally low, and eagerness to learn or to do creative work is usually stifled by the beginning of secondary school.[70] Women's enthusiasm for schooling in India may be hampered by the fact that employment rates are lower for females educated above the middle-school level. In Western nations with higher attendance rates, the importance of males' schooling is also emphasized. In Australia, according to Encel, Mackenzie, and Tebbutt, schools provide neither the encouragement nor the facilities for girls to study science or mathematics.[71] Further, Sampson observed that girls are not given the experience with geometric shapes and figures in primary school that may be a precursor to mathematics performance later on.[72] The one-sidedness in the encouragement of males has been documented many times, and is un-

[68] Vandra Masemann, "The 'Hidden Curriculum' of a West African Girls' Boarding School," *Canadian Journal of African Studies* 8, no. 3 (1974): 479–94.

[69] Audrey C. Smock, "Women's Opportunities for Education and Its Impact on Their Roles in the Philippines" (unpublished paper, Ford Foundation, New York, n.d.).

[70] Marie Eliou, "Scolarisation et promotion feminines en Afrique francophone (Côte-D'Ivoire, Haute-Volta, Senegal)," *International Review of Education* 19, no. 1 (1973): 30–47.

[71] Solomon Encel, Norman MacKenzie, and Margaret Tebbutt, *Women and Society: An Australian Study* (Melbourne: Cheshire, 1974).

[72] S. N. Sampson, "Egalitarian Ideology and the Education of Girls," *Australian Journal of Education* 20 (March 1976): 10–20.

doubtedly reflected in disproportionate numbers of males in scientific and administrative courses and careers.

There is also strong opposition to change. For example, in the United States, Fox arranged experimental mathematics courses for seventh-grade girls, to be taught during the summer by three female teachers in small-group and individualized instruction.[73] Conscious attempts were made to emphasize the social value of mathematical training and to develop students' study habits and skills. The experimental group girls scored significantly higher in their knowledge of algebra than girls in a mixed-sex control group. However, attempts to place the girls in advanced high-school classes were opposed by school personnel and from the girls as well, who saw a social stigma associated with high achievement in mathematics. The setting was not supportive, and the effects of beneficial models and increased curricular exposure were diminished. A study of American school counselors revealed further that both sexes resisted a female client's decision to become an engineer.[74] Unfortunately, these are the individuals to whom students often turn for direction.

Intrapsychic issues must be considered as well. In the United States, research has focused on the dimensions of female dependency. For example, there is evidence that girls, even more than their male counterparts, would benefit from increased levels of support and encouragement. Psychologists have observed that women are generally higher in social and affiliative interests than males. Maccoby and Jacklin, and Tyler, find that women, especially during the adolescent years, are more dependent on teachers and family for emotional support and more subject to suggestibility than males.[75] Thus they may respond both to positive and negative expectations held for them by "significant others"; this is Bandura and Walters's eliciting effect of role models. Recent work by Matina Horner posits a "motive to avoid success" on the part of young women.[76] While the concept has been subject to much controversy, its implications are important. If women do tend to experience discomfort when succeeding at educational or vocational tasks, then support to overcome this discomfort is necessary.

The traditional socioeconomic roles of women in many parts of the Third World make it unlikely that the same problems would arise. The broader question of the relationship between personality characteristics and attainment, however, cannot be neglected in examining sex differences. Everywhere, those females who wish to study male-dominated

[73] L. H. Fox, "Sex Differences in Mathematical Precocity: Bridging the Gap," in *Intellectual Talent: Research and Development*, ed. D. P. Keating (Baltimore: Johns Hopkins University Press, 1976), pp. 183–214.
[74] Pietrofesa and Schlossberg (n. 54 above).
[75] Maccoby and Jacklin (n. 24 above); Tyler (n. 24 above).
[76] Matina S. Horner, "Toward an Understanding of Achievement Related Conflicts in Women," *Journal of Social Issues* 28, no. 2 (1972): 157–75.

subject areas, in particular, require support that is both extraordinary in amount and of continuing duration.

Some research has been conducted on levels of academic and personal support as they relate to sex differences. Casserly reviewed programs to increase girls' performance in science and mathematics, and concluded that the most successful programs were the ones that relied on older girls to counsel, encourage, and tutor younger ones.[77] All-female schools may provide women with acknowledgments of their achievement and a stress on performance that cannot be attained in coeducational settings. According to Block, "male faculty members, like fathers, may provide less encouragement for women to achieve; may not offer collaborative opportunities to women because, like fathers, they place less value on the cognitive achievements of women."[78]

Many individuals may be in a position to provide the needed encouragement. The concern and support of older students in the work of their younger peers is commonplace in the Soviet Union, and peer tutoring is often encouraged in the United States.[79] The practice has not been documented with regard to actual or possible effects on sex roles, however. Further research may begin to identify the significant "decision points" in a child's education and study the roles of family, friends, and school personnel in formulating a course of action. Progress in understanding the relationship of academic and personal encouragement with the attainment of productive career lines should be given high priority.

Summary

The sources of unequal educational attainments for men and women are many and complex. Among them, formal schooling is a major institution through which limiting values may be transmitted or change implemented. It is in school that youth are exposed intensively to behavior models and materials which teach the range of possible adult behaviors; it is in school that alternatives to values learned elsewhere can be examined; it is in school that even a girl with limited aspirations can learn the specific skills necessary for employment.

The educational opportunity afforded females in most parts of the world is severely limited, thereby reducing women's life choices. Levin suggests four ways of viewing equality of opportunity: (1) equal access to the educational system for individuals regardless of social circumstance, (2) equal participation in the educational system, (3) equal educational

[77] Patricia Casserly, "Study Finds Girls Are Diverted from Careers in Math and Science," *ETS Developments* 25, no. 3 (Fall 1978): 4–5.

[78] Block (n. 22 above), p. 55.

[79] Urie Bronfenbrenner, *Two Worlds of Childhood: U.S. and U.S.S.R.* (New York: Pocket Books, 1973); Sophie Bloom, *Peer and Cross-Age Tutoring in the Schools* (Washington, D.C.: National Institute of Education, 1976).

results, and (4) equal educational effects on life chances.[80] In much of the world access to schooling is the predominant issue for females. This review focuses instead on participation; not to expose both sexes within school to the full range of course contents and adult sex-role models, or to the benefits associated with the highest expectations and support for their performance, is to deny them equal opportunity in the second sense. The possibility of equal results or equal life chances exists only when individuals can make their own "positive choices" from available alternatives, rather than "negative choices" from limited opportunity.

Participation may also be viewed in terms of the psychodynamics through which events are processed by the students. The social norms, school experiences, and attainments which are realized are accompanied by a set of personal values and expectations, internalized at an early age, which continue to mediate further congruent behavior. Children of both sexes carry rigid stereotypes of sex-appropriate adult roles; girls' attitudes toward school accomplishments are generally lower than boys, and girls often have lower aspirations than boys.[81] While it is beyond the scope of this paper to explore these or other attitudinal dimensions, their mediating role must be considered in further research into the effects of school process. Paramount among them, attitudes toward occupational roles and the job market are directly related to the educational attitudes and aspirations of women. These must be examined further on a cross-national basis and monitored closely in any attempt to bring about change through affecting school process.

[80] Henry M. Levin, "Educational Opportunity and Social Inequality in Western Europe," *Social Problems* 24 (December 1976): 148–72.

[81] I. D. Smith, "Sex Differences in the Self-Concept of Primary School Children," *Australian Psychologist* 10 (March 1975): 59–63; Marjorie M. Schratz, "Self-Esteem in Three Ethnic Groups: Differential Development for the Sexes" (paper presented at the Annual Meeting of the American Psychological Association, Toronto, March 1978); Margaret M. Marini and Ellen Greenberger, "Sex Differences in Educational Aspirations and Expectations," *American Educational Research Journal* 15 (Winter 1978): 67–79; Erma I. Muckenhirin, *Secondary Education and Girls in Western Nigeria* (Ann Arbor: University of Michigan School of Education, 1966); United Nations Economic Commission for Africa (UNECA), Women's Research and Training Center, "Women and Rational Development in African Countries: Some Profound Contradictions," *African Studies Review* 18 (December 1975): 47–70.

8. Church, State and Education in Belgian Africa
Implications for Contemporary Third World Women

BARBARA A. YATES

Colonialism embodied a heritage of attitudes toward women and their proper role in society. These attitudes and values were replicated in colonial school systems. Belgian colonialism was dominated by the "Big Three": the Roman Catholic Church, the colonial administration, and the large corporations. Through political trade-offs, schools became the special preserve of the church; at independence in 1960, nearly all of the 1.6 million Congolese pupils in school attended Catholic (77 percent) or Protestant (19 percent) institutions. The residual enrollment was in state vocational schools (established beginning in 1897), in secular primary and secondary schools (beginning in 1954), or in training programs financed by commercial firms (beginning in 1908).[1]

There were extraordinary differences between education offered to boys and to girls in the Belgian colonial education system. European educators sponsored a deliberate pattern of sex-differentiated roles the norms of which were embodied in the life of the schools. When the Belgian Congo became an independent republic in 1960 (later called "Zaire"), none of the several hundred Congolese students attending the two universities or the half-dozen post-secondary institutes were female. Furthermore, none of the 800 cumulative academic secondary school graduates were female.[2] The most educationally advanced Zairian female was a senior in an academic high school.[3] There was, of course, a connection between these low attainment rates and the Catholic domination of the educational system.

The predominance of missionaries as educators made their aims, values, and life styles central to the establishment of sex differentiation in education. Western colonizers brought with them a set of notions

---

[1] Betty George, *Educational Developments in the Congo (Leopoldville)* (Washington, D. C.: U.S. Government Printing Office, 1966), p. 20.

[2] High school graduates were estimated by the author in 1960–61, after interviews with the Director of Secondary Education at the Bureau of Catholic Education, and with the UNESCO statistical advisor at the Ministry of Education, both in Leopoldville. Higher education figures were ascertained from graduation lists provided in 1960–61 by the registrars of Lovanium University, the State University at Elisabethville (Lumbumbashi), and the postsecondary institutes.

[3] In early 1961, I interviewed this student, Mlle. Sophie Kanza, the daughter of the then mayor of Leopoldville. She became the first Congolese women to receive a high school diploma when she graduated from the *Lycée du Sacre Coeur*, in June, 1961.

Parts of this chapter appeared in Edna G. Bay, ed., *Women and Work in Africa* (Boulder: Westview Press, 1982).

about proper activities for women. While sharply differentiated sex roles have been a perennial theme in the Judeo-Christian tradition, Belgian Africa represented an especially clear-cut case of the influence of Christianity, especially that of conservative Catholicism, on educational practices. Belgium, from its inception in the early 1830s, was a repository of conservative European thought. England, it has been said, had the Reformation and France had the Revolution, but Belgium had little intellectual ferment. In Belgium, social patterns were little affected by the upheavals of the Industrial Revolution and the accompanying scientific age. The rural and working-class background of most missionaries who served in the Congo also reinforced their conservatism, especially among Catholic missionaries from rural Flanders, a stronghold of conservative Catholicism. Because of the conservative nature and the temporal power of the Catholic Church in Belgian colonialism, parochial attitudes and values were more pervasive and overtly reflected in government policy.

Belgian Africa, however, is not an isolated case study of the role of the church in colonial education. Christian missionaries, especially in the nineteenth and early twentieth centuries, spread throughout the world, dispensing their religious message and at the same time establishing schools. These schools, like those in the Congo, were vehicles for reflecting the missionaries' conception of acceptable sex roles. These church-related schools in many areas survived independence movements. In them, church-related attitudes and values persist today in many former European colonies in the Third World.

There were, of course, traditional differences in the roles of African men and women. These sex role differences were extensive as a result of the great number of ethnic groups in an area as huge as the Congo. Congolese women, thus, were caught in a double bind; they suffered from the dual differentiation of both traditional and colonial societies. Whether conservative Western concepts concerning appropriate gender roles were more restrictive than the various traditional African concepts they were meant to replace is a subject that needs further research, drawing upon anthropological literature.

This study, however, focuses on the superimposed colonial system. Whatever the local traditions, Belgian colonialism introduced the Western-type school and the modern economic sector and gave pre-eminence to conservative Western concepts about gender roles — even in agriculture, where Congolese women had clearly defined managerial responsibilities. As would be expected, strongly emphasized patriarchal traditions led to stereotyped linkages between sex differences in access to both education and employment in the modern sector. Finally, as also would be expected, sex differentiation during the colonial period has implications for the contemporary life of Third World women.

Western Patriarchy and Colonial Eduational Goals

Missionaries, bolstered by the government, sought to implant Christian patriarchy and white supremacy among the Congolese peoples. Missionaries dreamed of establishing a Christian nation in Central Africa. To accomplish this task, they strove first to establish the monogamous family and to instill Christian influences within African homes. These strategies were epitomized in the statement of a pioneer Belgian missionary leader:

> We missionaries are here to make the Congolese nation a Christian and civilized people. However, a people is composed of families. . . . When the young Congolese boy and girl are civilized and Christian, we will unite them into a Christian family from which will come the Christian people.[4]

Missionaries were not opposed to all African customs, despite their litany of derogatory comments designed to loosen the purse strings of metropolitan supporters. It was those customs that flouted the basic moral tenents of Christianity — polygyny, traditional religious beliefs, and premarital sexual relations — that were especially abhorred by churchmen.[5]

For creating a new type of society, as distinguished from merely creating new mines and plantations, women with a new character were as essential as men. As a Belgian Jesuit admonished: "It is Christian mothers who make a Christian society."[6] Missionaries viewed the taking of a pagan wife by male converts as a major cause of spiritual and moral backsliding; the unschooled country girl led a man back to paganism, while a sophisticated town girl led him into debauchery.[7]

In order to achieve the new Christian state, missionaries carefully

[4] Scheutist Father Superior Emeri Cambier, X/20/99 from Luluabourg, *Missions en Chine et au Congo*, August 1900, p. 486.
[5] Barbara A. Yates, "White Views of Black Minds: Schooling in King Leopold's Congo," *History of Education Quarterly* (Spring 1980): 27–50.
[6] Ivan de Pierpont et al., *Au Congo et aux Indes: Les Jesuites belges aux missions* (Brussels: Bulens, 1906), p. 96.
[7] Frère Gabriel, *Essai d'orientation de l'enseignement et de l'éducation au Congo* (Anvers: Stockmans, 1914), p. 14. Prostitution was evidently also an avenue of employment for some Congolese women. Catholic missionaries constantly harangued the government to enact more stringent laws on adultery and promiscuity for both whites and blacks, especially in the towns. By the beginning of the twentieth century, mulatto boys were being admitted to the state *colonie scolaire* at Boma. Soon a school for mulatto children was also opened by the Belgian Holy Ghost Fathers in the Kindu region, shortly after construction of the railway in that area was completed. See Marcus Dorman, *A Journal of a Tour in the Congo Free State* (Brussels; Lebeque; London: Kegan Paul, Trench, Trubner, 1905), passim.

129

delineated roles by race and gender. The conduct expected of European missionaries provided for the African role models of appropriate behavior between the sexes. While expectations varied between Protestants and Catholics, all agreed to follow the "teachings of the Bible where all authority comes from God through the Father."[8] In truth, the male missionary was a patriarch; he guided the work of subordinate female missionaries and African male assistants and established the rules by which the Christian community was to live.

Catholic priests welcomed female missionaries who would devote their efforts to preparing local girls to become Christian wives of male converts. Belgian Jesuits attributed the failure of the early Portuguese missionaries in the Congo and Angola to the lack of sisters for this duty.[9] Despite their indispensability to the apostolate, female missionaries must not fail to remain subservient, and they must not threaten priestly hegemony. The principal task of female missionaries (whether single Protestant or Catholic women or Protestant wives) was to teach in the elementary schools; secondary teaching and theological training were by and large white male domains.

Missionaries expected African men to take on the ideal character traits of white women: industriousness, docility, obedience, gentleness, and passivity — of course in relation to Europeans, especially to males. African women were to display the same humility but also toward African males. While the African wife was to be the foundation of her Christian family, devoting her time to tending the hearth and bearing and rearing a generation of African Christians, she would remain subservient to her husband.

Christian patriarchy was allegedly a blessing to African women for it would rescue them from polygyny and would confer vaguely stated benefits of Western civilization, such as "a healthy and comforting morality, which among other things, gives to the woman her real situation in nature. Polygamy will be replaced by the Christian family with all the rights that it confers."[10]

Both Christian missionaries and the colonial government attacked the traditional sex division of labor in agriculture, and their subsequent activities in agricultural education embodied this obtuseness. In the Congo, women were traditionally the major producers of food, especially

---

[8] Suzanne Comhaire-Syvain, quoted in Esther Boserup, *Women's Role in Economic Development* (New York: St. Martin's Press, 1970), p. 60.

[9] E. Laveille, *L'Evangile au centre de l'Afrique: Le Père Emile Van Hencxthoven, S. J., fondateur de la Mission du Kwango (Congo belge) 1852–1906* (Louvain: Museum Lessianum, 1926), p. 124.

[10] A. Devos, "Principes de civilisation," *Mouvement des Missions Catholiques au Congo* (December 1904): 349.

in the non-Muslim areas of the West and the South.[11] The new patriarchal aim, however, would move women out of the fields; men should
do the heavier work, because women were overworked while men
were lazy. Absence of a "proper" division of labor, the Jesuits (the
principal agricultural educators) contended, helped to make "all improvement in agriculture impossible,"[12] and so it was males who received
seeds, training, and supervision in farming.

The Christian "rights" of women were discussed endlessly by male
missionaries. Remarking, at the time of World War I, that there was
hope that in two or three generations the population around the Jesuit
missions in the Lower Congo would be Catholic and therefore well on
the way to "civilization," a leading Jesuit emphasized that, among other
things, it would be necessary "to establish the rights of fathers of families
over their children" and "to introduce more and more personal property
by agricultural cultivation."[13] Missionaries assumed that enhanced "personal property by agricultural cultivation" done by men would augment
male property and that somehow there would be a "trickle down" effect
to other members of the new Christian family. However, the Jesuits
reported a "strange phenomenon:" men, even Christian converts, refused
to cultivate traditional crops, although they were willing to grow new
European crops, such as rice and sweet potatoes.[14] The reason perhaps
was not so much laziness, as the missionaries claimed, as resistance to
uncomfortable sex roles. When agricultural education came to be provided by the state (1908), it was limited to males, who frequently
deserted these schools for a more academically oriented program. When
only an agricultural school was accessible, it was frequently used by
young men to acquire the literacy skills necessary for urban employment.[15]

Given all these deeply rooted attitudes, inevitably the provision of

[11] Report of the Committee on Education, in "Annual Report for 1893," *Baptist Missionary Magazine* (July 1894): 200.
[12] Joseph Van Wing (S. J.), *Le Vingt-cinquième anniversaire de la Mission du Kwango* (Bruxelles: Bulens, s.d. [1918]), p. 19.
[13] Ibid., p. 37.
[14] Ibid., p. 19. An interesting modern parallel is reported in an American magazine. East Coast air travelers complained of dirty airplaines. Management consultants found that maintenance men were using brooms instead of vacuum cleaners, which they considered "the tools of women." The solution was to make the machines heavier, paint them grey rather than pastel, and to label them "industrial vacuum cleaner." A "military-style competition" was under-taken to see who could best disassemble and clean his new industrial tool. The plan was suc-cessful. "It's now macho to vacuum efficiently." From *New York Magazine*, quoted in *MS.* (August 1978): 24.
[15] Jean-Jacques Deheyn [Director of Technical Education], "Realisations et objectifs de la Belgique en matière d'enseignement agricole au Congo Belge," *Bulletin Agricole du Congo Belge* 68, no. 1 (1957): 1–22.

educational opportunity mirrored Western patriarchal goals. The school became a powerful agency for socializing Africans into conservative Western views, especially about family life and occupation. A class of male "native intellectuals" was resisted, based on conclusions about the deleterious religious and political effects of "literary" education in older colonies, such as India and Sierra Leone. Recipients of academic education were said to lose their religious interest and to acquire an anti-colonial outlook, as well as to exhibit an arrogant desire for assimilation. Consequently, until after World War II, boys' postprimary and secondary education centered on preparation of religious assistants for evangelism and only secondarily on training subalterns for the administration. After World War II, secular elites were added to the preparation of priests, pastors, and subalterns.

While the purpose of the education of males would shift after World War II as political change came to the continent, the primary objective of girls' education at all levels remained unaltered from the opening of the first Western-type school in 1879 to independence in 1960: training Christian wives and mothers. The aim of education for girls was to implant Christian morality, an awareness of "proper" family relationships, and a favorable disposition toward children learning their religious duties. Accordingly, apart from the "sacramental" duties of wifehood, African girls needed to prepare formally for few new roles through attendance at schools.

Sex Differentiation in Education

These differential educational goals for boys and girls were reflected and reinforced in access to schooling, in curriculums, in the language of instruction, and in educational participation rates. The development of education in the Belgian Congo can be conveniently divided into three periods: (1) the Leopoldian period (1879–1908), when the Congo basin was the personal fiefdom of Leopold II, King of the Belgians; (2) the early parliamentary period, beginning in 1908 with the formal transfer of sovereignty from Leopold to the Belgian Parliament, and (3) the post-World War II period, until the Congo became independent in 1960.

The Leopoldian Period

The colonial educational system took form during the Leopoldian period. Neither the initial legislation, the 1890 and 1892 Education Acts and their implementing ordinances, nor the 1906 Concordat with the Vatican mentioned girls. This legislation promised state subsidization to Catholic educators for the training in *colonies scolaires* and mission schools of orphaned, neglected, and abandoned boys as French-speaking artisans, agriculturalists, or soldiers.[16] Protestant schools received no subsidies until after World War II. Beginning in 1897, a handful of secular, state vocational schools (*écoles professionnelles*) were also established for boys only, to train noncommissioned officers, artisans, clerks, male nurses, and plantation workers for the colonial administration.

While neither the 1890 and 1892 Education Acts nor the 1906 Concordat referred to girls, nonetheless separate Catholic-run and state-supported (Moanda and Nouvelle-Anvers) and government-authorized (several dozen locations) mission *colonies scolaires* were established for girls beginning in the late nineteenth century. They were to teach primarily domestic skills and Christian virtues. These schools were viewed by Catholic missionaries as "nurseries of virtuous young girls," hard-working and well-instructed, "where our boys can find faithful and devoted wives. Isn't this a work *par excellence* for extending the Christian religion and making it flourish in an infidel country?"[17] In recruiting pupils for these schools, executive orders required district commissioners to be sure they sent an equal number of boys and girls from each tribe so that they could later be joined in Catholic marriage.[18] Sex differentiation in the content of vocational education was vividly expressed by a visitor to King Leopold's Congo: "Boys are taught to cultivate, to work with wood and iron, to bricklay, to make bricks and tiles, and to construct a house; the girls learn to sew, wash clothes, cook, and keep house.[19]

Though artisan education was sponsored by the colonial administration for boys, and missionaries initiated home economics as the principal skills for girls, general literacy education and teacher training under missionary auspices for both boys and girls eventually arose. When missionaries opened schools in the late nineteenth century, Congolese boys demanded to be paid to learn reading and writing, perceiving no intrinsic or economic value in such skills. But, as railway construction opened up the interior and as Congolese became acquainted with the life styles of the literate West African craftsmen and clerks who had been brought in to assist with railway construction and colonial administration, local attitudes of males toward literacy changed from indifference to curiosity and finally to enthusiasm. Villages began to request that schools be established; enrollments, particularly of boys, soared.

[16] Etat indépendant du Congo, *Bulletin officiel* (1890): 120–22; (1892): 18–19; 188–95; 241–43.

[17] *Missions d'Afrique des Pères blancs* (December 1898): 360.

[18] Edouard Kervyn, "Les missions Catholiques au Congo belge," *La Revue Congolaise* (1912): 287. Boys at the *colonie scolaire* at Boma, for example, were regularly transported at government expense to the nearby Catholic-run girls' school at Moanda to choose wives. The boys' and girls' sections at Nouvelle-Anvers were in close proximity.

[19] Pierre Verhaegen, *Au Congo: Impressions de Voyage* (Gand: Siffer, 1898), p. 153.

The new interest of Congolese males in literacy led to intense intra-Christian rivalry for converts, using the school as an inducement to enter the mission orbit. Protestant and Catholic missionaries scurried to prepare more male teacher-evangelists and catechists in order to compete for villages. Some Protestant missionaries concluded that religious goals were fostered by teaching the wives of their evangelists at least to read. These wives could then assist with village schools as well as teach dressmaking to girls. Neighboring Catholic missions were not to be outdone, and conferred the direction of village work upon married catechists, whose wives had been trained by the sisters. Between 1898, when the railway was completed from Matadi (the seaport) to Leopoldville (the beginning of the navigable portion of the Congo River) and 1903, enrollments increased from approximately 9,000 to 27,000.[20]

The general education curriculum in these schools was very rudimentary, especially for girls. While religion was at the heart of every mission school program and manual labor to build character was required of all pupils, the curriculum for girls was more meagre than that for boys. At the better elementary schools, boys were exposed to the three Rs and perhaps a smattering of geography and French. Generally, Catholics viewed literacy as nonessential to religious goals, and their missions in the Leopoldian period seldom offered reading and writing to girls. Indeed, Catholic eduation for girls could best be described as resocialization, rather than instruction. Reading and writing were regarded by some Catholic missionaries as actually dangerous for girls: "To learn to read and write is usual for all our boys. But the majority of our female savages have none of it and it is reported even that certain ones, who have learned to read, neglect the care of their homes."[21] Catholics lagged behind Protestants in providing girls with opportunities for literacy, not only because of such male views but also partly because of an aversion to coeducation (single-sex schools became a continuing feature of Belgian colonial education) and partly because male catechists or priests were forbidden by most Catholic orders to teach girls any subjects other than religion.

Protestant schools provided more literacy education for girls because of the imperative for Bible reading and because of the coeducational nature of some Protestant schools. Some Protestant missionaries believed that if the school was taught by a missionary rather than by an African male, it was good to have boys and girls together; the boys would be spurred to better achievement by competition from the girls

---

[20] Estimated by the author from annual reports in missionary journals.
[21] *Missions belges de la Compagnie de Jésus* (September 1907): 328.

and at the same time become more respectful of the girls' ability.[22] Moreover, Protestant Bible schools usually required men to bring their families; these schools also admitted single women who were subsequently encouraged to marry evangelists or pastors. But Protestant missionaries, nonetheless, directed their main efforts to the conversion of boys and to training the most obedient and religiously pious of them as evangelists. Only after their staffs had expanded and station construction was completed did the intra-Christian rivalry lead Protestant missionaries to give more time to educating girls.[23]

Another continuing feature differentiating education for boys and girls was the medium of instruction.[24] Although the Education Act of 1890 emphasized the teaching of French, the administration endlessly berated Catholic headmasters of boys' schools for ineffectiveness at this task, while remaining unconcerned that school for girls taught no French.

By the early twentieth century, then, sex differences in education and in subsequent career opportunities were well established. By 1908, more than 46,000 Congloese attended school. Although educational statistics were not consistently disaggregated by gender, in 1908 probably well under 15 percent of pupils were female. The management of knowledge ordained that girls were to receive less literary training than boys and be limited to domestic science courses and teacher training, whereas boys were to prepare for artisan, military, nursing, clerical, teaching, and religious careers. Only boys (albeit a very limited number) would have access to French language training. This distribution of knowledge would be partly controlled through the provision of single-sex schools. Most important, the objectives of Belgian colonial education were firmly fixed during the Leopoldian era: Men belonged in the fields, the shop, the pulpit, and the market place, while women belonged in the home as good Christian wives and mothers. Men in limited numbers were schooled to enter the army, the colonial administration, trading firms, the railway, the missionary enterprise; women who ventured outside the home were limited to the elementary school and the convent.

---

[22] *Congo Missionary Conference 1906.* A report of the third General Conference of Missionaries of the Protestant Societies working in Congoland, at Kinshassa, Stanley Pool, Congo State, January 9–14, 1906 (Bongandanga: Congo Balolo Mission Press, 1906), p. 80.
[23] For example, of the 14 women, including wives, who were accepted for the first class in 1908 at the United Congo Evangelical Training Institution at Kimpese, the most advanced Protestant school in the Congo, only five could read or write, while the 19 men were literate. See George Hawker, *An Englishwoman's Twenty-Five Years in Tropical Africa* (New York: Hodder and Stoughton, 1911), pp. 315–24.
[24] Barbara A. Yates, "The Origins of Language Policy in Colonial Zaire," *Journal of Modern African Studies* 18, no. 2 (1980): 256–79.

Educational Legislation of the 1920s

The colonial Charter of 1908, which formally transferred sovereignty from Leopold II to the Belgian Parliament, incorporated the existing legislation on schools. While opportunities for both boys and girls grew slowly as more schools were opened and more years added to existing programs, differential opportunities based upon gender persisted, becoming explicit and official in the 1920s. Codifying educational practices of the previous four decades, the Education Code of 1929 recognized three levels of schooling: 2-year village schools (grades 1 and 2), 3-year upper primary schools (grades 3–5), and 3-year postprimary vocational schools (grades 6–9).[25] While the 2-year village schools could be coeducational, this code stated expressly that boys and girls in government-subsidized upper-primary schools ahd to be separated beginning with grade 3. Protestant schools, being unsubsidized, were not subject to the 1929 Code; consequently, some of their schools continued to be coeducational, although many followed the government curriculum.[26]

The general curriculum for girls continued to be a watered-down version of that offered to boys.[27] The section on girls' education in the code was introduced with the statement: "The domestic education of women is a factor of first importance in the elevation of a race and in the development of its needs."[28] The code provided that in grades 1 and 2 in village schools, some of which were coeducational, instruction would be the same for both sexes, with the exception of "manual labor"; girls were limited to light gardening, while boys participated in raising stock and

[25] A Commission, appointed after World War I, reviewed colonial education. The recommended plan appeared as *Projet de l'Enseignement Libre au Congo belge avec le concours des sociétés de Missions Nationales* (Brussels: 1925) and was put into practice by a code of government regulations, *Organisation de l'Enseignement Libre au Congo belge et au Ruanda-Urundi, avec le Concours des Sociétés de Missions Nationales* (Brussels: Dison-Verviers, 1929) (hereafter cited as 1929 Code). The former appears in English translation in David G. Scanlon, ed., *Traditions of African Education* (New York: Teachers College Bureau of Publications, Columbia University, 1964), pp. 142–60. See also the Royal Decree of July 19, 1926, regulating vocational education, Belgian Congo, *Bulletin Officiel* 1926, pp. 712–17, which was implemented by an Ordinance of September 11, 1926, Belgian Congo, *Bulletin Administratif*, vol. 15 (1926), pp. 376–78. This legislation did not create schools, but like the 1929 Code, it formalized existing practices.

[26] See *Report of the First Education Conference*, 2nd ed., December 18–23, 1931, mimeographed (Kimpese, Belgian Congo: 1934), and *Report of the Second Education Conference*, 25 July–2 August, 1933, mimeographed (Kimpese, Belgian Congo: 1934).

[27] Oswald Liesenborghs, "L'Instruction publique des indigènes du Congo belge" *Congo* 21, no. 3 (March 1940), p. 262. A school mistress at Ibanj frankly admitted that, when a sewing class for women began in 1901, "the object was not so much to teach sewing as it was to get them together for prayer and song." (See Mrs. Sheppard, *Missionary* (April 1905): 162–3.) It is interesting to note that missionaries in Kenya wrote to their supporters to send cloth cut into postcard size so that it would take a year to make a dress and thus provide ample time for the women to hear many gospel messages. See Yola Evans Connolly, "Roots of Divergency: American Protestant Missions in Kenya 1923–1946" (Ph.D. diss., University of Illinois, 1975), p. 68.

[28] 1929 Code, p. 10.

in the construction and repair of buildings. Beginning with grade 3 (when segregation by sex was required by law in government-subsidized schools), time devoted to the three Rs was reduced for girls in order to add needlework, sewing, and child care. While French was offered to boys as an elective (and was the language of instruction in schools to prepare male clerks), only African languages were used in girls' schools.

Opportunities for boys and girls in vocational education continued to diverge in the interwar years, as opportunities steadily widened for young men. Three kinds of postprimary job-oriented programs for boys were provided in the 1929 Code: clerk schools (*écoles de candidats-commis*, subsequently called *écoles moyennes*), normal schools (later called *écoles de moniteurs*), and vocational schools (*écoles professionnelles*). The clerk schools prepared young men to be office workers, customs agents, tax collector aides, or railway conductors. Normal schools prepared primary teachers for mission schools. In the vocational schools, four options were offered to boys: (1) wood-working (carpentry, cabinet making, joinery); (2) general mechanics (blacksmith, locksmith, foundryman); (3) metal-working (plumbers, metal-workers); and (4) agriculture.

The educational legislation of 1929 also reinforced the domestic role of women under the guise of vocational education. Postprimary vocational schools for girls remained limited by the 1929 Code to elementary school teaching (*écoles de monitrices*) and to home economics-agriculture (*écoles ménagères-agricoles*). The normal schools prepared elementary school teachers and later aides to European social workers in the new *foyers sociaux* (government-subsidized Catholic adult education centers for married women). The home economics-agricultural "vocational" schools led only to the hearth, not to employment in agriculture or to marketable domestic science skills; domestics in European households were generally males.

The agricultural portion of the curriculum in these postprimary home economics-agriculture schools differed from that in the postprimary vocational agriculture sections for boys. The girls' schools ignored tillage and focused on household work and the care of the sick and injured. The "agricultural" curriculum for girls focused on vegetable gardening, medicinal plants, and the care, not the husbandry, of barn-yard animals (such as upkeep of chicken coops, pig stys, pigeon cages, and rabbit hutches). In the vocational-agriculture schools for boys, the emphasis was on export and plantation crops, soils, irrigation, horticulture, animal husbandry, and agricultural machinery. Whereas the boys became qualified for employment in commercial agriculture, the girls had little alternative to homemaking and gardening.

Work in hospitals as midwives and nurses' aides now became accep-table for a few young women. The colonial medical service and the mis-

137

sions opened a handful of schools to train hospital personnel, including the soon-to-become prestigious male medical assistants; several sections to train female midwives and nurses' aides were also opened.

During the interwar years, colonial educators in Belgian Africa concentrated their efforts on training a religious, rather than a secular, elite in nongovernment-subsidized seminaries, Bible schools, and convents. While the White Fathers in the eastern Congo had pioneered the preparation of Congolese priests in the late nineteenth century and nuns in the early twentieth century, a shift in the Vatican policy of the 1920s toward Africanizing the clergy led to a significant expansion of schools to train priests and nuns.

Despite legislative provision for the postprimary education of girls, few opportunities were actually provided. During the interwar years, most of the expansion in girls' enrollment (as well as that of boys) took place in village schools (grades 1 and 2). Here the emphasis was on bringing more young people under missionary guidance through the attraction of rudimentary literacy. On the eve of World War II, no more than 20,000 girls were attending primary school and fewer than 2,000 were in postprimary schools, whereas over 50 percent of the boys of school age were attending formal classes. Catholic missions had only 24 postprimary schools for girls in all the Congo; nine *écoles de monitrices*, 12 *écoles ménagères-agricoles*, and three *écoles medicales*, [29] plus several dozen convent schools for training nuns scattered over an area the size of the United States east of the Mississippi. In addition, there were several dozen Protestant postprimary home economics and teacher training schools, the latter frequently coeducational. The few programs for nurses' aides and midwives, conducted by the colonial Medical Service and the missions, enrolled probably no more than 100 girls. Although data is sparse, estimated on the basis of the number of Congolese nuns in 1960, there were probably as many girls enrolled in convents preparing for religious vocations than in all these government-subsidized postprimary programs.

Belgian commentators conceded that these first postprimary programs for girls were not really secondary education but mainly filled the time between primary school and marriage (usually at 14 to 16 years). Even after girls began attending primary school at the usual European age, upon completing five years of primary education they still were not old enough to marry; further schooling might keep them out of mischief until they would find husbands.[30]

---

[29] E. P. Goetschalckx, *Situation des Ecoles Postprimaires pour autochtones 1952–1953* (Leopoldville: Bureau de l'éducation Catholique, 1953), pp. 6–73.
[30] Liesenborghs, "L'Instruction publique," p. 263.

Changes after World War II

World War II brought many changes to the Congo. New educational programs were initiated in two phases after the war. First, the Education Code of 1948[31] established the first full six-year academic secondary schools for black males as preparation for university studies, and in 1954 the Catholic-run Lovanium University opened with a solely male Congolese student contingent. Second, after 1954, secular state primary and secondary schools were established; these institutions now replicated the practice in Belgium of "parallelism" whereby parochial and secular schools coexisted and competed for pupils.

The patriarchal ideal, however, persisted. Missionaries were still asserting that one duty of the missionary educator was to instruct the people in their rights and duties according to the precepts of Christ: the abolition of polygyny, the establishment of the monogamous family as the primary unit of civilization, the inculcation in males of "their responsibilities as heads of families," and "enlightening" the African woman "on the mission of being a wife and mother in a new Christian society."[32]

The 1948 Code embodied no new aims for girls' education; they were still to become "good wives and mothers." The code stated that the government would have preferred that education of boys and girls proceed at the same pace. However, education for girls lagged because of (1) the "social organization" of native communities, (2) the "atavistic servitude" that burdened the Congolese female, (3) the generally lesser "intellectual receptivity" of girls, and (4) the "prejudices" and "opposition" of Congolese families to the education of girls. Consequently, "we cannot think of developing the instruction of girls at the same rate nor on a plan as widespread nor according to a curriculum as complete as that for boys."[33]

Indeed, the 1948 reorganization widened the sex disparity in educational opportunities, especially in general academic education and in teacher training. The 1948 Code stated that the instruction of girls must be "educative and practical." Not only was full academic secondary education denied to girls, but primary education was further differentiated by gender. Beginning with grade 3, primary schools for boys were now to be of two types; a 3-year "ordinary" program and a 4-year "select" program, the latter leading to the new 6-year academic secondary schools. Girls' upper primary schools were to be only of the "ordinary"

---

[31] Belgian Congo, Service de L'Enseignement. *Organisation de l'Enseignement Libre Subsidié pour indigènes avec le concours des sociétés de missions chrétiennes. Dispositions Générales,* 1948 (hereafter cited as the 1948 Code).

[32] L. Mottoule, "Les Missions et le développement économique du Congo," in *L'Eglise au Congo et au Ruanda-Urundi* (Brussels: Oeuvres Pontificales missionnaires, 1950), p. 74.

[33] 1948 Code, p. 26.

type. The 1948 Code provided boys with the first full academic secondary schools using French as the language of instruction, but teaching in all girls' schools continued to be in the vernacular only. Under the rubric *travaux féminin*, academic courses for girls continued to be replaced in part by sewing and housecleaning. Manual labor for boys involved development of school gardens, whereas girls continued to do only "light work" in these plots and were now to clean the classrooms as well.

Moreover, curricular differences for boys and girls in secondary-teacher training became even more rigid. The 1948 Code stated bluntly that the teacher training curriculum for girls was to be "more simple and more practical" than that for boys. Teacher training for girls (*écoles de monitrices*) continued the same emphasis on home economics and child care found in the primary schools for girls in which these graduates would teach.

While no new aims were set forth for the education of girls, and opportunities relative to boys declined, the reorganized educational system did embody a commitment to improve the schooling of girls as much as was "possible and opportune." In actuality this meant the ubiquitous presence of home economics. A new three-year secondary home economics program (*écoles moyennes-ménagères*) was established for daughters of *évolués* — chiefs, government clerks, medical assistants, teachers — who would marry the new secular male elite being trained in the academic secondary schools. The aim of the new secondary home economics schools was "to create a class of young girls capable of making a good appearance [*de faire bonne figure*] in the world of native *évolués*, as much from the standpoint of education (e.g, *savoir-vivre*, care of the home) as from that of instruction." To prepare this new feminine "elite," a transitional *class de 6ème préparatoire* completed their sixth primary year, qualifying them to enter the new secondary schools of home economics.

New postprimary programs in elementary-school teaching and in hospital work were also created by the 1948 Code, for girls (and boys) who completed the "ordinary" primary cycle. The 1948 Code provided for the establishment of two-year postprimary schools to train apprentice teachers (*écoles d'apprentissage pédagogiques*), with sections for boys and girls. Girls who were at least 16 years of age might enroll in the reorganized two-year schools for nurses' aide (*écoles d'aides-infirmières*) or midwife aide (*écoles d'aides-accoucheuses*).

The main change for girls following from the 1948 Code, however, was a reorganization of domestic science instruction. While the new secondary home economics schools were for daughters of *évolués*, the schools at the bottom of the educational ladder (*écoles ménagères periprimaires* and *écoles ménagères du 2è degré*) were designed to draw into the missionary orbit those girls who had not attended primary school at the usual age. Many of these girls came directly from the "bush." In the Lower Congo area these schools included only engaged girls, reflecting the missionaries' continuing desire to abolish cohabitation between engaged couples. The postprimary *écoles ménagères-agricoles* of the 1929 Code, which had prepared the female elite of the interwar years, dropped the agricultural label and became simply postprimary schools of domestic science (*écoles ménagères post-primaires*), catering to girls who had completed the "ordinary" five-year program and were of normal school age. As before, such schooling kept them "properly" occupied until marriage.

Thus, by the early 1950s, academically oriented female students or daughters from *évolué* families could enter (after primary school, including the *6ème préparatoire*) the secondary-teacher training schools (*écoles de monitrices*), or the secondary home economics schools (*écoles ménagères moyennes*) — together the apex of female education. Students who finished these programs, usually at about the age of 15, could teach in a primary or post primary homemaking school or become aides to European social workers in the *Foyers Sociaux*. Yet, by 1952 there were only 10 of the new secondary *écoles moyennes ménagères* and only 20 secondary-teacher training schools, which together enrolled slightly more than 1,000 girls.[34] The less gifted girls followed the "ordinary" upper-primary cycle and the younger ones could then go on, even after the fourth grade, to the two-year apprentice-teacher training schools (*écoles d'apprentissage pédagogiques*) or to schools for nurses' aide or midwife aide. Those who were left over entered the postprimary homemaking schools (*écoles ménagères postprimaires*) if they were of normal school age.

Catholic educators reported that only in 1952, after having been partly empty for years, were girls' postprimary schools finally filled.[35] The better postprimary and secondary schools for girls in towns suddenly acquired waiting lists. Curiously, at the same time, *évolué* families were reported to be dissatisfied with the quantity and quality of education available for girls. In 1952, the Council of the African Quarter in Leopoldville had unanimously asked that Congolese girls be given equal educational opportunities. Indeed, in the early 1950s several hundred daughters from educated Congolese families took the ferry across the Congo River to attend school in Brazzaville in the French Congo, where it was said they would at least learn French.[36]

[34] Goetschalckx, *Situation des Ecoles Post primaires*, p. 2.
[35] Ibid., p. 2.
[36] Belgian Congo, Ministère des Colonies. *La Réforme de L'Enseignement au Congo belge* (Brussels: Mission Pédagogique Coulon-Deheyn-Renson, 1954), p. 235 (hereafter cited as Coulon Report).

Further expansion of educational opportunities for both boys and girls came in the mid-1950s, after a Liberal-Socialist coalition government in Belgium replaced the Catholic Party in power. The new Minister of Colonies established the first secular primary and secondary schools for Congolese — on a coeducational basis — and inaugurated a secular university at Elisabethville. The introduction of "parallelism" expanded opportunities, particularly in secondary education. "Select" upper primary sections in parochial schools were finally provided for girls (as preparation for academic secondary education), and girls were finally admitted to both Catholic six-year programs of general academic secondary education and the senior technical high schools (usually to the normal or nursing sections). The original midwife schools were replaced by a higher, standard three-year school for maternity nurses (*écoles d'accoucheuses*), requiring at least four years of general secondary education for admission.[37] For the first time girls could receive an education in which French was both a subject and the medium of instruction. Although in principle girls could now prepare for study at the university, at independence in 1960 there were few "select" primary sections for girls, even in the principal provincial centers, and there were no Congolese women in the universities. In the early 1950s, for the first time thought was also given to creating vocational schools (*écoles d' auxilliares* and *écoles professionnelles*) to prepare girls for jobs in commerce and industry.[38] The few schools that were created specialized in clothing and textiles (*metiers féminins*).

The election of a non-Catholic coalition government in Belgium in 1954, however, neither equalized opportunities for schooling between the sexes nor changed the goals of education for girls. Appointed by the Liberal-Socialist coalition, the Coulon Education Commission, which visited the Congo in 1954, criticized education for girls, not so much because of sparse academic opportunities, but because it did not even teach home economics efficiently.[39] An official provincial director of education, serving under the coalition government, maintained even in 1957 that the "atavism of servitude" imposed on the Congolese female by her own culture could best be overcome by educating her "to occupy in a dignified manner her place in the true [i.e., Christian] home."[40] The Catholic Party, returned to power in the elections of 1958, spent the remaining few months of official colonialism grappling with the new and

---

[37] These new schools for maternity nurses gave a three-year specialized program that included science courses, but mainly ward work in obstetrics, pediatrics, and surgery, including the sole delivery of at least 25 babies, before awarding the diploma.

[38] M. Moffarts, "Enseignement secondaire," *Problèmes d'Afrique Centrale*, no. 36, 2ème trimestre, 1957, p. 120.

[39] Coulon Report, p. 238.

[40] Moffarts, "Enseignement secondaire," p. 120.

rising nationalist movement. Independence for the Belgian Congo, later called "Zaire," came in June 1960.

Implications of Colonial Education for Third World Women

Eighty years of Belgian colonial education through a Catholic-dominated system were immensely successful in reinforcing the social relations of conservative Christian patriarchy. Access to schools and educational attainment for girls were affected by the legal differentiation into single-sex schools, by the restriction of curricular choice for those schools, and by limitations on the use of a European language for instruction. The Belgian colonial example raises a number of issues concerning the social consequences of educational policies and practices, not only for contemporary Zairian women, but for all women, especially those in Third World countries.

Access to Education: Credit or Debit?

Lack of access to education certainly did not help the life chances of Zairian women. Enrollments in schools were sharply differentiated by gender: of the 1.6 million primary pupils in 1959–60 (the last school year before independence) only one-fifth were female, and of the 29,000 students in secondary schools, under 4% (fewer than 1,000) were girls.[41] The Belgian Congo had one of the highest Third World enrollment rates for males — and one of the lowest for females.[42] All in all, in 1960 there were some 350,000 girls in primary schools, but probably no more than 10,000 girls attended any postprimary or secondary school, about 1.5% of girls of secondary school age (15–19). More than half of the postprimary and secondary enrollments were in normal schools or in postprimary apprentice-teacher training programs. There were only 7 vocational schools (*metiers féminins*) with an enrollment of 430 girls and 16 hospital schools with about 350 girls. About 200 girls were taking academic general secondary programs, mainly in the urban centers of Leopoldville and Elisabethville. Thus, fewer than 9% of 2 million Congolese girls (aged 5–19 years) were attending a formal school at the time of independence.

Sex differences in educational participation were closely related to occupational outcomes. Specific educational credentials were required

---

[41] M. Crawford Young, William M. Rideout, Jr., and David N. Wilson, *Survey of Education in the Democratic Republic of the Congo* (Washington, D.C.: American Council on Education, 1969), p. 13.

[42] For example, by 1962 there were 11 female African college graduates in East Africa. See Guy Hunter, *Education for a Developing Region: A Study in East Africa* (London: Allen and Unwin, 1963), p. 102. UNESCO data indicate that in 1963 girls made up approximately one-third of the primary and secondary enrollments in most African countries. See figures quoted in David R. Evans, "Image and Reality: Career Goals of Educated Ugandan Women," *Canadian Journal of African Studies* 6, no. 2 (1972): 213, note 1.

for entry to skilled occupations, especially with government, which was a major employer. The sex-differentiated Belgian colonial education system meant that career opportunities for Africans in the modern sector were far broader for males than for females and that jobs were stereotyped by gender. For example, by 1960 males could enter several score occupations that required postprimary, secondary, or higher education. In religion alone, there were 600 Congolese priests, 400 Congolese brothers, and 600 ordained Protestant pastors.[43] All 136 of the prestigious *assistants médicaux* were male,[44] as were the agricultural (250) and veterinary (15) assistants.[45] There is no evidence that any of the more than 11,000 Africans in the administrative services[46] were female, nor were many of the thousands employed in industry. It should be noted that opportunities for boys or young men were limited by white views on the proper role of black males in colonial society. Other than the priesthood and ministry, the modern Congolese man was to have at best a subaltern position within the administration, the military, and commercial firms.

The black female was to be even lower in the colonial hierarchy; women and girls were prepared for the home and for the humbler occupations in the modern sector. On the eve of independence, Congolese women were employed mainly as Catholic Sisters (745) and as mission elementary school teachers (several thousand).[47] There were only 15 Congolese maternity nurses and 485 assistant midwives.[48] Even though both boys and girls were prepared for religious vocations, for school teaching, and for hospital work, their job titles varied (e.g., male nurse-maternity nurse, *moniteur-monitrice*, Catholic brother-sister, as did their tasks. Catholic nuns had neither the same tasks nor the same status as Catholic brothers. *Monitrices* were not employed in the more prestigious schools (those for boys only), as were male *moniteurs*.

Colonial attitudes toward women and work in the modern sector and the success of colonial education in limiting opportunities for Con-

---

[43] Ruth Slade, *The Belgian Congo*, 2nd ed. (London: Oxford University Press, 1961), p. 33; and Rene Lemarchand, *Political Awakening in the Belgian Congo* (Berkeley and Los Angeles: University of California Press, 1964), p. 126.

[44] Willy de Craemer and Renée C. Fox, *The Emerging Physician* (Stanford, CA.: The Hoover Institution on War, Revolution and Peace, Stanford University, 1968), pp. 3, 5.

[45] Young, Rideout, and Wilson, *Survey of Education*, p. 15.

[46] Catherine Hoskins, *The Congo Since Independence* (London: Oxford University Press, 1965), quoted in Tamar Golan, *Educating the Bureaucracy in a New Polity* (New York: Teachers College Press, 1968), p. 3. When in Kinshasa in 1960–61, I was struck by the absence of female secretaries in government offices and of sales clerks in stores. I observed female clerks only in the few modern supermarkets.

[47] M. Crawford Young, *Politics in the Congo* (Princeton, N.J.: Princeton University Press, 1965), p. 13.

[48] Figures for 1959. See Public Health Service, Department of Health, Education and Welfare, *Republic of the Congo, A Study of Health Problems and Resources* (Washington, D.C.: Government Printing Office, 1960), p. 48.

golese women are well-illustrated by reports on female education and employment in the three largest urban centers of the Belgian Congo. In a study of Stanleyville (Kisangani) in the 1950s, the differences between economic and social opportunities of African men and women were found to be probably more acute than those found in other African urban areas. "Most women had little or no involvement in either wage-earning or trading and were largely confined to work in and around their homes."[49] Moreover, Congolese women in Stanleyville also had little contact with Western education or culture as compared with Congolese men. "Only two or three" Congolese women could conduct even the "most ordinary conversation" in French, less than 5% worked for wages, only about 15% had ever attended school, compared with 50% of the men, and only about 35% of girls under 16 years of age in the city were then attending school, as compared with nearly 80% of the boys. Few Congolese women ever visited the center of the "European town." In addition, there was virtually no attempt on the part of *évolués'* wives to emulate the dress and public behavior of European women.[50]

The few women in Stanleyville who had received schooling were in great demand as wives for educated male *évolués*, but their supply was so scant that the "overwhelming majority" of men, even those with secondary education, married illiterate women. Even the few educated women were in a difficult situation. *Évolué* males complained that such women were not sufficiently educated, while uneducated men usually regarded women with some education "as less trustworthy than others."[51]

A study of Elisabethville (Lubumbashi) almost two decades later found similar results with regard to women and work. Out of a total adult female population of 66,000 in the city, it was estimated that there were only 70 female professionals, including nurses and school teachers.[52]

Sex differentiation in schooling during the colonial epoch has persistent effects on the lives of contemporary Third World women. First, the gap between male and female participation in education and the modern economy may widen as stringent budgets require cutbacks in educational investment and government employment.[53] As expansion of places in these institutions slows down, aspirations remain constant, and

[49] Valdo Pons, *Stanleyville: An African Urban Community under Belgian Administration* (London: Oxford University Press, 1969), p. 214.
[50] Ibid., pp. 214–15.
[51] Ibid., p. 217.
[52] Terri F. Gould, "Value Conflict and Development: The Struggle of the Zairian Woman," *Journal of Modern African Studies* 16, no. 1 (1978): 133.
[53] Young, Rideout, and Wilson, *Survey of Education*, p. 12.

145

competition for these places will become more intense. The percentage gains in school enrollments made by women since independence could diminish. Such reductions in opportunities for women probably would be justified on the "colonial" basis that women belong in the home and that investment in their further schooling in a period of stringent budgets is extravagant.

Second, the experience of racial and ethnic minorities generally has been that it is difficult to equalize opportunity, once some groups obtain an initial lead. For example, at independence there were no Zairian physicians, male or female. Through scholarships offered by Western nations, several hundred Zairian practicing male medical assistants (as well as younger men) were sent to Europe for medical training, and by the early 1970s there were almost 300 Zairian physicians—all male.[54] Even if quotas for women were to be established in medical programs at Zairian universities, it would be decades before there could be appreciable representation of women in the medical profession.

Third, 80 years of sex stereotyping of curricula (home economics for girls and artisan training for boys) and of occupations (trades for men and elementary schoolteaching for women) hold back efforts to broaden roles—as in many societies. When secondary education was finally offered to Congolese girls in 1948, the few females enrolled were in home economics, elementary teacher training, and nursing. This pattern persists. In a study of professional women in Lubumbashi (Elisabethville), almost two decades after independence, women were still engaged mainly in four occupations: nursing, teaching, directors of health clinics or home economics schools, and university assistants—the latter the only new occupation.

Finally, few data are yet available about the effect of educational and occupational stratification by sex on the self-concept and motivation of young Zairian women.[55] Research in Western societies indicates that women continue to congregate in "female" occupations because they receive more social approval and fewer negative social sanctions.

Some of the current literature implies that if barriers to the access of girls to education are lifted the problems of inequity in the wider society would be resolved.[56] Access to formal education, especially for rural girls, is said to be the "key to their integration" into modern development

<hr>

[54] Ibid., p. 15.

[55] In pedagogical writings, discussion of the relationship between single-sex schooling and differential psychological and social outcomes (e.g., self-concept, academic achievement, role models) is frequently contradictory and ambiguous. Belgium itself still has one of the highest percentages (88% at the terminal secondary level) of single-sex schools in the industrialized world. See L. C. Comber and J. P. Keeves, *Science Education in Nineteen Countries: International Studies in Evaluation*, vol. 1 (New York: Halsted Press, 1973), pp. 71–75.

[56] Mary Jean Bowman and C. Arnold Anderson, "The Participation of Women in Education in the Third World," *Comparative Education Review* 24, no. 2, pt. 2 (June 1980): S13–S32.

and to better employment opportunities and marriage options. Completion of primary school is considered "crucial" because (1) the education of a girl is the education of the next generation, (2) family nutrition improves, (3) women become more receptive to family planning, and (4) agricultural productivity increases.[57]

There are undoubtedly varying degrees of truth in these alleged benefits of access to education for girls. But there is also a debit side: Access to education does not necessarily lead to equal life chances. In such industrialized nations, as the United States, where girls have for some time participated in primary and secondary education on a par with boys, wide gaps still persist, for example, in income between men and women; and women still predominate in certain, frequently low-paying, occupations (e.g., nursing, elementary school teaching, secretarial work). Similar patterns of income differentiation are also found in Third World regions, such as the West Indies, where girls have a *higher* participation rate than boys in secondary schools.[58] In some of the countries of the English-speaking Eastern Caribbean, women even predominate in the professional sector of the labor force, yet on the average still receive less income than men. For example, in St. Lucia, in the 1979/80 school year, 56 percent of the pupils in secondary school were female.[59] Moreover, in the 1970 population census (the latest figures available), 58 percent of professional and technical personnel in St. Lucia were women, yet their median gross income was approximately half that of comparable men.[60]

The continuing relatively lower level of women's income in relation to that of men, even when their education is increased, reinforces the view that factors other than schooling are present in the process of income distribution. Schooling may be a necessary condition, at least at the entry level in the professions, but access to education is not a sufficient condition to explain or correct inequities in society on the basis of gender.

Differential Receptivity to Education

As we have seen, neither boys nor girls were interested in the first schools established in the Belgian Congo. Missionaries had to accept displaced youth or to repurchase domestic slaves as their first pupils in the late nineteenth century. If local children were to be enticed to attend

[57] Constantina Safilios-Rothschild, "Access of Rural Girls to Primary Education in the Third World: State of Art, Obstacles and Policy Recommendations" (Washington, D.C.: Office of Women in Development, U.S. Agency for International Development, 1979).
[58] See, for example, "St. Lucia, Final Report of the Committee on Educational Priorities," mimeographed (Castries, St. Lucia: February 1980) p. 42.
[59] St. Lucia, *Annual Statistical Digest, 1978/79* (Castries: Government of St. Lucia, 1980) p. 58, table 72.
[60] Ibid, p. 45, table 59.

school, they had to be paid. The attitudes of boys toward school rapidly changed at the beginning of the twentieth century, when they observed the material advantages of literate expatriate West Africans who were brought in to construct the railway and serve as subaltern clerks for the administration. Boys became eager to learn to read and write in the hope of emulating these expatriates.

Congolese girls, however, were far less eager to attend school than boys. The colonial establishment blamed this reticence on the girls and their families. Was this explanation realistic, or was there some relationship between the content of schooling and the uses of schooling that discouraged girls and their families from investing time in schooling? One could postulate that girls, in contrast to boys, resisted schooling because of its content and lack of economic utility. Home economics led only to the hearth of a father or a husband, not to well-paying jobs, such as domestic service to the white community. The limitation of literacy training to local languages, rather than French, effectively restricted opportunities in the modern sector. To become a nun was to give up one's culture and the traditional status accorded childbearing.

Particularly unfortunate was the undermining of women's position in agriculture. Agricultural education, which led to increased income from farming, might well have attracted women, but it was not provided in girls' schools. Well-illustrated by the Belgian Congo experience was the dichotomy in agriculture between food production and export crops. Colonial agricultural policy focused on the development of export crops, and agricultural education on the preparation of African males to assist with the task. Although female pupils were required to garden, they were seldom trained in modern farming techniques, despite their predominate role in domestic food production. This world-wide "colonial" blunder especially handicaps contemporary schemes of rural development in many Third World countries, which are now increasingly becoming food importers. Devoting disproportionate resources and attention to the rural male "can be attributed most readily to a tendency of some project planners and authorities to see African women in Western terms—i.e., essentially as domestic workers whose primary responsibility should be in the home and not in the fields.[61]

Ideological Issues

The ideas, values, and attitudes reflected in the school system also permeated the work place. The propriety of women working, and especially the experiment, begun in 1953, of employing Congolese women in textile-related industries were discussed at a meeting of

[61] Uma Lele, *The Design of Rural Development: Lessons from Africa* (Baltimore and London: Johns Hopkins University Press, 1975) p. 77.

148

Catholic business leaders (*Association des Cadres Dirigéants Catholiques des Enterprises du Congo Belge*) in Leopoldville in 1958. Several general attitudes prevailed in the discussion. Certain occupations were found more suitable for women than for men, such as "domestic service and shorthand typists." However, few Congolese women were capable of holding these jobs "best suited to their abilities" because of their general lack of education, poor skill in the French language, and vocational training. Thus, those women who wanted to work outside the home could find no jobs other than unskilled work in factories.[62]

Whether Congolese women belonged in textile factories, where, despite their lack of formal training, they operated sewing machines on the production line, or folded, ironed, and packed products, was discussed in economic and moral terms at the meeting. Economically, women were potentially cheaper to employ than men because a firm did not have to pay women family and housing allowances. But, given their lack of education, it was feared they would be less punctual and disciplined than men, and since most were illiterate, only a few could be utilized as forewomen-timekeepers. Moral concerns, however, were paramount. While the assembled Catholic industrial leaders agreed "in principle" that it was "unjustifiable antifeminism" to deny access to wage earning occupations to women, and counter to the "social teachings of the Church" to pay women differently than men for the same task, nonetheless, the Congolese woman's place was in the home, either that of her father or that of her husband. Working in factories meant that a woman's "moral standards" were "bound to suffer." It was "unanimously agreed" that men and women should be separated in factories and European women were preferable as supervisors. Although the shop foreman could be a man, he should not have African women working directly under his supervision.[63]

The assembled Catholic business leaders concluded their discussion by expressing their opposition to allowing women to engage in any kind of work, especially heavy work, "harmful to their physical health" and "types of work incompatible with their family duties," such as night work and long hours. While calling for Congolese schoolgirls to be "initiated to the problems of factory life," the Catholic business leaders insisted on "the need for social policy" to safeguard the "woman's family duties" and not to compel married women to take a job to balance the household budget. Especially they remained opposed to the employment of women in jobs where "moral precautions were inadequate."[64]

[62] Gerard Capelle, "Emploi de personnel féminin dans les Enterprises du Congo belge," *Bulletin of the Inter-African Labour Institute*, no. 2 (1959), p. 56.
[63] Ibid., p. 58.
[64] Ibid., pp. 58–59.

This discussion among male Catholic business leaders in the Belgian Congo illustrates several profound issues that should concern Third World women. First, the church is intimately involved in temporal affairs, and the Catholic Church is active in many contemporary developing countries, particularly in Latin America and the Caribbean. Note should be taken of the difference between principle — equal pay for equal work, "unjustifiable antifeminism" — and practice. St. Luica, the Caribbean example of income inequities for professional women cited above, is, like Zaire, a predominately Roman Catholic country, where the the church plays a major role in education and in the formulation of social policy.

Second, acceptance of male sexual harassment is implicit in this discussion by the Catholic business leaders as though it were the uncontrollable outcome of male-female interaction — something akin to the animal world's encounter of snake and mongoose. Since scientists tell us the human species is the only animal capable of speech and planned rationality, it appears that harassment between the sexes is deliberately learned, socially accepted behavior and can, therefore, be deliberately unlearned and considered socially unacceptable. That is, like other antisocial behavior, sexual harrassment in the workplace is subject to social approbation and control, irrespective of who supposedly precipitates such behavior. Third, the solution to aggressive behavior on the part of males was to "protect" the female victim by restricting her freedom of economic choice in a manner consistent with Roman Catholic social policy, i.e., to restrict her to the home as much as possible.

Conclusions

Thus, the consequences of colonial education affected the lives of Zairian women in at least three ways. First, Belgian colonial practices reinforced gender as a legitimate basis for differential treatment. Sex-segregated schooling and the related sex-segregated structure of jobs made it manifest to both children and adults that there was something profoundly different in what males and females could and should learn and in what work they could and should perform. Second, colonial education *superimposed* upon diverse traditional African views Western concepts of appropriate roles for men and women. The sex-segregated school system was relied on to ensure that women would be in the home and not in the fields, the office, the pulpit, or the workplace. Finally, Belgian colonial policies and practices in education affected women through *omission*. The transplantation of Christian patriarchy fostered economic marginality among women of the Congo. Women's opportunities to learn modern skills, such as literacy (especially in French), or marketable trades, were scanty. At the same time their traditional role in agriculture was ignored and undermined by lack of training in improved agricultural methods.

During 80 years of Belgian colonial rule in Central Africa, schools were used to socialize men and women to those European norms of Christian patriarchy that prevailed in Belgium, a distinctly conservative country. Christian patriarchy was transmitted to the Congo by colonial administrators and missionaries, and only now are developers recognizing the economic—and human—costs. As Judith Van Allen has noted: "African women have paid dearly for carrying the white man's burden."[65]

[65] Judith Van Allen, "African Women, 'Modernization,' and National Liberation," in *Women in the World*, ed. Lynne B. Iglitzin and Ruth Ross (Santa Barbara: Clio Books, 1976), p. 26.

9. An Action-Research Project on Universal Primary Education—The Plan and the Process

CHITRA NAIK

Editors' Note

In 1976 India reported having achieved nearly universal education of the country's boys in the early primary grades. There was, however, a persistent lag in the enrollment of girls; only 63.5 percent of India's girls aged 6–11 were in school, compared to 97.5 percent of the boys. In the higher grades, enrollments drop precipitously for both sexes, but even more so for girls. The proportion of girls in the upper primary grades is less than half that of boys (24.5 percent girls, 48.7 percent boys).[1] Despite the growing consensus among development experts that women's education leads to higher family income and to increases in health, nutrition, and family planning, little specific attention is directed at reducing this gap.

One can surmise several reasons for this comparative neglect of women's education. One reason is an unwillingness to see girls' access to schools as a distinctive issue that may require special ameliorative measures. The general rise in women's literacy and school attendance during each census decade, at rates roughly comparable to men's, prompts an evolutionary perspective from which it is assumed that the problem will be solved in time as the general level of education rises. The proponents of this view point out that there is little evidence of discrimination against girls with respect to school entry or facilities, particularly at the primary level. It is not known, however, how many older girls may be deterred from attending school by the lack of latrines in rural schools. One must also ask whether the nation can afford to wait for evolutionary progress to bring women to education if the linkages with other developmental goals are so strong.

On the other hand, there is a general sense of ineffectualness, if not despair, about the possibilities of reforming India's education. The educational system is mammoth, decentralized, bureaucratized, and part of a status culture that holds itself above rustic villagers and slum dwellers. It is also severely underfunded, particularly at lower levels. The many-faceted proposals of the distinguished 1965 Educational Commission of India have come to little, leaving educational reformers with little credibility. India's elites have largely opted out of the public school system in favor of private schools teaching in English, which is critical for admission to elite institutions of higher education. Compared to agriculture, where new technology is yielding good results, there are few apparent levers of change in education and little political will to create them.

The problems of girls' education are made more difficult by the overlay of commonplace assumptions which, added together, make a daunting argument about the impossibility of increasing their school attendance. Families' needs for girls to care for younger siblings, their reluctance to send prepubertal girls outside the house, early marriages, and the natal family's

---

[1] Department of Social Welfare, Government of India, *Women in India: A Statistical Profile*, (New Delhi: Government of India, 1978), p. 158.

unwillingness to invest in girls who will anyway leave for another family's household are the obstacles usually cited. These factors seem so deeply embedded in the culture's fundamental attitudes toward women that change can only be evolutionary.

It is against this background that the nonformal education project of the Indian Institute of Education which is reported below appears so exciting. This project was not designed for girls' education, but for universalizing primary education for all children. However, the institute has discovered that the largest number of children not reached by formal education are girls, and, more important, that these girls are able to attend school when it is adjusted to their needs. The most important of these adjustments is a change of the schedule to night classes, held after girls complete work and clean up after the evening meal. Until such classes began, however, no one knew whether families would allow their daughters to attend, since it involved leaving home after dark.

How the project was planned to gain the community trust necessary for this to happen is one of the contributions of this report. Other innovations reported are the use of untrained teachers, the development of techniques for peer-group teaching and mastery learning, and the replacement of annual exams with an "evaluation fair." The report details the thoughtful planning behind each of these innovations and shows how they are integrated into a comprehensive scheme of education, with important lessons for reform of formal schooling as well.

The project is being carried out in the State of Maharashtra in western India. Maharashtra is distinguished in India by its relatively independent women, by its wealthy industrial and trading center, the city of Bombay, and by its nineteenth century history of social reform, which focused on women's education. Although these factors make women's literacy in Maharashtra relatively high by Indian standards, literacy is only 21 percent in the dry rural hinterlands where the project is being carried out. Rural male literacy is 51 percent. [2]

It is hard to convey the excitement of visiting the project's night classes. One rides in a jeep for several hours from the district capital of Pune, fording streams created by monsoon rains. Suddenly in the distance there is a barely perceptible lantern glow amidst the dark forms of an unelectrified village. As visitors enter the usually windowless room of a temple or shed donated to the school, 10 or so scrubbed and beaming children pop up to greet them in unison. One finds nearly-moustached youths and little girls in pigtails singing loudly together the project song, "We are working children, we are learning children."

C.M.E.

An action-research project for universalization of primary education has been undertaken by the Indian Institute of Education, in Pune, India. The institute is a leading postgraduate center for research and teaching in education, with special emphasis on interdisciplinary approaches.

[2] Ibid., p. 138.

153

The project has been supported by the central and state governments, the local education authority of the Pune District, and UNICEF.

The Problem

The Indian Constitution requires that primary education be provided for all children between the ages of 6 and 14. Education is compulsory in most states for children through age 11. But in spite of all that has been done since independence, universal primary education remains a distant goal. Of children between 6 and 11, only 4 out of 5 attend school, and of those between 11 and 14 only 2 out of 5 attend. Dropout rates are high. Of every 100 children who enter grade 1, only 25 children reach grade 8. These average rates do not truly portray the distressing picture of educational deprivation prevalent in the rural areas. The worst affected are underpriviledged groups identified in the Indian Constitution as requiring special assistance such as tribals, nomadic tribes, scheduled castes, and other low-income groups. Among them, the educational status of girls is the lowest of all.

Most of the children who do not enter school, or drop out soon after entry, come from poor families where they are compelled to shoulder the burden of household chores or add to the income of the family. From age 7 onward, these children begin to share in adult tasks. They do not have the leisure to attend school for 6 hours in the middle of the day. A further problem is single-point entry: In the existing system of primary education, a child may enter the school only at grade 1, even if that child is 8 or 9 years old. Average children soon begin to feel uncomfortable among the younger lot and leave school. This insistence on single-point entry and full-time attendance has been a big hurdle in universalizing primary education for children from poor rural families, who constitute about 70 percent of the age group concerned. Of these, two-thirds to three-fourths are girls.

Children evade the compulsory law by enrolling in a nearby primary school, with almost no intention of attending. The teachers are ready to connive at this stratagem, for they prefer large enrollments on paper and a small class attendance. The arrangement is convenient all along the line—for children, parents, teachers, and even education offices, which revel in the statistically demonstrable progress of education. Although some of the names of absent children are occasionally struck off the register, this mutually satisfying game of inflated enrollments and deflated attendance continues without hindrance in the rural areas, where inadequate communication makes for minimal watchful supervision and maximum reporting of progress on paper.

Allied to the problem of nonenrollment and dropping out is the constantly deteriorating standard of primary education. Committees and commissions on education have established severe strictures on the increasing deterioration in the quality of instruction in primary schools and its irrelevance to life. It is often found that rural children who complete grade 3 or even 4 are barely literate. Failure in examinations is one of the causes of dropping out, but those who stay on in school as successful pupils are often no better than the deserters. They continue in school not so much because of their achievement as because of the financial ability of their parents somehow to see them through school. Here also, the parents' choice generally falls on boys rather than on girls.

The problem of universal primary education therefore presents itself in three aspects:

1. It concerns the education of poor children in the rural and tribal areas.
2. It concerns girls more than boys.
3. It is not only a question of the quantitative expansion of education but of its qualitative reshaping as well.

Purpose of the Project

The project was designed to test the assumption that universalization of primary education requires an alternative system of nonformal primary education functioning on a part-time basis according to the convenience of working children. This system will have to consist of ungraded classes and attend more to the requirements of the older age group, for younger children are relatively freer from work and able to join a formal primary school if it is accessible. Part-time primary education will have to be developed in a symbiotic relationship with the pattern of living and environment of the villages concerned, taking account of the work patterns of the children's families. Since working children can spare at the most about 1½ hours to 2½ hours in the evenings, the curriculum and teaching-learning techniques must be adjusted to the available time. Finally, ways will have to be found to link up the part-time with the full-time system so they will jointly meet the needs of all the children of primary school age in the community. Along with experimental part-time education for children not attending school, the project proposes to develop programs to reorient the teachers of formal day schools and help them undertake improvement of schools and self-development.

The involvement of the community is essential. Since the community must be convinced about the useful role of part-time primary education, even the earliest preparatory steps such as surveys and contact building must involve the local people. Most important, the teachers will have to be from the local community and be controlled by it. This step is necessary because: (1) educated persons and professional teachers from outside are unwilling to work in the interior villages; (2) an outside teacher working in an interior village is a stranger and the lack of rapport between him and the community is mutual, for he knows neither the local customs nor the idiom of the spoken language; (3) no teacher from outside would be prepared to conduct part-time evening classes for a modest honorarium.

Objectives of the Project

The objectives of this action-research project were set up as follows:

1. To strive to provide universal primary education for children in the age group 6–14 in selected rural areas of the Pune district, Maharashtra State
2. To strive to improve the quality of education in the primary schools in selected areas and to relate it more closely to the life and needs of the rural children and with rural development
3. To conduct experiments in urban slums of Pune city with a view to evolving similar programs for universalization of primary education in urban slums, to improve its quality, and to make it more relevant to the life and needs of the slum children
4. To produce improved educational materials for primary education in rural areas and in urban slums
5. To devise improved techniques for producing materials for the effective training of primary teachers
6. To devise more effective techniques of supervision

For the rural project, which began in 1979, five compact areas were selected in the Pune District on the basis of climatic conditions related to agriculture and of cultural characteristics. The areas range from intensively irrigated to dry and from flat to hilly, and they include tribal villages. The total population of the five experimental areas is 156,000, spread among 97 villages and 88 hamlets. In the area there are 185 multiteacher schools and 97 with a single teacher. There are 19,635 enrolled primary pupils, and the number of children of primary age who do not attend is estimated to be 19,374. The project's headquarters are located in a convenient and fairly large village in each area.

From the surveys conducted in the areas, it appears that about 400 evening classes will be needed within about three years, in order to bring all children between the ages of 9 to 14 within the stream of primary education. Only illiterate children in this age group are admitted in the first year of the project, and the literate dropouts will be covered in the second year. The classes are to be concentrated in a contiguous group of villages and hamlets in which primary education will be fully universalized. The rest of the experimental area will be covered progressively in a radiating manner.

The project team is small, consisting of five persons, whose work is guided and coordinated by the project director. They plan and conduct surveys, train the field staff, initiate action on the preparation of teaching-learning materials, and evolve techniques of teacher training, monitoring, and evaluation. At the field level each experimental area is looked after by a research officer and two or three project assistants, who live in a large, centrally located village and operate within a radius of about 15–20 km. The research officers are selected by open recruitment, but the project assistants are drawn from among the graduates of local schools who live in the project area.

The Project and the Community

Because this project seeks to accomplish in two years of part-time work what the formal primary school often cannot achieve in four years of full-time schedules, the process of learning must make use of a variety of nontraditional techniques and approaches. Initially, each of the five project areas was studied by the project team to get a feel for their life styles, language specialities, ideas about education, and attitudes toward the action-research project. The project assistants were the key persons in this exploration; having been recruited from among the few local school graduates they were known to the community. They provided information about the project to the local communities and gave back to the project team the focused insights it sought into the problems and pattern of living in the project areas. This helped to plan the location of classes, selection of teachers, collection of local folklore and language variations for use in teaching-training materials, and what is most important, set the communities thinking about the problems of education in their villages.

Questions about the relationship between formal schooling and the part-time classes were frankly discussed. That the nonformal system was going to place a good deal of managerial responsibility on the communities concerned—especially on the village leaders and educated youth—was made clear to the people. The short-term role of the experimenters whose presence in the project would be withdrawn in about four or five years, was placed before them and discussions were held as to how the community could make the entire activity its own responsibility by participating in a planned manner right from the start. Thus, in conducting the initial surveys of out-of-school children, selecting teachers from among the local inhabitants, securing accommodation for the classes, and mobilizing public opinion, the community was intentionally involved by the experimenters. An attempt was also made to involve the teachers of formal schools, but it met with only a limited response. For each village and hamlet, a local education committee was suggested, to look after those educational needs of the community that can only be identified and satisfied primarily through local effort.

To build in a capability for replication and adaptation, the district authorities responsible for the financing and administration of primary education have been fully involved in planning, implementing, monitoring, and evaluating the project. The project is also collaborating with specialized institutions to develop programs in science education, primary health care, and application of science and technology for rural development.

Classes

The 89 classes begun between November 1979 and January 1980 were reformed into 86 classes, held in 17 villages. The accommodation for the classes is provided by the community, free of charge. In the first phase of the project, the enrollment is restricted to the illiterate children in the age group 9–14, to facilitate the search for effective techniques of teaching beginning reading and numbers. The strategy is to enable the children to break the illiteracy barrier as quickly as possible and build up their self-confidence as learners. Restricting the class size to 20 is expected to establish good rapport between the pupils and their teachers. The smallest class would be around 10 pupils. The classes are planned on the ungraded model, using the principle of mastery learning. Individual attention given to the pupils is meant to help each one move ahead at his or her own speed in the various curricular and allied activities. Since it is mainly working children who enroll in these classes, classes are held between about 7 and 9 in the evening.

When the question of working days and vacations was raised by the project assistant, the teachers and students decided against vacations, pointing out that just as they could manage to work on most days of the year they could also learn on a similar schedule. The concept of vacations seemed rather strange to them. Holidays are taken only on the days of local fairs and festivals and a few days of national importance. The latter are used for recreational and other educational activities, if the children can get away from work for at least part of the day. Each class therefore works for about 300 days a year, depending on the accessibility of the classes in the rainy season and on the leisure available to the children in times of heavy agricultural work. Learning time is from January to mid-June and July to mid-December. The first half of June and the latter half of December are used for a children's fair and evaluation. During the 600 hours of class time each year, it is hoped to raise each child to the level of class 4 in the formal school, with a better knowledge of health, hygiene, and science.

A Profile of the Pupils

A study of the enrolled pupils was carried out when all the classes had begun to function, in January 1980. Among the 1,431 pupils, 1,040 were girls. Of the 89 classes started, 15 had only girls and 74 had both boys and girls. Since girls constitute three-fourths of the total nonattending children, their large enrollment was not unexpected. But such large numbers were a surprise, as was the villagers' acceptance of coeducational classes with a small proportion of boys.

Most of these girls come from families that have other children in school. In rural areas of Maharashtra, the proportion of families with not a single child in school is small, as is the proportion with every child in school. Commonly, some children (mostly boys) go to school and some (mostly girls) are kept at home. The evening classes substantially increased the proportion of families having every child in school.

Economically, these children come from the lower strata of the village, as table 1 indicates. The families are occupied as farmers, artisans and laborers. Guardians of some 850 children report no fixed occupation at all. The educational level of the children's guardians are also low, with illiterates predominating, as shown in table 2.

Within this generally poor group, however, the backgrounds of the girl students are somewhat more advantaged than those of the boys. As tables 1 and 2 reveal, a higher proportion of girls are from medium and more advantaged families, with fathers and mothers having primary education, as opposed to illiterates. Caste backgrounds bear this out: 58 percent of the girls are from the predominant farmer caste compared to 38 percent of the boys, whereas a higher proportion of boys than girls

TABLE 1

ECONOMIC CONDITION OF FAMILIES OF CHILDREN IN THE PROJECT

Economic Condition	Boys		Girls		Total	
	Number	Percentage	Number	Percentage	Number	Percentage
Very good	2	0.5	3	0.3	5	0.4
Good	2	0.5	35	3.5	37	2.6
Medium	155	40	449	43	604	42
Poor	180	46	480	44	640	45
Very Poor	52	13	93	19	145	10.1
Total	391	100	1060	100	1431	100

159

TABLE 2

EDUCATIONAL LEVEL OF PARENTS OR GUARDIANS OF CHILDREN IN THE PROJECT

Educational Level	Father		Mother		Other Guardian	
	Number	Percentage	Number	Percentage	Number	Percentage
Illiterate						
Boys	268	77	349	97	20	65
Girls	651	69	902	93	65	73
Primary						
Boys	73	21	11	3	7	35
Girls	285	30	72	7	19	26
Secondary						
Boys	7	2	-	-	-	-
Girls	10	3	-	-	5	7
Total						
Boys	348	100	360	100	27	100
Girls	946	100	974	100	89	100

are from the scheduled castes (untouchables) and tribes of Maharashtra. This difference probably arises because the brothers of the more advantaged girls are already in formal schooling. Project staff have noted that many of the pupils are eldest daughters of families having all the boys and the younger girls in school.

By design, the children were older than entrants to formal schools. Actually 174 children had once enrolled in school, but dropped out, usually in class 1 or 2, and were wholly illiterate. The girls tended to have dropped out at a lower level, with fewer years of schooling. The age range of the children in night class was from 9 to 14. The median age of girls was slightly lower (10–11) than for boys (11–12), reflecting the tendency for girls to withdraw as puberty approaches. It was very interesting, however, how many other children of both sexes enrolled, showing that older boys were not embarrassed to be in the beginning classes and that some parents were willing to send preadolescent girls out at night to school. This demonstrated their trust of the teachers.

Teachers

In order to avoid the rigidities of the regular school system, the project decided to train its own teachers rather than recruit teachers with formal credentials. This would also facilitate drawing teachers from the local community—important for building linkages with the community. Teachers are selected jointly by representatives of the project team and village leaders. This places the teachers under the control of the community. A roster of probable recruits is prepared for replacements as well, since occasional departures of a few teachers must be anticipated.

Eighty-six teachers have been appointed, 62 men and 24 women.

The teachers are full-time farmers, artisans, and construction workers, and the women primarily housewives. Their teaching assignment makes a welcome addition to their income, which is in most cases under 2,000 rupees ($250) per year. Most belong to the same social class as their pupils and use the same vernacular. Only one comes from the traditional literate Brahmin caste. Most are of the local farming caste, except in the tribal area, where a number of tribal teachers have been recruited.

The teachers tend to be young, averaging 32 years. Most have completed primary education and studied in secondary school but without completing the secondary course. Only eight have finished twelfth grade or entered higher education.

Women teachers are hard to find in the rural areas, particularly so in the interior. With the low enrollment and attendance of girls and their high dropout rates, even the spread of minimal literacy among women is relatively negligible. In Maharashtra, which claims 40 percent adult literacy, the percentage of women literates is just 18, including a high proportion of urban women. The project is very eager to recruit women teachers, in order to provide examples of rural women becoming independent professional workers. Therefore it accepts a lower educational qualification for women teachers and makes a special effort to improve their literacy and their mathematical skills.

Most (15 of 24) of the women teachers have completed the full primary course, which is seven years of schooling. Only one has completed secondary school. In age, they are between 20 and 30, though four are under 20. All but two are married and half earn some income in addition to family-based agriculture and household tasks.

Teacher training is organized in light of five factors: (1) All the teachers are fully employed during the daytime largely in farming and other rural occupations; (2) the education of the majority ranges from about Standard 7 to Standard 10; (3) teaching is a part-time job that makes only a marginal addition to their income; (4) they are residents of the village or hamlet where the classes are located; and (5) their only exposure to teaching techniques consists of their own previous experience as pupils in the normal, traditionally inclined full-time school.

The project team from the Indian Institute of Education camps for five days at the headquarters of each project area, at intervals of about six weeks, to conduct the training, in which it is assisted by the field staff. The training time of 11 A.M. to 5 P.M. enables the teachers to keep the evening classes going. The training team visits a few classes each evening to observe the teaching-learning process and to demonstrate new techniques. Parents and village leaders are also contacted at the

161

time of such visits in order to acquaint them with the objectives and approaches adopted in the project and to discuss other matters related to the conduct of the classes. Full feedback on the classroom process is obtained during the training sessions, with the help of the teachers' daily diaries, pupils' progress report cards, reports of the project assistants and research officers, plus discussions held with all these, with the leading villagers, and also with as many parents as possible.

On the training days, the teachers are compensated for the loss of their daily wages. They bring their lunch, but tea is provided from the project funds. Training sessions are held in a local schoolroom, temple, or other suitable place made available by the community.

The training process is structured but informal. The training materials are prepared by the team on the basis of the feedback of each previous training session and deal with the problems encountered by the teachers. In order to help the teachers improve their own language skills, special exercises are used in the training sessions. Teachers are also encouraged to study carefully the local language with a view to bringing the pupils gradually to an understanding and use of standard Marathi (usually understood to be the language of state-wide, popular newspapers). They collect vocabularies, local songs, and stories and write original stories in narrative or letter form for use in class. A circulating library is organized in each project area, containing Marathi literature and informative books. One Marathi science journal and one good children's journal are also supplied through this circulating library system. The training material, which consists of mimeographed notes on various aspects of the curriculum and the process of learning is revised from time to time. A series of teachers' instruction sheets and guide books are now emerging from this exercise. Emphasis is placed on training the teachers in their preparation and use of improvised teaching-learning materials. Some of these are expected to be prepared in collaboration with the pupils.

Discussions take place in face-to-face groups with the trainers, who avoid authority positions and demeanor. Everybody squats on the floor, in a circle around the books and materials, which are spread out within everybody's reach. The same arrangement and attitudes are expected to be transferred to the conduct of the evening classes.

The men teachers are not called "Guru" (teacher) but "Bhau" (elder brother). Women teachers are "Tai" (elder sister). This nomenclature establishes a family relationship between teacher and pupils, transcending class and caste barriers. It also helps to solve another ticklish problem inherent in a situation with female pupils of 12–14 — marriageable age in a traditional rural community — and the young male teachers of 20–22. The nomenclature was decided after discussions among the teachers, the leaders of the community, and the officials concerned. It emphasizes a new value also, that of the obligation of the educated rural youth to pass along education to the next generation, with whom they must ideally establish a protective relationship as older sibling.

Teacher-Learning Materials

The project believes that dropouts from formal schooling arise not only from children's obligations to work, but also because to them the curriculum of the regular schools is irrelevant and boring. Therefore it has devoted careful thought to the preparation of new curricular materials that are more interesting, as well as more suitable to the compressed time available for the night classes. The key concerns of these materials are self-learning and relevance to rural life. The materials are revised constantly as teachers and pupils provide reactions to them.

The materials have a clear value orientation toward creating a new consciousnes. Traditional prejudices and predispositions based on caste, sex, and occupations are avoided in favor of goal-based individual and group identities. The village community is ultimately envisioned as a well-organized, cohesive, and forward-looking entity as against its present constituency of groups bound by tradition, surviving together despite severe intergroup tensions and conflicts. Special songs and selections from the verses of three popular Marathi saints emphasize the need for an honest and intelligent examination of conflicts and an emotional commitment to a purposeful life, both individual and social.

By using scenes from daily village life and environment, the materials avoid a disturbing break with rural tradition. The project assumes that the pupils' frame of reference for learning is determined more by the circumstances of the rural situation than by chronological age. Therefore, abstract values are reflected in incidents narrated on story cards. This material has a familiar ring for the children, and they rapidly gain self-confidence as learners.

The project has a special group song that summarizes its approach to the children. The song speaks of their being both working children and learning children, who will soon take up responsibility for developing the country. In four stanzas it also highlights the major areas of the curriculum—reading, writing, arithmetic, history, geography, and science—and sets forth the intellectual and social values to which the classes are committed.

Whether to have a reading primer has been a difficult issue. Initially a primer was prepared; ploughed into it were some linguistics and assumptions about the interests and activities of rural children. Although there was debate about the relative value of learning reading with the help of cards and primers, the general opinion leaned toward

163

the primer to provide a graded introduction of the alphabet and vowel sounds. Proponents argued that villagers and pupils were familiar with the idea of starting school with a primer and that colored illustrations in the primer would make the learning process more attractive. As a tryout, pupils were given the first five lessons of the primer, well illustrated, showing 23 letters of the alphabet. At the same time, they were given their name cards to wear in class. This was done on the basis of experience in adult literacy classes where the learners unconsciously picked up reading skills by learning to decode one another's name cards. In a short while, this began to happen with the primary pupils as well. The majority also finished the primer lessons soon enough, along with language games and reinforcement cards. But they did not seem enthusiastic about the primer.

A critical evaluation of the primer, based on the evidence of the field staff and teachers, and tests administered to the pupils found that some of its contents and words were pseudorural and could not be grasped by the pupils. The primer was therefore withdrawn and replaced by three sets of reading cards containing familiar words and sentences based on vocabularies provided by the teachers. Similar cards were prepared for arithmetic. A set of four story cards and a story book (32 pages) for supplementary reading were also prepared, to reinforce the alphabet and vowel signs. The entire project staff and the teachers participated in the preparation of these materials on the basis of criteria evolved in staff workshops and teacher-training sessions. They have also devised literacy-arithmetic games that apply the skills acquired by the pupils.

As a matter of policy, the project has taken the line that rather than offer extrinsic incentives for enrollment and attendance, the part-time classes would search for and develop motivations intrinsic to the circumstances of the pupils. Accordingly, while deciding to provide free teaching-learning materials, a rule was also made that the pupils would take none of these home, but use them carefully in class and put them away tidily before class broke up.

The curriculum emphasizes a high level of skills in language, mathematics, and reasoning. History, geography, and science are treated as matters of general information — related to the child's past and present and significant for the future. Initially, most of this general information is imparted orally by means of observation and discussion. The pupils need not wait for the acquisition of literacy to examine the historical and geographical aspects of the village or the quest of man for food, clothing, and shelter. Such oral transmission of information and values is in keeping with the rural traditions of learning.

As a part of their reasoning exercises, the pupils collect specimens of different objects. The class collection is studied by the teacher and pupils in order to describe the objects and identify their similarities and differences. Along with exercises for developing inquiry and reasoning, language exercises are also often based on such collections. No learning is divorced from language development.

The Classroom Process

When the children return from work, they eat their evening meal and collect one another to go to class. There are no bells either to call the children or to dismiss them. Often the teacher makes the rounds of the village collecting children. Those who trek in from a hamlet normally come in groups, because, in the twilight hours, crossing the streams and walking through patches of jungle raises the fear of ghosts and wild animals. At the start, each class was given a bucket and some combs to help the children fetch water, wash, spruce themselves up, and then start class. In the span of one year, the bucket and combs have been retired. The children, particularly the girls, wash and tidy up at home before leaving for class.

When all the children arrive, the lanterns are lit, the teacher and pupils say "Namaste" (Greetings) to one another and settle down in a semicircle for prayers. The first prayer is selected from the verses of Tukaram, a venerated Marathi saint who, although a gardener by caste, is respected by all. The prayer does not address any particular god but rather the mystic presence that man feels whenever his troubled mind seeks strength and self-confidence. Briefly it says, "You are with me wherever I go, you hold my hand when I walk, you correct me when I lapse into wrong language, you take away my diffidence and make me bold. Now I play the game of life with pleasure and experience the happiness you have given me within and without." This is followed by an ancient Sanskrit prayer to the glowing lamp. It asks for happiness, health, and the training away of malice from the human mind. The prayers over, the class begins its chatting session, listens to a story lesson or one or two songs, and then divides into groups of four or five around each lantern. Reading cards and other aids are distributed by the teacher with the children taking turns helping. Each class has been supplied with four lanterns for group work. The teacher moves from group to group, teaching an item and showing the group how to carry on its practice. The pupils who are ahead teach and test those who are lagging behind. There is much learning from peers, which takes place naturally and informally in the manner of serious play.

With all kinds of odd accommodations in use for the classes, the

usual adjuncts of teaching, viz., the blackboard, wall charts, large flan-
nel graphs, etc., cannot be used. Therefore each class has been supplied
with one reversible, light-weight portable blackboard (12″ x 18″), one
folding cloth board with two flaps the size of foolscap and inner pockets
for keeping cards and cut-outs. These items of equipment have been
specially designed to ensure full utility and low cost. A set of wooden letters of the alphabets, the vowel signs, and numbers has been given to
each class. These were also designed by the project staff, along with a
canvas bag to hold all materials and teaching equipment. The teacher
carries this to class.

The pupils are given no homework in the traditional sense, but they
do receive suggestions for collecting specimens of wood, rocks, feathers,
weeds, etc. to bring to the class for an exhibition that can be spread out
in a corner of the classroom and studied critically. Most children are
clever with their fingers and make articles of clay, wood, grainstalks,
berries and seeds, and waste paper. They draw patterns on the floor
with colored powder—traditionally called "Rangoli." In the tribal area,
they draw and reproduce many beautiful tribal designs.

When the class is over, the children systematically collect all equipment and materials and hand them over to the teacher. No cards or
books are taken home. Reading materials are to be distributed to the
children for out-of-class use only when they reach the second year of
their studies; by then they will have come to know their value and learned
to enjoy them.

Before leaving the class, the children file past the teacher saying
"Namaste" and asking for any ointments or lotions they may need for
small wounds, cracked feet, scabbies, or lice. A small supply of mer-
curochrome, burnol, or sulphur ointment, etc., is available from the
teacher. Finally, the teacher picks up the canvas bag, the children carry
the lanterns, and, in a procession, they wend their way back home,
around ten o'clock in the evening.

Evaluation and Examinations

A continuous formative evaluation of progress is available from the
daily diaries of each of the teachers and from their fortnightly entries in
a detailed progress report card for each pupil. These documents are
discussed in the training sessions, and teachers are guided in dealing
with different types of cases. Since concepts of mastery learning and the
progress of each pupil at a different pace are major factors in the design
of the project, the idea of periodical or final examinations is incongruent. However, the parents, pupils—and even some of the
teachers, who are accustomed to the idea of annual examinations and
class-to-class promotions—have had to be oriented again and again

toward the concept of continuous evaluation. But it became apparent that nothing less than a "final" examination would satisfy them.

The project found an innovative way of meeting this demand by holding an "examination" accompanied by a children's fair. Teachers and children from all the classes in a project area are called to a central village for a children's fair, which was given the Marathi name "Bal Jatra." The project staff prepared evaluation tools, evaluation records, and instructions for teachers and pupils. On the appointed day, the children started early in the morning, arriving class-by-class, class in a procession, singing their group song. For half the day, they played group games, engaged in drawing and handicrafts, sang, danced, and listened to stories told by the teachers and members of the project staff. The latter half of the day was devoted to their playing with the newly prepared evaluation tools, such as literacy and arithmetic cards, and telling stories or answering a quiz. The performance of each pupil was observed by a a pair of teachers and carefully noted on an evaluation sheet, according to specific instructions. There is a significant correlation between the children's performance in the Bal Jatra and their fortnightly progress report cards prepared by classroom teachers. A detailed analysis of each child's performance in the Bal Jatra is now being conducted, to study its possible relationship with the child's personal, social, economic, and environmental conditions.

The Bal Jatra helps the children relax before they come to grips with the evaluation material. But they appear to treat the evaluation as a kind of play and take a keen interest in it. Although the project staff had asked the employers of the children who work as laborers to give them a paid holiday for the Bal Jatra, only a few employers agreed to this. But the children came anyway. One boy arrived hurriedly in the afternoon, saying, "Please let me take the test. I want to know how much I have mastered. Please hurry because I have come during lunchtime and must hasten back to work." In the same community, a child entrusted with the grazing of two ponies came cantering up on the back of one of them, tied the animal to a tree nearby, took the tests, asked for his share of the snacks, ate some, pocketed the rest to take to his younger brother, mounted the pony again, and cantered back to his grazing business.

Project Assessment

Pupils

A broad assessment of the achievement of the pupils became available from the Bal Jatra held in June 1980. These tests were directed toward finding out the number of pupils who had crossed the illiteracy barrier. The second Bal Jatra, held in December 1980, determined how

167

many pupils could read fluently, how many had reading difficulties, and why. It was found that 28.85 percent of the children could read any given material fluently. Another 24.29 percent had mastered the whole alphabet and vowel signs, read quite well, but did not reach the level of fluency. This means that 53.14 percent have adequately mastered reading skills in about one year. But 46.86 percent, who recognized the whole alphabet and read words with fair ease, stumbled on sentences. These pupils can be described as "just literate." From among them, 170 pupils were found to be still struggling with the alphabet. All such cases are being critically studied. Also, the reading materials and the teaching methods used by each individual teacher are being investigated.

As to arithmetic, after one year about 51 percent of the project's pupils can manage the various operations in addition and subtraction, arrangement of sets, and counting up to 50. Almost 26 percent have proceeded beyond this stage and count up to 100. Most of the children can do simple mental arithmetic in connection with their daily transactions. They can also recognize geometrical shapes, weights, and measures of daily use, and all the coinage.

Enrollments

In one year, enrollment fell by 282, a dropout rate of 19 percent. Among them were 196 girls (18.4 percent of enrollees) and 86 boys (20.4 percent of enrollees). Although this is far lower than the usual dropout rate of 50–70 percent in class 1, it still gives cause for concern. A detailed study of the dropouts revealed the individual reasons for leaving the classes and is shown in table 3. The causes can be divided into two categories: those that cannot be removed and those that can be tackled by the project. Causes 1 through 8 belong in the first category. These account for 207 of 282 pupils. (Perhaps a solution for the older and physically well-developed girls may be found in adult education, rather than in primary classes.) The causes in the second category are such that the teachers and project staff may be able to tackle them with tact and effort. The real problem of dropouts is, therefore, reduced to 53 girls and 22 boys, i.e., 75 pupils in all.

Another reason for the drop in enrollment was the closing of some classes. At the end of one year the number of classes was reduced from the original 90 to 78. Only two classes had to be closed because pupils failed to attend; these were the classes for children of migratory laborers. All other closings were due to the desertion or unavailability of teachers. Problems with teachers thus assumes great significance, and further experimentation is necessary to discover better and more effective solutions.

The experience of various villages shows the kinds of problems that

TABLE 3

PROJECT DROPOUTS AT THE END OF THE FIRST YEAR

	Reasons for Dropping Out	Girls	Boys	Total
1.	Shifted to another village	43	13	56
2.	Labor migration to another place	2	12	14
3.	Labor migration within the village	2	11	13
4.	Enrolled in formal schools	14	11	25
5.	No leisure because of household work	24	9	33
6.	Embarrassment due to older age or well-developed physique	15	6	21
7.	Betrothal and marriage	37	0	37
8.	Continually ill	6	2	8
9.	Difficulties in attending because of residence in distant hamlets	8	5	13
10.	Afraid of walking alone to the class	12	5	17
11.	Unwillingness of parents	19	0	19
12.	Pupils unwilling in spite of parents' willingness	14	9	23
13.	Waywardness	0	3	3
	Total	196	86	282

arise with teachers. One class was closed when the teacher left to take a job in Bombay. A substitute was found but could not join because this tribal area is infested by a man-eating tiger. The other class situated in a small hamlet closed down when the teacher found a job in another town. Another young man was appointed in his place but, he left soon after to seek government service. The hamlet has no additional educated persons who could continue this class, which has 21 enrolled pupils.

One area was particularly hard hit by teacher migration, losing six of 14 classes by December 1980. Two classes were closed because village factions prevented the teachers from functioning. One class continued until November but had to be closed when the teacher found a job in Bombay (a substitute may soon be found). Two other classes, conducted by two sisters-in-law, had to be closed because their mother-in-law objected to their attending the periodical training camps and made them resign. The villagers are helping the project staff to search for substitutes, as each of the classes has 16 girls on the rolls. One more class was ended because the teacher tried to manage her cooking and other chores during class hours. When the girls refused to attend this class, it was amalgamated with another class in the same village.

Attendance of Girls

Since girls' attendance was so much higher than had been expected, a sample survey of 154 households was conducted to find out why parents and girls wanted them to attend. An interview schedule, giving a jumbled set of reasons, was prepared for each group of respondents whom the research officers and project assistants had personally interviewed. The respondents were also free to offer any additional reasons. The interviewers were asked to prepare reports on the impressions they gained about the attitudes of the respondents to the project, and to the interview as well. Most interviewers were cordially received and a few were pressed to stay for a meal. Tea was supplied everywhere.

Parents noted their reasons as follows:

1. The girls will learn to keep accounts; to write and read letters; to read billboards, signs, receipts, and similar documents; and generally learn to manage daily transactions (134 responses).
2. Learning will help the girls to manage their life well. "They will become wise" (88).
3. The girl desired education, but we could not give it to her when she was young. Now that a facility is available, we want her to use it (77).
4. The girl has free time in the evening. Instead of being idle, she should learn something in the class (60).
5. The girl is eager to learn (45).
6. The girl will be able to marry an educated young man (37).

The checklist had stated one reason as: "We send the girl to the class because other people have started doing it." This received an extremely poor response, only two, as did another reason: "Well, we just send the girl to the class. We can't give a definite reason," with only three responses. Almost all agreed the most suitable time for the class was after 7 P.M., when the girls are free from their chores.

The girls' reasons for attending were:

1. Must learn to keep accounts, write and read letters, read road signs, receipts, etc., and manage daily transactions (135).
2. Did not get an opportunity to go to school when young. Now that the facility is available, I am keen to use it (75).
3. My parents say that I will become "wise" if I take the class (49).
4. My parents ask me to attend the class (42).

Each girl was asked to state specifically whether she attended the class because she wanted to or because of instructions from her father or mother. The responses were: "I want to attend" (115); "My father sends me" (96); "My mother sends me" (65). All agreed the most convenient time for the class was "evening" or "night," when they have finished their day's work.

Community Response

The community support for the project is indicated by the resources they have contributed to it:

1. The accommodation for all the classes is rent-free.
2. During an extreme shortage of kerosene, some villagers came forward to buy it in bulk and supply it to the classes to ensure that no class closed down for want of lighting.
3. Electric lights have been provided by the villagers for some classes.
4. Two hamlets built special sheds for the evening classes; they were constructed by the villagers, using tiles that the village leader had bought for repairing the roof of his own house.
5. In one village, the community has allotted a temple for the class and banned its use by devotees while class is in session.
6. In another village where the temple was being used by village youth as a dormitory, the class has been accommodated.
7. In order to solve a controversy in one village over which god should be installed in a newly constructed temple, the villagers have turned it into a community center and allotted it to the primary class in the evenings.
8. The youth club in one village has collected 200 rupees to provide a library and a small drum for the evening class.
9. The young men from a group of villagers have undertaken the responsibility to see that no one teases or gives any trouble to the girls when they walk to the class and return home late in the evening.

As the project progressed, villagers discovered that the teaching-learning methods were different from those of the formal primary schools. Instead of the usual chanting of multiplication tables and letters of the alphabet, they heard rhythmic songs, much story telling and the reading of whole words with the help of cards. The parents questioned the wisdom of postponing writing. In some villages a rumour was spread that the project was meant for training the girls to become singers in folk drama (Tamasha) and not for giving them school education.

However, the progress of the pupils was a reassuring factor. When the first evaluation of their performance was held in May and June 1980, the villages where the Bal Jatra was held provided facilities like sheltered space, drinking water, and even some snacks for the children. In August 1980, the classes celebrated India's Independence Day in collaboration with the local schools, and the villagers were impressed by the little speeches and dramatic performances of the pupils from the nonformal classes. In all these activities girls had taken the leadership, which was an unusual and amusing—but gratifying—spectacle for their parents. The resistance to the new techniques has now diminished because almost 75 percent of the pupils have become fairly good readers, can do the expected arithmetic, and have also begun to write a little. That they have grown relaxed, bold, and acquainted with techniques of self-learning is a matter noticed more by the project staff and the teachers than by the parents. Yet it is obvious that the classes and the Bal Jatra are filling the cultural vacuum that was oppressing these working children, and that some community leaders have perceived the glimmerings of change. In one area, programs of postprimary education for girls are being promoted by a community leader, and he has begun to give suggestions to the project staff on how to plan and organize it.

What the project planners have been hoping for has, therefore, begun slowly to emerge from within the community. Resistance from the established structures and processes is expected. New types of tensions within the community are also possible. But these are some of the inevitable aspects of this project, even though its objective of universal primary education sets certain limits to its intervention in the process of social change and development.

10. Images of Men and Women in Indian Textbooks

NARENDRA NATH KALIA

In 1965, the Government of India proposed to create a curriculum conducive to sex-role equality. Recognizing the fundamental equality between men and women, it envisioned an educational system that would
pave the way for a new society where individuals would not be forced to
follow sex-based patterns of behavior: ". . . it is unscientific to divide tasks
and subjects on the basis of sex and to regard some of them as 'masculine'
and others as 'feminine.' Similarly, the fact that the so-called psychological differences between the two sexes arises, not out of sex but out of
social conditioning, will have to be widely publicized and people will have
to be made to realize that stereo-types of 'masculine' and 'feminine' personalities do more harm than good."[1]

This commitment was reiterated a decade later in a proposed
amendment to the Indian Constitution which, among other fundamental
duties, called upon Indian citizens to ". . . remove any practice derogatory to the dignity of women."[2]

The Indian government has had a very important means for implementing this educational policy since 1955, when the preparation and
approval of Indian textbooks became a highly centralized and mostly
state-controlled enterprise. Ever since 1953, when the Secondary Education Commission found serious flaws in textbooks published by private
concerns, the government has steadily increased its direction of the
textbook industry. The National Council of Educational Research and
Training (NCERT) and the National Board of School Textbooks developed guidelines for the states, and by the end of 1971, all states had set
up appropriate agencies to produce the texts.[3] As a result, the Indian
educational policymakers today enjoy almost complete control over the
content and format of Indian school textbooks.

I would like to acknowledge the help I received from professors Lou Kriesberg, Agehananda
Bharati, Raymond Waxmonsky, and JoAnn Wypijewski in completing this paper.
    [1] Education Commission, India, *Recommendations on Women's Education* (New Delhi: Education
Commission, 1965), p. 5.
    [2] *Overseas Hindustan Times* (September 16, 1976), p. 1.
    [3] Initially, the private publishers controlled the Indian textbook market. Then the Secondary
Education Commission (1952–53) found serious flaws in the prescribed textbooks. As a result,
various state governments set up organizations to lower the prices and upgrade the quality of
textbooks by: (1) taking over the production of textbooks, and/or (2) improving the machinery for
approving textbooks submitted by private publishers. At the national level, the Central Bureau of
School Textbooks, the National Board of School Textbooks, and the National Council of Educational
Research (NCERT) were entrusted with the task of preparing and prescribing textbooks that conform to state policy. See A. Biswas and J. C. Aggarwal, *Education in India* (New Delhi: Arya Book
Depot, 1972).

Reprinted from the *Comparative Education Review* 24, no. 2 (part 2)(June 1980): S209–23.

Yet a content analysis of Indian textbooks shows that the government has not utilized its control to produce textbooks conducive to its promise of sex-role equality in education. In the following pages, we shall demonstrate that Indian school textbooks promote an ideology which refuses females equal access to opportunities and rewards even in areas where the sex of a person is totally irrelevant. More subtly, Indian textbooks prepare males for a bustling world of excitement and decision making, while conditioning the females to seek fulfillment in the background where servitude and support are the only requirements.

In treating the content of school textbooks as an instrument of socialization for adult aspirations, we do not deny the role of other factors that may subsequently affect the realization of such aspirations. Variations in aptitudes, individual socioeconomic status, and economic conditions governing employment affect entry into the job market. But these factors do not minimize the importance of formal schooling in developing adult attitudes.

As in other societies on the path of industrialization, formal education is a particularly strong factor in occupational role modeling of Indian youth. Because the world of adults and children was contiguous in preindustrial societies, the young could acquire their occupational role models with relative ease. Today, daughters watching their mothers at work may have a similar opportunity, but even this opportunity lends itself only to adopting nonmarketplace roles. As India becomes more industrialized, boys and girls will be increasingly excluded from any direct involvement in the professions of their working parents. Given this separation, the occupational role models presented in the textbooks for Indian youths will have a significant impact on their occupational socialization.

Sample and Methodology

The findings reported in this paper are based on a content analysis of 41 Indian textbooks. Our sample included 20 Hindi and 21 English language instruction textbooks used in high school, higher secondary, and preuniversity curricula (classes 9–11) in five areas of India: Haryana, Punjab, Rajasthan, Uttar Pradesh (all states), and Delhi (a union territory). Also included were the textbooks prepared by NCERT. The NCERT texts are used by the Central Board of Secondary Education and many states other than those included in our sample.[4] The textbooks in our sample had an annual readership of more than 1.3 million students.

[4] The textbooks contained a total of 740 lessons. We excluded all lessons which were (1) poetry, (2) contained no human characters, (3) deployed an abstract focus on theoretical topics with no or an insignificant role assigned to human actors, or (4) contained no plots involving social situations with human actors. Following the exclusions, 353 lessons were selected for content analysis. More than half of these lessons (58 percent) were stories. The remainder were plays, biographies, essays, memoirs, and commentaries.

These texts were subjected to a number of quantitative analyses. We counted (1) male and female characters, (2) males and females as leading figures, and (3) males and females as subjects of biography. We also listed and counted the frequencies of the favorable images by which men and women are portrayed in Indian textbooks.

To study occupational stereotyping, we counted the frequency of occupations assigned to male and female characters and examined the range of occupations open to each sex.[5] Finally, we selected a subset of textbooks prescribed in 1978–79 for a more intensive qualitative analysis of themes and images. Included in this analysis were six Hindi and twelve English language instruction texts, all of which were in use for classroom instruction in 1978–79 in high school/higher secondary or preuniversity curricula.

Quantitative Findings

Male characters were in a clear majority. In 75 percent of the lessons they were the leading figures (see table 1). The males also dominated the biographical lessons in the textbooks. There were only seven biographies of women, compared with 47 of men (see table 2).

The attributes of men and women portrayed in the textbooks were heavily stereotypical. Females were most often described for their beauty, obedience, and self-sacrifice; men for their bravery, intelligence, and achievement. While some of the most common favorable images of men and women were similar, as shown in tables 3 and 4, the differences between the male and female lists show a clear sexist bias. Images not found in the top 10 category of the female list—popular, strong, achiever, innovative, and adventurous—are all the attributes conducive to success in the marketplace.

TABLE 1

SEX RATIO OF LEADING ACTORS

	%	N
Lessons with males as leading actors	75	265
Lessons with males and females as leading actors	17	60
Lessons with females as leading actors	8	28
Total	100	353

[5] Since our main purpose was to determine the range and diversity of occupations, the frequency count of an occupation in a lesson was limited to one instance in each text, regardless of the number of characters belonging to that occupation. For example, if there were six farmers, one soldier, and four housewives in one lesson, each occupation was entered only once in the frequency count for that lesson. The cumulative frequency of an occupation in the total sample determined its frequency score (e.g., King—89 signifies that the occupation of king appeared in 89 lessons: 89 is the frequency score for occupation King).

175

TABLE 2

BIOGRAPHIC SUBJECTS AND OCCUPATION BY SEX

	Male (N)	Female (N)
King/Queen, Warrior, Army Leader	4	1
Author, Philosopher, Prophet, Teacher	13	1
Scientist, Doctor, Nurse	13	2
Adventurer, Explorer	5	0
Political Leader, Social Reformer	12	2
Housewife	0	1
Total	47	7

Range and Diversity of Occupation by Sex

We counted a total of 463 occupations in the textbooks. Of these, 84 percent ($N = 391$) are filled by males, while 16 percent ($N = 72$) are filled by females. A similar distribution emerges in the frequency scores, which total 2,083 for all occupations. Males in occupational roles occur in 85 percent ($N = 1,761$) of the total number of instances, while females take up the remaining 15 percent.

To examine the range and diversity of occupations, we divided the total count of occupations into three lists: (1) occupations assigned both to the male and female, (2) occupations assigned only to the male, and (3) occupations assigned only to the female. Table 5 lists occupations assigned commonly to the male and female characters in the Indian texts.

Table 5 demonstrates that many high-prestige occupations are held by both males and females. As gods and goddesses, holymen and holywomen, both sexes guide and manipulate divine forces. Males and females appear as members of the nobility and as professionals in the service and production industries. The two sexes are also represented in such low-prestige occupations as beggars, cooks, shepherds, servants, and slaves.

However, the occupations common to both sexes represent only a meager 13 percent of the total occupations in the textbooks. Once we examine the differences in the frequency scores for the two sexes, table 5 loses most of its positive impact. There are male and female governors, but the male governors have a frequency score of 8, while the frequency score for female governors is only 1. Other similar disparities transform the list of common occupations into a catalog of tokenism at best.

List of All Occupations Assigned to the Male and to the Female

The contrast is even more striking when the total lists are examined. Among the 72 occupations held by women, with the exception of occupation Housewife (118), only four occupations have double-digit frequency

TABLE 3

LIST OF FAVORABLE IMAGES ASSIGNED TO MALES
(Descending Order of Frequency)

Frequency	Images	Frequency	Images
82	Brave	14	Patriotic
75	Popular	13	Duteous
54	Strong	13	Faithful
51	Kind	13	Friendly
50	Achiever	12	Idealist
49	Innovative	12	Self-respecting
48	Adventurous	11	Liberal
44	Hard working	11	Studious
40	Generous	10	Gallant
39	Educated	10	Heroic
38	Clever	10	Just
34	Compassionate	10	Peace loving
32	Honest	10	Respected
31	Intelligent	9	Disciplinarian
30	Noble	8	Orator
30	Wise	7	Thankful
29	Determined	6	Earnest
29	Political activist	6	Gentle
28	Commanding	6	Humorous
26	Humble	6	Polite
24	Civic spirited	5	Diplomatic
24	Loyal	5	Rational
24	Self-sacrificing	5	Tall
24	Simple	4	Agile
24	Smart	4	Innocent
21	Persevering	4	Romantic
21	Proud	4	Secular
20	Loving	3	Introspective
19	Handsome	3	Philosophic
18	Accommodating	3	Practical
18	Scholarly	3	Protective
18	Skillful	2	Competitive
17	Humanitarian	2	Divine
16	Hospitable	2	Inspirational
16	Resourceful	2	Persuasive
15	Ambitious	2	Saintly
15	Careful	2	Spiritualist
15	Cheerful	2	Vigilant
15	Confident	1	Aristocratic
15	Independent	1	Beautiful
15	Religious	1	Big
14	Brilliant	1	Classicist
14	Cultured	1	Immortality seeker
14	Devoted	1	Universalist
14	Patient		

scores. Of these, two, Princess (24) and Queen (30), are occupations where status is more a matter of ascription than achievement. Just as a lowly Maidservant (27) may have accomplished very little to qualify for her position, the status of a queen/princess is usually derived from being the wife or daughter of a king. The textbooks contain only three in-

TABLE 4

LIST OF FAVORABLE IMAGES ASSIGNED TO FEMALES
(Descending Order of Frequency)

Frequency	Images	Frequency	Images
42	Beautiful	5	Persevering
23	Brave	4	Adventurous
23	Kind	4	Duteous
20	Loving	4	Honest
19	Faithful	4	Humanitarian
19	Hard working	4	Humorous
18	Compassionate	4	Patriotic
17	Generous	4	Respected
17	Loyal	3	Affectionate
14	Educated	3	Careful
14	Independent	3	Confident
13	Determined	3	Innocent
13	Hospitable	3	Inspirational
13	Self-sacrificing	3	Scholarly
12	Political activist	3	Self-respecting
10	Accommodating	3	Smart
10	Devoted	3	Wise
10	Innovative	2	Brilliant
10	Popular	2	Holy
9	Cultured	2	Just
9	Proud	2	Practical
9	Religious	2	Propitious
8	Agile	2	Simple
8	Clever	1	Artistic
8	Noble	1	Child prodigy
7	Cheerful	1	Diplomatic
7	Civic spirited	1	Disciplinarian
7	Skillful	1	Divine
6	Achiever	1	Earnest
6	Friendly	1	Gentle
6	Protective	1	Humble
6	Strong	1	Liberal
5	Ambitious	1	Orator
5	Commanding	1	Peace loving
5	Idealist	1	Persuasive
5	Intelligent	1	Poetic
5	Motherly	1	Serious
5	Patient	1	Thankful

stances where the queen appeared as a ruler rather than as a wife or daughter.

On the other hand, of the 391 total male occupations, 19 occur in double-digit frequencies. Their range is more interesting. While men do hold the positions of King (89) as well as Servant (44), they also score high in a variety of professions: Teacher (42), Doctor/Medical (42), Poet (30), Farmer (28), Writer (28), Scientist (19), and Prime Minister (11). The diversity of these achievement-oriented occupations stands in sharp contrast to the female list. The very number of occupations ascribed to men signifies the choices *unavailable* for female occupational achievement in the Indian textbooks.

TABLE 5

FREQUENCY OF OCCUPATIONS FILLED BY BOTH MALES AND FEMALES
(Descending Order of Frequency Scores)

Males		Females	
89 King	9 Peasant	30 Queen	1 Fairy queen
52 Soldier	8 God	27 Maidservant	1 Farmworker
44 Servant	8 Governor	24 Princess	1 Godfairy
43 Student	8 Lord	8 Student	1 Governess
42 Doctor,	8 Shepherd	6 Leader,	1 Gypsy
medical	8 Washerman	political	1 Marchioness
42 Teacher	7 Holyman	4 Farmer	1 Milliner's
36 Prince	7 Scholar	4 Goddess	apprentice
30 Poet	6 Commander, army	4 Witch	1 Minister,
28 Farmer	6 Saint	3 Cook	political
28 Writer	6 Tailor	3 Poet	1 Priest
27 Priest	5 Duke	3 Queen/ruler	1 Prime minister
19 Leader,	5 Farmworker	3 Teacher	1 Professor
political	4 Beggar	3 Writer	1 Pupil
19 Scientist	4 Pupil	2 Holywoman	1 Saint
18 Minister,	3 Artist	2 Housekeeper	1 Scholar
political	3 Milkman	2 Kitchenmaid	1 Scientist
15 Laborer	3 Street hawker	2 Lady (lord wife)	1 Scullion
13 Traveler	3 Weaver	2 Nanny	1 Seamstress
12 Professor	2 Angel	2 Peasant	1 Seller, bangle
12 Warrior	1 Apprentice	2 Teacher, violin	1 Shepherdess
11 Cook	1 Gypsy	1 Artist	1 Slave
11 Prime minister	1 Social worker	1 Beggar	1 Social worker
11 Shopkeeper	1 Teacher, music	1 Commander, army	1 Soldier
11 Slave	1 Warlock	1 Court Lady	1 Teacher, deaf
10 Courtier		1 Dealer, hair	1 Traveler
		1 Deliverer, milk	1 Warrior
		1 Doctor, medical	1 Washerwoman
		1 Duchess	1 Weaver
		1 Factory worker	
		1 Fairy	

We found 343 occupations assigned exclusively to the male. The significance of this list becomes clearer when we compare it with the list of 12 occupations assigned exclusively to the female. These are: Cleaning Woman, Dancer, Dietician, Housewife, Landlady, Matron, Nun, Nurse, Pathologist, Prostitute, Reverend Mother, Sweeper. Of these, only the occupations of the Reverend Mother and, to a limited degree, that of the Nun involve the exercise of leadership or power over others. In all other cases, the females operate in a service-oriented capacity. Barring the occupations of dietician and pathologist, the occupations assigned only to the females are essentially low prestige and semiskilled, neither requiring extensive training nor bringing substantial rewards in the marketplace. The highest number of females in the Indian textbooks appear as Housewives (118), an occupation that defines their identity in terms of domesticity and economic dependence on the male.

Perhaps as a tribute to the power of patriarchy, prostitution is also listed as a female occupation in the textbooks. In a society that treats prostitution as both illegal and immoral, a textbook for impressionable youths is a rather unusual place to find it as an occupation for the female.

Analysis of Themes and Images

In order to develop a fuller picture of the sex-role stereotypes in the Indian textbooks, I subjected a smaller sample of 18 texts to a deeper content analysis by concentrating on four components of sex-role modeling: (1) male-centered language, (2) traditional sex-role expectations, (3) derogation of women, (4) victimization and acquiescence.

Male-centered Language

By identifying both men and women in masculine terms, male-centered language discriminates against women. To assess the extent of male-centered language, I analyzed lessons in my sample with attention to the usage of masculine nouns and pronouns as all-inclusive terms for both sexes.

The texts often begin with a general form and refer to it thereafter with a masculine pronoun. Pronouns of the masculine gender are used to designate both men and women.[6] "If anyone rides [this horse] I shall give him a rich reward. If, however, he fails, he will be put in prison."[7] Though this sentence begins with a neutral pronoun "any," it soon changes to a masculine gender.

The words "mankind" and "brotherhood" are used to signify all people, including women.[8] Just as a text uses the term "boys" to denote all the students in a coeducational school,[9] other lessons in the textbooks consistently use the word "man" as a substitute for "person," "individual," "people," or "someone."[10]

In its plural form, "men" as a collective noun is used to refer to "masses of men *and* women."[11] The editors of the *New Radiant Reader Book VIII*, now in its twenty-second printing, tell us, "the world and its

[6] T. C. Collocott, ed., *New Radiant Reader Book VIII*, 22d impression (New Delhi: Allied, 1974), lesson 5; prescribed for standard 8 classes in Uttar Pradesh, 1978.
[7] National Council of Educational Research and Training, eds., *English Reader, Book IV* (Haryana: Board of School Education, 1978), lesson 8; prescribed for class 9 in Haryana, 1978; 567,000 copies in print.
[8] K. R. Chandrasekharan and K. N. Acharya, eds., *The Threshold*, 11th impression (Delhi: Oxford University Press, 1978), lesson 1; prescribed for preuniversity classes in Himachal Pradesh, 1978.
[9] Central Institute of English and Foreign Languages, eds., *An English Course for Secondary Schools* (Delhi: Central Board of Secondary Education, 1978), lesson 1; prescribed for class 9 in Delhi, 1978.
[10] J. C. W. Rust, B. D. Srivastava, and D. E. McFarland, eds., *Olympic English Course Reader* (Madras: Macmillan, 1977), lessons 3 and 13; prescribed for class 9 in Rajasthan, 1978; 77,000 copies printed in 1977.
[11] Board of School Education, ed., *A Text Book of English Prose* (Chandigarh: Board of School Education, 1978), lesson 3; prescribed for secondary classes in Haryana, 1978; 485,000 copies in print.

180

goods are the common property of all men."[12] Similarly, while casting his beloved's bust, a sculptor remarks, "Men will remember my beautiful little Yupi for thousands of years."[13] Describing the process of education for boys and girls at the Tolstoy farm in South Africa, Mahatma Gandhi, as an author, does use terms like youngsters, children, and once, "boys and girls." But whenever it comes to discussing the specific problems of teaching, the "Father of the Indian Nation" reverts to the masculine gender.[14] A story about Abraham Lincoln extols "the chance of any little backwoods boy to become president of the United States."[15] Apparently, the backwoods girls are not in the running.

When used to describe a woman, "man" is usually intended as a supreme compliment,[16] because in the Indian textbooks the best of humanity is masculine. An essay, "The Recent Past of Man,"[17] included in a textbook now in its eleventh impression, deifies the "nineteenth century man" who singlehandedly bolstered civilization through the Industrial Revolution, "the fourth greatest advance in man's life" wherein "applying the discoveries of the men of science . . . men learned to tap the hidden forces of the earth." The one instance in which this essay mentions women does not apply to any definite action: ". . . the invention of the internal combustion engine which has done more to change the surface of the earth and the habits of the men and women who live on it than any other single discovery." In light of what precedes and follows this sentence, there is but one conclusion: men act; women merely exist.

Such male-centered language is hardly consistent with goals of equality between the sexes. In a society where every action and actor is assumed male unless otherwise specified, access to power, opportunities for meaningful action, and even qualities of complete humanity will seem distant to females.[18]

Traditional Sex Roles

In the traditional model, home maintenance was considered the major responsibility of females. Indian textbooks continue to judge a female's success by her proficiency at household chores. "Supposing you learn plain cooking," advises one character. "That's a useful accomplishment which no woman should be without."[19] In a dramatization based on fantasy, prescribed by the Central Board of Secondary Education, vari-

[12] Collocott, *New Radiant Reader Book VIII*, lesson 9.
[13] Rust et al., lesson 3.
[14] G. Bagchi and B. Nag, eds., *English Prose and Poetry Selections* (Delhi: Central Board of Secondary Education, 1976), lesson 4; prescribed for classes 9 and 10 in Delhi, 1978.
[15] T. C. Collocott, ed., *New Radiant Reader, Book IX*, 24th impression (New Delhi: Allied, 1976), lesson 16; prescribed for class 9 in Bombay, 1978.
[16] Board of School Education, lesson 5.
[17] Chandrashekharan and Acharya, lesson 16.
[18] C. Miller and K. Swift, *Words and Women* (New York: Doubleday, 1976).
[19] Collocott, *New Radiant Reader Book IX*, lesson 39.

ous characters from children's books —Alice, Huck Finn, Tom Sawyer — recite their ambitions. This is what a female character states: "(Dreamily) I should like a lovely house full of all sorts of luxurious things —nice food, pretty clothes, handsome furniture, pleasant people, and heaps of money. I am to be a mistress of it, and manage it as I like with plenty of servants, so I never need work a bit."[20] The contrast with male ambition is striking: "I want to do . . . something heroic or wonderful that wouldn't be forgotten after I'm dead. I don't know what, but I'm on the watch for it, and mean to astonish you all some day. I think I shall write books and get rich and famous."[21]

While most males strive to realize similar high goals, the core of the woman's concerns lies in her worries over how to prepare a new dish. The culmination of her achievements is the compliments she receives from males for her looks and her cooking. The living proof of her good fortune is the fulfillment she realizes in "woman-talk" with her daughters: "When my husband, with more blind faith than perspicacity, assures me that I am the most charming lady at the party; when my lemon meringue pie emerges from the oven perfect for praise; when my nearly grown-up daughters come to me at night, combing their hair and talking in low voices of the things only women talk about together —then I know what I believed all along is truth. Women are the fortunate people."[22]

This traditional model requires the ideal Indian wife to treat her husband as the polestar of her existence. More than one lesson advises how important a husband is. A wife ". . . can give her life for him. But she cannot even imagine a situation where she might hurt him in order to placate somebody else. If she does so, she is a sinner."[23]

Such imagery firmly ensconces the female in her home, where she is subservient to the male. When males are present, the plot is most often dominated by men and boys. As "masters" in their homes, most males in the texts consider it unnecessary to consult the females on household affairs, such as giving away the wife's property, controlling children's lives, treatment of guests, household budgeting, adoption, and marital arrangements. When the male and female actors differ on an issue, only the female is chastised for disagreeing with the males. Often, the male's right to dominate a decision is derived from his sex-role prerogatives rather than from his problem-solving capacity. Women are socialized into compliance by command and dependence upon male approval.

[20] P. V. Mehrotra and B. M. Datta, eds., *English Rapid Reader* (Delhi: Central Board of Secondary Education, 1975), lesson 1; prescribed for classes 9 and 10 in Delhi, 1978.
[21] Ibid.
[22] Bagchi and Nag, lesson 11.
[23] Haryana Vidyalaya Shiksha Board, ed., *Gadhya Saurabh* (Chandigarh: Haryana Vidyalaya Shiksha Board, 1976), lesson 18; prescribed for high school classes in Haryana, 1978; 285,000 copies in print.

To train females for self-abnegation from early childhood, the textbooks promote the desirability of female subservience. The students in New Delhi and other schools under the jurisdiction of the Central Board of Secondary Education read: "There is a picture in Bapu's hut. Tired, he has returned home. He is sitting on the chair, while Ba is washing his feet. *This* is Indian womanhood! Those of my sisters who are galvanized by the glitter of civilization, may call her a simpleton. But the course of Indian history glows with the pious character of such females."[24]

The nature of available male support determines a woman's social existence. Most girls are taught to depend upon males not only for economic support but also for guidelines on how far to study and whom to marry. Even in their simple, day-to-day chores, princesses and housewives appear helpless when no or limited male support is available.[25] When such support is withdrawn, as in the death of her husband, a woman has no social place. Therefore, ". . . every Hindu woman prays to die before her husband."[26]

Women can benefit little from formal education. "There are certain things in this world that are meant for the males, and higher education is one such thing." If such a privilege was extended to women, the same lesson states, it would upset the society: ". . . if the females too . . . begin to read English newspapers and discuss politics then what would happen to the domestic chores!"[27]

According to the Indian textbooks, an educated daughter means trouble for her parents, who risk losing control over her. Further, an educated woman is an unattractive marriage partner. The father of a prospective bridegroom says, "We don't need an overly educated girl. Who would cater to her whims? We don't want a mem-sahib. At the most a matriculate."[28]

To make such subservience palatable, the texts either ignore the marketplace achievements of women or use different standards of role performance to define success for females. While mentioning various inventions in technology made during the latter half of the nineteenth century, one lesson prescribed for Rajasthan students credits men alone for scientific achievements.[29] Another lesson for Bombay students, entitled "Choosing a Career," reads: "Very often a career may seem interesting

[24] National Council of Educational Research and Training, ed., *Gadhya Bharati* (Chandigarh: Haryana Vidyalya Shiksha Board, 1978), lesson 5, sec. 2; prescribed for high schools in Haryana; 285,000 copies in print.

[25] S. C. Gupta and O. Prakash, eds., *Lalit Sankalan* (Delhi: Central Board of Secondary Education, 1978), lesson 1; prescribed for classes 9 and 10 in Delhi, 1978; 265,000 copies in print.

[26] Board of School Education, lesson 1.

[27] Haryana Vidyalaya Shiksha Board, lesson 19.

[28] Ibid.

[29] Rust et al., lesson 2.

and glamorous, but does the boy have an aptitude for it? . . . A boy may
have an aptitude for engineering. . . . Both boys and girls can become
laboratory technicians and girls can take up nursing. . . . If a small factory
is built in your village, a clever man will open a small tea shop or a tobacco
shop next to it. . . . Girls who prefer to stay at home can also have a job
other than housekeeping. They can learn tailoring and dress-making and
make a lot of money."[30]

The careers suggested for women only complement their traditional
roles. The possibility that a woman might have an aptitude for engineering or hotel management or a full business outside the home is never
allowed. If she should venture beyond the home, she had better find a
situation where she is looked after or where her duties are no better than
the extensions of her domestic chores.

Derogation of Women

While the textbooks appear to praise women for their subservience
and devotion to domestic duties, there is frequently an undertone der-
ogating women for just these traits. For instance, the female narrator of
"I Wish I Were a Man" labors over the advantages and disadvantages of
being female.[31] She had always thought that women did the "truly creative things, like having babies or adding a bit of curry to Saturday's roast
for a Monday masterpiece," until her failure to hail a cab is magnified by
a man's ease at summoning a fleet of them. Then the narrator enumer-
ates the male traits she envies: men whistle through their teeth; they run
gracefully for trains; they have more pockets than they will ever need;
they are not encumbered by a handbag; they are not slaves to their
hairdressers. She concludes, however, that the female's disadvantages are
a small price to pay for male chivalry.

Often the women are so weak and frivolous that they appear no more
than overgrown children. The female is described as faithless, while the
child is devoted to self-centered pleasure. Among Typees, for example,
while men undertake activities essential for the survival of the society, the
girls idly anoint themselves with fragrant oils, dress their hair, and compare their trinkets.[32]

Women's frivolity is associated also with their inability to cope with
modern ideas. In *Lalit Sankalan* (265,000 copies in print), the Central
Board of Secondary Education enlightens the Indian students as to how
"outwardly the Indian woman may wear high-heeled sandals, don nylon
saris, walk upright, fancy a high coiffure, run around in a car, write the
washerman's accounts in English, but deep down where it counts, she

[30] Maharashtra State Board of Secondary Education, Pune, ed., *English Reader* (n.p., n.d.), lesson
17; prescribed for class 10 in Bombay, 1978.
[31] Bagachi and Nag, lesson 11.
[32] Collocott, *New Radiant Reader, Book VIII*, lesson 32.

continues to be our same old aunt-type."[33] The character referred to as the aunt is a fad-infatuated, superstitious, orthodox, irrational female.

The underlying tone in women's subservience is manipulation. They are often portrayed as jealous creatures who demand that men devote all their energies toward them. A statement ascribed to Indian nationalist leader Lala Lajpatrai reads, ". . . the practice of law is like a jealous woman and a lawyer has to serve her twenty-four hours a day."[34] Similarly, in the *English Rapid Reader*, the "Man in Asbestos" describes women as manipulating and exploiting men. "She did not work . . . half of what you had was hers," he says. "She had the right to live in your house and use your things. At any moment [she] could inveigle you into one of those contracts."[35] Young girls are viewed the same way. In Jainendra Kumar's story *Khel*, included in the NCERT-produced *Kahani Sankalan*, which has been in circulation since 1968, a boy topples a little girl's sand creation. She suffers silently.[36] The author tells us that her reaction is typical of a female who is not really angry at the insult inflicted upon her. Rather, she views it as a perfect opportunity for manipulating the male by embarrassing him through her silence.

Other derogations abound. The *New Radiant Reader*, now in its twenty-fourth impression, tells students that women are fussy do-nothings. "Oh! you women, you make such a fuss over everything."[37] Women are described as weak. A lesson in *Olympic English Course Reader* (77,000 copies printed in 1977) for Rajasthan students calls Christianity "a soft religion for women and children, not for men and soldiers."[38] Women are irrational. To fulfill their sex roles, they resort to superstition.[39] Women are despicable. Even coach drivers "swear in the name of the horse's grandmother establishing intimate relationships with her."[40] Women are vain. "Her hair isn't a woman's crowning glory. It's the pivot around which her life swings."[41] Educated or not, women must look pretty. A text repeats the hackneyed joke that the state should tax the beauty of females to increase its revenue. Every female should be allowed to determine the amount of her own assessment. The assumption is that, vain and naive as females are, they would compete with each other to pay the highest taxes to legitimize their claims to beauty.[42]

[33] Gupta and Prakash, lesson 1.
[34] Haryana Vidyalaya Shiksha Board, lesson 10.
[35] Mehrotra and Dutta, lesson 9.
[36] Himachal Pradesh School Shiksha Board, ed., *Kahani Sankalan* (Simla: Himachal Prakashan Nigam, 1968), lesson 7; prescribed for high school and higher secondary classes in Himachal Pradesh.
[37] Collocott, *New Radiant Reader, Book IX*, lesson 1.
[38] Rust et al., lesson 9.
[39] Himachal Pradesh School Shiksha Board, lesson 2.
[40] Haryana Vidyalya Shiksha Board, lesson 13.
[41] Bagchi and Nag, lesson 11.
[42] Haryana Vidyalya Shiksha Board, lesson 19.

Victimization and Acquiescence
I studied the incidence of sex-role victimization as an indicator of authority relationships. Sex-role victimization was defined as an individual's persecution because of role restrictions inherent in gender-based social placement.

The plots of texts project an exaggerated view of male power. As in the traditional sex-role model, the *sarvagunasampanna maryaada-apurush* —strong, handsome, generous, achieving —males dominate the texts. In the traditional model, it was vital for the male to maintain a posture of strength to assure his manhood. The Indian textbooks seem obsessed by the ideal of muscle-bound masculinity. The male must prove himself, and how better to do it than with his fists. The Central Board of Secondary Education curriculum, used in classrooms throughout the country, includes a story in which students at an all-boys school test their new teacher by pitting him against the local Hercules in a boxing match. The teacher wins the bloody match, securing a badge of honor in the boys' subculture.[43]

It is considered proper to physically punish the female for her deviation from the traditional roles. A woman may be punished or even killed for failing to fulfill her "inherent" role as the object of male concupiscence. Males often use violence as an instrument to assert their power over women and children, to vent their frustrations, to establish their territorial imperative. In a story prescribed for Rajasthan students, a young sculptor demands that his fiancé abandon her career. She refuses, declaring that even marriage cannot usurp her passion for dance. To prevent her from ever dancing again, he casts a spell on her. He makes a statue in her likeness and then breaks the statue's feet. Now she will not dance again.[44] Another story portrays an educated, successful businessman who feels no qualms about abusing his wife at whim.[45] And, in one of the plays, a beautiful woman is disfigured in a railway accident. Her husband cannot endure her imperfection, so he strangles her in her hospital bed. The lesson describes this murder as the ultimate tribute to beauty.[46]

The most poignant victimization, however, is the message given to little girls that they are not as wanted as their brothers. Women in the Indian textbook often pray for many sons.[47] More than one textbook portrays a daughter as a liability. Haryana students are told in *Gadhya*

[43] Bagchi and Nag, lesson 7.
[44] Rust et al., lesson 3.
[45] Haryana Vidyalya Shiksha Board, lesson 17.
[46] S. Aggarwal, ed., *Ekanki Sangrah* (Chandusi: Bhargava & Sons, 1977), lesson 40; prescribed for Rajasthan higher secondary classes, 1978.
[47] Board of School Education, lesson 1.

Saurabh (285,000 copies in print) that ". . . be she a doctor or a sister [she] is born as a Rs. ten thousand penalty" for her family.[48]

Female characters in the textbooks do not generally retaliate against their physical and verbal degradation. In portraying their humility and forebearance, the textbooks imply that the Indian woman should endure an abusive male, accepting his violence as "natural." The texts never condemn the male for his violence against the female. Rather, the female's silent suffering is highlighted, as if canonization for sainthood is compensation enough for beatings.

Boys, on the other hand, are given no such acquiescent model. In my sample, I came across only one instance of male victimization. Here, the finicky wife of a retired police officer squanders a substantial part of his pension on religious rituals, leaving little for the upkeep of the house.[49] But unlike other female characters, this man's destitution is not lauded. Rather, he stands as an admonition to such males who are foolish enough to let control of their households slip into their wives' hands.

Conclusion

Instead of fostering the basic equality between men and women, the messages given to school children in the Indian textbooks sanction the dominance of males. Instead of freeing individuals from conformity to sex roles, the Indian texts fortify a sex-based division of labor in which men venture into a bustling world of excitement and decision making while women remain in the background providing service and support. Instead of inspiring each sex to develop a respectful attitude toward the other, the texts condone the use of physical and verbal abuse against women who fail to comply with archaic sex-role expectations. While I do not contend that all texts are totally devoid of themes conducive to sex-role equality, it is clear that the overall stance of Indian textbooks is decidedly patriarchal and male favored.

Such texts do not serve modern India well. To foster the exclusion of one-half of India's population from contributing to the tasks of modernization is a waste of human talent which India cannot afford. Nor do these texts reflect the Indian tradition well. The history and literature of traditional India have countless examples of strong, brave, wise, and achieving women, a few of which do appear in the texts as queens and warriors. Before these admirable models, the textbook portrayal of the "traditional" woman is a pale reflection. What we find in the texts is not an accurate depiction of the many roles historically assigned to Indian women, but what sexist educators and textbook writers have selected.

[48] Haryana Vidyalaya Shiksha Board, lesson 19.
[49] Gupta and Prakash, lesson 1.

11. The Impact of Western Schools on Girls' Expectations: A Togolese Case

KAREN COFFYN BIRAIMAH

Literature on the effect of Western education on Third World women's role expectations has taken two distinct courses. Some scholarship suggests that the relative economic and political position of women, as well as their social status and independence, has declined as modernization occurs. Van Allen, for example, tries to dispel the widely held belief that Western influence has increased non-Western women's status.[1] She argues that modernization (and Western schools, which are a part of modernization) has a regressive effect on women's political, economic, and social status. Van Allen believes that colonization and modernization in Africa have undermined traditional female patterns of authority and power. Discrimination inherent in European Victorian values joined with African customs limiting female participation in selected social functions, thus severely limiting female education and career opportunities.

Kenneth Little, in his study of urban African women, expands upon this theme by emphasizing the effectiveness of social pressure applied by schools, husbands, and workers in channeling women into the narrow roles of wife and mother.[2] Little believes that women use education solely to obtain an influential and wealthy husband. He assumes that educated women internalize attitudes and roles to which they were exposed during their years of schooling.

An alternate approach to the theme of schools effectively determining the goals and expectations of their female students is found in the scholarship of Vandra Masemann.[3] In her study of a Ghanaian secondary school, Masemann suggests that females use their education as a tool for upward social mobility and as an efficient means of fulfilling obligations and responsibilities traditionally held by women, such as child support and care of relatives.

The current literature leaves us with two opposing interpretations of the impact of Western education on the formation of female role expec-

Funding for this research was provided by a graduate research fellowship from the State University of New York at Buffalo. This article is part of my doctoral dissertation.

[1] Judith Van Allen, "Modernization Means More Dependency," *Center Magazine* 7 (May–June 1974): 60–67.

[2] Kenneth Little, *African Women in Towns: An Aspect of Africa's Social Revolution* (Cambridge: Cambridge University Press, 1973).

[3] Vandra Lea Masemann, "Motivation and Aspiration in a West African Girls' Secondary School" (Ph.D. diss., University of Toronto, 1972); Vandra Lea Masemann and Mary P. Maxwell, *Gender, Roles and Aspirations, a Comparative Study: Females in Canada and Ghana* (Toronto: Canadian Sociology and Anthropology Association, 1974).

Reprinted from the *Comparative Education Review* 24, no. 2 (part 2)(June 1980): S196–208.

tations. On the one hand, we are told that the Western school experience, with its "hidden curriculum," serves to demean and devalue the traditional position of women.[4] Yet another school of thought suggests the inability of Western schools to influence or alter Third World women's role expectations.

In order to obtain a clearer understanding of the school's ability to affect female role expectations, it is necessary to study the school environment itself, to identify aspects within the school which promote specific role models, and to determine the extent to which these role expectations are actually internalized by the students. This article is an in-depth study of a government secondary school located in Lome, the capital of Togo. It focuses on whether students internalize teachers' attitudes, classroom interaction messages, and the messages implicit in the school's authority structure.

The secondary school I studied was open to all male and female students who successfully passed the elementary school-leaving examination. It served both as a point of termination and as preparation for the prestigious lycée (or other postsecondary training schools) which might be attended after the successful completion of both the 4-year secondary program and the *brevet* examination. Only those students who completed their lycée program and passed the baccalaureate examination could attend university.

Though the school was located in the suburbs of Lome in Ewe tribal land, 30 percent of the students were from non-Ewe tribes (approximately 55–65 percent of Togo is comprised of non-Ewe people). Although 70 percent of the students said they had spent at least one-half of their lives in Lome, 53 percent reported leaving the capital during school vacations to return to homes located in rural areas or small towns. Based on an inventory of household items, it also appears that the student body represented various economic backgrounds. Fifty-eight percent came from medium-income families, while the remaining 42 percent were equally divided between the low- and high-income brackets. While the school was composed mainly of Ewe students with extended exposure to the urban environment, the student body came from diverse tribal and economic backgrounds and had considerable roots in rural Togo.

The school itself is representative of Togolese secondary schools, which are generally located in or near large urban areas throughout the country. (This urban relationship was further strengthened by recent governmental decree which closed all dormitory facilities, thus forcing students to board with family or friends located near a secondary school.)

[4] Vandra Lea Masemann, "The Hidden Curriculum of a West African Girls' Boarding School," *Canadian Journal of African Studies* 8, no. 3 (1974): 479–94.

Data for the study included classroom observation, teacher questionnaires, and interviews with the entire third-year (4ème) female student population as well as interviews with a similar sample population of final-year elementary school girls.

This article will examine factors within the secondary school — specifically, the authority structure, teacher attitudes, and classroom interaction patterns — to determine messages and expectations inherent within the school environment. The expectations of the female students exposed to this environment will then be analyzed to determine if internalization has occurred and to what extent factors within the school appear to have affected these expectations. Data from a sample population of elementary school girls will also be analyzed to determine how increased exposure to Western schools affects attitudes and expectations.

The School Environment

The secondary school studied was composed of four levels (6ème, 5ème, 4ème, 3ème) which followed the successful completion of a 6-year elementary school program. The level studied, 4ème, was the third year in this secondary school program. The total school enrollment was 1,548 students, with females comprising 44 percent of the student body. Students were assigned to one class for the year (averaging 90 male and female students per room), while teachers rotated among the classes. Every 4ème student studied the same subjects (French, English, history-geography, mathematics, physics-chemistry, geology, and sports). Boys and girls attended the same classes together, including sports. The only exception to this pattern was a weekly homemaking class which was required only for girls, though the boys were free to remain as observers. All 4ème instructors were male, with the exception of one English teacher, one geology teacher, and one homemaking teacher.

Student Body Composition

While the secondary school under consideration had not fully met the government's guidelines for sexual equality in education, girls made up a significant part of the school population. According to school records, 44 percent of the student body and 46 percent of the 4ème class were females. While they fell short of these official figures, the 4ème class I observed had a student body which was 41 percent female.

However, one must be careful to look beyond such figures in evaluating the quality of these experiences. In the case of this school, strong trends of differential treatment of female versus male students were present with regard to student responsibilities and leadership roles. Of the 20 class and school prefects, who held much responsibility and power, only one was female.

School Staffing Patterns

In both the school's administrative structure and its actual teacher assignment roster there appeared to be definite patterns of sex-role stereotyping. Men held most positions of responsibility and authority in the teaching staff and school administration. In the case of nonteaching and administrative posts, men held not only the majority (five out of eight, or 63 percent) but also the most important positions, including that of director. The three women on the nonteaching staff filled the posts of assistant secretary and typist (two).

While at first glance the official teacher roster appeared more equally balanced than that of the nonteaching staff with regard to male/female participation (14 females and 16 males), the actual full-time nonleave personnel roster listed eight females and 15 males (a drop in female participation from 47 percent to 35 percent).

This basic staffing pattern was further reinforced through assignments to academic committees and other nonteaching responsibilities. Positions such as departmental chairs were dominated by male staff (73 percent of all nonteaching academic positions were held by male teachers). Only female staff, on the other hand, were assigned as housekeeping monitors.

The staffing pattern of the school meant that students had less contact with female teachers. In the 4ème classes I observed, students were exposed to female teachers for only 24 percent of their classroom time. While it is, of course, impossible to draw conclusions from such data, my observations call into question the official school statistics which suggest that students are exposed to female teachers 47 percent of the time.

Thus, while the school officially had a reasonably equal male/female staff ratio, the actual exposure of students to males and females in roles of responsibility greatly underscored the dominant male position.

Teacher/Student Interactions

Though the authority structure of the school tended to place women in roles subordinate to men, it does not necessarily follow that teachers and students believed that females themselves should be allocated to such positions, or that student/teacher interactions themselves reinforced the messages implicit in that authority structure. To find out whether teachers' and student/teacher interactions were consistent with the staffing pattern, I administered a questionnaire to staff members and recorded student/teacher interaction patterns within the classroom over a period of several months.

The Teaching Staff: Its Subjective Values and Expectations

Through a questionnaire, the teaching staff was asked to record their own personal opinions and values regarding their students. Of particular importance were their views on future careers and the efficacy of female education. This was done in order to determine the existence of obvious male/female stereotype patterns.

First, the teachers were given a list of 37 characteristics which might describe their male and/or female students. Table 1 lists the terms teachers most often used to describe their male and female students. The table shows that the teaching staff held little regard for the ability, character, or potential of their female students. Teachers most often described their female students in negative terms, such as "disruptive behavior" or "lacks interest in school." The few positive terms teachers used to describe their female students had little to do with actual academic success. Teachers most often said that the girls had a "neat appearance." In contrast, they described male students as "responsible," "hard working," and "scholarly."

While it may be impossible to determine how or why these images were formed, they appear not to have been shaped by the actual academic performance or behavior of the students. While the teachers believed that the boys had much more potential than girls for academic success, only 39 percent of the 4ème male students passed their examinations in the 1978–79 school year, while the female pass rate stood slightly lower at 32 percent. Similarly, teachers believed boys had a lower absentee rate than girls, despite the fact that there was little difference in their absentee rate. In the classes I observed, 90 percent of boys versus 85 percent of girls consistently attended class.

Teachers' expectations of their female students' projected careers were appreciably different from those they held for their male students. When asked to list the most likely careers to be pursued by their female students, the secondary school teachers relegated them to low-status, low-paying, less skilled, and nurturing occupations. They ranked the

TABLE 1

TEACHER SELECTED STUDENT CHARACTERISTICS
(Ranked)

Female Students	Male Students
1. Neat appearance	1. Likely to succeed at higher education
2. Below-average work	2. Good attendance
3. Does not follow instructions	3. Good in math
4. Lacks interest in school	4. Likely to obtain a good job after education
5. Does not profit from attending school	5. Responsible
6. Family well educated	6. Aware of current events
7. Handles school property carefully	7. Hard working
8. Quiet/submissive	8. Above-average work
9. Very emotional	9. Scholarly
10. Disruptive behavior	10. Leadership qualities

192

following as the most likely careers to be held by their female students: nurse, office worker, housewife, hairdresser, seamstress, primary school teacher, and midwife.

Observed Teacher/Student Interactions

Are teachers' different attitudes toward their male and female students transmitted in the classroom? To determine this, I conducted a series of detailed classroom observations over several months. During this time, I kept a log of academic participation and teacher reinforcement patterns. Of specific interest was the possible development of patterns which might be interpreted as establishing role models or acceptable achievement potentials. For example, did teachers of the arts encourage female participation? Were math classes dominated by male students? Were female students responsible for only housekeeping chores, or were they undertaking equally challenging and responsible classroom roles?

In the actual observation instrument, seven categories were listed; as the class progressed, the number of male and female students participating in each category was noted. Participation rates based on male/female attendance were calculated; using the male rate as a benchmark, the girls' participation rates were calculated.[5] Thus in table 2 a score of 100 would mean that, based on attendance, both boys and girls participated equally. Numbers over 100 indicate more female than male participation, and numbers less than 100 indicate less female participation.

Table 2 shows that the female students' academic participation in class fell far behind that of their male counterparts, with the exception of the girls' participation in the arts courses. Although the female students generally played a marginal academic role in the classroom, they were not forgotten when housekeeping duties were assigned. Not only did the girls do all the sweeping before class (supervised by female staff members), they were also called upon three times as often as their male counterparts to do in-class maintenance tasks such as cleaning the boards or returning papers.

In an analysis of classroom interaction, however, it is necessary to look beyond a strictly statistical interpretation for two important reasons. First, while the statistics which compare boys' to girls' participation generally underscored a much larger rate of male participation, it must be pointed out that in actual number of responses, neither the male nor female students had any significant degree of participation or interaction with the teacher. Table 3, which is based on the actual percentage of classroom participation (number of participations divided by the number of students in attendance) underscores this low rate of involvement by both male and female students.

[5] Girls' participation rate = N female participations/actual female attendance. Girls' rate, with boys' taken as benchmark, = (girls' participation rate/boys' participation rate) × 100.

TABLE 2

PARTICIPATION RATE OF GIRLS

Item	English	French	History-Geography	Total Arts	Geology	Physics-Chemistry	Math	Total Science	Total Arts and Sciences	Total All Subjects*
Chosen to answer	61	42	113	58	20	17	30	22	49	47
Chosen to read/recite	87	132	102	106	0	65	63	62	88	88
Allowed to ask questions	12	21	100	13	8	14	14	13	15	32
Positive academic reinforcement	91	69	68	80	11	0	94	40	70	64
Negative academic reinforcement	55	65	115	71	0	0	50	25	64	60
Negative behavior reinforcement	1,400	168	500	317	0	0	27	19	113	100
Class maintenance	275	648	367	463	275	0	485	282	394	316

NOTE.—Adjusted to enrollment, with male participation rate as benchmark.
* Includes arts, science, sports, and homemaking.

TABLE 3
ACTUAL CLASSROOM PARTICIPATION RATES (%)

Item	Arts		Science		All	
	Boys	Girls	Boys	Girls	Boys	Girls
Chosen to answer	25	14	6	1	13	6
Chosen to read/recite	7	8	3	2	6	5
Allowed to ask questions	4	2	8	1	6	2
Positive academic reinforcement	8	6	2	1	4	3
Negative academic reinforcement	12	11	1	0	6	5
Negative behavior reinforcement	2	4	2	0	2	2
Class maintenance	2	10	1	3	2	6

This low observed rate of student classroom participation is further underscored by a daily classroom procedure which highlighted only the teacher's activities, not that of the students. For example, in most of the classes I observed, a majority of the time was spent on classroom lectures and dictations. The students, both male and female, accepted a role of listener and/or notetaker, though some students chose to demonstrate their displeasure with (or disinterest in) particular classes through activities such as talking, inattention, or sleeping (mostly done by female students).

A second point which should be discussed when analyzing the apparent negligible role of females in the classroom is teacher/student interactions. While statistics show that girls participated to a lesser degree than boys, it appears to be of their own choosing and not an act of exclusion by the classroom teacher. During my observations it was not apparent that the low rate of female participation was a deliberate attempt on the part of the teacher to ignore female students who wished to participate, but, rather, an observed habit of most teachers to choose from those students who volunteered. Since few girls ever volunteered, few were ever called upon to participate. The teachers were rarely observed attempting to involve students who did not wish to be involved.

Another point to be discussed is that when the girls were called upon to participate academically, they did not appear to be shy or withdrawn. Though the girls were not always correct, they did not appear to perform any more poorly than their male counterparts and, in some cases, were able to correct a male student's error.

Therefore it is my opinion that, based on actual classroom observation, the female students have opted to behave in a particular manner which limits their interaction with the teacher, but when actively engaged in classroom activities, they performed at least as well as, if not better than, their male counterparts.

Based on these observed classroom interactions one must conclude that few messages or teacher expectations are being communicated to the girls, and, with the possible exception of classroom maintenance tasks, neither girls nor boys experienced any significant degree of interaction with their teachers.

Student Expectations

While teachers hold negative attitudes concerning the academic abilities and career potentials of their female students, it is questionable that students internalized teachers' attitudes about themselves. To explore further this question of effective internalization, secondary school girls' expectations with regard to both their education and future careers will be examined.

In order to determine if increased exposure to Western schools increases the internalization of these expectations, a sample population of final-year elementary school girls was administered the same mother-tongue interview schedule given the secondary girls. While the secondary population comprised the entire female 4ème class ($N = 137$), the elementary sample of 25 students was chosen at random from the final-year female population. As both schools were located in similar suburban areas of Lome and both were coeducational, government day schools, the two populations proved to be well matched, with the exception of age and exposure to Western schools.

Expected Level of Education

While an earlier discussion of staff expectations with regard to female success in education appeared quite negative, this pessimism was not shared by the girls themselves. If one studies the data obtained through personal mother-tongue interviews with both secondary and elementary school female students, several tentative conclusions can be drawn.

With regard to expected (not desired) educational goals, 79 percent of all secondary students and 80 percent of all elementary students polled expected to enter a lycée or university at some time in the future. This self-assessment by the girls appears to negate two important arguments. First, it questions whether expectations and different treatment of female versus male students by classroom teachers (demonstrated in the staffing assignments) are effectively internalized by the girls. Second, if one compares the closeness of results in both the secondary and elementary samples, which were administered identical questionnaire instruments, one must question whether increased exposure to Western schooling has any real effect on attitude and expectation formation. The high correlation between elementary and secondary replies to all questions seriously questions the assumption that increased exposure to Western schools produces increased internalization of attitudes and expectations found within that school's environment. It also questions a more basic assumption that Western schools have a measurable impact on the formation of girls' attitudes and expectations.

While the discussion above has dealt with expected educational performance as a whole, it may be of interest to test the ability of classroom teacher/student interaction, and the total school environment itself, to affect patterns of success or failure. One might examine, for example, the actual performance in two classes, history-geography (where the girls experienced the most academic interactions and positive reinforcement) and geology (where the girls experienced the least amount of interaction and reinforcement). Based on the results of a student self-ranking of best subjects (which lists geology first, followed by French, history-geography, math, English, and physics-chemistry) and on ranked examination results by subject (which again lists geology first, followed by French, English, history-geography, math, and physics-chemistry), there appears to be little correlation between classroom environment and academic performance.

This statement is made on the grounds that geology, the class where the girls received the least interaction and reinforcement, was chosen as their best subject in the interview process and also came in first with regard to the best female examination pass rate. History-geography, on the other hand, with the best overall interaction and reinforcement rates, only ranked as the third best subject by the girls and placed fourth in successful examination results.

It is interesting to note in passing, however, the close association between what the girls perceived as their best subject and the actual examination results posted after the interviews were concluded. This suggests a highly realistic view held by the girls with regard to their ability in the various subjects.

Expected Careers

While it appears that the secondary school environment and experience is filled with differential treatment and overtones of female inability and weakness, to what degree does this environment actually appear to affect female students' role expectations?

With the exception of nursing and clerical careers, a comparison of students' career expectations listed in table 4 with those most often selected by their teachers (wife, hairdresser, seamstress, and primary school teacher) reveals that female students have come away from the Western secondary school environment with career expectations quite different from those of their teachers. Although it is beyond the scope of this paper to prove causation, the close agreement between teachers and students on nursing and clerical careers may not be due to the school

197

TABLE 4

STUDENT CAREER EXPECTATIONS
(Ranked)

Female Secondary Students	Female Elementary Students
1. Nurse-midwife	1. Nurse-midwife
2. Clerical	2. Clerical
3. Doctor	3. Doctor
4. Professional*	4. Don't know
5. Semiprofessional†	5. Teacher
6. Lawyer	6. Lawyer
7. Sales-service	7. Semiprofessional†
8. Teacher	8. Sales-service
9. Don't know	
10. Skilled trades	

* Requiring university or other professional training, such as druggist.
† Requiring partial or complete university training; includes careers such as journalist.

environment but, rather, to the high visibility of these two careers in Lome.

The length of exposure to Western education does not apparently affect these expectations, as results obtained through the elementary school interviews show (see table 4). While the secondary population appears to have been more diverse than the elementary sample, neither patterned itself more closely than the other to teacher-held expectations, thus calling into question the ability of the Western school to alter role expectations.

An interesting side issue in this discussion of role expectations concerns the role of "housewife," a theme emphasized by Little from literature on education as a tool for acquiring a husband. Although the teachers have ranked housewife as the fourth most likely career for their female students, not one female student mentioned it as a possible life's occupation.

In fact, when asked why they were attending school, the girls' remarks were decidedly career oriented, with not one interviewee stating that "finding a husband" was a suitable reason for attending school. In analyzing the results of both the secondary and elementary school interviews, one notices that with age and increased exposure to Western education, the female student appeared to see school as a more important means of obtaining a career and good life, although the goal of being educated and the felt need to help family members declined. For example, 66 percent of the secondary population, compared with 44 percent of the elementary sample, stated that school should be attended in order to get a job, while only 6 percent of the secondary population and 19 percent of the elementary sample saw education itself as being the main reason for attending school.

198

Conclusions

In attempting to discuss the possible causes for the lack of congruity between teacher attitudes and student expectations, it is necessary to examine the environment within and outside the school.

Classroom Interactions Which May Have Contributed to the Incongruent Results

The degree to which the teacher can effectively transmit values and expectations is severely hampered by the formal classroom procedure which limits teacher/student interactions of any kind. Thus a major cause for the apparent lack of internalization on the part of the female student may simply be lack of directed classroom communication.

A second observed phenomenon which might help explain the incongruency between teacher and student expectations is the extrovert behavior on the part of the girls who did participate in classroom interactions. Though the girls did interact to a lesser degree than the boys, the quality of this interaction appeared equal, if not better, than that of the male students. From my observations it appeared that the girls had not effectively internalized the teachers' limited expectations, for they performed at least as well as, and in some cases superior to, the boys when responding to questions or executing problems at the board. On the basis of my observations it appears that the girls who sought to participate and excel in the classroom did so, while those who chose to resist passively or to ignore the classroom procedures were left to themselves.

Student Values Which Might Tend to Limit Internalization of Expectations in the School Environment

From preliminary tabulations drawn from the student interviews, it appears that two factors might directly affect the discrepancy between teacher and student expectations. These include a declining respect for the role of teacher as exposure to school increases and a high degree of awareness of and interest in careers outside the school environment. More specifically, increased exposure to Western education only appears to weaken the ability of teachers to function as positive role models. For example, when asked if there was anyone on the school staff they would most want to be like, 39 percent of the elementary sample and 62 percent of the secondary population answered "No one." This represents an 88 percent increase in the rejection rate of careers in education as girls progress from elementary to secondary school. Thus, with increased exposure to Western schools, girls appear to have become more disinterested in patterning themselves after their teachers or school administrators, and this rejection may help to explain why internalization of expectations held by the teaching staff appears not to have taken place.

In negating the effectiveness of the Western school environment (as represented by teachers' attitudes, classroom interaction messages, and

TABLE 5

POTENTIAL CAREERS OUTSIDE THE SCHOOL (%)

Item	Secondary Girls	Elementary Girls
If you could be like anyone, whom would you most want to be like?*		
Important female	39	44
Important male	32	44
No one	29	12
Do you know any famous women?†		
Togolese political minister	32	70
Director, national midwife school	24	15
No one	21	0
Togolese lawyers	13	0
Miscellaneous	10	15

* All important male and female figures cited by the girls were involved in prestige careers outside the school or home (i.e., president, lawyer).

† Knowledge refers to a girl's awareness of the individual, not a personal knowledge.

the school's authority structure) to alter female expectations, it seems only fitting to suggest possible alternatives. As table 5 suggests, careers outside school appear to be more effective, though their potential for affecting role expectations does appear to decrease with an increase in the girl's age. Thus, while 88 percent of the elementary sample would like to pattern themselves after a variety of public figures, this decreases to 71 percent by the third year of secondary school. However, when compared with the 30 percent who expressed a desire to pattern themselves after a teacher, this 71 percent still remains impressive.

Of equal interest is the girls' ability to know, by name, important women figures within the Togolese society. As the results of table 5 suggest, the girls are extremely aware of the adult women who have succeeded in highly visible, prestigious careers.

While this article has suggested that factors such as personal determination or outside role models may be effectively regulating the internalization of attitudes and expectations found within the school environment, further research in the areas of peer-group relations, formal curriculum, or the impact of female role models outside the school would be valuable in a reassessment of the impact of Western schools on Third World women's expectations.

PART III
Outcomes of Women's Schooling:
Women and Work

12. Sex Differences in the Labor Market Outcomes of Education

RATI RAM

This article discusses the major approaches to an analysis of sex differences in the labor market outcomes of education and the main dimensions along which such differences do or may occur. Do the labor force participation effects of schooling differ for males and females, and, if so, what explanation could be offered for the difference? How do the income effects of education differ by gender and why? To what extent may a similar educational distribution lead to different occupational distributions of men and women and why? Put a little differently, I discuss some theories of sex differences in educational outcomes, point out their main implications, and relate these to the observed differences in the labor markets. The study focuses on the developing countries. Due to the paucity of theories and scarcity of data pertaining specifically to the developing countries, I often draw upon the models developed in the Western context and occasionally even rely on the empirical patterns observed in the United States and other industrialized countries.

The subject covered is wide and rather difficult and unsettled. Several important limitations concerning the scope of the study should be noted. First, it does not go into the question of sex differences in educational access or achievement. More important, it does not consider the consequences of female education in relation to household production, including fertility. (Other articles in this book deal with these questions.) This article also avoids a discussion of male-female differences in the effects of schooling in agricultural production situations characterized mainly by self-employment or work on the family farm.[1] Even within the labor market, the focus is on differences that relate to educational outcomes and not on all sex differences in wages, occupations, and so forth. In short, this article deals with the differences in the educational outcomes of men and women in labor market situations involving wage or salary payments. It is confined largely to economic perspectives and avoids a consideration of any approaches that are primarily sociological or cultural.

C. A. Anderson and M. J. Bowman made numerous useful suggestions and provided many relevant references. Robert E. Evenson, Elinor Barber, and Carolyn M. Elliott offered several comments that helped me organize the article.

[1] See Rati Ram, "Male-Female Differences in Educational Outcomes, with Special Reference to the Labor Market" mimeographed (New York: Ford Foundation, June 1978).

Reprinted from the *Comparative Education Review* 24, no. 2 (part 2)(June 1980): S53–77.

The broad plan of the article is as follows. It begins with a survey of the major approaches to studying sex differences in the labor market outcomes of schooling. The approaches include several forms of the theory of sex discrimination and the human capital view as extended by the more general household-production models. The article then discusses the major dimensions along which sex differences in the labor market consequences of education are observed. These include market-activity rates, wages, earning profiles and rates of return, and occupational distribution.

Major Theoretical Approaches to Sex Differences in the Labor Market

Sex differences in the labor market outcomes of schooling can be modeled in several different ways.[2] These approaches are often not mutually exclusive but overlap in varying degrees and sometimes differ in emphasis rather than in their basic contents. Nevertheless, it seems useful to distinguish between two divergent approaches in explaining why the education of males and females may have quite different outcomes in the labor market. These two views are not inconsistent with each other but reflect quite different postulates concerning the sources of sex differences in the labor market. One of these approaches is based on the theme of sex discrimination in the labor market, particularly on the part of employers. The other, which may be called the "human capital" or the "household-production" model, relies primarily on the postulate of maximizing behavior on the part of males and females in relation to their educational and labor market decisions, coupled with differential comparative advantage of each sex in the household and the market sectors. I shall discuss the two approaches in the following sections, but it may be useful to note that the major difference between the two is that (a) the "discrimination" approach regards the discriminatory behavior of employers as the primary source of sex differences in the labor market and (b) the human capital approach makes no such assumption (while being able to deal with discriminatory employer behavior) and can explain sex differences in the labor market with reference to the different comparative advantage (or "productivity") of the two sexes in market and the nonmarket activities. Both approaches may be partially correct. The observed differences may be due to discrimination (whatever its source) as well as to sex differences in what may be called "adaptability" to market and household activities.[3] While the two approaches are distinct, they do not have to be regarded as mutually exclusive.

[2] Ibid.
[3] "Adaptability" refers to the notion of comparative advantage mentioned earlier. Note that it might be possible to *derive* the implication of employer discrimination against females on the basis of the household-production model along with a postulate of different comparative advantage for males and females in the market and nonmarket activities; for an attempt at such a derivation, see

Discrimination Models

A major objective of the various sex-discrimination models is to explain two observed phenomena: lower wages of females, and concentration of females in certain occupations and activities and their relative absence in others. These models do not deal directly with sex differences in educational outcomes, but they do suggest some implications in that regard.

One can identify several types of theories based on sex discrimination. At a straightforward level one can postulate a "taste" for discrimination against females on the part of employers, employees (including unions), consumers, or all of them. Given such a taste, a rational profit-maximizing employer would pay lower wages to females as compared with males. Such a wage differential would reflect the psychic cost to the employer of hiring females (if the employer has the taste for discrimination), or the higher cost of hiring male employees if they do not like to work with females, or the possible reduction in sales if it is the customers who discriminate against females. The foregoing framework in relation to sex discrimination is formally similar to the now-standard models of racial discrimination.[4]

The simple framework described above is useful in several ways. Not only does it predict a male-female wage differential for different educational levels, but it can also imply different occupational distributions for males and females. Given that male employees have a strong distaste for working under female supervisors, it can yield the prediction that female wage disadvantage is likely to increase with more schooling or training.[5] There are, however, at least two problems with this framework. One problem pertains to the persistence of discrimination for long periods even in the presence of the pressures of a competitive market, particularly when the discrimination is postulated to be primarily on the part of employers. Given some fairly plausible assumptions, one would expect the profits of the discriminators to be lowered, thus providing incentives to others to add to their profits by not discriminating. There is a cost involved in discrimination, and there should be competitive pressure on the discriminators in terms of reduced profits.[6] Therefore, even if discrimination does not disappear altogether, one should observe a tendency toward its attenuation as a result of the market pressures.

Robert E. Evenson, "The Allocation of Time by Adult Women: An International Comparison" mimeographed (New Haven, Conn.: Yale University, 1979).

[4] See Gary S. Becker, *The Economics of Discrimination*, 2d ed. (Chicago: University of Chicago Press, 1971); Kenneth J. Arrow, "Models of Job Discrimination," in *Racial Discrimination in Economic Life*, ed. Anthony H. Pascal (Lexington, Mass.: Lexington, 1972), pp. 83–102.

[5] Arrow, p. 88.

[6] Ibid.

It is possible to explain persistence of discrimination in various ways. One can postulate noncompetitive markets: monopolies in the product market, monopsonies in the labor market, or a combination of these. In the context of racial discrimination, Arrow has sought to explain existence of discrimination as an equilibrium characteristic by focusing on employee discrimination as a major factor in the market place; the argument also applies to sex discrimination.[7] However, the model raises a problem in that discrimination by employees, reflected in higher employee costs if both males and females are hired, does yield the prediction of occupational segregation, but it also carries the empirically inaccurate prediction of no wage differential. To rationalize the existence of *both* wage differentials and occupational segregation, Arrow postulates "personnel costs" which prevent an employer from switching from an all-white (male) to an all nonwhite (female) work force or vice versa. Thus, by postulating both employee discrimination and personnel costs, it is possible to set up a model which can yield the prediction of wage differential along with a tendency toward segregation as the attributes of an equilibrium state.

Even if the objection concerning the reasons behind persistence of discrimination can be overcome by an argument of the type mentioned above, there is another serious problem with such models. By treating the tastes for discrimination as being exogenous, the models are assuming away an important part of the phenomenon. The problem obviously exists even in regard to racial discrimination. However, in the case of racial discrimination, it might make sense to postulate that white employers, employees, or customers seek to maximize physical or social distance from nonwhites; but, as Thurow also points out, such a postulate makes very little sense in regard to male behavior relative to females.[8] It is true that, with certain assumptions, average male income might be expected to increase if there is discrimination against females. But since the income of almost every female is shared with some male, why would males as a class be interested in increasing their incomes by reducing females incomes? Even assuming that males in general do want such a redistribution, why would rational employers act so as to increase the average male income at the cost of that of female employees? It is not easy to postulate a plausible mechanism by means of which males could, as a class, be perceived to be acting to reduce female incomes through discrimination, even if that was what they wanted.

A special version of the taste-related theories of discrimination is contained in the "overcrowding" hypothesis, which postulates the effect of

[7] Ibid., pp. 92–96.
[8] Lester C. Thurow, *Generating Inequality* (New York: Basic, 1975), pp. 177–81.

discrimination on the demand and supply sides.[9] Simply stated, it suggests that, on the demand side, women are denied entry into certain (prestigious) occupations, and that therefore (from the supply side), most women seek jobs in those occupations where such barriers do not exist or are minimal and thus create overcrowding there, causing wages to fall even more in these occupations.

In the pure discrimination models described above, we mentioned the difficulty relating to motives for discrimination and concerning explanation of the persistence of discrimination in reasonably competitive markets. Perhaps partly because of these difficulties, models of "statistical discrimination" have been proposed.[10] The core of the theory of statistical discrimination is that while employers have no taste for discrimination against females, they evaluate a potential female employee on the basis of their perception of the average performance of female employees. Thus, if the employers perceive a typical female employee to be more likely to quit or to have a higher absenteeism rate, or to be otherwise less productive than a typical male applicant, their hiring practices will be governed by such perceptions, and thus females not conforming to such a stereotype will be unfairly treated. In this theory, the employers' cost of acquiring information about an individual applicant is considered too high and so the employers go by statistical averages.

There seems to be one problem with this view. Either an employer's perception about the statistical average is correct or it is incorrect. If it is correct, then while some female employees (better than average) will be unfairly treated, others (below average) will be more than fairly treated. Therefore, on the whole there may be no discrimination against females as a group. If any employer's information about the average is, however, incorrect, there will be others who can increase their profits by having a better perception of the average, and so a grossly erroneous perception will—like the pure discrimination taste—constitute an unstable state. However, in an era characterized by rapidly changing female attitudes toward market work, employer perception of female employees' productivity and performance could be very much outdated. While employers may go by statistical averages for both males and females, the practice may operate harshly or unfairly against females for quite a long time simply because their market-activity patterns are changing, while the male patterns are stable. As Thurow has pointed out, statistical discrimination can be self-reinforcing in the sense that if a group starts with less favorable characteristics for whatever reason, statistical discrimination

[9] Barbara Bergmann, "The Economics of Women's Liberation," *Challenge* 16 (May–June 1973): 11–17.

[10] Arrow, pp. 96–99; Thurow, pp. 170–77; Francine D. Blau and Carol L. Jusenius, "Economists' Approaches to Sex Segregation in the Labor Market: An Appraisal," in *Women and the Workplace*, ed. Martha Blaxall and Barbara Reagan (Chicago: University of Chicago Press, 1976), pp. 181–99.

will retard acquisition by the group of better characteristics and thus prevent their escape from such discrimination.[11]

The start and continuance of statistical discrimination can be explained in several different frameworks. Thurow's model of job competition can easily explain such a phenomenon. Statistical discrimination is also an aspect of the so-called internal labor market approach to employment and wage determination.[12] According to this approach, jobs in any enterprise fall into two categories. In one category are the jobs which are filled from outside through hiring of new workers; in the other are jobs filled internally from among the existing employees on the basis of seniority or other promotion rules. The usual market forces of supply and demand are supposed to operate at the entry level. For the second category, the external market forces operate minimally, and allocation of jobs and the wage structure are determined in the internal labor market of the firm. The extent to which a person would get access to the more highly paid and more prestigious jobs in the internal market depends largely on the sort of entry level position at which the person is hired. The approach suggests that females and other disadvantaged groups usually have access to entry level positions that have low promotion possibilities. Such a situation could arise due to employer perceptions regarding the background characteristics and qualifications of different groups of people in regard to their suitability for training and other forms of skill-formation for absorption in the internal-market positions. The approach can thus predict earnings differentials by sex and also a tendency toward sex segregation. Although there is some plausibility in the internal-market hypothesis, its applicability on a wide scale is not clear; nor is it obvious how some of its propositions can be derived from a set of plausible employer behavioral postulates.

There is the extreme radical view of discrimination in terms of the theme of class exploitation. It holds that women constitute a "class" which is exploited by the male class in a capitalistic economic system. Women constitute a "reserve army" which enters the work force when there is a shortage of workers and is pushed out when such a shortage ceases. Women are exploited or discriminated against in much the same way as other members of the proletarian class. In short, male-female differences in the labor market are due to class exploitation inherent in capitalistic economic systems, and the only way to end this discrimination is to end the capitalistic systems. Aside from the more general attacks on the radical approach, it seems to have some obvious problems in terms of rationalizing the motivation for exploitation of females by males and of

[11] Thurow, p. 181.
[12] Blau and Jusenius.

explicating the mechanism through which such exploitation is started and maintained.

A rather special model, and the one based on what might be called "semidiscrimination," is suggested by Madden.[13] She proposes that females are exploited, or unfairly treated, in the labor markets due to a combination of two factors: First, there is a certain degree of monopsony power with the employers; second, the elasticity of female labor supply is lower than that of males because of the constraints operating on female labor force participation. These two factors enable the employers to exploit female workers to a greater extent than they can exploit male workers. While Madden's model incorporates a possibility, it is not obvious how widely applicable it is to real-life labor market situations in the developing or the developed countries.

Even though the theories of discrimination described above do not deal directly with sex differences in schooling outcomes, as mentioned earlier, they do have implications in that regard, and these implications are broadly similar for most theories. They imply, directly or indirectly, (a) lower wages and lifetime earnings for females than for males with comparable schooling levels; (b) possibly a flatter age-earning profile for females, indicating limited opportunities for promotion and career development even though they may have the same education as males; and (c) different occupational distributions for the two sexes with the general characteristic that females dominate in low-paid and less prestigious clerical occupations, while men dominate in those occupations and professions that are highly paid and involve greater authority, more power, and higher prestige.

Human Capital Models

A useful approach to the study of male-female differences in the labor market outcomes of schooling is provided by an application of what is commonly called the "human capital" theory of schooling.[14] In its simplest form, the approach suggests that people obtain education and training with reference to the costs of acquiring such skills and the benefits expected from them in the form of higher market earnings or direct consumption gains. The theory suggests that given different costs of or benefits from schooling, different people or groups will acquire different amounts of schooling which will be reflected in differences in the market earnings of such persons or groups.

Although good as a starting point, the theory is not directly useful in understanding differences in the labor market consequences of the

---

[13] Janice Fanning Madden, *The Economics of Sex Discrimination* (Lexington, Mass.: Lexington, 1973), chap. 5.

[14] See the articles in *Journal of Political Economy*, vol. 70, pt. 2 (October 1962) for pioneering and illuminating discussions of the various aspects of the human capital theory.

schooling of the two sexes. An extension of the theory is, however, quite straightforward by using Gary Becker's theory of the allocation of time or the so-called household-production model.[15] Using the household-production framework, it is possible to model consumption, investment in schooling, and labor-supply behavior of males and females and to study differences across the two sexes. Although the basic model was developed and has been used mainly in the context of high-income countries, the framework is quite general and has recently been adapted by Robert Evenson for a cross-national comparison of the allocation of time by males and females.[16] It is, of course, obvious that for generating predictions of sex differences in the aspects we are considering, some difference between males and females should be postulated to serve as the basis for differential behavior of the two sexes in regard to education and the consequences of schooling in the labor market. One assumption that can be made is that women have a comparative advantage, relative to the males, in bearing, and possibly in rearing, children.

Given the assumption that females have a comparative advantage in bearing and rearing children, it can be proposed that the pattern of labor force participation would generally be different for males and females, and marital status could have diametrically opposite effects on the market-activity behavior of males and females. A major part of the difference between married males and females would lie in the lower market-activity rate for the females and, possibly, in a "discontinuous" participation pattern characterized by a five-point spectrum consisting of entry (before marriage), exit (at first childbirth), entry-exit (second or later child), and final entry after the period of childbirth and child care is over. Important implications can be drawn from such participation-sequencing concerning male-female differences in wage rates in general, relative levels of investment in schooling by males and females, type of schooling (e.g., more "home-oriented" and/or less obsolescence prone for the females), investments in the on-the-job training (OJT), and occupational distribution. First, reduced market participation implies lower market return to female schooling and, therefore, smaller investment in female education. Second, during the period of nonparticipation there may be depreciation of market-oriented human capital of females who may in any case have a weaker incentive to acquire OJT. Therefore, a lower wage rate would be observed for females with comparable schooling levels. Finally, greater emphasis may be predicted during female schooling on areas leading to occupations with low depreciation and low obsolescence rates. It is also possible that there would be greater emphasis by females on those areas

[15] Gary Becker, "A Theory of the Allocation of Time," *Economic Journal* 75 (September 1965): 493–517.
[16] Evenson.

of study that complement well both market and nonmarket activity since, unlike the males, some periods of complete "specialization" in the household are foreseen by females if they intend marrying.

Starting from a simple premise, the human capital approach enables one to derive implications of lower schooling levels for females, different choice of educational fields for males and females, lower market-activity rates of females with given educational levels, lower observed wage rates for (married) women with comparable educational levels more or less throughout their labor market experience, concentration of women in some occupations (e.g., where skill depreciation rates are low or the OJT component is lower), and, on the whole, a less remunerative position of women in the labor market. Most of these predictions seem in accord with the empirical facts in developed countries and possibly some developing countries. Also, the predictions are qualitatively similar to those generated by discrimination models.

Although plausible in terms of its basic analytical framework, the human capital model may need some modification when it is applied to developing countries. For example, in some low-income countries in Asia and Africa, women have traditionally been active in production activities on family farms or in local trade. In some cases production structures have allowed females to combine work in the household with that for the market. The so-called cottage industries are one example of such structures. Thus the market participation discontinuities observed in respect of several female cohorts in the United States and some industrialized countries may not be found in many developing countries, and the implications based on the market activity behavior of females in the United States would not be entirely applicable to them. Modified versions of the human capital model would then be more useful for understanding sex differences in the labor market outcomes of schooling. Of course, there are attacks on the basic human capital approach itself, either in terms of the "screening" hypothesis and the postulated divergence between private and social consequences of education or in terms of the low empirical predictive power of the model.[17]

Variations in the applicability and the operationality of the two major theoretical frameworks discussed in this paper may be noted. The human capital models are largely based on market behavior and would not apply directly either to socialist countries or even to public-sector (government) enterprises in developing countries. Moreover, the core of the human

---

[17] See Mark Blaug, "The Empirical Status of Human Capital Theory: A Slightly Jaundiced Survey," *Journal of Economic Literature* 14 (September 1976): 827–55. For a critical review of the human capital approach in relation to the treatment of females in the labor market, see Cynthia B. Lloyd, "The Division of Labor between the Sexes: A Review," in *Sex, Discrimination and the Division of Labor*, ed. Cynthia B. Lloyd (New York: Columbia University Press, 1975), pp. 1–24; and Blau and Jusenius.

capital models, being related to the childbearing responsibility of women, might not be easy to apply, and therefore not very useful when differences between *unmarried* males and females are analyzed, even though theoretically the models posit a behavior based on lifetime optimization. The need for some modification of the predictions of the human capital models in situations involving a tradition of continuous market work by women has already been mentioned. The discrimination models may have a wider applicability, but, to the extent that the socialist or the radical argument for the existence of sex discrimination is premised on class exploitation inherent in capitalistic systems, the framework would be conceptually inapplicable to noncapitalist economies.

Having taken a brief look at the main theoretical approaches, we may now turn to a consideration of the major dimensions along which male-female differences in educational outcomes are or may be observed.

Main Dimensions of Differences in the Labor Market Outcomes of Male and Female Schooling

Labor Force Participation or Market-Activity Rates

Theoretical predictions concerning male-female differences in the effects of schooling on market-activity rates are not exactly straightforward. In terms of the human capital framework, though, it is relatively easy to predict that, as for men, market-participation rates of women should rise with schooling, with some exceptions.[18] The prediction can be premised on the proposition that increased schooling of females—like the increased schooling of males—raises their market earning power (potential wage) and thus provides a stronger inducement to seek market work. Other points not directly suggested by the human capital model can be added. Education may raise female occupational aspirations, change their attitudes toward sex roles, and/or vest them "with the formal qualifications needed for participation in many aspects of modern society."[19] Thus education may favorably affect both their willingness and ability to do market work. Education may also enable them to find more interesting or more respectable jobs which may receive greater social acceptance. On the other hand, the prediction in terms of the discrimination model is not clear. Existence of sex discrimination would generally tend to discourage market activity by females, but the effect of schooling on activity rates is not evident. If educated females are subject to a greater degree of

[18] One exception would be the situation in which increased education of a female results in her marrying a higher-income husband, and the family income effect on market participation (which is likely to be negative) dominates the positive (substitution) effect of increase in her potential wage due to more schooling. Another (though unlikely) possibility, of course, is that schooling raises the female productivity in the household as much as or more than it raises her market productivity.

[19] Audrey C. Smock, *Women's Education and Roles* (Chicago: University of Chicago Press, in press), chap. 1.

discrimination, education may not raise the female market-activity rate at all or may raise it to an extent smaller than in the case of males. If, on the other hand, discrimination against educated females is less than that against uneducated females, the positive effect of education on female participation rate may be stronger than in the case of males. Within the discrimination framework, Guy Standing, in his extensive discussion of the effects of education on female market-activity rates, proposes the "sexual dualism" hypothesis, which suggests that a dualistic structure of the labor market could result in education having different effects on the market-activity rates of men and women.[20] Standing also suggests that, unlike male education, female education may generate a strong "status-frustration" effect, especially because of the prevalence of high unemployment rates in urban areas of developing countries, and may thus cause women to withdraw from the labor market.[21]

The empirical situation concerning sex differences in the effect of schooling on market-activity rates is mixed. Broadly speaking, one can say that (despite some apparent exceptions), the effect of male schooling on labor force participation is positive in both industrialized and industrializing countries. The effect of female schooling also seems positive in the United States and possibly in other high-income market economies.[22] For the low-income countries, a rather rich compendium of studies has recently become available.[23] The countries covered in these studies include Argentina, Brazil, Chile, Colombia, Costa Rica, Ecuador, Egypt, Ghana, India, Jamaica, Kenya, Mexico, Nigeria, Pakistan, Papua New Guinea, Peru, Philippines, Singapore, Sri Lanka, Sudan, Venezuela, and Yugoslavia. These show a generally mixed picture regarding the effect of education on labor force participation rates (LFPR) of women. The effect seems to vary with the educational level considered, rural/urban residence, marital status, presence of children, and husband's or family's income. As a rough generalization, it can be said that the female market-participation rate does have a tendency to increase with education. It can be said that, in several cases, the relationship between education and female participation rate seems to be "curvilinear" in the sense that at low levels of schooling (e.g., a change from illiteracy to bare literacy) the effect of education on female market-activity rate is small or negative, while at somewhat higher educational levels the effect is more clearly positive. There are, of course, exceptions to these generalizations.

[20] Guy Standing, "Education and Female Participation in the Labor Force," *International Labor Review* 114 (November–December 1976): 281–97.
[21] Ibid.
[22] U.S. Department of Labor, *U.S. Working Women: A Data Book* (Washington, D.C.: Department of Labor, 1977).
[23] Standing; Guy Standing and Glen Sheehan, eds., *Labor Force Participation in Low-Income Countries* (Geneva: International Labour Office, 1978); Smock.

Before the empirical patterns are discussed in detail, some methodological points should be noted. First, a simple relationship between education and labor force participation may indicate correlation, not causation. Even if a positive covariance between education and female market-activity rate is observed, it would not necessarily reflect the effect of education; the correlation may be due to the operation of other variables that affect both education and labor force participation, for example, aspiration levels, connections, or opportunities. If, on the other hand, a multiple-regression model is used, high correlation between regressors like education, income, and family background may lead to high standard errors of the estimates. Different results could be obtained by varying the sample period or sample coverage, changing the functional specification or estimation procedure, and altering the variables included in the estimating equation. Sometimes different measures of market-activity rates (e.g., hours worked vs. activity status) can yield different results. Finally, one faces the problem of lack of uniformity in the concept of "labor force participation" in different countries. One should, therefore, keep these limitations in mind when comparing the results across countries. Strictly speaking, these results are not comparable; but the broad patterns revealed by the comparisons are still useful if one does not overlook the fact that the sample periods, variable definitions, functional specifications, and estimation procedures are not quite the same in different studies.[24]

The studies relevant to the issue may be broadly classified into four groups: those that indicate a more or less uniformly positive relation between education and female market-activity rate, those that indicate a curvilinear relation, those that suggest a mixed pattern, and those that suggest a negative relationship. The only country to fall in the last, and unusual, category is Colombia. Based on a 1970 sample of 3,000 women aged 15–50, a multiple-regression analysis of market hours worked by females indicates a negative effect of education (except in the eastern region), and the negative coefficients are statistically highly significant.[25]

For many countries the data suggest a more or less uniformly positive effect of schooling on female participation rates. For both Mexico and Costa Rica (rural and urban areas), a tabular analysis suggests the relationship to be positive except for the relatively less important group of females aged 15–19.[26] The aforesaid position in respect to Mexico is to be contrasted with the analysis by Smock, which suggests that primary

---

[24] Standing and Sheehan, pp. 1–11.

[25] Alejandro Angulo and Cecilia L. de Rodriguez, "Female Participation in Economic Activity in Colombia," in Standing and Sheehan, pp. 17–26.

[26] Andras Uthoff and Gerardo, "Mexico and Costa Rica: Some Evidence on Women's Participation in Economic Activity," in Standing and Sheehan, pp. 43–50.

schooling has little impact on female market-activity status.[27] In regard to Kenya, consistent with Smock's findings, the study by Richard Anker and James Knowles, based on a national sample of 3,180 households taken in December 1974, indicates that in urban Kenya education has a positive effect on the labor force participation of married females.[28] Moreover, a regression based on "willingness to work away from home" in respect to married females aged 20–49 indicates a positive effect of schooling in both rural and urban areas.[29] In both cases, the coefficients of higher-levels of education are larger and more significant.

Similarly, K. T. de Graft Johnson finds that the relationship between education and labor force participation in both the rural and urban areas of Ghana is positive, and, as for urban Kenya, the coefficients rise with the level of schooling.[30] This finding, based on multiple-regression analysis, also differs somewhat from that of Smock, who found a cur-vilinear relationship between women's educational attainment and eco-nomic activity rate in Ghana.[31] In fact, it is interesting to observe from Johnson's analysis that when a composite education variable is included in the regression, its coefficient in the female activity-rate equation is much higher than that in the male activity-rate equation.[32]

For Sudan, the multiple-regression analysis indicates a high and posi-tive coefficient on female secondary education.[33] The Yugoslav case indi-cates a divergence between the tabular and regression-analysis results. The tabular analysis shows a positive effect of female education on mar-ket activity (as opposed to a mixed effect of male education), but the regression estimates reveal a mixed position in respect to both male and female educations.[34] The effect of female education on market activity is observed to be positive in Singapore.[35] For Jamaica, the human capital variable is seen to have a strongly positive effect.[36] In the Philippines, the effect of female education is almost consistently positive, although male schooling has a mixed effect.[37] For Costa Rica, too, the effect of female

[27] Smock.

[28] Richard Anker and James C. Knowles, "A Micro-Analysis of Female Labour Force Participa-tion in Africa," in Standing and Sheehan, pp. 137–63.

[29] Ibid.

[30] K. T. de Graft Johnson, "Factors Affecting Labour Force Participation Rates in Ghana, 1970," in Standing and Sheehan, pp. 123–28.

[31] Smock.

[32] De Graft Johnson.

[33] Glen Sheehan, "Labour Force Participation Rates in Khartoum," in Standing and Sheehan, pp. 165–75.

[34] Miroslav Rasevic, "The Determinants of Labour Force Participation in Yugoslavia," in Stand-ing and Sheehan, pp. 191–213.

[35] Pang Eng Fong, "Labour Force Growth, Utilisation and Determinants in Singapore," in Stand-ing and Sheehan, pp. 215–34.

[36] Guy Standing, "Female Labour Supply in an Urbanising Economy," in Standing and Sheehan, pp. 87–122.

[37] R. Wery, G. B. Rodgers, and P. Peek, "A Model of Labour Supply in the Philippines," in Standing and Sheehan, pp. 327–38.

215

education on market activity is uniformly positive when one looks at all the income groups together, although the position does differ across the various income groups. Qualitatively, the effect is also positive in Turkey, Syria, and Egypt, where about 4 percent of women with primary schooling, 21 percent of those with secondary education, and 66 percent of those with university education are in nonagricultural or professional employment.[38] In rural Kenya and Venezuela, the effect of female education on market activity is mixed without any clear pattern.[39] In Chile also, the ordinary least squares (OLS) and maximum-likelihood estimates (MLE) for the total sample show a mixed picture.[40] However, when estimation is done separately for the "modern" and "traditional" sectors, both OLS and MLE show positive coefficients, although their significance varies.[41] For Ecuador (table 1), Papua New Guinea, and Sri Lanka the broad pattern appears to be that of a curvilinear relationship.[42] For Pakistan also Smock reported a curvilinear relationship.[43] Some studies for India also suggest a curvilinear relationship, and a similar relationship seems to hold for Peru.[44]

Just to give an example of the patterns discussed here, table 1 gives the 1970 female participation rates in Ecuador and Costa Rica by income ranges and educational levels.[45] Looking at the aggregate picture, Costa Rica's is a case of positive relationship, while Ecuador represents a curvilinear relationship between female education and labor supply; understandably, the position differs across the various income groups in each case.

Besides considering male-female differences in the overall effect of education on market-activity rates, one can also look at sex differences in the effect of schooling on age-specific LFPR. An understanding of the effect of female education on age-specific LFPR is useful, not only for getting a better insight into the effect of education on market activity, but also for perceiving more clearly sources of sex differences in regard to the effect of education on age-earning profiles. In many Western countries, age-specific participation rates of females are bimodal: The partici-

[38] Nadia Youssef, "Women in the Muslim World," in *Women in the World*, ed. Lynne B. Iglitzin and Ruth Ross (Santa Barbara, Calif.: ABC-Clio, 1976), pp. 203–17.

[39] Waldomiro Pecht, "Participation of Married Women in the Urban Labour Market in Selected Latin American Countries: Chile, Costa Rica, Ecuador and Venezuala," in Standing and Sheehan, pp. 27–41; Anker and Knowles.

[40] Peter Peek, "Family Consumption and Married Female Employment," in Standing and Sheehan, pp. 51–74.

[41] Peek; Peter Peek, "A Simultaneous Equation Model of Household Behavior," in Standing and Sheehan, pp. 75–86.

[42] Standing and Sheehan, pp. 239–41; Glen Sheehan, "Labour Force Participation in Papua New Guinea," in Standing and Sheehan, pp. 247–70.

[43] Smock.

[44] Standing, "Education and Female Participation in the Labor Force," pp. 290–92.

[45] Of course, for some of the countries discussed in this section, one can find other studies which suggest a different position; Standing mentions several such studies.

216

TABLE 1

PARTICIPATION RATES OF URBAN WOMEN AGED 25–34, MARRIED AND IN CONSENSUAL UNION,
ACCORDING TO INCOME OF THE HOUSEHOLD HEAD AND EDUCATION, 1970

A. ECUADOR

Income (Sucres/Month)	Education (Years)							
	0	1–3	4–5	6	7–9	10–12	13+	All
0– 390	0	0	16.7	0	0	0	···	3.9
391– 886	27.5	9.2	34.3	11.2	42.2	74.9	···	20.5
887–1,600	26.2	8.9	7.1	15.7	11.9	50.9	100.0	17.2
1,601–4,800	50.0	0	9.9	4.2	15.1	47.0	52.2	20.9
4,801 +	···	···	0	0	0	16.6	28.8	13.2
Total sample	25.4	7.4	20.2	10.5	13.7	41.4	43.5	18.5

B. COSTA RICA

Income (Colones/Month)	Education (Years)							
	0	1–3	4–5	6	7–9	10–11	12+	All
0– 300	6.6	8.4	13.5	15.6	33.1	···	100.0	14.0
301– 400	35.8	16.2	4.8	19.2	33.3	24.5	100.0	18.4
401– 600	0	13.0	17.0	22.8	16.1	28.8	100.0	18.3
601–1,000	0	9.9	12.7	13.6	30.7	48.2	92.1	25.8
1,001+	0	0	10.5	11.4	5.4	19.1	58.1	21.5
Total sample	7.3	11.5	12.7	15.7	20.2	29.1	74.7	20.9

SOURCE. —Guy Standing and Glen Sheehan, eds. *Labor Force Participation in Low-Income Countries* (Geneva: International Labour Office, 1978), pp. 36–38.

pation rates are high for younger age groups in the range 16–25, the rates then fall for age groups in the range 25–35, and, finally, the rates rise again for older age groups.[46] In terms of the human capital model, such bimodality or participation discontinuity is an important source of sex differences in the labor market outcomes of schooling. One would, therefore, like to know whether the bimodality observed in the United States, United Kingdom, and other Western countries also occurs in low-income countries and, if so, how female schooling affects such bimodality. Data on age-specific LFPR are readily available for many countries. The studies compiled by Standing and Sheehan include fairly recent data for Costa Rica, Kenya, Mexico, Nigeria, Papua New Guinea, Singapore, Sri Lanka, Sudan, Tanzania, and Yugoslavia.[47] In these countries the picture regarding bimodality in the age-specific female LFPR appears mixed; in fact, it seems quite accurate to say that the bimodality observed, if any, is small. Out of the 10 countries listed above, age-specific female LFPRs do not seem to have any bimodality in Costa Rica, Mexico, Nigeria, Papua New Guinea, and Tanzania. In Sri Lanka, Singapore, Sudan, and Yugo-

[46] See Jacob Mincer and Solomon Polacheck, "Family Investments in Human Capital: Earnings of Women," in *Economics of the Family*, ed. T. W. Schultz (Chicago: University of Chicago Press, 1974), pp. 397–429; Ruth Ross, "Tradition and the Role of Women in Great Britain" in Iglitzin and Ross, pp. 163–74.
[47] Standing and Sheehan.

slavia the bimodality is only slight. It is only for Kenya that bimodality is observed for both the rural and urban areas. However, the effect of schooling on the age-specific LFPR pattern is not quite clear. It is noticed, though, that in Yugoslavia the age-specific LFPR is slightly bimodal for females without schooling, but the bimodality is rectified when one looks at the sample of all females, both with and without education. It might appear, therefore, that schooling has some effect toward attentuating the female LFPR bimodality.

Somewhat older data on age-specific LFPRs of both males and females are reported by Durand for most countries of the world.[48] Since Durand's work does not indicate age patterns in LFPRs by education levels, we cannot study the effect of schooling on these patterns, but we can still look at the overall patterns and see how widely prevalent bimodality is in age-specific participation rates of females. Durand classifies the patterns into four categories: central peak or plateau, late peak, early peak, and double peak (bimodal). Table 2 contains a summary of the number of countries in each category classified by the five levels of development (from a low level I to high level V). It seems that roughly one-third of all countries have bimodality in the age pattern of female LFPR; also bimodality is more common in high-income than in low-income countries. Durand states,

> The central peak or plateau and late peak patterns . . . are found mainly in little-developed countries, where most of the women in the labor force are unpaid family workers or employed at home in handicraft industries, retail trade "in the front room," and other such activities that combine easily with the role of the housewife and mother. The double-peaked pattern that has evolved recently in the United States and some other highly developed countries seems especially fitting to the small size of families, the early termination of child-bearing and the predominance of wage labor in the modern urban-industrial society . . . , but such patterns are found also in a number of less developed countries.[49]

In short, it seems that the bimodality in age-specific LFPRs observed in the United States and some other high-income countries is perhaps not widely prevalent in low-income societies. That means, on the one hand, that the sex differences in wages and earning profiles that may be caused by such bimodality may be less severe in developing countries; on the other hand, education may not have much effect in attenuating the bimodal pattern in low-income countries simply because the pattern is not as much in existence there as one might think on the basis of the position in the United States.

Further research in regard to age patterns in female LFPRs and effect of schooling on these patterns appears to be useful. Durand's work can

[48] John D. Durand, *The Labor Force in Economic Development* (Princeton, N.J.: Princeton University Press, 1975).
[49] Ibid., pp. 133–34.

TABLE 2

PATTERNS IN AGE-SPECIFIC LFPRS OF FEMALES IN DIFFERENT COUNTRIES CLASSIFIED BY LEVELS OF ECONOMIC DEVELOPMENT (*N* Countries)

Patterns	Level of Development: I (Low)	II	III	IV	V (High)	Total
	National Totals					
Central peak of plateau	7	5	...	2	...	14
Late peak	3	2	1	2	...	8
Early peak	2	5	12	8	8	35
Double peak (bimodal)	1	7	4	6	9	27
Total	13	19	17	18	17	84
	Rural					
Central peak or plateau	3	3	...	4	...	10
Late peak	1	2	1	...	...	4
Early peak	...	2	5	2	1	10
Double peak (bimodal)	...	4	3	2	3	12
Total	4	11	9	.8	4	36
	Urban					
Central peak or plateau	1	2	...	1	...	4
Late peak	3	1	...	...	...	4
Early peak	...	5	6	5	1	17
Double peak (bimodal)	...	3	3	2	3	11
Total	4	11	9	8	4	36

SOURCE.—Based on John D. Durand, *The Labor Force in Economic Development* (Princeton, N.J.: Princeton University Press, 1975), p. 134.

perhaps be updated by considering the data generated by national censuses of or around 1970. Also, studies of the type compiled by Standing and Sheehan could be attempted for other low-income countries.

A slightly different way of looking at sex differences in the effect of education on market activity is to consider some index of lifetime participation and relate it to education. For the United States, Polacheck did a pioneering analysis based on data from the 1967 National Longitudinal Survey of Work Experience for Females 30–44 Years of Age.[50] He estimated that the "lifetime labor force participation" (LLFP), defined as the total number of years worked divided by "total exposure" to the labor force, is 30.1 percent for females with elementary schooling, 36.9 percent for those with high school diploma, 41.4 percent for those with college degree, and 59.1 percent for those with graduate education. Such esti-

[50] Solomon W. Polachek, "Discontinuous Labor Force Participation and Its Effect on Women's Market Earnings," in Lloyd (n. 17 above), pp. 90–122.

mates, though perhaps not difficult to make, seem to be lacking for most other countries. There is, however, an exception in respect to India. Working mainly with data from the Indian National Sample Surveys, Visaria not only compared the age-specific participation rates of men and women with various education levels but also estimated "gross years of active life" for both males and females with different educational levels.[51] Besides the expected finding that the female participation rate is lower than the male rate, and the interesting finding of a U-shaped (curvilinear) female LFPR profile by education groups, his calculation of gross years of active life shows a higher figure (9.3 – 13.5 years) for illiterate females than for nonmatriculated literate females (3.1 – 4.9 years), although the figure for college graduates is the highest (9.8 – 17.1 years). These figures are nothing but a refined reflection of the U-shaped relationship between education and LFPR. Therefore, it seems that, at least in the Indian samples examined by Visaria, education at the lower (elementary) level does not increase the female commitment to the labor force, but higher schooling levels do seem to increase such commitment. The type of study done by Visaria for India appears quite useful for understanding the effect of schooling on female work participation patterns which have an important influence on male-female wage differentials.

Wage Rates, Earning Profiles, and Rates of Return

Whenever one thinks of male-female differences in educational outcomes, the wage-earning picture is generally uppermost in one's mind and rightly so. Male-female differences in wages, earnings, and earning profiles are substantial and more or less universal for all age and education groups. While a study of the pattern of male-female earning differentials by age and marital status is important, what is more relevant to this article is an analysis of the effect of schooling on such differentials.

We may first recall the theoretical position in terms of the human capital model. In that framework, the principal sources of male-female earnings differentials are (*a*) smaller female investment in human capital, especially in OJT, due to a smaller anticipated labor force participation; (*b*) depreciation and obsolescence of such capital during periods of nonparticipation in market work; (*c*) female investment heavily focused on fields which have a low OJT component, low depreciation/obsolescence rates, and high complementarity with nonmarket work—which fields presumably have lower market returns. Therefore, one important component of the answer to our question concerning the effect of schooling on male-female differentials depends on what schooling does to market participation by females. If, as the human capital framework broadly suggests, schooling raises the overall level of female LFPR, attenuates the

[51] Pravin Visaria, "Labor Force Participation by Age, Sex, and Education," *Journal of the University of Bombay* 40 (1971): 200–201.

bimodality (discontinuity) in their age-specific LFPRs, increases the hours/weeks worked, and generally strengthens their commitment to the labor force (making them more "able and willing" to work in the market), then schooling should reduce male-female wage/earning differentials and should also narrow down the discrepancy between the age-earning profiles of men and women with similar age and educational background. It is important to note, however, that since forgone earnings constitute an important part of educational costs, the human capital framework does not yield a clear prediction regarding male-female differentials in the rates of return to schooling. To the extent that male-female earning differentials decline with schooling, rates of return to female schooling could be *higher* than the male rates of return.

The discrimination theories do not seem to offer any major insights into the effect of schooling on male-female earning differentials or on the differences in age-earning profiles of males and females or in regard to sex differences in the rates of return to schooling. If the degree of exploitation/discrimination declines with schooling, the wage/earning differentials should narrow down, but if exploitation or discrimination increases with schooling, the sex-related differentials in wages/earnings may be accentuated.

At the empirical level, one may begin with some general remarks. First, although there appear to be numerous studies of male-female differences in wages, earnings, and even age-earning profiles, there are not many dealing with the effect of schooling on these differentials. Second, even the studies that deal with male-female earning differentials are mainly for the developed countries, and there are very few significant studies dealing with the developing countries. We do, however, have studies for a few developing countries on rates of return to the schooling of males and females, and we shall have to limit our empirical discussion to this available information. In addition, a Canadian study on male-female earning ratios for different schooling levels will be mentioned.

We shall draw principally on two sources for male-female differences in rates of return to education. One is the article by Woodhall and the other a list of studies prepared by Psacharopoulos.[52] The countries or areas for which some information is available include (besides several high-income countries) Brazil, Colombia, Greece, Kenya, Malaysia, and Puerto Rico. The position is summarized in table 3, which shows that the return to female schooling is not always lower than that on male schooling; in some cases it is higher and in some others, lower. In other words, in some cases education reduces the male-female earning disparity, while

[52] George Psacharopoulos, *Returns to Education: An International Comparison* (San Francisco: Jossey-Bass, 1973); Maureen Woodhall, "Investment in Women: A Reappraisal of the Concept of Human Capital," *International Review of Education* 19 (1973): 9–28.

RAM

TABLE 3

RATES OF RETURN TO SCHOOLING OF MALES AND FEMALES IN SELECTED COUNTRIES FOR DIFFERENT
SCHOOLING LEVELS (%)

	Primary		Secondary		Higher/ University		Vocational	
	M	F	M	F	M	F	M	F
Brazil	17.9	38.6	···	···	···	···	···	···
Colombia	···	···	26.5	13.5	2.9	3.6	35.4	39.8
Greece	···	···	3.0	5.0	···	···	···	···
Kenya	21.7	7.1	23.6	19.5	···	···	···	···
Malaysia	9.4	9.3	12.3	11.4	10.7	9.8	···	···
Puerto Rico	17.1	17.2	21.7	20.9	16.5	6.3	···	···

SOURCES. — George Psacharopoulos, *Returns to Education: An International Comparison* (San Francisco: Jossey-Bass, 1973), p. 69; Maureen Woodhall, "Investment in Women: A Reappraisal of the Concept of Human Capital," *International Review of Education* 19 (1973): 11.

in others it accentuates such disparity. That the position is mixed is not surprising since we have already noted that theoretically it is not obvious how rates of return to female schooling should compare with those on male schooling, although one may generally expect male-female earning differential to decline with increased schooling. It is important to point out, however, that a higher rate of return on female schooling does not mean that educated females are in any way better placed than educated males; they are indeed usually worse off than males with similar levels of education in terms of earnings and other employment benefits. The rate-of-return differential in favor of females only means that the position of more educated females is somewhat better than the position of less educated females. It is also useful to remember that there are well-known problems in the computation and interpretation of rates of return to schooling.

The Canadian study by Holmes on male-female earning differentials by schooling level is important partly because of the direct information it conveys, but largely because it suggests a simple model that can be applied to many developing countries for assessing sex differences in the effect of schooling on earnings. Holmes first compares the estimated present value of potential lifetime earnings of males and females and then calculates the "gross" lifetime-earnings ratio. Then he adjusts for male-female differences in weeks worked, marital status, occupation, residence, and other relevant characteristics and calculates the "adjusted" ratio of lifetime earnings. He finds that for lower education levels (up to high school) the gross female-male earnings ratio varies roughly between 0.35 and 0.40, and the corresponding "adjusted" ratio ranges between 0.45 and 0.55. For higher educational levels (college and graduate education), the gross ratio ranges between 0.45 and 0.55, and the adjusted ratio

222

varies from 0.60 to 0.65.[53] These results support the intuitively appealing proposition that education reduces the relative male-female earning differentials.

To summarize, although the theoretical position is not clear, one generally expects schooling to reduce the relative disadvantage of females in terms of wages and earnings. The empirical position for the developing countries is hard to judge because of the lack of studies in this area. The few rates-of-return studies that compare the position for male and female schooling present a mixed picture. The Canadian study by Holmes does suggest an attenuation of female earnings disadvantage with increase in schooling. Studies for developing countries using Holmes's simple model should be very useful.

Since male-female differences in earnings and wages are closely related to sex differences in occupational distribution, I now consider the latter aspect.

Occupational Distribution

A preliminary point may be clarified before we discuss male-female differences in educational outcomes in terms of occupational distribution. For whatever reasons, women may not get the necessary educational training for certain occupations or may get such training on an extremely limited scale. Engineering and dentistry are two possible examples; business management and law may also belong to this group in some countries. With respect to such occupations, male-female differences lie primarily in educational access or achievement and not in educational outcomes.

However, it is still important to consider male-female occupational differences for the conventional, general schooling levels, namely, the elementary school, high school, college, and graduate levels. After all, an overwhelming majority of educated males and females in almost all countries can be classified as belonging to one of these levels, and it is instructive to observe how males and females with similar education are distributed over the various occupations.

Theoretically, both the human capital and discrimination theories lead to fairly similar predictions. In terms of the human capital models, one can see that if females have, or perceive, a comparative advantage in nonmarket activity, their human capital investments are likely to (i) be less obsolescence prone, (ii) complement nonmarket work, and (iii) have low depreciation rates, especially during periods of complete specialization in nonmarket work. Therefore, their occupational choice will be in keeping with the orientation of their training and, in addition, they would join those occupations in which the OJT component is smaller.

[53] R. A. Holmes, "Male-Female Earnings Differentials in Canada," *Journal of Human Resources* 11 (Winter 1976): 109– 17.

The discrimination theories would suggest an underrepresentation of women in prestigious and well-paid occupations and overrepresentation in low-paid occupations even if they had the same schooling as men. These latter occupations may well be the ones which have low OJT components and which are less prone to obsolescence.

Empirically, there appears to be overwhelming evidence of striking male-female differences in occupational distributions all over the world. The differences are probably as well documented and as pervasive as the wage/earning differentials, and the two sets of differences are obviously related.

While an awareness of differences in the overall occupational distributions of men and women is useful and relevant, the more important aspect for this study is an analysis of such differences for comparable educational levels. If, for example, the educational distribution of female workers is different from the educational attainments of male workers, the observed differences in occupational distribution of the two sexes may be a function of the educational differences as well of sex-related differences in educational outcomes. Studies of male-female occupational differences holding education constant are not numerous for any country and are even fewer for the developing countries. The exercise is simple and valuable, but it does not seem to have been attempted on any significant scale. What needs to be done is to compare the occupational or industrial distribution of males and females for similar education levels. An example is given here from India to illustrate how the analysis can be done for almost any developing country on the basis of the census data, which should be easily available, or with reference to survey data.[54]

Table 4 gives the distribution of male and female urban workers in India in selected industrial groups by education levels. It is clear from the table that, *within each schooling level*, women are grossly underrepresented in transportation, communications, trade, and commerce and are grossly overrepresented in "other services." It is thus reasonable to say that, in relation to occupational entry, schooling seems to have dramatically different effects for females and males.[55] Although table 4 depicts the position for India, it seems likely that the picture is similar for many developing (and developed) countries. A more detailed study in this direction should be useful.

[54] Since the focus is on developing countries, we avoid mentioning here in detail the U.S. case which in some ways is truly extraordinary. The U.S. Department of Labor (n. 22 above) indicates that in 1977 the median years of school completed by males and females in the labor force were identical (12.6; p. 11). However, the distribution of male and female workers across occupations was dramatically different. The percentage of women workers to the total ranged from a low of 1.8 percent in engineering, 4.8 percent in craft, and 9.2 percent in law to a high of 90 percent among bookkeepers, 91.1 percent among bank tellers, 96.6 percent among registered nurses, and 98.5 percent among secretaries and typists.

[55] It is, of course, true that occupational distribution is not an outcome of education alone, and therefore some caution is needed in interpreting the results of such a tabular analysis.

TABLE 4

DISTRIBUTION OF MALES AND FEMALES IN SELECTED INDUSTRIAL GROUPS, BY BROAD EDUCATION
LEVELS: INDIA, 1971, URBAN AREAS ONLY
(% of Total Male or Female Workers with Each Education Level)

Schooling Level	Industrial Groups							
	Manufacture, Servicing, etc. (Nonhousehold)		Trade and Commerce		Transport and Communications		Other Services	
	M	F	M	F	M	F	M	F
Primary	27.6	21.9	25.9	7.9	9.1	1.2	17.7	33.8
Middle	27.5	17.7	26.5	5.3	10.8	1.5	22.4	62.3
High school or more	15.3	6.4	23.1	6.3	10.6	3.9	40.5	82.9

SOURCE. —*Census of India* 11971, ser. 1, India, pt. 2, Special All India Census Tables (estimated from 1 percent sample data) (New Delhi: Registrar General and Census Commissioner, n.d.), pp. 1–6.

To sum up, the theoretical approaches predict quite different occupational outcomes of male and female schooling, and, although explicit studies seem few, the empirical position probably conforms to what the theories suggest.

Other Dimensions

Besides the three dimensions discussed in this paper, there are others that are not insignificant and are related to the three discussed. These include sex differences in educational outcomes in respect to unemployment rates, quit and absenteeism rates, and migration propensity. A brief discussion of these can be found elsewhere.[56]

Concluding Remarks

Male-female differences in regard to the labor market outcomes of schooling can be considered through several different theoretical approaches. The human capital approach, assuming different areas of comparative advantage for the two sexes, relates male-female differences in educational outcomes to different levels and types of human capital accumulation by members of the two sexes, especially if they are or intend to be married.

Discrimination theories attribute male-female differences to unfair or exploitative treatment of females in the labor market. The several variants of the discrimination hypothesis include (*a*) a postulate of taste for discrimination on the part of employers, employees, or consumers even though the factor markets are competitive; (*b*) a belief that employers act on the basis of their statistical or stereotyped perception of female labor behavior and productivity; (*c*) discrimination attributable to a stronger

[56] Ram (n. 1 above).

225

monopsonistic power of the employers caused by a lower supply elasticity of females; and (*d*) existence of a dual labor market in which females and other minorities have access to low-status secondary jobs (the market for which may be competitive) while the well paid, high-status primary job market, which is not competitive, is not accessible to females for reasons of statistical discrimination or otherwise.

Although the theoretical approaches mentioned above have been formulated largely in the context of developed countries, they do have relevance to low-income countries which constitute the focus of this study. However, the human capital (or the household-production) approach which appears promising may need some adaptation to take account of those features of the female labor markets in the developing world that differ from those in high-income countries.

Market-activity rates constitute a major dimension along which sex differences in educational outcomes may be analyzed. The theoretical position in this respect is not entirely clear in the context of discrimination theories. In the human capital view, however, male-female differences in the rates of market activity should generally diminish with increase in schooling. Empirically, the position is known (though with varying degrees of accuracy, precision, and detail) for a fairly large number of developing countries. The broad position seems to be that, like the male activity rates, female market-activity rates increase with schooling. However, besides a case of negative relationship, there are several countries where the direction of effect is ambiguous and quite a few others where the relationship is curvilinear, that is, an increase in schooling initially lowers the female market-activity rate, but at higher schooling levels the effect is positive. The evidence on age patterns in female market-activity rates is quite substantial. It seems that the bimodality in age-specific female LFPRs observed in the United States and other high-income countries is not as pervasive in the developing world. Evidence on the effect of schooling on age patterns in female market-activity rates is meager and mixed, although one may offer the guess that schooling perhaps attenuates the bimodality in female age-specific LFPRs wherever such bimodality exists. It should be useful to do a wider study on male-female differences in regard to the effect of schooling on participation rates by age and marital status, which should include as many developing countries as possible and should try to find patterns in these differences.

Another important dimension concerns male-female differences in wage rates, earnings, and earnings profiles for various education levels. The human capital theories suggest that the differences should become narrower for higher education levels, but the discrimination models do not generate any clear prediction. Empirically, while there are numerous works dealing with male-female earnings differentials, there are but a few studies relating these differences to schooling, and even these are mainly for high-income countries. For the developing world, the few available studies on rates of return to male and female education reveal a mixed picture; in some cases the rates of return are higher for males, while in others, higher for females. There would seem to be a handsome payoff, in terms of theoretical insights and empirical information, to studies of male-female earnings differentials by schooling level in the various developing countries. The Canadian study by Holmes should provide a useful framework for such studies elsewhere.

Male-female differences in occupational distribution constitute an extremely important aspect. There are many general studies of male-female occupational differences; but studies of such differences by schooling levels are only a few, although the differences in many cases are possibly as dramatic as in the Indian and the U.S. cases mentioned in this article. Paucity of studies on this aspect is somewhat puzzling because for many, perhaps most, countries the relevant data should be directly available from the population census records. Studies of male-female occupational differences in various countries for different education levels should be fruitful. These studies should, of course, try to find cross-national patterns and relate these patterns to the patterns in sex roles and other factors, like educational access and achievement.

In short, although there is clearly scope for adaptation of the available conceptual frameworks to special situations in the various developing countries, the major direction for future research seems to lie in the empirical domain. The areas that appear to offer the greatest promise are: sex differences in the effect of schooling on market-activity rates (including age patterns in these rates) and earnings profiles, male-female differences in the rates of return to education, and sex differences in occupational distributions by schooling levels.

13. Women, Schooling, and Work in Chile:
Evidence from a Longitudinal Study

ERNESTO SCHIEFELBEIN AND JOSEPH P. FARRELL

When considering the education of women in developing nations, Chile is an extremely interesting case. It enjoys, and has long enjoyed, relatively high levels of female participation in the educational system. Also, female participation in the labor force, especially in semiprofessional and professional positions, is very high compared with other societies. This article analyzes women's participation in the educational system and their entrance into the labor force. It draws upon data from an ongoing longitudinal study of Chilean young people and advances some tentative explanations for the unusual phenomenon which Chile represents, using both current and historical data.

Historical Antecedents

Chile has throughout its history been at the forefront of "liberal" social thought in Latin America and the translation of that thought into policy. It was the first Latin American nation to establish a system of public instruction (in 1842). Elementary education was declared to be free of cost in 1860. Chile established the first normal school in Latin America only 2 years after the first such institution appeared in the United States. Early in the present century Chile developed the first social security system in Latin America and, in 1920, enacted the first law for compulsory elementary education.

The Chilean historical experience is unique in Latin America in several respects which are salient to this article. Because it was a distant, isolated, and relatively poor part of the Spanish empire, metropolitan Spanish institutions and patterns of social thought were less firmly established in colonial Chile. Also, the indigenous population fiercely resisted European domination until late in the nineteenth century. Thus for more than 2 centuries men were regularly away from home, at war on the expanding frontier. Because of these two factors, sex-role divisions of labor emerged differently than in the rest of the continent. Women often assumed economic roles traditionally assigned to men, such as, depending on their class, laboring in the fields, managing farms, running commercial enterprises, and organizing households.[1]

[1] Agustín Venturino, *Sociología Chilena* (Barcelona: Editorial Cervantes, Colección Sócrates, 1929), pp. 20, 67. While Chilean historians often note the roles played by women, there is little in the literature which attempts specifically and systematically to account for their unusual degree of economic and educational activity. Thus our brief analysis must be regarded as tentative. Our under-

Reprinted from the *Comparative Education Review* 24, no. 2 (part 2)(June 1980): S160–79.

At the time of its struggle for independence (1810–23), the Chilean colonial aristocracy was less wealthy and less firmly entrenched than in Latin America generally.[2] The nascent state's provisional governments were willing to innovate in both politics and education in an attempt to build a new and democratic society.[3] As early as 1813 the provisional government enacted a statute calling for the establishment of locally supported schools for both boys and girls in all towns with more than 50 inhabitants.[4] During the long fight with Spain such a statute could only be an expression of intent, but soon after self-government was secured education for both sexes expanded. By 1853, 25 percent of all enrolled students were girls; by 1876 girls constituted 43 percent of the student population.[5] This trend was both ratified and stimulated by the Organic Law of Primary Education of 1860 which decreed that at least one primary school for each sex be established in all departments with more than 2,000 inhabitants, with the curriculum for both sexes being, in most respects, identical.

Secondary education for women grew more slowly, remaining almost entirely in private hands until the 1870s. However, in 1877 a milestone in the development of women's education was achieved, with a presidential decree granting them equal rights to secondary and higher education and access to the professions. Within 10 years the first women doctorates were awarded, in medicine.

The expansion of educational opportunities for women met with fierce conservative opposition, especially from the church, which believed that advanced schooling and entry to the professions would detract from women's natural roles as wives and mothers. Indeed, one official church journal predicted in the 1870s that state-controlled secondary schools for women would "be nothing more than mere brothels financed by the taxpayers."[6] Liberal Chilean intellectuals nonetheless continued to argue that women should receive the same education as men, and over time their views prevailed.[7]

That such views won out in Chile, while they lost, or gained ascendency much later, in many other Latin American societies, appears to be

---

standing has benefited greatly from consultations with two noted Chilean historians, Ricardo Donoso N. and Juan Gomez Millas.

[2] Federico Gil, *The Political System of Chile* (Boston: Houghton Mifflin, 1966), p. 38.

[3] K. Silvert and L. Reissman, *Education, Class and Nation: The Experiences of Chile and Venezuela* (New York: Elsevier, 1976), pp. 107, 109.

[4] Ricardo Anguita, *Leyes promulgadas en Chile hasta el 1° de Junio de 1912* (Santiago: Imprenta Barcelona, 1912), 1:36.

[5] N. Fisher, "Chile: The Evolution of an Educational System," (Ph.D. diss., University of Nottingham, 1974), p. 201.

[6] Cited in ibid., pp. 189–90.

[7] "Liberal," that is, for their time and place. Throughout this period Chile remained fundamentally an oligarchical society. The working classes were severely oppressed and did not gain an effective political voice until well into the present century.

traceable to Chile's unique political development. Partly as a consequence of the unusual colonial experience, a political accomodation was worked out early in the postindependence era between traditional Mediterranean corporatism, with its emphasis on fixed class orders, tutelary government, and clericalism; and the "new" social philosophies of the Protestant West (e.g., utilitarianism, libertarianism, positivism, social Darwinism) which had powerful adherents among Chilean intellectual leaders. Although the first strong postindependence government (starting in 1830 under Portales) was very conservative and corporatist, by the 1840s liberalism had strongly established itself, particularly in the field of education. This trend was reinforced by the early growth of a strong middle class, with a large admixture of non-Mediterranean Europeans. Politically, this class expressed itself in the Radical party, which was ideologically related to the French Radical Socialists and was strongly influenced by the anticlerical Masonic lodges. Middle-class Masonism became a powerful political force in Chile, again accommodated in the political system, and was influential in promoting female education. Available records suggest that a large share of women who entered university in the early epoch were the daughters of middle-class Radical Masons.

Because of peculiar historical factors, then, Chile has a long-established and persistent pattern of providing educational opportunities for women. In 1930, 49.4 percent of primary and 43 percent of secondary students were female; by 1970 women accounted for more than half of all secondary students.[8] The Chilean record is all the more impressive when taken against the rest of Latin America and when one considers that higher-level occupational opportunities are unusually available to women. The proportion of females in semiprofessional and higher-level occupations in Chile (32 percent) exceeds the rates in Australia (31 percent), Japan (28 percent), New Zealand (23 percent), Hungary (21 percent), Belgium (20 percent), the United States (20 percent), France (19 percent), the Netherlands (7 percent), and Iran (3 percent).[9]

Why and how the contemporary Chilean schools provide greater educational equality for women and articulation between education and higher-status employment than elsewhere is the focus of this article. We shall try to explain this phenomenon in terms of both the school system and the Chilean job market.

---

[8] For a detailed statistical account of female participation in the educational system from 1930 to the early 1970s, see Manuel Barrera, "La mujer en la estadística educacional y en la fuerza de trabajo Chileno" (Santiago: Programa Interdisciplinario de Investigaciones en Educación, PIIE Estudios, 1976).

[9] A. H. Passow et al., *The National Case Study: An Empirical Comparative Study of Twenty-One Educational Systems* (New York: Wiley, 1976), p. 182.

A Framework for Analyzing Educational Equality

In previous articles dealing with social class stratification in Chilean schools we have developed a multifaceted conception of educational equality by class,[10] which can usefully be applied to the analysis of educational equality by gender. Four types of equality can be distinguished: (1) equality of access —the probabilities of children of different sexes getting into the school system; (2) equality of survival —the probabilities of children of different sexes staying in the system to some defined level, usually the end of a complete cycle (primary, secondary, higher); (3) equality of output —the probabilities that children of different sexes will learn the same things to the same level at a defined point in the school system; and (4) equality of outcome —the probabilities that children of different sexes will live relatively similar lives subsequent to and as a result of schooling (have equal incomes, have jobs of roughly the same status, etc.).

The first three types of equality refer to the flow through the school system itself. They represent mechanisms by which the formal educational system screens children, and they operate at each level or cycle of a school system. The fourth type refers to the junction between the school system and adult life —in the present case, the labor market. The analyses presented below will follow the chronology of this framework, tracing the destiny of boys and girls as they pass through the Chilean schools. First, however, it will be useful to describe briefly the study from which the data derive.

The Study

The data to be considered here are taken from an ongoing longitudinal study of a cohort of Chilean young people. The investigation began in 1970, when the subjects were in grade 8, the last year of primary school. Its original objective, as part of an effort to evaluate the effects of a massive reform of the educational system implemented between 1965 and 1970, was to identify the factors which most influenced performance on a national achievement test administered to all students at the end of primary education. To that end, questionnaires were administered to a random sample of 10 students in each of 353 eighth-grade classrooms throughout the nation, to their teachers, and to the directors of their schools. Codable data were received from 3,469 students, 2,340 teachers, and 353 school directors. Combining the questionnaire responses with the test results and other information routinely collected by the ministry

[10] E. Schiefelbein and J. P. Farrell, "Selectivity and Survival in the Schools of Chile," *Comparative Education Review* 22 (June 1978): 326–41, and "Social and Pedagogical Factors Influencing Survival in the Schools of Chile," *Canadian and International Education* 7 (June 1978): 59–87.

of education produced, for each subject, more than 500 separate measures of characteristics of the students themselves, their classmates, their teachers, their schools, their families, and their communities. These data form the baseline for the study.

These students completed primary schooling in December 1970, and those who continued in the educational system (in Chile almost all primary graduates enter secondary schooling) began secondary education in March of the following year. Near the end of the 1971 school year a follow-up study was undertaken, attempting to identify the type of secondary school in which the students had enrolled and their academic success during the first postprimary year.

Those students who stayed in school and did not repeat a grade were in the last year of secondary in 1974. In that year an additional follow-up was undertaken. Using the records of the university admissions systems it was possible to locate effectively all of the original cohort who were in the fourth year of secondary education. Questionnaires were again administered to students, their teachers, and school directors. Of the original group, 1,369 were in the last year of secondary. Of these, 986 returned usable questionnaires, as did 684 teachers and 252 school directors.

Finally, in 1977 another (and to this point in time, the latest) attempt was made to contact the original subjects. Because most of them were out of school by 1977 and were in a variety of life circumstances —working, unemployed but searching for work, undertaking nonformal education, housewives raising families, etc. —the process of locating individuals was extremely complex, involving teams of researchers working throughout the nation during a 10-month period. Eventually 1,205 were located and provided usable data on a complex questionnaire which included information on current family socioeconomic status and living conditions, a year-by-year (1971–76) history of all formal and nonformal educational experiences, and a complete history of all employment since 1970, focusing on characteristics of each job, job search behavior, and reasons for and the process of job change. Comparisons of the group located in 1977 with the full 1970 cohort indicate no significant sampling biases.

Sexual Equality within the Educational System

Given the data regarding female participation in Chilean education presented earlier, one would expect that sex is not a powerful determinant of a child's educational destiny in Chile. This is generally the case. However, a particular advantage of using the equality framework discussed above with longitudinal data is that it permits us to identify precisely where in the educational system sex does begin to "make a difference" and thus to provide more cogent explanations of the behavior of

232

women in the school system (and the behavior of the system toward women) than would otherwise be possible.

Equality of Survival at the Primary Level

Although almost all Chilean children enter primary school (thus there is no major problem of equality of access), only about 50 percent of an entering cohort will complete 8 years of primary schooling.[11] Our concern here is whether girls are more or less likely than boys to be among those survivors to a complete primary education. Since this study started with students in grade 8, we cannot directly calculate survival ratios by sex. However, it is possible to estimate retroactively the composition of the grade-1 cohort from which the eighth-grade students in our sample started. Since we know that 50 percent of a grade-1 group completed grade 8, we assume the original group to have been twice the size of the eighth-grade sample and to have consisted of equal numbers of boys and girls. In order to specify the analysis by social status, we assume that the grade-1 students were distributed by father's education, as were the adult males in the work force in 1960 (the census year nearest to when these students started school). We can then estimate the number of children in the grade-1 cohort by sex and social status and compare that number with the number found in the eighth-grade sample.

Overall, a higher proportion of girls than boys complete primary schooling in Chile (53.3 percent vs. 46.6 percent). When the figures are specified by social status, however, we find that the sex differences are smaller among children whose fathers have high levels of education — secondary or more (87.4 percent vs. 84.4 percent) —and greater among those whose fathers have low levels of education (40.4 percent vs. 32.3 percent). This pattern may suggest that the forgone earnings for boys of upper-primary age, when most drop out, are higher than those for girls, and thus lower-status families are more likely to withdraw boys from school. Whatever the explanation, it is clear that there is no discrimination against girls at this level of the system, for either high- or low-status children.

Equality of Output at the Primary Level

Even though girls are more likely than boys to complete primary schooling, it is possible that they learn less. On the national achievement test administered at the end of primary schooling (a 100-item test divided equally between a verbal and a mathematics section), boys scored about two points higher on average than did girls. However, in regression analysis on test scores, sex is not a significant predictor. It did not survive preliminary screening to identify the 12 best predictors to include in a

---

[11] See Schiefelbein and Farrell, "Selectivity and Survival in the Schools of Chile," p. 339.

final regression equation.[12] Specifying the analysis by social status produces no important changes in this pattern. We conclude, then, that sex has no significant independent effect on achievement at the end of primary schooling.

Equality of Access at the Secondary Level

Since almost all Chilean students who complete primary schooling continue on to some form of secondary education (95 percent of this sample did so), the salient equality question at this level is related to the type of secondary school entered: the prestigious, academically oriented, and university preparatory *liceos* or one of the technical/vocational schools which are available (e.g., commercial, industrial, agricultural). Girls are substantially more likely than boys to enter *liceos* rather than vocational schools. Indeed, in a multiple discriminant analysis on type of school in 1971, sex is the second strongest of 17 predictors, its strength being surpassed only by an index of social status.[13] Sex is a more powerful predictor among lower- than among higher-status children (indeed, among higher-status youngsters there is little difference between the percentage of boys and girls who enroll in *liceos*). Several factors are likely to be at play here. First, lower-status boys tend to enroll in vocational schools which are supposed to prepare them for middle-level technician jobs that are regarded as appropriate for males and inappropriate for females. Second, some higher-status girls attend commercial schools to prepare themselves to work as secretaries. Lower-status girls who have been successful in their primary schooling recognize that they must attend *liceos* in order to have a chance to enter university to prepare themselves for nursing, teaching, and similar sex-appropriate occupations which are in Chile, as in many societies, often the first step into the white-collar middle class. Again, whatever the full explanation, the educational system does not relegate girls to the less desirable types of schools.

Equality of Survival at the Secondary Level

The percentages completing secondary school have been directly calculated from the sample data. The same proportion of girls as boys completed on time, without repeating a grade (34.5 percent of girls and 34.9 percent of boys). Even with delayed completions taken into account, the equality holds. In discriminant analyses comparing (1) those who completed on time with those who did not and (2) those who eventually completed with those who dropped out without completing, sex is not a significant predictor. Specification by social status does not notably alter these patterns.

[12] E. Schiefelbein and J. P. Farrell, "Expanding the Scope of Educational Planning: The Experience of Chile," *Interchange* 5, no. 2 (1974): 18–29, esp. p. 22.

[13] E. Schiefelbein and J. P. Farrell, "Resultados de un estudio de seguimiento" (paper presented at the annual National Educational Research Meeting, Lo Barnechea, Chile, 1973).

Equality of Output at the Secondary Level and Equality of Access to University

These two aspects of equality should be considered together, since the prime determinant of acceptance to university in Chile is a student's score on an achievement test administered at the end of secondary schooling. Actually, university admission involves several steps. First, students in the last year of secondary decide whether to sit for the admission test. Those who take the test submit a rank-ordered list of faculties and universities in which they wish to enroll. Using the test scores, the university faculties select the best-qualified applicants for admission until they have filled their quota for new entrants, and the students then decide whether they wish to (and are financially able to) enroll in the faculty for which they have been selected.

Sex is not an important determinant of the decision to take the admission test. Indeed, it is the least powerful of 24 predictors in a discriminant analysis between those eligible students who did and did not take the test. However, there are significant differences in the actual test scores of boys and girls. In the 1974 application of the test, 18-year-old males had an average score of 563.0, compared with 453.7 among females. There was a similar, but slightly smaller, difference among 17-year-old applicants (550.4 for males and 467.8 for females). In a regression analysis on the test scores for all subjects who took the test in whatever year, sex is a significant predictor, the sixth strongest of 19 variables. This, then, is the first point at which we find a noticeable *negative* educational result among females in the Chilean system.

This does not translate, however, into a serious disadvantage for women in terms of university entrance. Although women are slightly less likely than men to enter university, sex is only the fourteenth strongest among 21 predictor variables in a discriminant analysis comparing those who did and did not enter university (among those who were eligible to do so).

We have here an interesting pattern. Women are as likely as men to complete secondary schooling and are as likely as men to sit for the university admission test. Sex is not a powerful independent predictor of actual university entrance. However, women score significantly lower than men on the university admission test itself.

One explanation could be that women are provided with an inferior education during secondary school (remembering that sex had little effect on achievement test scores at the end of primary schooling). However, a higher proportion of females attend the academically oriented *liceos*. There is evidence also that girls in all-female schools achieve higher test scores than do those in coeducational schools. There is no difference between sexes in educational "quality" variables such as class size and textbook availability during secondary school, which are themselves important predictors of university admission test scores (the first and third most powerful predictors in regression analysis).[14] Moreover, when asked to estimate their own academic ability (relative to classmates) and to indicate to what extent they enjoyed various academic subjects, the responses of men and women are alike. This evidence does not suggest that women are provided with a systematically inferior quality of education at the secondary level.

A more plausible explanation for the lower average test scores among women relates to anticipatory socialization, to a perceived low need to achieve high test scores in order to be admitted to those university programs in which most women enroll. The number in our sample who have entered university is too small to permit detailed analysis by program of study. However, other data are available showing the male-female enrollment by field of university study in Chile and the lowest test score which permitted admission to various fields of study. The fields of study for which both kinds of data are available are displayed in table 1. There is a clear tendency for lower admission standards to be associated with those fields which enroll the most women. Almost two-thirds (62.6 percent) of all female students are in education and nursing, which have the lowest minimal admission scores. Although men are not so highly concentrated in a few fields, the two areas (after education) which enroll the most men, engineering and economics and finance (these are also among the three areas with the smallest percentage of female enrollment), have the second and fourth highest cutoff points. We suggest that it may well be the case that women achieve average lower scores on the university admission test because they know that they do not have to score as high to get into the faculties which traditionally enroll most of the females.[15]

This suggests that for no type or stage of education considered above is there systematic discrimination against women within the Chilean educational system. At the one point where women appear to be at a disadvantage (equality of output at the secondary level), their lower scores

---

[14] E. Schiefelbein and J. P. Farrell, *Determinantes de la supervivencia escolar y el ingreso al mercado* (Santiago: Centro de Investigaciones y Desarrollo de la Educacion, 1979), p. 81.

[15] The "cutoff point" in admission test scores is not predetermined and will vary from year to year depending on the number of postulants to various faculties, their test scores, and the number of available places for new entrants in each faculty. However, the relative ranking of various faculties in terms of lowest score admitted remains quite constant over time, and this information is widely known among prospective university entrants. An alternative explanation of the lower scores could be that women, anticipating that they will score less well, apply predominantly to those faculties known to have lower admission standards. While this kind of adjustment of aspirations almost certainly occurs *within* each sex (e.g., neither men nor women who expect to do poorly on the test are likely to apply to a faculty of medicine), two pieces of evidence counter this as an explanation of *between-sex* differences. First, as noted above, women secondary students do not perceive themselves to be less academically capable than do men. Second, professions such as nursing and teaching (especially preschool and primary teaching) have long been predominantly female occupations, since well before the implementation of the current university admission system (indeed, since well before university studies were required to enter these occupations).

TABLE 1

FEMALE ENROLLMENT AND MINIMUM ADMISSION SCORES BY UNIVERSITY FIELD OF STUDY

Field of Study (in Order of % Female)	Female Enrollment (%)*	% of All Enrolled		Lowest Test Score Admitted†
		Males	Females*	
Engineering	6.3	18.3	2.0	616
Agronomy and				560
Veterinary medicine	14.6	5.0	1.4	589
Economics and finance	19.2	11.5	4.4	647
Natural science (except chemistry)	22.8	.9	.4	655 (biochemistry)
				611 (biology)
Law	25.2	4.8	2.6	533
Medicine	27.1	4.4	2.6	713.5
Architecture	30.1	3.0	2.0	557
Chemistry	37.8	.8	.7	557
Dentistry	43.4	1.2	1.5	638
Pharmacy	45.6	.7	.9	599
Education	60.9	19.8	49.3	501 (pedagogy)
				501 (preschool)
				477 (primary)
Social sciences (except economics)	67.6	3.1	10.1	573 (political science)
				568 (anthropology)
				538 (sociology)
Nursing	90.2	1.0	13.3	502

* *América en cifras, 1974: Situación social* (Washington, D.C.: Organization of American States, 1975), table 501-77; data refer to 1970.

† E. Schiefelbein, "Selectividad del sistema universitario," in *Universidad contemporanea: Un intento de análisis empirico*, ed. E. Schiefelbein and N. McGinn (Santiago: Ediciones CPU, 1974), p. 261; data refer to 1972.

reflect perceptions of the performance levels required to enter those professions traditionally defined as socially acceptable occupations for well-educated females in Chilean society. We see, then, that the critical differences between men and women relate to what we have called equality of outcome and operate at the juncture between the formal schooling system and the labor market.

We have explained the differential behavior of women and men within the educational system in terms of anticipated occupational roles. We now turn to an examination of differential labor market entry patterns among those men and women who, by 1977, had left schooling and sought employment.

Equality of Outcomes: Labor Market Entry

When the 1977 follow-up was being designed, it was assumed that most students who had not completed secondary schooling on time, in 1974, had either already left school or, because of grade repetition, would soon do so. However, these young people stayed in school generally much longer than had been expected. Consequently, fewer had taken up occupations than anticipated, and those with jobs had been working for a relatively short time. Two consequent limitations on the analyses reported below should be noted. First, certain complex multivariable cross-tabular analyses which had been planned could not be carried out due to small-cell-size problems. Second, we have been unable to consider systematically patterns of job change and within-career mobility. Rather, we have had to concentrate on labor market entry, considering only the first job obtained.[16]

A few features of the Chilean labor market during the time when these young people began to search for jobs, which are necessary to interpret the data presented below, should also be noted. First, the Chilean economy is primarily industrial and urban based. In the 1960 census only about one-third of all economically active males were reported employed as agricultural laborers, a figure which had dropped to one-quarter by the early 1970s.[17] Second, throughout the 1970s Chile has experienced severe economic difficulties. Those of our sample who left school early, before 1974, entered the labor market at a time of great economic (as well as political and social) turmoil. The public sector expanded very rapidly owing to extensive nationalizations, the remaining private sector stagnated, work stoppages were endemic, a vast black market flourished, and inflation reached record annual rates of near 1,000 percent. Whatever one may argue regarding the causes of those conditions, one consequence was a chaotic employment market. Those who left school thereafter came into the employment market at a time when the "shock treatment" economic policies of the military government which had overthrown the Allende regime were producing a severe economic depression, one of whose results was very high unemployment rates, especially among young people.[18]

In analyzing the linkage between schooling and work among Chilean women we wish to advance the following argument. We have already noted that female participation rates in higher-level occupations (semi-professional and above) in Chile are quite high. Chilean women have a much greater probability than women in most societies of acquiring relatively prestigious jobs. Such jobs, however, especially those which are traditionally socially defined as appropriate for females (e.g., secretarial work, teaching, nursing, government service), typically require at least a complete secondary education and in many cases a university degree.

[16] This may not be a serious limitation. A recent study suggests that mobility within careers in Chile is rather limited (esp. between the broad occupational categories used here). Thus the first job may be a fairly good indicator of the level of occupation an individual will have throughout his or her life (see D. Raczynski, "Opportunidades occupacionales: Origen socioeconomico versus educación en Chile," *Revista Latinoamericana de sociología 1* [1974]: 66–93).

[17] K. Steenland, "Rural Strategy under Allende," *Latin American Perspectives* 1 (1974): 121–33, esp. p. 129.

[18] A. Acevedo, E. Marshall, and M. Silva, *La capacitación de los jovenes marginados en relación con la pequeña y mediana empresa* (Montevideo: CINTERFOR, 1977), p. 17.

Employed women earn less than men with the same level of education,[19] and it is somewhat more difficult for women than for men to acquire the same type of job, especially in tight economic circumstances. Yet it has been demonstrated that the private rate of return to university education (in two regions of the nation where the calculations were made) is higher among women than among men (principally because the forgone earnings of women are less than those of men.)[20] Moreover, for the same type of job, female applicants tend to need higher levels of education than do men in order to be employed.[21] These factors together motivate Chilean young women who have any chance to do so to stay in school as long as possible.

The interplay between education and labor market entrance can be seen clearly in the data presented below. We will focus attention on two aspects of the labor market entrance of women: (1) differences between those who have and have not found employment and (2) predictors of the level of the first job obtained.

Finding a Job

Here we will be attempting to identify those factors which best predict whether a woman, once having left school, will locate a job. An important conceptual limitation should be noted. When considering males, we assume that those who have left school but are not working are actively seeking employment —they are "unemployed" in the standard sense of the term. We cannot make the same assumption for women, since it is socially appropriate for females to be neither studying nor working. The available data do not permit us to distinguish clearly between those without jobs who are actively seeking work and those who have never done so. With this limitation in mind, the results of a discriminant analysis[22] comparing those out-of-school women who have found a job and those who have never worked are presented in table 2.

The first thing to be observed in table 2 is that the most important discriminators between women with and without jobs relate to the quality of education received: average test score of the eighth-grade class at-

[19] E.g., among employed persons in Santiago with 7–12 years of education, the average salary of females is 57.8 percent that of males (E. Schiefelbein, "Educación y empleo en diez ciudades de América Latina," *Revista del centro de estudios educativos* 8, no. 3 [1978]: 112).

[20] E. Schiefelbein, J. Rodriguez, and J. Morales, "Rentabilidad privada y social de le educación superior en la I y II region del país," *Estudios sociales* 14, no. 1 (1977): 59.

[21] Schiefelbein.

[22] Discriminant analysis can be thought of as an analog of regression analysis for use when the dependent variable is not continuous but is categorical —in this case, dichotomous. The objective is not to predict an individual's score on the dependent variable but to predict the category in which the individual will fall. The discriminant weights associated with each predictor variable indicate the relative power of that variable, independent of the effect of other variables, to accurately predict the category for an individual subject. The overall accuracy of the total "discriminant function" is determined by the calculation of the percentage of cases correctly classified. To give an indication of the direction of effect of each predictor the average scores among the two groups are also noted for each variable.

TABLE 2

DISCRIMINANT ANALYSIS COMPARING OUT-OF-SCHOOL WOMEN WHO HAVE WORKED AND WHO HAVE NEVER WORKED

Variables (in Order of Discriminant Weights)	Discriminant Weights	Averages	
		Never Worked	Worked
Average test score eighth-grade class	.77	51.87	54.85
Textbook availability secondary level	.67	1.72	1.77
Personal estimate of academic success	.49	1.87	2.05
Pedagogical excellence eighth-grade school	.46	.35	.37
Lives with spouse	.44	1.37	1.18
Verbal part score eighth-grade class SD	.35	6.66	6.71
Textbook availability eight-grade class	.29	−.14	−.06
Urbanism of province where currently lives	.26	2.03	2.19
Average class size secondary	.25	28.77	28.23
Education of father	.25	3.23	3.43
Eighth-grade test score individual	.25	49.35	52.15
School type 1971	.20	2.42	2.55
Average liking for academic subjects	.20	2.96	3.25
Direct stimulation by parents	.14	2.09	2.13
Eighth-grade class SES SD	.13	.56	.55
Last school year entered or completed	.11	2.98	3.41
Personal estimate of academic ability	.11	2.35	2.47
Preservice training eighth-grade teachers	.03	3.13	3.27

NOTE.—Significance = .015, N never worked = 131, N worked = 74, percentage correctly classified = 68.3%.

tended, secondary level textbook availability; the subject's personal estimate of her own academic success, pedagogical excellence of the eighth-grade school. On the other hand, length of schooling is not a powerful independent predictor, although those with jobs do have more schooling. Similarly, socioeconomic status is a weak predictor, although those who have found employment score slightly higher. Of particular note is the fact that for all of the important education-related predictors, those women who have found work score more positively than those who have never worked. (Among men the result is quite different—those who have found work score higher on some predictors and lower on others, in a pattern which is difficult to interpret.) This is consistent with the argument advanced above, suggesting that women who have received a "better" education are more likely to seek jobs and find them.

Two other pieces of evidence are consistent with our argument. The fifth strongest predictor (and the first noneducational variable) is "lives with spouse." Women who are married less often take a job (the converse is true among men). This is in spite of the fact that 52.9 percent of female respondents stated that they wanted "by all means" to work after they married, and another 31 percent claimed that they would very much like to work after marriage. We may be observing here the intervening effect of social status. Lower-status women tend to leave school earlier and to get married sooner than their higher-status peers. At the age of these subjects, out-of-school married women would be predominantly from the lower social strata with relatively low levels of education. They would thus be less likely to qualify for female-appropriate occupational roles and would be inclined to seek employment only out of economic necessity. The next most powerful noneducational predictor is "urbanism of the province where currently lives." Women in the more urbanized provinces are more likely to have found employment. It is in the urban areas where one is most likely to find the kinds of jobs defined as most acceptable for females. Indeed, in the capital city of Santiago, with its high concentration of head offices of private-sector firms and of major public-sector enterprises (the national government, the major universities, the largest medical centers, many international agency offices, etc.), 51.3 percent of the out-of-school women in our sample had found employment, compared with 36.7 percent in the rest of the nation.

Determinants of First-Job Level

Because of the relatively small number of subjects who left school and found employment, analyses related to the type of job acquired have had to involve broad occupational categories and use restricted sets of predictor variables. We should first note a distinct difference in the kinds of first jobs acquired by men and women. Almost two-thirds of the employed women in this sample have jobs as office workers or sales personnel, compared with 39.4 percent of men. More than half of the males are employed in some form of manual labor, compared with less than one-third of the females. This last figure also indicates, of course, that, in spite of the social definition of appropriate female roles, a significant proportion of women do end up with manual occupations.

A woman's schooling has a powerful effect on her probability of acquiring an "appropriate" job. To demonstrate this, table 3 relates duration of studies to job type, dividing the sample into those who left school in 1973 or earlier (and thus could not have completed secondary schooling) and those who left in 1974 or thereafter. In order to attain acceptable levels of statistical significance, occupations have been grouped into two categories: manual and nonmanual. For each sex there is a clear relationship between duration of schooling and level of first job. The relationship is stronger among women than men (γ = .36 vs. .26). Indeed, one can note that among women who left school in the earlier period, 60 percent had manual jobs, a figure which is only 9.4 percent lower than that for men who left school in the same time period and higher than the overall figure for men (55 percent). That is, a woman who drops out early in secondary has about as great a probability of becoming a manual worker as does a man who drops out early and a greater probability than male primary graduates overall.

241

TABLE 3

LEVEL OF FIRST JOB BY YEAR LEFT SCHOOL AND SEX

	Level of First Job							
	Males*				Females**			
	Nonmanual		Manual		Nonmanual		Manual	
Year Left School	N	%	N	%	N	%	N	%
1973 or before	11	30.6	25	69.4	14	40.0	21	60.0
1974 or later	60	49.6	61	50.4	108	73.5	39	26.5

* $P > .05$.
** $P > .001$.

The same pattern can be observed when job type is related to level of schooling eventually attained, categorized as incomplete secondary, complete secondary, or incomplete university. (Since this analysis considers only those who had definitively left school at the time of the contact with them, in 1977, none of the sample would have completed university and entered the labor market with their degree.) For each sex the probability of acquiring a nonmanual first job is considerably higher among those who have completed secondary education than among those who entered the labor market with an incomplete secondary education. For neither sex does an incomplete university education provide an advantage over having a complete secondary education. Here, too, we find that the percentage of women with incomplete secondary education who have acquired manual jobs (54.2 percent) is almost identical to the percentage of all males with such low-level occupations (54.4 percent). Both measures of educational attainment show the importance for women of acquiring at least a complete secondary education if they are to achieve white collar, nonmanual occupational status.

As one would expect, parental status also affects the level of the first job obtained (γ relating job level to father's education = .51 for females and .42 for males). To control for the effect of socioeconomic status on educational attainment, both variables have been entered into a regression analysis on first-job level. In order to compare the results with classical models of the occupational attainment process,[23] level of occupational aspirations has also been entered into the equation. The results for men and women are found in table 4. In addition to standardized regression weights, the results of commonality analyses, which correct for problems

[23] See, e.g., W. H. Sewell and R. M. Hauser, *Education, Occupation and Earnings: Achievement in the Early Career* (New York: Academic Press, 1975). Mental ability, which is often included in models of the occupational attainment process, cannot be used here, as we have no independent measure of intelligence. Regression equations including larger numbers of variables were also run, but they produced nonsignificant weights for many predictors.

TABLE 4

REGRESSION, WITH COMMONALITY ANALYSIS, ON LEVEL OF FIRST OCCUPATION: MALES AND FEMALES

	Males		Females	
	% of Total Variance (Total R^2 = .160)	% of Explained Variance	% of Total Variance (Total R^2 = .152)	% of Explained Variance
	Commonality Analysis			
Unique effects:				
Occupational aspirations (A)	.049	30.6	.006	3.9
Education of father (B)	.012	7.5	.034	22.4
Last school year entered or completed (C)	.021	13.1	.044	28.9
Joint effects:				
AB	.006	3.8	0	...
AC	.033	20.6	.009	5.9
BC	.013	8.1	.051	33.6
ABC	.026	16.2	.008	5.3
	Variable Weights in Regression Equation (β)			
Occupational aspirations	.243**		.082	
Last school year entered or completed	.164**		.235**	
Education of father	.115**		.202*	

* $P > .05$.
** $P > .01$; total equations $P > .01$.

of multicollinearity (intercorrelations among predictor variables, which can confound interpretation of regression results), are also reported.[24]

For neither sex is the percentage of variance in occupational levels explained by the equation large ($R^2 = .16$ for males and .152 for females).[25] Nonetheless, the contrasts between males and females are quite sharp. While for each sex length of schooling is more important than father's education, both variables are more important among women. Conversely, occupational aspirations are the most powerful predictor for men and the least powerful for women.

Part of this difference between sexes may be accounted for by the interaction between aspirations and length of schooling. Among women the effect of this interaction (joint effect AC in the commonality analysis, table 4) is small, but among men it is quite strong (20.6 percent of explained variance). It may be that for men schooling operates not only directly but indirectly by increasing their occupational aspirations, while

[24] For these analyses the occupational codings have been regrouped into five ordered categories: (1) agricultural laborers; (2) other workers, transportation workers, and personal service workers; (3) artisans and skilled tradespeople; (4) office workers and sales personnel; and (5) professionals, technicians, managers, and administrators.
[25] This is not surprising. The nature of the study to date has eliminated the extreme values on both occupational attainment and the major predictor variables.

243

for women it does not have this indirect effect. A corollary to this is that women's occupational aspirations vary less than do those of men; for example, 66 percent of women and only 41 percent of men aspire to nonmanual occupations. Indeed, we have been arguing that it is this predominantly high level of occupational aspirations among women which compels them to stay in school as long as possible. Another part of the difference between men and women reflects the interaction between length of schooling and father's education. This interaction (joint effect BC in commonality analysis, table 4) is weak among men but very strong among women. That is, for women, both of these variables have strong unique effects on first-job level, with educational attainment a slightly more powerful predictor, while the effect of the interaction between them is even stronger. Put another way, more than two-thirds (68.4 percent) of the explained variance for women is accounted for by the direct or indirect influence of educational attainment (unique effect C plus joint effect AC and BC). The comparable figure for men is much lower (41.8 percent).

All of these data, then, are consistent with the argument we have developed above that the labor market for women in Chile is much more socially predetermined than for men, with a woman's acquisition of a "socially acceptable" higher-level job being heavily dependent on her completion of a relatively high level of schooling.

Conclusion

As we noted at the outset, with respect to the education of women Chile is a highly unusual case. There is no evidence of systematic discrimination against women within the educational system. Women in Chile have more access to high-level occupations than do women in most other societies, and schooling is a more powerful determinant of that access among women than it is among men. We have argued that the latter phenomenon strongly influences the behavior of women in the Chilean educational system. Because these findings derive from a complex longitudinal study, they have more analytical detail and explanatory power than they would have if we were dealing with cross-sectional data. However, what this study highlights most strongly is the need to develop a much fuller explanation of the educational and occupational situation of Chilean women than has been possible within the scope of this paper. The Chilean situation is so striking in a comparative context that it begs for further research. A few potentially promising lines of enquiry may be noted.

1. Sex-role stereotyping in curricular materials and differential teacher attitudes toward and expectations of boys and girls are frequently

mentioned in the literature on women's education. It may be that these phenomena are less present in Chilean schools than in other societies. Some careful examinations of didactic material and observational studies of classroom behavior are warranted.

2. Part of the explanation of the degree of access which Chilean women have to high-level occupations (with its attendant effect on educational participation) may lie in the nature of the Chilean economy itself. We have already noted that the economy is highly urbanized, although many societies which are even more urbanized and industrialized have poorer records of female occupational participation. However, within this generally urbanized economy, the fact that basic social services such as education and health, which attract large proportions of female employees, are more widespread than in most nations at a comparable level of development may account for some of the female employment. In a similar vein, the Chilean civil service generally is very large in relation to total population and attracts many female professionals. Detailed studies of the nature of the female employment market in Chile, in comparison with other societies, would be very useful.[26]

3. In the opening section of this article we advanced a brief historical explanation of the development of high levels of educational and occupational participation among women in Chile. That treatment is not only brief but must be regarded as very tentative, as little work has been done regarding the educational, and especially the occupational, history of women in Chile. Our hunch is that this may be the most promising line of investigation.

Whatever may be the eventual explanation of the special Chilean case, we suggest that further studies of the status of women in that nation may be one of the best ways to advance significantly our understanding of the education and employment of females not only in developing nations but in developed societies as well.

Appendix

A number of variables are used as predictors in the analyses reported in this paper. These are listed below. In cases where the nature of the variable is not self-evident, or where necessary explanation is not provided in the text, explanatory notes are provided.

[26] Some work has already been done in this area, but much more is needed. See, e.g., Programa Regional de Empleo para America Latina y el Caribe (PREALC), "Participación laboral feminina y diferencias de remuneración según sexo en América Latina" (Santiago: Organización Internacional de Trabajo/PREALC, 1978); M. Teresita de Barbiere, "Acceso de la mujer a las carreras y ocupaciones tecnológicas de nivel medio" (Santiago: Facultad Latino-Americano de Ciencias Sociales, 1972); "La Mujer Chilena en la fuerza de trabajo: Participación, empleo y desempleo (1957–1977)" (Santiago: Universidad de Chile, Facultad de Ciencias Económicas y Administrativas, 1979).

Characteristics of the Individual Student

1. Sex.

2. Eighth-grade test score: These are the scores for each student on the national eighth-grade test, which was taken by this cohort of students in 1970. The test consisted of two parts (50 questions each) assessing verbal and mathematical achievement.

3. Liking for academic subjects: All students were asked to indicate on a four-point scale how well they liked each academic subject in the curriculum. The score represents the arithmetic mean for the subjects taken at the secondary level.

4. Personal estimate of academic success: For each year in secondary school students were asked to estimate whether their grades were higher than, lower than, or around the average of the grades of all students in their class. The score represents the arithmetic mean of the responses for each year in which a student studied.

5. Personal estimate of academic ability: Students were asked to assess on a three-point scale their own academic ability relative to that of their classmates in secondary school.

6. Textbook availability at the secondary level: All students were asked whether they had a textbook for personal use, and whether the professor had required a text, in each academic subject they studied in each year in which they were in school. In cases where the professor asked for a text, they were coded 2 if they had a text, 1 if not. The scores are the arithmetic mean of the responses for all subjects and years studied.

7. Education of the student's father.

8. Direct stimulation by parents: Students were asked a series of questions regarding the interest and help received from their parents in schoolwork. The responses were combined, using weights derived from factor analyses, to form a single score.

9. Occupational aspirations: Subjects were asked what types of occupation they desired to have in 1983. The responses were coded into the same categories used for regression analysis on current occupations (see text).

10. Lives with spouse: Those living with a spouse were coded 2, others 1.

11. Last school year entered or completed: Coding ranges from 1 = completed eighth grade to 6 = entered university.

School and Teacher Characteristics

1. Pedagogical excellence of the eighth-grade school: This is a complex variable derived from factor analysis. It includes measures of such teaching-learning facilities and characteristics as laboratories, workshops, library, and various kinds of specialized teaching personnel. Scores are scaled to have a mean of 0 and a range of − 1.0 to 1.0

2. Textbook availability in the eighth-grade class: Responses to a series of questions regarding textbook availability by subject at the eighth-grade level were weighted and averaged using a scaling program (with scores scaled to have a mean of 0 and a range of − 1.0 to 1.0) which produced a single score for each student. These scale scores were then averaged over all students in a class to produce an index of general textbook availability.

3. Average class size at the secondary level.

4. School type 1971: Coded as: *liceo* = 3, commercial = 2, other = 1.

5. Level of preservice training of eighth-grade teachers: Eighth-grade teachers were asked to indicate the level of their preservice training on a five-point scale, ranging from incomplete normal school to a university degree in pedagogy. These scores were then averaged for all of a student's teachers.

Characteristics of the Eighth-Grade Class

In order to assess the "peer group" effect on educational behavior, the average and standard deviation of the scores of all students in each eighth-grade class for whom we had data were calculated, for a number of individual student characteristics. The average or standard deviation was assigned as a class score. The following are used in this article:

1. Total eighth-grade test score, average.

2. Verbal part score on the eighth-grade test, standard deviation.

3. Socioeconomic status of the student's family, standard deviation: At the individual student level this is a complex variable derived from factor analysis. Component variables include education of the student's father and mother, a family consumption scale, and an index of father's occupational prestige.

Community Characteristics

1. Urbanism of the province where currently lives: The province in which a subject lived in 1977 was recorded. Provinces were scored according to the percentage of their population living in urban areas.

14. Women, Work and Science in India

MAITHREYI KRISHNA RAJ

In a developing country the obvious inequality of women vis-a-vis men in society must be subsumed under the more pervasive inequality between various sections of the people. What sense does equality have if the content of that equality means only equal privation, deprivation, subjugation, and general misery for both men and women? Therefore our first question must be, "How many are better than before?" and the second "Among these sections have women equal advantages compared to men?" One must also ask the reverse question, "How many are worse off than before, and among them are women more disadvantaged?" Both situations apply to India. General inequality is not unique to developing countries but its magnitude there is distinctive. This means that any study attempting to evaluate the position of women will face difficulties of definition and measurement. Not only will one have to bear in mind the reference group but also changes over time within that group. Where massive social changes are taking place and the influences at work are diverse and complex, there are many anomalies and contradictions that cannot be easily resolved. The tentative findings of a field study of employed, scientifically educated women presented here may be disappointing in their lack of a clear-cut answer to the equality issue, but they will provide clues to qualitative changes over time for the group.

Education is widely assumed to be a fundamental prerequisite for participation in the advanced sectors of society. Higher skills, greater information, and knowledge are essential for administration, improvement in productivity, and citizenship in a modern democracy. Great hopes have been pinned on education to bring about social change toward modernization. Education not only enables an individual to adjust to changes already taking place but it is itself the means whereby he/she can accelerate such changes. Third World countries hold as an axiom that education will result in changes in values and attitudes conducive to development. After three decades of development, however, it is not clear how such changes take place or fail to take place. How education and employment in science has affected the lives and status of women in service may provide insight into this general question.

This study was undertaken in Bombay in 1976–78, under a grant from the Council of Scientific and Industrial Research, India's largest scientific establishment in charge of directing, guiding, and undertaking

249

development of science and technology.[1] Though confined to Bombay, the study has a broader significance, for several reasons. Most of the scientific establishments in India have similar organizational structures and are in urban areas where 80% of the scientifically educated women live. The group tends to be homogenous also across the crucial variables of class, caste, and level of education, making it possible to generalize about the group as a whole. Science-educated women represent an advanced sector by virtue of their scientific knowledge and their employment in the modern sector. Whether these women who are apparently successful are actually faring well is our concern. We shall focus on two areas: (1) the career status and the support systems available to science-educated women, and (2) how a scientific education has affected them.

While India displays all the classic features of underdevelopment of Third World countries, it also boasts a sizable advanced sector. Though Indian women in the aggregate have a low status by measurable development indicators, such as income, employment, health, and education, there are many women in visible positions of power and prestige.[2] This situation is less paradoxical when viewed against the historical circumstances that have resulted in women in some sections of the populace gaining advantages. In the nineteenth century, men who were exposed to Western education and liberal ideas turned a critical eye on their own society.[3] One of their major concerns was the position of women in Hindu society. Through legislation and stirring public opinion, they sought to remove such evil practices as child marriages, "Sati" (self-immolation of widows on their husbands' funeral pyres), and the cruel treatment of widows. These social reformers saw education as the main instrument of women's emancipation. Hence, throughout the late nineteenth and early twentieth century, women's education was ardently and consistently fought for.

The formal education of women in India began a hundred years ago.[4] Despite this early start, improvement in general literacy was painfully slow and quickened only after independence, with a growth rate ranging between 40% and 60% per decade.[5] Though a success of some sort, this progress was severely qualified by the uneven coverage of different classes and groups. A corollary of the rapid expansion was an even faster growth in university education. Both government policy and

[1] Maithreyi Krishna Raj, "Working Women: Science Degree-Holders in Bombay," (Bombay: SNDT Women's University: 1978).
[2] Government of India, Ministry of Education and Social Welfare, *Women in India: A Statistical Profile* (New Delhi: 1978); *Towards Equality: Report of the Committee on Status of Women* (New Delhi: Government of India, 1974).
[3] Neera Desai, *Women in Modern India*, rev. ed. (Bombay: Vora and Co., 1977).
[4] N. B. Sen, *Development of Women's Education in New India* (New Delhi: New Book Society, 1969).
[5] University Grants Commission, *Annual Report, 1979–80* (New Delhi).

250

public investment supported the social demand by the middle and upper classes for higher education. The proportion of school graduates who enter college is 15% higher than in the United Kingdom and West Germany, although not in the United States and the Soviet Union.[6] Women from the middle class benefitted from this opportunity for higher education not only because the climate for women's education had been made favorable by the reform movement, but also because of the rising age of marriage for boys and girls and the value education acquired as a marriage-enhancing attribute for brides.

University-educated women now form only 3% of the female population, but the size of the educated class is large enough to make it significant. In 1973–74, university enrollment of women was 520,825, and women constituted 23% of total enrollment, which surpasses all Asian countries, including Japan. Of this, science enrollment of women was 101,244. The present total estimated *stock* of scientific personnel is 2.5 million, of whom women constitute over 500,000.[7] This places India third in the world in scientific manpower.

The entry of women to science can be attributed to three factors: (1) general and rapid growth of university eduation, (2) a planned program of development, which gave a prominent place to science education and research, and (3) merit selection of college entrants into science courses, based on high school grades. There are no *visible* constraints as between women and men at the point of entry. Because college admissions to science courses are restricted by the paucity of laboratory facilities, the female entrants must be high achievers. Because development plans led to the creation of many scientific establishments, these women also have had good job opportunities.

There is considerable looseness in the definition of the term "scientist." Usually, it refers to a person doing research and making a creative contribution to science. Since science in India is a fairly new activity, this would be a very restrictive definition. Therefore, the definition given by the Indian National Science Documentation Centre has been adopted, viz., anyone engaged in teaching, research, or testing or standardizing in scientific establishments that serve any of these functions. Holders of degrees, B.A., M.A., and Ph.D in natural sciences are included.[8] Since university departments list only the natural sciences

[6] Association of Indian Universities, *Higher Education and Development* (New Delhi: Association of Indian Universities, 1977).

[7] Planning Commission (India), *Sixth Plan, 1980–85* (New Delhi, 1981).

[8] For other studies of this group, see: R. P. Jaiswal, "Women Scientists and Engineers" (Ph.D. diss., in preparation; preliminary findings presented at the National Conference on Women Studies, SNDT University, Bombay, April 1981); A. S. Seetharamu, "Women in Organized Movements: Cast Study of the Participation of IAS Women, Women Advocates, Doctors, Engineers and University Teachers in their Professional Organizations in Bangalore City," mimeographed, 1981.

among the science disciplines in India, medical, engineering, and technical degree-holders are excluded. Both public and private establishments were covered. By a process of two-stage sampling, out of 110 establishments located in Bombay and employing 1,304 women holding science degrees, a sample of 400 was drawn, which gave 95% confidence level.

The sample consisted of 80% Hindus, 8% Christians, 2% Muslims, and 10% others. There were 120 women from teaching institutions, 124 from research centers, 91 from hospital laboratories and other laboratories involved in testing standardization of products, and 65 from industry. One hundred ninety had the B.Sc. degree, 180 the M.Sc., and 30 the Ph.D. There were 60% married (of whom two-thirds had children), 37% unmarried, and 3% widowed or divorced. Most of the group was 26–40 years of age. They came from well-educated families; 18% of the parents had college degrees, and only 10% of parents had no formal education. Many (68%) had other members in the family with science degrees. The married women had husbands equally or better educated than themselves, but usually in other occupations. Generally the group was of high status: well-to-do middle class families, educated parents, and educated husbands earning good salaries.

Each respondent was asked for a full career history. Then a detailed questionnaire with 5 sections and 60 items was administered in person. After analysis of the survey results, 15 cases each of high achievers and low achievers were selected for in-depth interviews. The survey examined the following questions:

1. What is the social background of this group of science-qualified women working in scientific establishments?
2. In what kind of jobs and at what levels are they working?
3. What is their career advancement?
4. To what extent do they receive support from their families and the organisations where they work?
5. How do they perceive their career and the value of science education?

Career status was measured by the level of post held, salary drawn, chances for promotion, recognition obtained, tenure, the authority vested in the position in terms of leadership, initiative, and policy making, and the correspondence between the woman's qualifications and her present post. Qualifications included degrees held, special training if any, and publications (if the scientist held a position in teaching and research). In addition to the personal career histories, information from each scientific establishment was obtained on the categories and ranking of jobs in the cadre. Although salary scales differ between the public sector and the private sector, the hierarchy is broadly comparable across establishments. With these two sets of data—the career status of individual respondents and the establishment data on job structure—we assessed the career achievement of the women in our sample.

The limitation of self-reporting was overcome by designing a series of questions that interlocked, rather than by a single point question. For instance, career history questions covered many areas, step by step. The question, "Do you feel satisfied with your career?" was followed by a series of queries on what they expected from their jobs, what their unrealized ambitions were, whether they felt being a woman imposed obstacles, etc. Likewise, family support was gauged through detailed questions on what kind of support was given in which ways; who performed what kind of duties and how regularly, and so on. These provided a contour that helped in the assessment of their replies to the first direct questions.

Studies of professional women elsewhere report discrimination and role conflict as major problems. Male bias, accumulation of disadvantages along a career route, and lack of old-boy support systems are perceived as the components of discrimination.[9] Role conflict arises because of competing demands for time, or a psychological inability to decide which demands should receive higher priority. This study examined these issues among employed science-educated Indian women. Their opinions on whether they faced discrimination are compared with actual inequalities, and possible explanations are suggested. Their attitudes toward work and family roles are examined as an exploration of how they perceive their career status.

Of the women scientists holding teaching positions 73% were on the lowest rung of the ladder. Among those in research positions there was no one at the highest level, 50% being middle level, and the rest below. Of those holding administrative responsibility, 90% were in the clerical category, and among laboratory technicians, 80% were at the junior level.

In salary, most were in the middle or lower middle range. The majority had not received any promotion, and those who had had obtained it after many years. Some had made a special contribution but received

[9] U.S. studies on women scientists include: Jacqualyn Mattfield and Carol A. Van, "Women in the Scientific Professions," MIT Symposium Papers (Cambridge, Mass.: MIT Press, 1965); Margaret Rossiter, "Women Scientists in America before 1920" (Ph.D. diss., in preparation); Sally Gregory Kohlstedt, "In from the periphery: American Women in Science: 1930–1880" *Signs* 4, no. 1 (1978).

no recognition. Of the women 28% said they had never received any recognition, and one-third reported only praise without material reward. Lack of promotion may not be evidence of unequal treatment, however, for in India promotion is based on a vacancy arising. Higher posts are few and given only on the basis of seniority, with the exception of some major research establishments where promotions are given on merit. On the whole, the women did better in research organizations, especially in the public sector. Tenure was available to almost all, for in India public sector organizations and many private units grant tenure after a year's probationary service. While some teachers, researchers, and executives in industry had a degree of supervisory authority (e.g., heads of departments) there was not a single woman in a policy making body. The career profile is not a happy one.

Because a cohort study of men and women such as Cole's was made impossible by resource constraints and other practical difficulties, one cannot establish direct evidence of inequality.[10] Indirect evidence does exist in aggregate national statistics, however.[11] The 1971 census, which produced a special volume on holders of degrees, shows that (1) women are in the lower posts in all establishments vis-a-vis men with equal or better qualifications; (2) women are concentrated in a narrow range of occupations; and (3) salary differentials between men and women widen with age.

How did the women scientists perceive their status? There were many who had not received their due but felt no qualms. Typical was a senior researcher with 45–50 papers to her credit and two decades of service who had never risen very high. She explained, "I am too involved in my work to notice discrimination." There were many who felt they were happy doing what they were doing. They regarded achievements in their career as "satisfactory" and did not see any special difficulty in being a woman, nor did they want any special benefits for women. They saw no need for a special women's organization to press their cause.

Only a small minority with definite ambitions felt there was discrimination. Among those who did (5%), only one or two were annoyed by it, while the rest accepted it. A 40-year-old senior programmer, holding a M.Sc. degree, said: "There is discrimination. Two years ago, I was bypassed when promotions were given. Both by seniority and merit, it should have come to me. The reason given was that I, being a woman, did not need the money." She declared, however, that she was

[10] Jonathan Cole, *Fair Science: Women in the Scientific Community* (New York: McMillan, The Free Press, 1979).

[11] There are some studies of individual scientific establishments but these were not accessible to the researcher, nor was unpublished data of the Council of Scientific and Industrial Research.

"satisfied" because her work was challenging and rewarding. More resentment was expressed by an unmarried executive in a pharmaceutical company who supports her family. She said, "I got this post after 15 years. I have 20 men under me. No matter how capable a woman is, men are reluctant to accept her competence. I never knew what beng a woman meant to my career till I joined the workplace. In school and college I did not anticipate this."

These scientists who saw discrimination pointed out many subtle forms of it. Women are bypassed in selections for committees, conferences, seminars; when training programs are conducted, circulars do not reach them; recommendations may not be enthusiastic when they apply for better posts; and so on. However, without detailed enquiry it is hard to establish whether such incidents represent discrimination, for Indian establishments are generally accused of being bureaucratic. These omissions may produce as many men victims as women.

The strength of the career motivation of these women scientists was revealed by questions regarding career plans and efforts to find a satisfying position. Most reported that they had made "plans" for a career, but their answers to detailed questions about how they selected their specialty, how they analyzed job prospects, and what efforts they made to get jobs indicated that they had not thought carefully about a disciplinary specialty in relation to a career. Most said they chose jobs to "use" their "education and training" or "to do something useful." Except for the laboratory technicians who had taken a short vocational course, it appears that what the women really meant by "career plans" is that they had meant to "work" but had not trained or planned for a specific line. Many had gotten their jobs through personal contacts.

Their career satisfaction was a mixed picture. While 76% said they were satisfied with their present jobs and thought them equal to their qualifications, they also said they "would have liked a more interesting job." None have applied for better jobs elsewhere, or joined unions or professional associations to increase the rewards of their present position. In the Indian context, however, the absence of efforts to seek better jobs elsewhere cannot by itself be regarded as showing a weak career motivation, for the scarcity of jobs makes security a highly prized value.

Did family responsibilities makes a career difficult? Families supportive of their working and cooperative husbands were reported by 65% of the group.[12] Further probing as to what they meant by this

[12] For other studies of career women in India, see: "College Women," *Indian Journal of Social Work* 38, no. 1 (1977); Raj Mohini Shethi, *Modernisation of Working Women in a Developing Society* (National Publishing House, 1976); Premila Kapur, *Marriage and the Working Woman* (New Delhi: Vikas, 1970); Kiran Wadhera, *The New Bread Winners* (New Delhi: Vishwa Yuvak Kendra, 1976); Urmila Phadnis and Indira Malani, *Women of the World, Illusion and Reality* (New Delhi: Vikas, 1978).

brought out that husbands generally did not resent their wives' working. Assistance with domestic tasks was given only in emergencies. Husbands seldom helped in the housework but did help children with their studies and in marketing. The women categorically said they bear the major responsibility for housework and child care.

Among the nonsupportive husbands, there were two major patterns: 83% of these husbands were in the same career line as their wives. Upper-middle-class husbands of higher professional standing with intense career demands were also less helpful.[13] In these families the wives' incomes were less critical than in lower middle-class families, where the husbands usually worked at a level only slightly above that of the wife.[14]

On the other hand, many felt their career stood in the way of home responsibilities, although they declared their families did not say so. Their sense of family obligation was high. In a few cases, the family pressure was also high. Said a botanist, "My in-laws are eager enough to benefit from my income but did not make a single concession to me. For 20 years, I have risen at 4 A.M. and gone to bed long past midnight, finishing the chores, and yet I was on trial all the time to see how 'dutiful' I was. Every ritual, ceremony had to be performed in the prescribed manner. At work I had to establish my credentials over and over again." This determined woman finished her Master's and Ph.D. degrees years after she joined the department and finally rose to be its head. But the price? Thus, when the women said, "husbands did not mind," "husbands helped," or "families cooperated," it appears this support was given because the women continued to maintain a full family role. Would such support have been forthcoming had they been more ambitious?

Why are professional scientifically educated women satisfied with modest career rewards?[15] Socialization into sex-role stereotypes is not an adequate explanation, for there are several institutional and historical bases for their gender identity.[16] The women's perception of their current status is derived by comparing their present status to women's status in their mothers' generation rather than to the status of men in ur-

---

[13] Usha Nayyar, "Women Teachers of South Asia: Case Study of Empirically Based Comparative Education in Non Western Societies" (Paper presented at the National Conference on Women Studies, SNDT University, Bombay, April 1981).

[14] Barbara Ward, *Women in New Asia* (New York: UNESCO, 1963).

[15] For other discussions of professional women and role conflict, see: Karuna Ahmad, "Trishankus: Women in the Professions," mimeographed (Paper presented at the Seminar on Sex Discrimination in Gainful Employment, Indian Institute of Education, Pune, 1976); J. C. Aggarwal, *Indian Women: Education and Status* (New Delhi: Arya Book Dept., 1976); A. Ramanamma, *Graduate Employed Women in an Urban Setting* (Pune: Dastane Ramchandra & Co., 1979).

[16] U.S. Department of Health, Education and Welfare, NIE, "Sex Role Socialization and Sex Discrimination: A Synthesis of Literature and Critique of Literature" (Washington, D.C.: Government Printing Office, 1979).

ban middle-class families who now "permit" women to work outside the home, but there is less change in other directions. The acceptability of women working depends on the social prestige of the occupation. White-collar work, especially teaching, is regarded as respectable, and the heavy concentration of women professionals in teaching reflects this social preference. Women are expected to play their traditional roles alongside the newly gained occupational role, as an extension of responsibility rather than a shift.

Work at home has become qualitatively different for these women. They have a greater concern for the raising of their children. While for rural women, agricultural workers, and working-class women, child care involves primarily physical care, educated mothers feel responsible for the psychological and intellectual development of children. They need more time to supervise them, arrange stimulating activities, plan their leisure hours, assist in their studies, and so on. These things a "servant" cannot do.

Yet, the traditional burden of housework remains heavy because technological improvements are inadequate. A considerable amount of food processing is still done at home, for preprocessed foods are unavailable or of uncertain quality. The component of hard labor is high because there are few kitchen gadgets. Daily preparation of the staple bread (chapattis), for example, requires five different processes: cleaning grain, getting it ground, making dough, rolling it out, and cooking individual portions. An average middle-class Indian housewife spends at least four hours a day in food preparation. A woman doing this work feels she is making a clear contribution to family survival, which brings an intrinsic reward.

In India, solidarity and identification with one's gender is strong. Women relate to women constantly at birth, marriage, festival rituals, and so on. This sense of connection and embeddedness in social life provides security and worth to women as women. It also reinforces the value of motherhood, a very important base of a woman's esteem. Motherhood and feminine-gender identity may be sufficiently rewarding for women to obviate their seeking competitive rewards in the workplace. The jobs they have provide them with intellectual and social stimulation and an outlet for their education and skills. Working also brings additional income for a more comfortable family life and contributes to women's sense of fulfilling their family obligation. That they perceive rewards at work and at home is not therefore surprising. "So much only for work," and the rest is for the home, creates a feeling of having done one's duty.

These women are largely first generation professional women. Their college education and work outside the home have given them opportunities for interaction with the outside world that were unknown before. Perhaps when they, or their daughters, become accustomed o this, they will ask for more.

These women are in the forefront of the modern sector. How do they see the value of science to society and to themselves? Can they be sources of change and carriers of new knowledge to their families? This is really part of a larger question. To what extent does education bring about change? What kind of changes occur and why?

Third World countries attempting to transform their societies through science and technology pay insufficient attention to science as a social movement and do not often distinguish among the three dimensions involved in scientific development: practical application of the fruits of scientific research, the spread of scientific knowledge, and the acceptance of a scientific outlook.[17] While all three are inextricably bound up with the social structure and cultural context, it is critically necessary to separate them.

In this study of women with a scientific education, the primary concern was with the second and third dimensions. Have women who are exposed to university level science imbibed a scientific outlook to such an extent that their lives and behavior are influenced? As daily practitioners of science, do they carry a scientific frame of mind to other areas of their lives?

The basis for expecting scientific education to influence individual behavior lies in the contrast between traditional and scientific outlooks. Traditionalism implies attitudes and values that give preeminence to authority and custom in the modulation of behavior. It makes for stability and maintenance of the status quo in social institutions and social relations. The mechanism of progressive change has usually been conceived of as a noncontentious process of acculturation, diffusion, and trickledown of the benefits of growth from a progressive, modern sector to the traditional sector. While there is increasing doubt about this model, there is not adequate theory to relate development to cultural change.[18] A variety of cultural forms coexist with economic development, and the kind of social changes that can clearly be labeled as "development" is unclear. Despite these limitations, one can assume that science and scientific attitudes are associated with universalistic criteria that are conducive to "development," while Third World countries in general have social structural relations that are regulated by particularism, functional diffusion, and ascription, especially in the orientation of people. We know

[17] R. Varadarajan, "The three planes of Science in Society," *Impact of Science on Society* 25, no. 1 (1975).

[18] A. Inkeles and D. M. Smith, *Becoming Modern: Individual Changes in Six Developing Countries* (Cambridge, Mass.: Harvard University Press, 1974).

from the experience of advanced societies that science in the form of technological artifacts is imbibed more easily than a scientific outlook. Nevertheless, one may assume that prolonged exposure to science would generate a scientific outlook, and a rational appraisal of old knowledge in the context of the new.[19] One would expect in India that a scientific outlook would eradicate superstition, prejudice, and blind belief.

In the absence of an accepted scale to measure rationality, we asked open-ended questions about what science meant to these women scientists. Was their behavior at home traditional or did they discard rituals/customs usually observed by women in India? We also asked how they thought science helped them, how they ranked the scientist's profession, and how they ranked three commonly held uses of science to society: improvement in productivity, increase in knowledge, and the generation of a scientific outlook.

The scientists' assessments of the value of science emphasized an instrumental view. The majority thought it gave them better job opportunities; 30% thought it helped them in homemaking by instilling better health habits; and 20% thought scientific training helped women to work as equals with men. Their practical orientation to science was reflected also in their assessments of the value of science to Indian society: 50% gave first priority to "science for production," and 26% to "science for practical knowledge." Those who gave topmost priority to "science for promoting a scientific outlook" constituted only 26% of the whole sample of 400 women.

There was a minority with a larger vision. The value of a "scientific outlook" was mentioned by 30%. By this they meant "logical thinking" or "giving up superstitions." A typical response was that of a senior programmer with a M.Sc. degree in mathematics:

> It is difficult to define a scientific outlook. It is an attitude of mind which tries to see an event in a logical way. Traditionally all that our ancestors did or gave us is not always worth transferring in toto. Perhaps some customs were useful in those days, but if we do not find them necessary, we should have the courage to discard them. I do not personally believe in rituals or horoscopes or anything like that. I do not take seriously God-men and miraclemongers. Philosophy is different from rituals. Scientific education does make one ask questions and changes one's outlook.

[19] For discussions of the scientific outlook, see: Gerald Holton, ed., *Science and the Modern Mind* (Boston: Beacon Press, 1958); Philip Frank, "Contemporary Science and Contemporary World," in *The Philosophies of Science*, ed. Saxe Commins and Robert Linscott (New York: Modern Pocket Books, 1954); Bertrand Russell, *The Impact of Science on Society* (London: George Allen and Unwin, 1951); idem., *The Scientific Outlook* (London: George Allen and Unwin, 1931); Jacob Bronowski, *Science, Its Method and Outlook*, ed. Directorate of Education, Aligarh Muslim University (Asia Publishing House, 1965); Alexander Varoulis and Wayne A. Colver, eds., *Science and Society* (Holden Day, Inc., 1970); James Newman, ed., *What is Science* (New York: Washington Square Press, 1962).

In contrast, a forty-three-year-old chemical analyst working in a pharmaceutical company dismissed the question of scientific outlook by saying, "I do follow traditional customs. These taboos and rituals are good. Seclusion gives rest to a woman; vows are good for health. God-men and miracles belong to religion. Rituals, one's daily customs, are part of religion and have nothing to do with science."

    What was the behavioral outcome in their daily lives? In India, women observe many rituals, customs, and taboos. Fasts are observed for a husband's long life; vows are kept to cure illness; menstrual taboos are observed with regard to touching others, using the kitchen, and abstaining from worship; horoscopes are consulted for marriage and for predicting the future. Among the scientists, there was a distinct weakening of these traditional practices: 36% never observed any menstrual taboos (some 46% desisted from acts of worship); 45% never observed vows or fasts to achieve special effects; and 56% of the group never consulted any horoscope for whatever purpose. Of those who did follow these practices, most claimed to do so out of habit or in order not to displease elders in the family, without belief in the outcome of the rituals. However, there were many interesting intermediate gradations of belief. Many (46%) abstained from such religious acts as worship but otherwise did not practice taboos. Those who consulted horoscopes said they did so in times of crisis and for marriages. One research scientist always consulted her horoscope before beginning an experiment.

    As for applying scientific knowledge to daily practices, the respondents were asked about activities that most absorb women's time—food preparation and child care. Women in India usually have older women assisting them during childbirth, after care and child rearing. In this way, traditional modes of bathing, dressing, making herbal concoctions, etc. are passed along, and expert advice from books is rarely sought. Educated mothers, in our experience, however, do prize modern knowledge about food and hygiene. The scientists did so as well. The scientists also stressed the importance of the mother's presence for the infant, even if other help is available, and the need for a less authoritarian relationship with children. When they talked of teaching science to their children, however, they revealed their limited view of science. The majority viewed science teaching in terms of books and information, while only 8% felt that observation and curiosity needs to be promoted. Over-all, the emphasis was clearly on acquiring information rather than changing attitudes.

    The most progressive were not necessarily the most well-educated, but those who valued a scientific outlook. They were younger women, often with only a Masters' degree, from families where education was valued as a liberating force, and where the emphasis was on freedom to think and become independent. These attitudes were found not only among the fathers, who were usually well educated, but also among mothers, who were progressive for their times and wanted their daughters to benefit from education. By contrast the emphasis in traditional families was on "getting good marks" or "qualifying for a job." The following are examples from each set: A young chemist said: "My family is progressive. They have never observed rituals, customs, practices. My parents gave me full freedom, encouraged me to explore, to think. We shared many activities. I was encouraged and coaxed into reading widely." And this, from another chemist:

> My family was religious and orthodox. I was never allowed even to join college picnics. I was always expected home immediately after college. I never took part in any extracurricular activities. My mother was in the kitchen and observed many rituals. My father was a businessman and was rarely at home. Coming from an orthodox Jain family, I follow all the rituals and I have great respect for them.

Over-all, there is a moving away from tradition, but it is partial. The adaptation of knowledge to immediately useful areas like food, health, hygiene, and child care is more prevalent than to other areas of belief. It appears that for most of these women science means useful knowledge rather than a scientific outlook.

Are male scientists different?[20] One might expect so because men have greater exposure to the outside world. But studies show male scientists regard their laboratory activities as a sphere separate from the rest of their lives. They retain strong adherence to caste, rituals, and heirarchical values. While the ethos of science as an intellectual activity is wholeheartedly accepted, it is not extended to other areas of life. Outside their work, scientists accept the dominant aspects of traditional society and refuse to confront differences between the value systems of science and traditional religion.

In India, there is no confrontation between the scientific community and the older social values or philosophical cultural framework because science is still an isolated activity, restricted in scope, character, and structure. There are special cultural and historical factors that explain this. The history of science in India has suffered two major discontinuities. The older scientific tradition in Sanskrit was broken by invasions in the medieval period. The later colonial introduction of science through the English language strengthened the existing stratification by excluding the bulk of the people.

---

[20] On male Indian scientists: Surajit Sinha, ed., *Science, Technology and Culture* (New Delhi: India International Centre, 1970); A. Ahmad and S. P. Gupta, *Opinion Survey of Scientists and Technologists* (New Delhi: CSIR, 1967).

261

The earliest to benefit from Western education in India were the upper castes, whose tradition of doing no manual labor was reinforced. Those educated in English took to the new white-collar occupations. Since then, higher education has been seen primarily as a route to white-collar jobs and prestige. Education has a status value for women also, because educated men need educated wives for compatibility. A scientific education, like higher education in general, is mainly a status-giving acquisition, and it is more valued for this than for its particular ethos.

Generally in Third World countries, especially excolonial countries, where science was introduced without any restructuring of the social system, the linkage between science, technology, and society is less through the ideational nature of science as a system of knowledge and more through the relationship of scientific enterprise with the social system. Because the instrumental value of science has immediate and direct relevance, it is more easily perceived and absorbed. National economic development stresses adaptation of technology and absorption of units of scientific knowledge produced elsewhere. Even the diffusion of science-based knowledge is constrained in these countries by the severe inegalitarianism.

India has scientists, but not a scientific community.[21] The institutions that generate and keep alive such orientations as curiosity, the pleasure of discovery, and the readiness to discard previously held views in the face of new observations and theories—these are difficult to create. They involve an intricate structure of relations among scientists, scientific bodies, policy makers, the normative and motivational systems, and the models of action—past and present—which underlie and permeate social relationships. A few scientists cannot by themselves impose or recreate in their society these orientations, as they are part of that society.

The two forces, those who build a scientific community to make it creative and productive and those who spread science to the people at large, are mutually interactive. Science can permeate the cultural ethos only with a different model of development and genuine mass education. Scientists need support from an educated public to build a well-articulated scientific enterprise. Where scientists themselves are tradition-bound, and the scientific establishments are strongly hierarchic and opposed to innovation, this process cannot even begin.

The study of women educated in science shows that even though career achievement is modest and unequal to their efforts, they are

[21] Steven Dedijer, "Underdeveloped Science in Underdeveloped Countries," in *Education, Scientific Policy, and Developing Societies*, ed. A. B. Shah (Bombay: Manak Talas, 1967).

satisfied and do not press for equality with men. A career is not the primary goal because the family role is seen as more important. Role conflict is thus not experienced in any acute form. Though they are in the modern sector these women value the instrumental value of science more than the benefits of a scientific outlook.

Science-educated women have strong familial values because the family in India is the major social, economic, and moral base of one's identity. A scientific education leads to some absorption of useful knowledge, but within limits only, because the scientific enterprise in India has so far had a limited role in society — conferring status within the existing social structure rather than changing the social structure.

15. The Impact of Education on the Female Labor Force in Argentina and Paraguay

CATALINA H. WAINERMAN

In her book *Women and Work in Developing Societies*, Nadia Youssef points out that there are at least four factors influencing female employment in nonagricultural work.[1] From the demand side (1) the level of economic development and (2) the specific organization of the economy, and from the supply side (3) the level of educational achievement and (4) the marital and fertility characteristics of the female population.

In this paper I shall focus on the factors impinging on the supply. How do education and family characteristics affect the supply of women to the labor force? Having different educational levels, which depends on the insertion within the socioeconomic structure, implies different interests, values, and attitudes. These show up, among other behavioral spheres, in reproductive and marital patterns. These patterns are, in turn, closely related to female involvement in economic activities. Actually, the more educated a woman is, the higher the probability that she will remain single, marry later and, having married, postpone childbearing longer and have fewer or no children. In societies where females bear the primary responsibility for sociological as well as biological reproduction (as is the case in most known societies), participating in the productive structure implies taking on a double role. Therefore, at each stage of the life cycle, the woman's decision to join the labor force cannot be independent from the characteristics of the family: with or without husband, with or without small, adolescent, or adult children.

Regardless of the relationship to marital and reproductive patterns, a higher level of education improves the competitive position of women in the labor market and increases the information about job opportunities and the probability of getting better-paid jobs that are also more gratifying and have more flexible working hours. In other words, it increases the (subjective and objective) opportunity cost of staying outside the labor

This paper deals extensively with part of the results arrived at in the research project "La participacion de la mujer en la actividad economica en la Argentina, Bolivia y Paraguay: Un estudio comparativo" [Female participation in economic activity in Argentina, Bolivia and Paraguay: A comparative study]. This project was sponsored by the International Development Research Center (IDRC) of Canada under contract no. 3-9-76-0009-02 and carried out jointly by the Centro de Estudios de Poblacion (CENEP, Argentina), the Centro de Investigaciones Sociales (CIS, Bolivia), and the Centro Paraguayo de Estudios Sociologicos (CPES, Paraguay). This article is based on a paper presented at the Workshop on Women's Roles and Fertility sponsored by the International Development Research Center, Ottawa.

[1] Nadia Youssef, *Women and Work in Developing Societies* (Berkeley: University of California Press, 1974).

Reprinted from the *Comparative Education Review* 24, no. 2 (part 2)(June 1980): S180–95.

market. Furthermore, a longer exposure to formal education usually raises economic aspirations, stimulates a redefinition of domestic duties to make housekeeping easier, and tends to change the position of women within the family structure. Personal fulfillment through extradomestic activities becomes meaningful as an alternative to fulfillment through the role of mother-homemaker.

Summing up, whether due to its effects on family composition or on life conceptions, or to the economic opportunities it opens up, education plays a central role in the explanation and prediction of female labor force attachment. This point is agreed upon both by researchers enrolled in neoclassical economics (*New Home Economics*) as well as by those who subscribe to other approaches when dealing with female supply to the labor market.[2] Jaffe and Ridley review a large number of studies of the factors affecting female labor force membership and fertility.[3] They point out that even though the significance of education is acknowledged, little or no attention has been paid to the interrelationship among the three variables.

In this paper, while focusing on the two supply aspects brought out by Youssef, I shall move in the direction suggested by Jaffe and Ridley. The context of the inquiry is Argentina and Paraguay in 1970, and the objective is twofold. I shall attempt to identify which females, in different educational levels and "family situations," defined in terms of the presence or absence of husband and of children, have a greater propensity to participate in the labor market. I shall also try to evaluate how formal education and family situation influence that propensity. The data for this study are drawn from the latest available population censuses of Argentina (1970) and Paraguay (1972). The analysis is made at the national level. Because of lack of comparable data, no analysis is undertaken for urban versus rural areas.

Even though this study includes only two countries, the substantial structural differences between them will enable us to generalize the findings beyond these two cases. Argentina and Paraguay, though sharing a common cultural tradition and historical circumstances, represent two clearly different cases in demographic, economic, and sociological terms.

By 1970 Argentina was among the 10 most highly urbanized countries in the world. It was one of the most urbanized in Latin America, with almost 80 percent of its population residing in cities. It differs from most countries in the region because of its relative racial homogeneity and the

[2] See Guy Standing, *Labour Force Participation and Development* (Geneva: International Labour Office, 1978), chap. 6.
[3] A. J. Jaffe and J. C. Ridley, "Fertility and Lifetime Employment—non-Spanish White Women," *Industrial Gerontology* (Winter 1976).

265

existence of a large middle class. The population age structure is relatively old and the literacy level considerably high. The country is now at a comparatively high level of industrialization for Latin America. By 1970 the agricultural sector contributed only 15 percent of the gross domestic product, and 15 percent (3.8 percent of females and 18.5 percent of males) of the total labor force was engaged in agriculture.

Paraguay is a predominantly rural country, with slightly over 37 percent of its population living in urban areas. It has one of the highest birthrates in the region, almost double that of Argentina, and its literacy level, though substantially increased since 1950, is still relatively low compared to Argentina. Paraguay's economy is based on agriculture and handicrafts. By 1970, the agricultural sector contributed 37 percent to the gross domestic product and employed 51 percent (13.2 of females and approximately 62 percent of males) of the total labor force.

In spite of these structural differences, by 1970 the refined labor force participation rates of women aged 12 and over were fairly similar in both countries (25.3 percent in Argentina; 21.1 percent in Paraguay). These are relatively high levels for Latin America, though they are low rates compared with the United States and several European countries. The major difference in female participation between the countries lies in the structure of the labor force membership. In Argentina, over two-thirds of active women are employed in the tertiary sector—in domestic service and as professionals and technicians engaged in jobs related to health and education. In Paraguay, a substantial number of females are employed in the agricultural sector, and most of the rest work in domestic service or as artisans and operatives in small-scale activities which are usually carried out at home.

General Background

Education Drives Women toward the Labor Market

Illiteracy has long ceased to be a serious problem in Argentina as a whole, although there are regional variations. Among persons age 10 and over, it is 7.4 percent for females and 5.6 percent for males. Most of the population has some primary education, but secondary and higher education is still the privilege of a minority, although it has expanded in the past decades.

The situation in Paraguay is different. Even though illiteracy has dropped almost by one-half since 1950, it is still relatively high in the population age 12 and over: 17.7 percent of females and 9.7 percent of males. In younger age cohorts the gap between males and females is narrowing as education expands.

As in Argentina, most of the population in Paraguay has not gone beyond primary education. The number of primary school dropouts is substantially higher in Paraguay, resulting in a lower level of education. For instance, in Paraguay, only 20 percent of women age 12 and over who entered primary school completed it; in Argentina, 40 percent of women age 10 and over finished primary school. The same is the case for the secondary level: only 23 percent of Paraguayan females completed it, as compared with 41 percent of Argentinian females. (In both countries, the number of dropouts is higher among males than among females.) To summarize, even though in both countries there is an absolute majority of females who did not receive more than primary education, completion of primary school is more unusual for Paraguayan than for Argentinian women.

In spite of the above differences—less average formal schooling and greater difference in education between the sexes in Paraguay than in Argentina—in both societies formal education is an important credential for entry into the female labor market. Clearly this credential benefits the most highly educated. The average educational level of working women surpasses that of nonworking ones. In Argentina, 31.4 percent of the females active in the labor force had primary education or above, as opposed to only 20.8 percent of all the females of working age. The equivalent figures for Paraguay are 22.2 percent and 12.0 percent, respectively.

Level of education does not function as a recruitment criterion in the labor market in the same way for men as for women. This does not mean that education has no effect on the positions men hold in the economic structure, but that for the males the level of education does not affect their entry into the labor market.

An analysis of the participation profiles of groups with different educational levels clearly shows, in the case of females, that the probability of participating in the labor market is closely related to years of schooling. The higher the level of education attained, whatever the age group, the higher the probability that women will participate in the labor force. This is the most frequent pattern both for developed and developing countries.[4] Among the latter, however, there are several instances where a U-shaped nonlinear pattern has been found. This is the case, for instance, in India, Colombia, and Bolivia, where the percentage of active females among illiterate women has proved significantly higher than among literates, though activity rates among the latter increase as schooling in-

[4] United Nations, *The Determinants and Consequences of Population Trends* (New York: United Nations, 1973), 1:317; Juan C. Elizaga, "Participacion de la mujer en la mano de obra en America Latina: La fecundidad y otros determinantes," *Revista Internacional del Trabajo* 89, nos. 5–6 (1974): 569–88; Edith A. Pantelides, *Estudio de la poblacion femenina economicamente activa en America Latina, 1950–1970* (Santiago: CELADE, 1976).

creases.[5] In other cases, the relationship between education and labor force participation is either mixed or, in a few countries, negative.[6] The diversity of universes studied (countries, regions, states, urban and rural population, female population of different ages and marital status, etc.), definitions, measurement techniques, and quality of the data used precludes solid conclusions. All these studies support the conjecture, however, that the relationship between educational attainment and participation of women in the labor force is conditioned by the educational level of the total population (male and female) and by the structure and organization of the economy and, therefore, by the size and structure of the labor force demand.

Notwithstanding the fact that the labor force participation (total as well as for the various sectors) of Argentinian females is higher than that of Paraguayan females, in both countries and almost with no exception in each age group, the activity rates of the females with higher education (complete for Argentina, complete and incomplete for Paraguay) are four or five times as high as the activity rates of illiterate females. For females who reached the highest educational levels, participation in the labor market is a very frequent experience, nearly as frequent as it is for males of any educational level. For females who did not receive several years of primary education, it is a rare experience. These females differ substantially from males at all educational levels. Thus the women at both ends of the educational scale show very clear work behavior: the majority of the most privileged group participate in the labor market, the majority of the least privileged group refrain from doing so. The remainder of females, which are a majority within the active population of central ages, appear to face more frequently the choice between domestic and extradomestic work.

The high participation propensity of the most educated females should not be mistaken with their share in the labor market. In 1970 the overwhelming contribution to the female labor market was made by the least educated; this, however, was not due to their high work propensity but rather to the fact that, in terms of sheer size, they represented the absolute majority of the female population of active age.

In short, a high investment in schooling seems to draw women into the labor market, while a low investment seems to draw them away from it. In the first case, about 80 percent of the females in Argentina and about 60–70 percent of those in Paraguay, in each age group, who are in the central range of the life cycle (ages 25–50) participate actively in the

[5] J. N. Sinha, *Dynamics of Female Participation in Economic Activity in a Developing Economy* (Belgrade: World Population Conference, 1965); Hugo Torrez, *La mujer boliviana y sus caracteristicas demograficas en la fuerza de trabajo, 1975* (La Paz: Ediciones CIS, 1977); United Nations, *Methods of Analyzing Census Data on Economic Activities of the Population* (New York: United Nations, 1968).

[6] Standing, chap. 6.

labor force; in the second case, no more than 20 percent in Argentina and 15 percent in Paraguay, in each age group, do not enter the work force.

The similarity of trends (though not of levels) in both countries should not obscure a difference certainly related to the diverse educational structure of their female populations of active age. The educational thresholds associated with the greatest increases in female activity rates differ for each country: in Argentina, they lie at the transition between the primary and the secondary levels and, still more markedly, at the completion of secondary school; in Paraguay, the equivalent threshold lies at a lower level, coinciding with the completion of the primary level. As stated above, completion of primary school is more exceptional for Paraguayan than for Argentinian females.

Family Burdens Keep Women Away from the Labor Market

The influence of formal education on female work behavior is mediated in part by its effects on marital and reproductive patterns. Even though education, generally acquired prior to family formation, tends to modify family structure and dynamics and the definition of the domestic role, the family situation imposes restrictions on labor force participation regardless of the women's educational level.

Age changes during working life accompany changes in the marital status and in the stages of the family cycle that condition the enactment of mother-homemaker and labor force roles. Therefore, we shall now look into the similarities and differences in the work force participation of females in different kinds of family constellations.

By 1970, in Argentina and Paraguay as well as in most societies, more than half of the females in the work force were single; one-third were married, legally or consensually; and the rest were widowed, divorced, or separated females. In both countries, single women were overrepresented in the labor force, while married women were underrepresented. Separated and divorced women followed the same pattern as single women, and the widows the same as married ones.

This pattern, which holds in both countries, suggests that it is the presence or absence of a husband which influences women's entry into the labor market. The effect is so strong that even between ages 40 and 49, and between 50 and 59, when the demands arising from the presence of small children have disappeared and family burdens become more similar for single, married, widowed, divorced, or separated women, the differential participation in the work force remains at similar levels as among the younger groups.

The presence of a husband is not the only family factor which negatively affects female participation in the labor market; the presence of children has a similar influence. The age-specific activity rates of females with different numbers of children outline a very clear pattern in both

269

countries: regardless of the presence or absence of a husband at home, the presence of children has a negative influence on female work force participation. Except for females under 20, among whom it is irrelevant to analyze the effect children have (95 percent in Argentina and 94 percent in Paraguay are childless), in each age group between ages 20 and 60 the activity rates of females with larger numbers of children are lower. In Paraguay, the labor behavior of the females with husband and no children shows practically no differences from that of one-child females.

Aside from the fact that, in general, the female participation rates in Argentina are higher than in Paraguay, in both countries the lowest participation profile corresponds to the females with husband and two or more children. Under no circumstances do the labor force rates of women with a husband surpass those of women with no husband. It should be pointed out that, at the same ages, even the rates of childless married females (whose domestic burdens are closer to those of single childless women) are lower than those of single, widowed, divorced, or separated women with two or more children.

These findings lead to the conclusion that the discouraging effect of husband presence outweighs that of children. (Note that within the more active age group, 30–39, the activity rate of females without a husband but with two or more children is far higher than that of females with a husband and no children.) Different economic needs is a major explanation. However, this pattern also reveals cultural orientations with respect to the behavior regarded as appropriate for men and women, and particularly for married women. In Argentina, for instance, labor laws sanctioned for women early this century, and still in force in their basic ideational contents, have consistently discouraged female labor force participation.[7] Participation has only been accepted when regarded as inevitable, either because of the inadequacy of the spouse's income, or in the case of marital disruption or of single women with needy parents. Even though no equivalent information is available for Paraguay, the similarities observed in other Latin American countries suggest that the situation is probably similar.[8]

The negative relationship observed in Argentina and Paraguay between fertility patterns and female activity rates does not, however, suggest a causal model. It should not be inferred that there is a simple and direct causal relationship from participation in the labor market to reduced family size. Despite an abundant literature, it has not yet been

[7] Catalina H. Wainerman and Marysa Navarro, *El trabajo de la mujer en la Argentina: Analisis preliminar de las ideas dominates en las primeras decades del Siglo XX* (Buenos Aires: CENEP, 1979).

[8] Marly A. Cardona, "Subsidios do Direito do Trabalho para um debate sobre a situacao da mulher," in Cadernos de pesquisa, no. 15 (Sao Paulo: Fundacao Carlos Chagas, 1975); Ligia Chang and Maria Angelica Ducci, *Realidad del empleo y la formacion profesional de la mujer en America Latina*, Estudios y monografias, no. 24 (Monte video: CINTERFOR, 1977).

established whether working women tend to reduce their number of children, or whether a selection takes place in which childless women or women with few children tend to have a higher labor force attachment, due to more time available to them, fewer social restrictions, their making up for a social deficit, or some other reason. Nor is the negative relationship clearly established. There are a number of studies which have found no relationship between fertility and female economic activity; others, though very few indeed, have found that for some specific groups of females the relationship in question becomes positive.[9]

In short, it is not only that the direction of the relationship is obscure, but also that the relationship itself has not been sufficiently described. This might be due to analyses being restricted to the association between number of children and work force participation rates without taking into account the children's age, the level of family needs and income, the presence of other adults in the household, the type of the mother's activity, etc.

Some economists argue that the increase in family size and the decrease in per capita income may drive the mother, and other members of the family, toward the labor market so as to keep up the family's standard of living.[10] Sweet, for instance, controlling for the mother's age, the number of children under 18, and the youngest child's age, has found that the participation propensity of the mother increases as the "income adequacy" of the family decreases, that is, as economic pressures increase.[11] One of the characteristics which has proved more relevant in the specification of the relationship between fertility and female economic participation is the type of occupation, or what Darian calls "the convenience of work."[12] This is related to the fact that the burden of children differs for mothers depending on whether they work at or away from home, in the modern or in the traditional sector, with flexible or rigid working hours, full or part time, etc. In general, the studies agree in pointing out that the relationship between fertility and female economic participation is no longer negative when the domestic and the productive roles are not too incompatible.

The Varying Family Situation of the Most and the Least Educated Women

We have shown above that females' propensity to participate in the labor market varies according to their level of formal education and to their type of family situation. But, as stated at the beginning of this paper,

---

[9] For an exhaustive review of this literature, see Standing, chap. 7.

[10] Ester Boserup, *The Conditions of Agricultural Growth* (London: Allen & Unwin, 1965); Albert O. Hirshman, *The Strategy of Economic Development* (New Haven, Conn.: Yale University Press, 1958).

[11] James A. Sweet, *Women in the Labor Force* (New York: Seminar, 1973).

[12] J. C. Darian, "Convenience of Work and the Job Constraint of Children," *Demography* 12 (1975): 245–58.

marital and reproductive patterns are not independent of the educational level achieved but, on the contrary, vary systematically with it.

As regards marital patterns, both in Argentina and Paraguay, by 1970 the percentage of married women in each age cohort decreases as educational attainment levels increase. The most educated women tend to marry later. Between ages 20 and 24 in both countries, about half the females with primary schooling are already married, while the percentages are one-third lower among those with secondary schooling and fall to 15–16 percent among those with higher education. The same regularities hold among females active in the work force. These findings add to the frequent evidence existing in many countries on the pattern of marriage delay among the most educated females.[13]

With reference to reproductive patterns, both in Argentina for females aged 50 and over, and in Paraguay for those aged 40 and over, the average number of children of illiterate females is more than double that of females with secondary and higher education. A concurrent trend is observed among childless females: they represent only 10–12 percent of the illiterate group aged 50 and over, but the childless group is three and even four times larger in Argentina and twice as large in Paraguay among those with secondary and higher schooling. Since a level of 10 percent of childless couples seems to be a biological constant, a significant deviation from that figure should be taken to express extrabiological reasons, among which life patterns, attitudes, and values occupy a major place.

The regularities found for the total female population of active ages hold for the active sectors in both countries. Thus, for instance, among women aged 20 years and over, the percentage of married women with two or more children is several times higher among those who had access to secondary schooling. The respective figures are 16.0 and 1.5 percent in Argentina and 22.4 and 1.0 percent in Paraguay. These trends are observed without exceptions in each age group.

The negative relationship observed in Argentina and Paraguay between women's educational achievement and fertility is the most frequent pattern in other countries as well, but it is not the only one found. The relationship between these factors is relatively complex, and it keeps neither the same direction nor the same intensity through time or through space.[14]

It seems relevant to ask now whether the greater tendency to enter the work force on the part of better-educated women is due to the

[13] R. Dixon, "Explaining Cross-cultural Variations in Age at Marriage and Proportions Never Marrying," *Population Studies*, vol. 25, no. 2 (1971): 215–33.

[14] Serim Timur, "Demographic Correlates of Women's Education: Fertility, Age at Marriage and the Family" (paper presented at the International Population Conference, IUSSP, Mexico City, 1977).

facilitating or driving effects of education itself or to the fact that their family situation is more compatible with holding a job. The data presented in tables 1 and 2 show that, whatever the females' age and family situation, almost without exception, in both countries the activity rates of the most educated females are higher than those of the least educated ones. This means that education itself influences female work behavior.

Education Equalizes the Propensity to Participate in the Labor Market

Even though the regularities described refer to both countries, there are differences between them. In Argentina, for example, in the 30–34 age cohort that did not complete or go beyond primary education, the labor force participation rate of females with neither husband nor chil-

TABLE 1

AGE-SPECIFIC FEMALE ACTIVITY RATES BY SCHOOLING AND FAMILY SITUATION, ARGENTINA, 1970

No. of Children and Schooling	Age					
	20–24	25–29	30–34	35–39	40–44	45–49
Two or more children, with husband:						
Incomplete primary or less	8.5	10.4	12.4	12.8	13.1	12.7
Primary	9.5	11.4	12.8	13.4	12.5	12.1
Secondary	23.5	28.1	34.1	36.5	33.3	31.5
Higher	33.3*	52.9	59.1	62.1	60.5	58.4
One child, with husband:						
Incomplete primary or less	11.5	15.3	18.4	21.3	18.9	17.2
Primary	13.6	16.1	21.7	18.8	18.1	16.7
Secondary	29.1	40.5	46.7	47.6	40.9	34.5
Higher	40.3	62.6	75.0	77.4	77.4	65.2
No children, with husband:						
Incomplete primary or less	22.4	29.4	30.0	30.9	26.6	23.1
Primary	32.4	32.6	41.0	39.7	29.2	28.2
Secondary	49.0	56.8	62.3	63.9	58.4	48.3
Higher	60.9	79.1	83.3	72.5	71.4	57.1*
Two or more children, without husband:						
Incomplete primary or less	42.1	54.4	70.4	54.4	50.7	39.7
Primary	44.6	63.6	66.9	67.8	61.2	47.9
Secondary	57.1	63.3	80.6	80.2	64.0	63.8
Higher	.0	83.3*	83.3	95.2	94.1	77.8
One child, without husband:						
Incomplete primary or less	55.5	60.8	65.4	70.3	67.5	49.3
Primary	59.8	61.4	76.7	73.1	66.9	64.2
Secondary	59.2	81.7	82.1	81.0	74.2	63.6
Higher	75.0*	80.0*	88.9*	71.4*	85.7*	90.0*
No children, without husband:						
Incomplete primary or less	59.1	60.8	60.8	56.0	53.6	52.8
Primary	65.2	73.4	71.2	72.2	71.7	65.2
Secondary	70.8	83.0	87.2	86.3	83.7	74.4
Higher	45.6	78.8	88.0	90.8	95.3	83.0

SOURCE. —Unpublished table elaborated by CELADE (Omuece 70).
* Small frequencies.

TABLE 2

AGE-SPECIFIC FEMALE ACTIVITY RATES BY SCHOOLING AND FAMILY SITUATION, PARAGUAY, 1972

No. of Children and Schooling	Age					
	20–24	25–29	30–34	35–39	40–44	45–49
Two or more children, with husband:						
Incomplete primary or less	7.1	8.1	10.5	10.5	12.0	11.9
Primary	15.3	18.6	22.2	22.2	24.2	18.2
Incomplete secondary to						
complete higher	25.6	36.7	44.1	41.0	38.2	25.3
One child, with husband:						
Incomplete primary or less	9.5	18.6	13.9	12.1	17.3	16.0
Primary	25.1	28.8	40.6	50.0	45.0	31.3
Incomplete secondary to						
complete higher	33.2	52.1	52.8	58.0	41.5	36.7
No children, with husband:						
Incomplete primary or less	17.1	17.6	19.1	15.5	14.6	15.2
Primary	31.4	40.5	36.9	22.2	40.0	21.4
Incomplete secondary to						
complete higher	36.0	77.3	73.6	66.7	65.0	54.6
Two or more children, without husband:						
Incomplete primary or less	29.0	32.9	40.0	37.4	39.2	30.7
Primary	38.4	47.0	61.9	61.2	58.1	41.9
Incomplete secondary to						
complete higher	37.5	58.8	75.0	70.0	64.4	70.3
One child, without husband:						
Incomplete primary or less	36.1	39.5	37.9	50.0	41.4	34.3
Primary	52.0	52.0	74.4	69.2	57.1	38.5
Incomplete secondary to						
complete higher	56.4	73.1	84.9	90.5	66.7	40.0
No children, without husband:						
Incomplete primary or less	38.2	37.1	45.1	37.7	41.6	33.6
Primary	56.2	63.8	60.4	67.4	53.9	51.6
Incomplete secondary to						
complete higher	55.1	78.1	84.0	86.8	84.9	68.1

SOURCE. —Unpublished table elaborated by CELADE (Omuece 70).

dren is almost five times higher than those with similar levels of education who had a husband and two or more children. This difference drops to one and a half among the most highly educated females. The same trend is observed in Paraguay, though at lower levels of schooling. In other words, having or not having a husband and children has smaller effects on the labor behavior of Paraguayan than on Argentinian females. Circumstances related to the occupational composition and the family structure probably account largely for that difference. Agricultural and handicrafts employment, which is more prevalent among Paraguayan females, provides less conflict with childbearing. Argentinian women are more frequently employed in the modern sector of the economy as professionals, technicians, or clerical workers in jobs usually carried out away from home and with rigid working hours. Furthermore, there is reason to believe that the extended family is more prevalent in Paraguay than in Argentina. If this is the case, then Paraguayan females would have greater opportunity to share their domestic duties with others. Even though Paraguayan women have larger numbers of children than Argentinian women, which implies a greater burden of household work, older children can help take care of the younger ones, relieving women of this responsibility.

If education influences the probability of females participating in the labor market regardless of family situation, under what condition do the effects of education surpass those of the family situation, and under what circumstances do the latter surpass the former? To answer this question, we shall focus our attention on two particular groups of females, those for whom family situation and education have opposite effects on labor force participation. We shall compare the rates of the females who have a husband and two or more children and who have the highest educational attainment with those who have neither husband nor children and who have not completed primary school. It should be kept in mind that, in terms of family circumstances, the former group has the lowest rate of labor force participation and the latter the highest. If the most highly educated (but with greater family burdens) show higher activity rates than the least educated (but with smaller family burdens), we could then conclude that the driving effects of education surpass the retracting ones derived from family situation.

For Argentinian females, as shown in figure 1, the effects of education and family situation vary between age cohorts. In the youngest, those aged 20–24 and 25–29, the influence of the family surpasses that of education. These young females have two or more children who for the most part have not yet entered primary school and make greater demands on mothers. At this stage, family burdens keep a high proportion of these women out of the labor force. This trend is strongest among women who are still in school. At these ages, the effects of education surpass those of family situation. (The shaded area in fig. 1 shows the extent to which these females' activity rates are higher than those of females who have neither husband nor children and are in the lower extreme of the educational scale.) At about ages 30–34, the relative influence of the driving and retracting factors becomes even. In short, having two or more children, though quantitatively constant for females of different ages, has qualitatively different meanings along the family cycle.

The changing interaction between education and family situation can be more fully appreciated in the sequence of figures 1, 2, and 3. These illustrate the consequences of the decrease in filial demands, a decrease now due not only to the decreased attention required by the older chil-

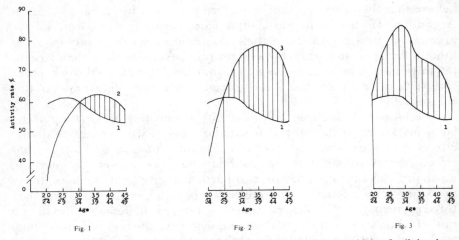

FIGS. 1–3.—Activity profiiles of women, Argentina, 1970. Fig. 1, Women with low family burdens, low education and women with high family burdens, high education. Fig. 2, Women with low family burdens, low education and women with middle family burdens, high education. Fig. 3, Women with low family burdens, low education and women with low family burdens, high education, 1 = no husband, no children, incomplete primary education or less; 2 = husband, one child, higher education; 4 = husband, no children, higher education. Source: table 1.

dren but also to the presence of fewer children. In these figures, the labor force activity rates of females with neither husband nor children and primary education or less are compared with those of women with a higher educational level and a husband at home and with two or more, only one, or no children. These three last sets of women correspond to the groups that, in terms of family circumstances, show the lowest labor force participation. The trend is very clear: the effects of education increasingly surpass those of the family, and they do so in younger and younger age groups. Among females with two or more children, the age group where the effects of both factors become even and counterbalance is that of 30–34 (fig. 1). Among the females with one child, this situation is found in the 25–29 age group (fig. 2), and among childless females, in the 20–24 age group (fig. 3). The smaller the number of children, the shorter the portion of the life cycle where females face greater filial demands. Among married childless females, the driving effects of education appear earlier.

In Paraguay, the participation profiles of the equivalent groups of females are more irregular. The low frequencies of females with high education levels and of married childless females in that country account for much of this irregularity. Even though the patterns arising from the analysis of figures 4, 5, and 6 are not as clear as those for Argentina, the

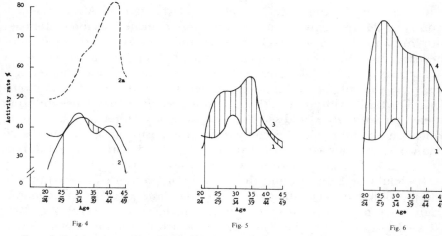

Fig. 4   Fig. 5   Fig. 6

FIGS. 4–6.—Activity profiles of women, Paraguay, 1972. Fig. 4, Women with low family burdens, low education and women with high family burdens, high education. Fig. 5, Women with low family burdens, low education and women with middle family burdens, high education. Fig. 6, Women with low family burdens, low education and women with middle family burdens, high education. 1 = no husband, no children, incomplete primary education or less; 2 = husband, two or more children, incomplete secondary to complete higher education; 2a = husband, two or more children, higher education; 3 = husband, one child, incomplete secondary to complete higher education; 4 = husband, no children, incomplete secondary to completed higher education.

general trends in both countries are similar. As shown in figure 4, in the youngest groups, ages 20–24 and 25–29, the retracting effects of domestic burdens in homes with a husband and two or more children surpass the driving effects of secondary and higher education. Starting at ages 25–29, however, the activity profiles of these females are almost the same as those of females with neither husband nor children and with primary education or less. This suggests that starting at those ages, the intensity of the drive toward the labor market characteristic of the most educated females counterbalances, though it does not surpass, the intensity of the retraction from the labor market typical of females with husband and two or more children. Nevertheless, when examining the labor behavior of the few females with husband and two or more children and higher education exclusively, the "advantage" of the influence of education over family situation is clearly outlined all along the central ages of the life cycle, as illustrated by the comparison with the dotted curve in figure 4. Because of the low frequencies of females with higher education among those with husband and only one or no children, for the purposes of the analysis in figures 5 and 6, females with secondary and higher education were considered together.

In Paraguay as well as in Argentina, when family pressures originating in filial demands decrease (figs. 2 and 3), the driving effects of education easily surpass the retracting effects of the family. Already at age group 20–24, the activity rates of the most educated sector of females with husband and one or no children are the same as the activity rates of the least educated sector of females with neither husband nor children.

Summing up, it would seem that among females with husband, education plays the role of overcoming the negative influence of family burdens. For those without a husband and especially if they have children, when a paid activity would seem to be a necessity rather than an option, education plays the role of accompanying the positive disposition toward paid work. In other words, the driving effects of education have different meanings for females with different family situations.

It should be kept in mind that education keeps a close relationship with position in the class structure. Those who due to their socioeconomic origin have had access to higher education have, in general, a greater likelihood of getting higher and more satisfactory employment with better pay and more flexible work hours as well as greater economic means to purchase in the market the substitutes for part of the domestic chores (domestic service, child care, etc.).

These data also show that children have different meanings for women in terms of economic orientations. Children prevent those women from entering the labor market who are from the lowest educational level who have access to the least privileged positions in the economic structure. Children push into the labor market those women who have the same low educational level but must support the family due to the spouse's absence. Children have little influence on the labor force participation of those women who, on account of their high educational levels, have access to more privileged positions, whether they share the responsibility for economic family burdens with a spouse or not.

Conclusions

This study has demonstrated that formal education exerts a strong influence on labor force participation of women, over and beyond that of family situations, in both Argentina and Paraguay. Research in other countries, both in Latin America and elsewhere, is needed to see if the relationships demonstrated here are generalizable.

The implications of this study for both educational policy and human resource development are clear: education of females has a definite relation to their entry into the work force, and educating women, in this sense, will in the long run contribute to the development of national economies.

There are several issues that remain unresolved by this study and need further investigation. For example, this study did not take into account specific types of employment and the impact of education and the family on them. We do not know, for instance, whether some occupational roles are more accessible to women with certain familial characteristics than other occupational roles. Further study should distinguish full-time from part-time work, work at home from work away from home, and work with rigid hours from work with flexible hours to see how these clearly affect women's propensity to take one type of employment or another.[15] In addition, research needs to refine the impact of different family constellations on women's work force behavior. This study merely discriminated between women with husbands and without them and women who had two or more children and who had one or none. It did not distinguish between women who had infants, preschool children, or adolescents. It also left unanswered the question of variation in education's impact on labor force participation among similarly educated women with children whose filial demands may differ.

In short, new case studies are needed that will detect for what values of certain structural parameters the relationship found here among education, family, and female employment is valid. In order to understand better that relationship, it will be necessary to advance along the study of the characteristics of female activities and the characteristics of their family situations. This task may mean resorting to data sources other than censuses and turning to sources frequently used by anthropologists, social psychologists, and historians.

[15] Darian calls these characteristics "conveniences of work."

PART IV
Outcomes of Women's Schooling:
The Family

16. Influences of Women's Schooling on Maternal Behavior in the Third World

ROBERT A. LE VINE

This is an interim report on some effects of an ongoing historical process: the spread of Western schooling among the peoples of Asia, Africa, Latin America, and the Pacific. This process of institutional diffusion began on a significant scale more than a century ago, has accelerated since World War II, and will certainly continue for a long time. In most places the schooling of women has lagged far behind that of men and is thus a more recent phenomenon; yet enough progress has been made for an early assessment of effects.

The notion that educating women in the Third World has potent and beneficial effects on child care and family life is appealing because it fits in with many of our cherished beliefs and values. Our task in this paper, however, is to set ideology aside and consider whether and to what extent this idea is true, by identifying the research questions involved, reviewing empirical studies, and interpreting their results with as little bias as possible. We must emphasize at the outset that we do not believe educated women make "better mothers" in any general sense. Indigenous patterns of infant and child care throughout the Third World represent largely successful adaptations to conditions of life that have long differed from one people to another, and the values embodied in these patterns have long been effectively transmitted by parents who had no formal education.[1] Nonliterate women were "good mothers" by the only relevant standards, those of their own culture. The hypothesis central to this paper is that women with formal schooling will show a greater tendency to prepare their children for participation in a new socioeconomic order found in the urban sectors of Third World societies. We do not ignore by-products or concomitants of this hypothesized tendency, but we do not assume they will be beneficial or adaptive.

This paper's focus on maternal behavior or "mothering" should not be interpreted to mean that only biological mothers are or should be

This report was produced with the support of the National Science Foundation (BNS 77-9007) and the Ford Foundation. I acknowledge with gratitude helpful comments on the first draft by Elinor Barber, Sara Harkness, Cigdem Kagitcibasi, Jerome Kagan, David C. McClelland, Christine Oppong, and participants in the Aspen-Gajareh Workshop, "Modernization and Culture Change: The Family," June 1978; useful suggestions on the second draft by Ronald Dore, Carolyn Elliott, Gail P. Kelly, Richard Krasno, and William Sewell; and constructive advice on the third draft by Elinor Barber. I am grateful for the assistance and data analysis of Amy Richman, Barbara Welles, Shelagh O'Rourke, and James Caron.

[1] Robert A. LeVine, "Parental Goals: A Cross-cultural View," *Teachers College Record* 76 (December 1974): 226–39.

Reprinted from the *Comparative Education Review* 24, no. 2 (part 2)(June 1980): S78–105.

responsible for the early care and development of their children. Multiple caretaking of infants and fostering and adoption of young children are traditional in many human societies, including some discussed in detail below. It remains true, nevertheless, that women are the primary caretakers of preschool children almost everywhere and that among the majority of peoples they manage the care of their own offspring for at least the first 2 or 3 years. We recognize this fact without granting it normative weight or attempting to predict its future.

The education of women in the Third World is part of a process of social change often called "modernization," and its effects are, as Whiting and Edwards[2] have pointed out, difficult to disentangle from those of concomitant changes in socioeconomic participation, income, urbanization, household design, and media exposure. Where women's schooling is confined to segments of the population high in income, social status, urban residence, and media exposure —as is true in some countries — then it is especially difficult to isolate its effects. In this report we shall nevertheless consider schooling as a psychological variable, that is, as a type of experience that might have direct effects on the attitudes and behavior of women if their social and economic positions were held equal. What effects on maternal attitudes and behavior are theoretically conceivable? The following list represents some hypothetical possibilities.

1. The more educated mother might be more likely to adopt parental investment strategies designed to maximize the life chances of her children, that is, their probability of survival, health, and economic success, under the new conditions of life brought about by urbanization, economic development, and the introduction of Western schools and medical services. This could include the decision to bear fewer children so as to allocate more resources to each one, resulting in more living space, material goods, and access to parental attention for each throughout the years of immaturity, and more social and financial sponsorship in young adulthood. In specific regard to health and survival, it could mean the more educated mother might be more likely to provide a healthy diet, seek appropriate medical help, and follow medical advice in the treatment of her children. (This is not a trivial point in the Third World, where child mortality is frequent and chronic malnutrition can reduce the child's adaptive performance through the debilitating effects of diseases such as anemia as well as through heightened susceptibility to infection.) In specific regard to economic success, it could mean the more educated mother might be more concerned and knowledgeable about obtaining educational credentials for her children: supervising their school attend-

[2] Beatrice B. Whiting and Carolyn P. Edwards, "The Effect of Age, Sex and Modernity on the Behavior of Mothers and Children" (progress report submitted to the Ford Foundation, January 1978).

ance, transferring them to better schools, arranging supplementary tutoring when necessary, providing them with contacts helpful to obtain employment. Furthermore, she might be more likely to purchase goods and services for her children to help prepare them for participation in modern adult environments: books and other reading materials, toys, clocks and calendars, radios and phonographs, competent caretakers and companions from whom they can learn skills, etc. In all of these ways, it is conceivable that more educated mothers could improve the life chances of their children.

2. The more educated woman might be more likely to choose a husband who shares some of the tendencies mentioned above or who is wealthier and therefore better able to provide the resources needed to enact them.

Up to this point we have considered possibilities in which the mother functions as decision maker and manager of her child's environment, with her own schooling affecting the decisions (marital, reproductive, economic, medical) she makes concerning fateful aspects of their lives. She could theoretically have some of those decisions implemented by others, and some mothers do so. Thus without the assumption that mothers exert a lasting influence on the psychological development of their children through direct contact, it is easy to imagine maternal influence on the child's life chances operating through decisions concerning health, education, and resource allocation.

3. The more educated mother might provide her child with more useful forms of instruction, encouragement, interaction, and exposure, transmitting skills and shaping his or her psychological development in distinctive, perhaps adaptive ways. The permanence of such influence is a major question in developmental psychology.

These hypothetical possibilities represent general questions for research on the consequences of women's education for the development of children in Third World societies. They cannot be asked or answered in the same ways everywhere, for we would not expect differences in mother's education to have the same impact on maternal attitudes and behavior at different levels of schooling. In some Third World societies, the most educated mothers have had postsecondary schooling and the least educated have completed primary schooling; in others, the most educated mothers have had a few years of school and the least have never gone at all; in many others, the full continuum from illiterates to university postgraduates is present. The psychological consequences of becoming literate should be different from those involved in getting a university degree. There is then no reason to expect a linear relationship between schooling and maternal variables across the full range of Third World populations, and research designs must be sensitive to the educational contexts of specific regions and communities. The case studies presented below illustrate this point in detail.

Maternal Schooling, Fertility, and Mortality

We begin our review with the question, Does a woman's schooling affect her reproductive decisions and how she provides for the health of her children? This question takes us outside the perspective of the mother as psychological environment for her child and into the domains of demography, economics, health, and nutrition, where we lack competence. A mother's fertility and medical-nutritional practices, however, seem as likely as her other behavior to influence the psychological development of her children; in the case of fertility, by determining how many other children there will be to share domestic resources, including maternal attention; in the case of medicine and nutrition, by their impact on health and chances of survival. This is particularly likely in the Third World, where there are extreme variations in fertility, disease, and diet. If mother's education makes a difference in those factors, it should be visible there.

In the case of fertility, Cochrane has recently produced a comprehensive review and analysis of the research literature on the relationship between education (male and female) and fertility in Third World countries.[3] Reviewing the results of several dozen surveys carried out in Third World countries (very few in sub-Saharan Africa), she found a tendency for women with more schooling to have fewer children. This inverse relationship between years of school and number of children holds for their husbands too, but less strongly and hardly at all when income is held constant. For women, however, the relationship between schooling and fertility is increased when income is held constant, indicating that it is not simply a function of their economic position. In other words, within a particular economic level, women with more education bear fewer children than women with less education. This is a fairly sturdy finding, though it must be qualified as indicated below, and it suggests the possibility that schooling changes women's attitudes in favor of having fewer children.

Three qualifications to this generalization and the attitudinal implications we have drawn from it are the following: (1) To some degree, women's education affects actual fertility through age of marriage, simply by keeping girls in school and out of marriage longer so that they are older when they begin giving birth; this does not involve a shift in their reproductive attitudes. (2) To some degree, women's education affects

---

[3] Susan H. Cochrane, *Fertility and Education: What Do We Really Know?* (Baltimore: Johns Hopkins University Press, 1979).

actual fertility through employment, by providing women with qualifications to obtain jobs which interfere with their bearing as many children as women who are less educated (and nonemployed); this helps account for the finding that the inverse relationship is stronger in urban areas (where jobs are concentrated) than in rural areas (where educated women are more likely to be nonemployed). This qualification does not eliminate the possibility of an attitudinal shift, since the decision of an employed woman to curtail childbearing is not automatic but depends in part on her attitude toward integrating work with child care. It does mean, however, that the causal path from schooling to reduced fertility runs through the labor market, and if there are few jobs, the coupling of greater education with fewer children may be weakened. (3) In countries with low literacy rates, including those of tropical Africa, the relationship between women's education and fertility is more likely to be direct; women with more schooling bear *more* children than their uneducated age-mates. Thus even though there is unquestionably an inverse relationship between women's education and fertility in the Third World, a whole group of societies represent exceptions to it —at least so far.

The central problem we see in studies of women's education and fertility in the Third World lies in the role of personal attitudes. How general is the change in a woman's beliefs and values brought about by schooling, and how does the change influence her fertility? The evidence supports a variety of answers. The reduction in fertility resulting from prolonged schooling does not necessarily involve change in a woman's attitudes. If she deliberately curtails her fertility in the pursuit of an occupational career for which schooling qualifies her, this suggests attitudinal change, though it is often treated as a constrained and circumscribed economic decision. Insofar as schooling affects her ideology of family life and the place of mother-child relationships in it, however, attitudinal change may play a central role in fertility decisions. There is no denying the demographic and economic factors that help account for the correlations between women's education and fertility in the Third World. At the same time, attention should be paid to personal attitudes in order to understand the channels by which schooling affects individual fertility, a point Cochrane correctly emphasizes. As more sophisticated research attention is paid to personal attitudes, it becomes clear that they are quite important in combination with the other factors and in their own right. This has been the central concern of the Value of Children study, a cross-national investigation, the first phase of which has been admirably summarized by Espenshade.[4] Its results generally support the association between education (of both sexes) and attitudes favorable to

[4] Thomas Espenshade, "The Value and Cost of Children," *Population Bulletin* 32, no. 1 (1977): whole issue.

reduced fertility, particularly a greater interest in and expectation of nonmaterial rewards from children rather than economic support for the parents in old age. But its relatively small sample sizes did not permit women's education to be as effectively disentangled as the second phase of the study.

In its second phase the Value of Children study involved national samples of 2,000–3,000 respondents in each of nine countries: Indonesia, Korea, the Philippines, Republic of China, Singapore, Thailand, Turkey, Germany, and the United States. We have had access only to a paper by Kagitcibasi reporting some of the Turkish results.[5] In a sample of 1,763 married women, she found that "wife's education . . . shows a negative relation with numbers of children wanted ($r = -.11$, $P < .05$), even when the influence of age, income and family type is controlled. [Education] is also strongly related to parity (number of existing children). . . . When the effect of age is controlled, the correlation between wife's education and parity increases from $-.26$ to $-.31$ ($P < .05$)."[6] For Turkish women, then, fertility aspirations and accomplishments are inversely correlated with amount of schooling, even when other relevant factors have been statistically controlled. We would emphasize the fact that attitudes of educated women favoring a smaller number of children are not simply a function of income but hold up when income is held constant. Maternal education is related to family income but exerts an independent effect on personal attitudes. Though we have not seen the relevant correlations, the Turkish study seems to indicate that schooling affects fertility at least partly through modifying the attitudes of women. The final results from this and the other eight studies should shed a great deal more light on this question. At this point, however, we have no hesitation in claiming that the relationship between women's schooling and fertility shows evidence of psychological change that cannot be simply reduced to economic change.

The evidence relating the education of women to the mortality of their infants and young children is as striking as that concerning fertility. Here we rely on a recent report by Caldwell on his Nigerian study and research conducted elsewhere in the Third World.[7] He states, "Evidence has accumulated that maternal education plays a major role in determining the level of infant and child mortality, but little attempt has been made to explain this phenomenon and it frequently seems to have been assumed that maternal education is merely a reflection of the standard of

[5] C. Kagitcibasi, "Value of Children: Women's Role and Fertility in Turkey" (paper presented at Turkish Social Science Association Seminar on "Women in Turkish Society," Istanbul, May 1978).
[6] Ibid., p. 30.
[7] John C. Caldwell, "Education as a Factor in Mortality Decline: An Examination of Nigerian Data," *Population Studies* 33, no. 3 (1979): 395–413.

living."[8] Caldwell challenges the validity of this latter assumption with the results of his 1973 research in western Nigeria, where he and his colleagues surveyed 6,606 Yoruba women in Ibadan and 1,499 Yoruba women in the surrounding areas, rural and urban. They found differences in infant and child mortality by education of mothers which are consistent across categories differing by age, socioeconomic background, and current socioeconomic situation. For example, 27.6 percent of the children born to all women 45–49 years of age were reported to have died, but for unschooled women in that age bracket the figure was 29.6 percent, for women with primary schooling 24.8 percent, and for those with some secondary schooling 11.8 percent. Younger women as a whole reported smaller proportions of children who died, presumably reflecting improved health facilities over time, but within each age category those with more education showed a smaller proportion of deaths. The life expectancy of a child whose mother had some secondary education was between 10 and 17 years greater than a child whose mother did not go to school, depending on the age cohort of the mother.

Caldwell shows that those differences in child mortality by mother's schooling are not attributable simply to the better material conditions in which more educated women find themselves. Even among the wives of men with secondary school education in white-collar occupations, for example, the inverse relationship between level of women's schooling and child mortality remains strong. Among the daughters of men who had white-collar jobs the relationship is very strong.[9] Area of residence and ease of access to health facilities were of little independent consequence. Caldwell states that "in terms of child mortality, a woman's education is a good deal more important than even her most immediate environment."[10] At the end of the analysis, he concludes, "[When] five . . . control variables are employed, there is still a downward trend in child mortality so that children of mothers with secondary schooling average little more than half the chance of dying than children with mothers similar in terms of the other five characteristics but who have not had any schooling."[11] "The preceding analysis has shown that maternal education is the single most significant determinant of these marked differences in child mortality. These are also affected by a range of other socioeconomic factors, but no other factor has the impact of maternal education, and in their totality they do not even come close to explaining the effect of maternal education. Clearly maternal education cannot be employed as a proxy for gen-

[8] Ibid., p. 396.
[9] Ibid., p. 404, table 4.
[10] Ibid., p. 405.
[11] Ibid., p. 407.

eral social and economic change but must be examined as an important force in its own right."[12]

How general are these Nigerian findings? Caldwell reviews data from other parts of West Africa, India, Indonesia, the Philippines, Ecuador, Chile, Costa Rica, and the United States —all of which point in the same direction, though apparently without the same statistical controls. He notes that in a United Nations study of 115 countries, maternal literacy showed a higher correlation with life expectancy at birth than any other factor, adding support to the hypothesis that schooling has an effect on mothering that does not simply reflect material affluence.[13] More analyses like the Nigerian one are needed, but the trend of evidence to date clearly suggests that women with more schooling prevent the deaths of their small children more frequently than do women with little or no schooling.[14]

How does the schooling of a woman become translated into an enhanced likelihood that her children will survive to maturity? No one has the answer to this question, as far as empirical evidence goes. The Caldwell study shows that neither affluence nor proximity to health facilities accounts for it in western Nigeria and some other places where it has been examined. Caldwell believes that a woman who has been to school is more likely to feel personal responsibility for the health and welfare of her children, to enlist her husband and mother-in-law in this effort, and to initiate a change in intergenerational relations in the family such that children get a larger share of family resources, give less labor, and incur fewer risks.[15] He does not indicate what happens in school to make Yoruba women assume more personal responsibility for their children's health and welfare.

Extending Caldwell's speculations, we might advance the following hypothesis: The Yoruba girl, like many African children, learns early in life to take her place at the bottom of a family hierarchy in which she follows parental commands, rarely seeks the attention of adults, and does not expect her expressed thoughts or feelings to be taken seriously by them. Participation in the school classroom represents entry into a new world of values and becomes a form of assertiveness training, overcoming her reticence to speak as an adult, inducing her to display what she knows and thinks for public evaluation, and encouraging her to view her asser-

[12] Ibid., p. 408.
[13] Ibid., p. 398.
[14] This well-documented but inadequately explained finding has its parallel in research by health economists in the United States, where years of schooling is the most powerful correlate of good health (much better than income), but the connections remain matters of speculation (see Victor R. Fuchs, "The Economics of Health in a Post-industrial Society," *Public Interest* 56 [Summer 1979]: 3–20, esp. pp. 6–7).
[15] Caldwell, p. 412.

tions and attention-seeking tendencies as positive aspects of her self rather than breaches of etiquette. The consequences of this training in adulthood, we hypothesize, is a greater tendency to take one's own opinions seriously, act upon them, believe in the efficacy of one's own actions, and refuse to be intimidated by others. Additional years of schooling mean more practice in self-assertion, within the limits of the classroom, and increased confidence in the positive effects of one's judgments and actions. This leads educated mothers to pursue the health and survival of their children (a traditional goal) more persistently and with greater determination than women of the same age with less schooling.

This conjecture could be tested by empirical research if we knew more about the measures by which mothers with more schooling were reducing the death rate of their children —hygiene, nutrition, use of medical facilities, etc. —for until we can specify the behavioral outcomes of education, it is difficult to investigate the process which leads to them. We shall return to this problem in the final section of this article.

Does Mothering Influence Psychological Development?

Before exploring the relationships in Third World populations between years of maternal schooling and mother's attitudes and actions regarding the behavior of her children, it is necessary to ask whether there is reason to believe that mothering influences psychological development. Developmental psychologists have been conducting research related to this question for decades, with varying results; the pendulum of scientific opinion has swung back and forth between "yes" and "no," and continues to do so. Short-term effects of maternal behavior on the behavior of infants and young children have been demonstrated with increasing specificity and replicability;[16] it is the stability of these effects in individual development which is currently at issue. On the whole, it has been difficult so far to demonstrate long-term effects of maternal behavior on psychological development. Some investigators attribute this to the immaturity of developmental psychology as a science, that is, the crudity of its methods, particularly in the older studies for which we now have data on adults. The assumption is that with improved methods and perhaps improved conceptualization, it will be possible to show how maternal behavior in the first few years affects psychological development permanently. Others argue that the evidence as it stands is sufficient to call into question the general notion that early experience has a permanent effect on psychological development. We cannot settle this matter here, but we can provide a perspective on it for the present context.

[16] For example, K. Alison Clarke-Stewart, *Interactions between Mothers and Their Young Children: Characteristics and Consequences*, in *Monographs of the Society for Research in Child Development*, vol. 38, nos. 6–7, serial no. 153 (Chicago, 1973).

Much of the cross-cultural discussion concerning maternal influence on psychological development has been focused on cognitive development as measured by tests devised for use in Western settings. This is understandable, since the diffusion of schools based on European and American prototypes in the Third World has resulted in a linkage of school and examination performance to employment and income, a linkage which is much tighter in many Third World countries than in the West. Thus children in Asia, Africa, and Latin America increasingly go to school, are evaluated by some of the same standards as their Western counterparts, and are increasingly dependent on such evaluation for their economic adaptation. It is consequential for them if they perform less well on academic examinations and on the conventional intelligence tests designed to predict examination performance. Children from isolated, rural, and illiterate communities perform less well (on the average) on standard intelligence tests based on Western academic prototypes.

The conclusions of a previous review on this topic, though based on earlier evidence, still hold and are worth repeating in the present context:

> From this perspective, intelligence test scores measure a population's degree of intellectual adaptation to a modernized socioeconomic environment that includes Western-type educational institutions; they tell us little or nothing about the population's intellectual adaptations to other aspects of its environment past or present. For the least modernized peoples in the world, the intelligence tests tend to yield negative information, indicating what we already know, that they are not adapted to the intellectual norms of modern institutions, to which they have been recently or only partly exposed. There is no reason to believe that this information indicates a lack of long-run potential for making such an adaptation under the right educational and economic conditions; on the contrary, the diffusion of Western education provides numerous examples of large-scale adaptive changes within a few generations. In the case of the Japanese, as reported in the international study of mathematics achievement (Husen, 1967), change has involved surpassing European and American norms.[17]

Cross-cultural differences in scores on academic achievement tests and standard intelligence tests, then, are due less to inherent cognitive capacity, innate or acquired, than to the child's verbal fluency, responsiveness to elicitation by adults, self-confidence in independent problem-solving situations, willingness to display ability to others —social skills that strongly affect test performance and are affected by early experience. Mothers throughout the world play an important role in organizing the social experience of their infants and young children. As we read the available evidence, their influence on the development of these social skills operates not through providing a stimulus-rich environment in the

[17] Robert A. LeVine, "Cross-cultural Study in Child Psychology," in *Carmichael's Manual of Child Psychology*, 2 vols., ed. P. Mussen, 3d ed. (New York: Wiley, 1970), vol. 2.

manner of the old animal experiments on sensory deprivation, but through their own interaction with the child.

The Boston study of Tulkin and Covitz, for example, shows positive relationships between amount of mother-infant interaction, including reciprocal vocalization, at 10 months and cognitive performance of the same American children at 6 years of age.[18] Kagan believes these data "imply that experience that accelerates aspects of cognitive development during the first year may facilitate a slight precocity that is moderately stable through preschool years."[19] A mother who engages her baby in interactive play approximating conversation and who encourages the child to converse with her as he gets older is, deliberately or not, preparing the child to respond effectively in classroom and test-taking situations. At the other extreme, a mother who quickly soothes the baby's crying, but does not encourage conversational reciprocity in infancy or childhood, will, other things being equal, probably have a school-age child who does not respond easily to adults in the interactive situations of the classroom or test taking. It is not that the former child is brighter or more competent linguistically (in terms of knowing the grammar and vocabulary of his native language), but simply bolder about speaking to and seeking the attention of an adult, more habituated to reciprocal interaction with an adult. The second type of mother is much more likely to be found in rural areas of the Third World, partly because infant mortality there creates a chronic emergency in which maternal responsiveness to infant distress is an adaptive strategy to prevent death,[20] and partly because, as Harkness and Super[21] have shown for the Kipsigis of Kenya, domestic agricultural production requires a child who responds to adult speech with obedient action rather than reciprocal speech. As Kipsigis mothers increase their commands and insults after age 2, the children speak less frequently; in later childhood they are relatively unresponsive to simple questions on psychological tests administered in their own language. From evidence of this type it seems that mothers can and do influence the adaptive social skills their children develop in preschool years, by the quantity and quality of their interactional attention, and that cross-cultural variation in mother-child social interaction might account for concomitant variations in performance on Western tests designed originally to measure cognitive capacities.

[18] Steven Tulkin and F. Covitz, "Mother-Infant Interaction and Intellectual Functioning at Age Six" (paper presented at the meeting of the Society for Research in Child Development, Denver, April 1975).
[19] Jerome Kagan, "The Role of the Family during the First Decade," in *The Family —Can It Be Saved?* ed. V. Vaughan and T. B. Brazelton (Chicago: Year Book Medical Publishers, 1976).
[20] LeVine, "Parental Goals: A Cross-cultural View."
[21] Sara Harkness and Charles Super, "Why African Children Are So Hard to Test," in *Issues in Cross-cultural Research*, Annals of the New York Academy of Sciences, no. 285 (New York: New York Academy of Sciences, 1977), pp. 326–31.

The pattern of evidence from studies of both cultural and individual differences warrants the tentative conclusion that maternal behavior can influence the social development of young children in ways relevant to their subsequent adaptation. The question that most interests many developmental psychologists, namely, how reversible are these maternal influences on social development, cannot be answered on the basis of presently available evidence. In other words, if mothers were to engage their infants and toddlers in a great deal of reciprocal vocalization and interactive play but withdraw attention from them afterward, it is not at all clear that the unaugmented experience of the first 2 years would have a measurable effect at 12 years of age. Insofar as mothers behave consistently across a period of years, the exact "critical period" for maternal influence (if there is one) cannot be unambiguously identified in a testable hypothesis; hence the problem of reversibility remains with us as a source of controversy. If we leave the purely psychological issue and take the perspective of social adaptation, maternal influence appears more significant, because even if its impact were limited to the child's initial adjustment in school, the positive or negative nature of that adjustment might set the direction for his or her long-term academic experience, affecting performance long after maternal behavior was no longer relevant. Thus it is easy to conceive of mothering having a variety of indirect but important effects on development, mediated not through intrapsychic processes in the child but through other persons and institutions in the child's later environment.

This discussion has been limited to maternal influence on social skills relevant to performance in cognitive tests because cognitive performance is relevant to education, the new common denominator of individual adaptation throughout the world. In the acquisition of moral values, norms for the display of emotions, styles of conversation, and meanings attached to interpersonal relationships and cultural symbols, the impact of early experience may be even more enduring and the role of mothering greater. The evidence is suggestive rather than definitive, and questions of reversibility have not been resolved. But available evidence does not refute the idea that maternal behavior affects psychological development, and it remains our most plausible way of conceptualizing early experience.

Schooling and Mothering in Africa

The literature relating women's education to interpersonal and interactive influences on the psychological development of the child in the Third World is, with few exceptions, comprised of studies that have examined different aspects with different methods in different places, so that direct comparison of results is impossible. Rather than attempt a composite review, we present four studies in some detail and discuss their findings separately and then in comparative perspective.

This section reviews findings from two such studies conducted by the author in tropical Africa. The first was carried out in collaboration with Barbara Lloyd among the Yoruba of Ibadan, Nigeria, in 1961–63; its results appear in articles by Lloyd and by LeVine, Klein, and Owen.[22] The Yoruba were one of the first peoples in tropical Africa to send children to Western schools, and the education of women was by 1960 probably more advanced among the Yoruba than anywhere else. Our study compared two samples of 30 women each from Ibadan, the largest Yoruba town: one drawn from a traditional neighborhood in which we were conducting ethnographic research (these women were largely illiterate); the others were from scattered suburban families; these women had gone to secondary school, many had completed it, some had lived abroad. Though both groups of women and their husbands were Yoruba, they were far apart in schooling and sophistication —as well as wealth, housing, and husbands' occupations. To compare them is to juxtapose extremes of schooling, with other aspects of modernization inevitably and heavily confounded; it may nevertheless be instructive concerning the directions in which schooling shifts maternal attitudes.

Each of the 60 mothers was interviewed at length concerning her beliefs and behavior toward a child of hers, 5 or 6 years old at the time of the interview.[23] We regard mothers' retrospective accounts of their own behavior as attitudinal data, reflecting how they think and feel about child rearing rather than what they did to these particular children.

Table 1 (rows 1–5) shows differences in factors relevant to infant care between the traditional illiterate mothers and the highly educated mothers of the modern elite group. All of the traditional mothers and half of the elite mothers reported conforming to the lengthy prohibition on postpartum sexual intercourse; other evidence confirms this reported practice, which is associated with prolonged breast-feeding (and acts as a restraint on fertility). The traditional mothers reported breast-feeding three times as long on the average as the modern elite, also confirmed by independent evidence. The modern elite mothers are career women working in bureaucratic settings from which infants are excluded; less than a quarter considered themselves the primary caretaker of the child

[22] Barbara Lloyd, "Education and Family Life in the Development of Class Identification among the Yoruba," in The New Elites of Tropical Africa, ed. P. Lloyd (London: Oxford University Press, 1966); "Indigenous Ibadan," in The City of Ibadan, ed. P. Lloyd, A. Mabogunje, and B. Awe (Cambridge: Cambridge University Press, 1967); and "Yoruba Mothers' Reports of Child-Rearing: Some Theoretical and Methodological Considerations," in Socialization: The Approach from Social Anthropology, ed. P. Mayer (London: Tavistock, 1970); Robert A. LeVine, Nancy Klein, and Constance Owen, "Father-Child Relationships and Changing Life Styles in Ibadan, Nigeria," in The City in Modern Africa, ed. H. Miner (New York: Praeger, 1967).

[23] The interview schedule appears in Lloyd, "Yoruba Mothers," pp. 98–105.

TABLE 1

YORUBA MATERNAL ATTITUDES TOWARD INFANTS: TRADITIONAL AND MODERN ELITE MOTHERS
REPORTING SELECTED BEHAVIORS

	Traditional	Modern Elite	Group Differences
1. Postpartum taboo: practicing	30 (30)	15 (30)	$\chi^2 = 16.1, P < .001$
2. Mean duration of breast-feeding (months)	22.2 (30)	7.4 (30)	Student's t, $P < .001$
3. Force-feeding	18 (30)	3 (30)	$\chi^2 = 16.3, P < .001$
4. Primary caretaker: mother	22 (30)	7 (30)	$\chi^2 = 13.1, P < .001$
5. Deliberately talk to baby	6 (30)	12 (24)	$\chi^2 = 5.40, P < .025$
6. Strongly discourage aggression	27 (31)	15 (35)	$\chi^2 = 13.9, P < .001$
7. Praise for schoolwork	10 (30)	29 (30)	$\chi^2 = 26.45, P < .001$
8. Expect immediate obedience	27 (30)	15 (30)	$\chi^2 = 9.60, P < .01$
9. Physical punishment for slight offenses	12 (30)	1 (30)	$\chi^2 = 9.80, P < .01$

NOTE.—Numbers in parentheses are number of respondents.

during infancy. The majority of traditional mothers named themselves as primary infant caretaker and also reported force-feeding, a Yoruba custom in which gruel is fed to the baby while his nostrils are blocked. We interpret this and the prolonged breast-feeding as reflecting the traditional mother's concept that a baby needs to be fed a great deal and it is her job to do it. It is not unusual to see year-old children in traditional Ibadan fed on the average of every 30 minutes while the mother is present, with an alternation between breast and supplementary foods. Finally, half of the elite mothers reported deliberately talking to their babies to encourage speech, while only a fifth of the traditional mothers did. This suggests the educated women take a more interactive and instructional stance with their infants.

This pattern of group difference is consistent with the idea that traditional Yoruba mothers view infancy as a period in which the child's survival is jeopardized, physical nurturance is the primary means to survival, and they are the primary agents ministering to the child's needs by feeding and keeping him close. The modern elite mothers, by contrast, seem more confident of the child's survival with other caretakers and less feeding, which leaves them freer to pursue their careers. They are more likely to see the baby as requiring instruction and verbal interaction. The emphasis on physical care and feeding in infancy seems to be common in the Third World, while emphasis on interaction and instruction is more typical of the Western middle class.[24]

Table 1 (rows 6–9) shows differences related to the preschool child. The traditional mothers much more frequently gave responses classified in the category "mother strongly discourages aggression against other

[24] Le Vine, "Parental Goals: A Cross-cultural View."

children (excluding siblings)," from Sears, Maccoby, and Levin;[25] they were also much more likely to report expecting immediate obedience from their small children and punishing them physically for slight offenses. The modern elite mothers, on the other hand, much more frequently report, in answer to a question that asked them to imagine their response to their own child's bringing home a good report card from school, that they would give praise or a tangible reward, or both; most of the traditionals said they would thank God or feel happy. In the postinfancy period, it appears that the traditional mother's goal is to make the child tractable and obedient in the household labor force, whereas the modern elite mother, more tolerant of fighting and other misbehavior, and more willing to give positive reinforcement for good performance, wants a more active and self-confident child who will do well in school.[26] Here again, these trends resemble differences between working-class and middle-class samples in Western studies.[27]

To what extent can these attitudinal differences be attributed to mother's education? There is no question that the modern elite responses resemble those of educated middle-class mothers in other countries, and that the traditional mothers gave responses widely found among less educated women of the lower classes in many places. But there is no way of showing in this study that the education of the mother has an effect on her child-rearing attitudes that is independent of her economic position in life. Both groups of women live in a large city, engage in remunerative work (the traditionals as market traders), speak the Yoruba language, and hold to some of the more basic Yoruba values. Their life-styles and material positions in life are so different, however, and their prior experience has differed in so many ways other than schooling, that their attitudinal differences cannot be reliably attributed to the influence of school. Furthermore, since they are such extreme groups, it could well be that the more educated came from families different from those of the less educated (e.g., more likely to be Christian, Western-oriented, well-to-do) and that the variations in maternal attitude reflect their family backgrounds rather than (or inextricably with) their educational experience. We need to examine a less polarized sample to assess the effect of schooling on maternal attitude.

In a recent longitudinal investigation of infants and their parents among the Gusii of Kenya, we studied a less polarized sample that gives the hope of teasing out the effects of mother's education with greater

[25] Robert R. Sears, Eleanor E. Maccoby, and Harry Levin, *Patterns of Child Rearing* (Evanston, Ill.: Row, Peterson, 1975), p. 246.
[26] Lloyd, "Yoruba Mothers," pp. 83–86.
[27] Melvin Kohn, *Class and Conformity: A Study of Values* (Homewood, Ill.: Dorsey, 1967).

precision, at least for infancy.[28] Unlike the Yoruba, the Gusii have been a strictly rural people, isolated from the mainstream of modernization in Kenya, and with relatively little socioeconomic differentiation. Few men and hardly any women had gone past primary school before Kenya's independence in 1963. As late as 1968, when Nerlove conducted a study in the Gusii community described by LeVine and LeVine, she found that all of the mothers of her sample children were illiterate.[29] Our infant study, which included women from surrounding communities and was conducted in 1974–76, after the expansion of school in the area, took in 28 mothers, seven of whom had completed primary school (7 years of schooling). They ranged in age from 21 to 43, with the more educated women tending to be younger. The inverse correlation between age and education ($r = -.56$) is not as high as one might expect, because while most of the older women had no schooling, so did some of the younger ones. This study, then, examines maternal schooling at its lower levels, contrasting illiterates with women who have had partial or complete primary education.

The Gusii sample mothers, however differentiated by their educational backgrounds, are neighbors, inhabiting the same area, cultivating their fields, and mothering infants during 1974–76. (They were selected randomly within a sex-balanced design of three overlapping age cohorts of infants.) Their differences in life-style, unlike those of the Yoruba samples in Ibadan, are not immediately apparent to the outside observer. They are all working mothers who do their agricultural work at home. Table 2 shows the family characteristics associated with mother's schooling. The more educated women tend to be married to men with more schooling, but wife's education is more strongly correlated with husband's occupational prestige (in local terms), suggesting that women with more schooling marry men with better prospects of community status. Husband's income is only moderately related to wife's education, presumably because the young husbands of higher occupation or schooling have not yet translated these intangibles into material rewards. This cluster of relationships means that the schooling of a woman becomes confounded through mate selection with her husband's occupation, education, and income, though at a moderate level of correlation.

The education of a Gusii woman affects her life-style and consumption patterns in ways related to the infant's environment. One important choice facing a woman is whether she will spend money on alcoholic

[28] The field research was carried out during 1974–76 with the support of the National Science Foundation (SOC74-12692) and the National Institute of Mental Health (Research Scientist Award).
[29] Sara B. Nerlove, "Trait Dispositions and Situational Determinants of Behavior among Children of Southwestern Kenya" (Ph.D. diss., Stanford University, 1969); Robert A. LeVine and Barbara B. LeVine, *Nyansongo: A Gusii Community in Kenya* (Huntington, N.Y.: Krieger, 1977).

TABLE 2

CORRELATES OF MATERNAL CHARACTERISTICS IN THE GUSII INFANT STUDY
(N = 28)

	Maternal Characteristics				
	Education	Age	Modern Attitudes	Education with Age Controlled	Education with Income Controlled
Family characteristics:					
Maternal age	−.56**	...	.25	...	...
Husband's education	.43**	−.55**	.12	...	...
Husband's occupational prestige	.52**	−.21	.31	...	...
Husband's income	.29	.13	.01	...	...
Maternal drinking (frequency)	−.41*	.13	−.17	−.41*	−.33*
Media-contact consumption	.50**	−.45**	.32*	.34*	.48**
Maternal beliefs:					
Age baby sees	.11	−.57**	−.37*	−.30	.21
Age recognizes mother's face	−.14	−.20	−.13	−.31	−.14
Age responds to mother's voice	−.20	−.14	−.19	−.34*	−.21
Child nurse as teacher	.38*	−.33*	.00	.25	.40*
Mother/child behavior:					
Play (all)	.18	.43**	.38*	.55**	.10
Social play (frequency)	.26	.36*	.41*	.59**	.14
Social play (proportion)	.31*	.21	.26		.20
Breast-feeding (frequency)	−.19	.21	−.42*	−.08	−.22
Breast-feeding (proportion)	−.16	.33*	−.41*	.04	−.33*
Bayley Mental Score (1 year)	.28	−.02	−.38*	.33*	.21

NOTE.—Pearson r's are presented, despite difficulty of estimating normality of distributions with such a small sample. Nonparametric correlations yield essentially the same results.
* P = .05.
** P = .01.

beverages, a form of self-indulgence that diverts scarce resources from their possible use in providing for the needs of children. A four-point scale of frequency of maternal drinking is inversely correlated with mother's education, suggesting that more educated women may be sacrificing their own immediate pleasures for the welfare of the family. The other consumer decisions on which we have information are related to the education level of both parents. We divided the inventory of physical objects in the home into items of comfort and convenience (furniture, roof material, well) and items relating to media contact (newspaper, radio, calendar, photographs on wall). The first set is not related to maternal schooling, while the latter is. Media-contact items are as strongly related to husband's education ($r = .54$), suggesting that men make some or all of these consumer decisions. The strong partial correlation of mother's education with media-contact items when income is controlled indicates that this pattern of consumption is more a function of education than of income.

Table 2 also shows the relation of mother's education and other characteristics to her beliefs about infants. The Gusii traditionally conceive of infancy in terms of physical care rather than communication and learning, and elderly women claimed that young infants had little or no capacity for sensing or responding to their maternal environment. We asked our sample mothers at what age a baby could see, recognize his mother's face, and respond to his mother's voice. Our hypothesis was that more educated mothers would give younger ages, that is, that schooling would lead them to conceive of the infant's capacity to sense and respond as beginning earlier. The expected inverse correlations between maternal education and these age attributions did not materialize, as table 2 shows. Although controlling for age brings one correlation up to significance and the other two close to it, they are eliminated when income is controlled. The mother's score on a Modern Attitudes questionnaire is a slightly better predictor of these age attributions. The Modern Attitudes questionnaire consists of 11 items adapted from the work of Inkeles and covering club membership, knowledge and interest in the outside world and current events, and beliefs and preferences concerning reproduction. It is not correlated with mother's education ($r = -.14$), which means that some educated women scored low on it and some uneducated ones scored high. Thus maternal education and modernity as measured by the questionnaire are not equivalent in this sample, and it is attitudinal modernity rather than education that tends to be correlated with the mother's beliefs that infants are capable of sensation and communication at a younger age.

The last item under Maternal Beliefs, "Child nurse as teacher," shows a different pattern. Each of the mothers was asked, "What does a child nurse do for a baby that a mother does not do?" Some mothers mentioned playing, others teaching; we classified them into those who mentioned teaching and those who did not. This answer is correlated with mother's education (point biserial $r = .38$, $P < .05$) and is not diminished when income is controlled (partial $r = .40$, $P < .05$). Thus more educated mothers seem to conceptualize infant care in more educational terms, even when someone else is doing it.

The bottom third of table 2 shows the correlation with maternal characteristics of several behavioral items. The first five, covering play and breast-feeding, are scores derived from the spot observations made by a native observer who visited each infant's home more than 80 times over a 15-month period. The first item, "Play (all)," represents all the instances in which the baby was found playing with physical objects, other persons, or self; the second, "Social play," represents those in which he was found playing with other persons; "Social play (proportion)" represents the proportion that social play is of all play. Mother's education is only significantly correlated with the third of these ($r = .31$, $P < .05$), and even this is reduced below significance when income is controlled. Mother's Modern Attitudes are a better predictor of play, being significantly correlated with two of the items. The first of the breast-feeding variables represents all the observed instances in which mother was found nursing the infant; the second is the proportion these constitute of all instances of maternal holding. We predicted that mother's education would be negatively correlated with the latter of these, on the supposition that educated mothers would more frequently do something other than feed when holding the baby. This was not confirmed. There is a negative correlation when income is controlled (partial $r = -.33$, $P < .05$), but not when age is controlled (partial $r = .04$). Mother's Modern Attitudes are a much better predictor than her education.

Finally, there is (at the bottom of table 2) the Mental Score from the Bayley Infant Scales, standardized in the United States, which we administered to all the sample children. Using their performance at approximately 12 months of age (some were older, but the scores are age adjusted), we find a nonsignificant correlation with mother's education ($r = .28$), which increases when age is controlled (partial $r = .33$, $P < .05$) but declines when income is controlled (partial $r = .21$). Age is unrelated and Modern Attitudes are inversely correlated ($r = -.33$, $P < .05$).

Figure 1 shows one way the education of these Gusii women might be influencing the development of their children. While mother's education

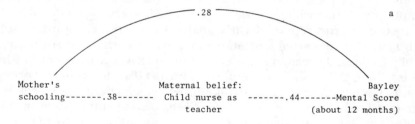

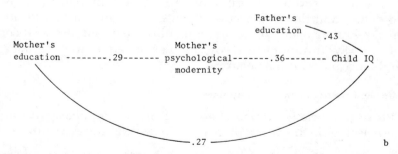

FIG. 1.—a, Correlations (Pearson's r) of maternal variables with Bayley test scores of Gusii infants; b, correlations (Spearman's rho) of parent variables with WPPSI scores in Manila.

is correlated with baby's 1-year Bayley Mental Score at a nonsignificant level ($r = .28$), it is connected with those scores through sturdy relationships with a third variable, "Child nurse as teacher" (see description above). The correlation shown between maternal education and the belief that the child nurse teaches the baby better than the mother ($r = .38$, $P < .05$) is, as mentioned above, undiminished by controlling for income (partial $r = .40$, $P < .05$). The belief variable in turn is strongly correlated with the Bayley Mental Score ($r = .44$, $P < .01$), and this correlation also holds up when income is controlled (partial $r = .46$, $P < .01$). Thus while mother's schooling is not strongly related with the baby's test performance in a direct way, it may be influencing it through a belief factor that is strongly correlated with the Bayley test results. This illustrates the need to use causal inference procedures for this type of problem. It throws no particular light on what it is that mothers who think of the child nurse as a teacher might be doing to their babies or to the child nurses that affects the babies' performance. The maternal behavior link in the causal chain, however, is missing. We suspect that spot observations are too crude to detect the qualitative factors in the infant's interactions with his caretakers that are making this difference. If those factors include reciprocal vocalization or other forms of contingent interaction, for example, identifying them requires examination of our naturalistic observations on the infants' interaction with their caretakers, which are being analyzed.

In this interim report of early analyses from the Gusii infant study with respect to maternal education, we have seen that the education of women is strongly related to aspects of the family environment in which she is raising children, for example, her husband's education and occupation, her media contact, and drinking behavior. There is also evidence that educated women, irrespective of wealth, see infant care in more educational terms and that this is related to infant test performance. On the other hand, the aspects of maternal behavior examined so far seem to be heavily influenced by the family income. We conclude that the independent effects of women's education are difficult, though not impossible, to detect, and that it is necessary not only to control statistically for income and other material factors to identify them but also to focus on causal pathways through which education exerts an indirect but measurable influence on maternal behavior.

Schooling and Mothering in the Philippines

This section briefly presents findings from an unpublished study by Salvador-Burris in the area of Manila in which she grew up.[30] Sixty

[30] Juanita Salvador-Burris, "Modernization, Social Class, Childrearing and Cognitive Performance: Their Inter-Relationships in an Urban Community in the Philippines" (Ph.D. diss., University of Chicago, 1977).

families (30 "middle class," 30 "lower class") were chosen, the mothers interviewed, and children tested during 1970–71. By contrast with the African studies just reviewed, in the lower-class sample 40 percent of the mothers had been to high school or beyond, the rest to primary school; in the middle-class sample, 37 percent had attended college, 50 percent went as far as high school, and only 13 percent had only primary schooling. Even the less educated mothers were literate, reported reading an average of one newspaper and one magazine regularly, as well as listening to the radio; one-third of the lower-class mothers own television sets. This is a different world in terms of urban sophistication, media exposure, and women's education. What is most significant from the perspective of this report is that the lower-class mothers in Manila have more schooling on the average than the best-educated rural Gusii women, and even those Manila women with the least education are likely to use their literacy more regularly than their Gusii equivalents. When we make comparisons of Manila groups defined by social class or mother's education, we are examining the effects of secondary and postsecondary education rather than those of literacy.

Salvador-Burris interviewed the 60 mothers about their child-rearing attitudes and practices, and she constructed a role-playing situation interview to assess their "psychological modernity," specifically, their sense of efficacy, readiness for new experience, and risk taking. She tested their 4–7-year-old children with a Tagalog translation of the Wechsler Preschool and Primary Scale of Intelligence (WPPSI). The WPPSI has not been standardized in the Philippines, and even though one section was dropped as culturally biased and the test was administered by experienced local testers, the middle-class mean was only 85.63 and the lower-class mean 77.8. Salvador-Burris interpreted the scores as assessments of cognitive performance reflecting acquired skills related to Western norms of academic achievement. Her analysis is focused on differences between the samples defined by social class, but it is possible to see in her dissertation findings relevant to the effect of mother's schooling.

Figure 1b shows some of these relevant findings. Mother's education is correlated moderately with child's WPPSI score but not as strongly as is her psychological modernity. The correlation between maternal schooling and child IQ disappears entirely when social class, income, or father's education is controlled. The correlation of mother's psychological modernity with IQ, however, holds up even when other factors are controlled. This is also true of father's education, the strongest correlate by far of child's IQ. This finding may seem surprising, but it can be partly explained by three factors: the fathers are highly educated (more than half of the middle-class fathers have at least a high school education); they

303

have more schooling than their wives; and they spend time in interaction with their children, in contrast with fathers in other parts of the Third World. Thus the Tagalog fathers are in a position to affect the psychological development of their children, and they apparently do so.

Another unusual finding from the Salvador-Burris study is that the mother's child-rearing attitudes and practices, including tolerance of aggression and educational values, were unrelated to the psychological modernity responses, child's IQ, and social class. It is clear, however, that the sharp differences in child-rearing attitudes found in earlier studies between unsophisticated and disadvantaged mothers on the one hand and sophisticated, privileged, and educated ones on the other are not easily replicated where all the women are literate, urban, and in contact with the mass media. The Manila mothers seem to have less exclusive control over the early education of their children than those Third World mothers with absent or indifferent husbands and no television. Nevertheless, the correlation of .36 between the psychological modernity of the mother and child's WPPSI score, which holds up even when father's education is controlled, suggests a maternal influence related to her education without indicating the nature of the influence process. Further analysis of these data might reveal possible paths of influence.

The major lesson we draw from the Salvador-Burris data as they have been analyzed is that when the factors of maternal illiteracy and paternal noninvolvement are removed, the relationships between women's education, maternal behavior, and child performance become more complicated and somewhat more difficult to assess. At the upper end of the scale on mother's schooling in the Third World, environmental influences on child development may show a substantially different pattern.

Schooling and Mothering in Los Angeles: A Mexican-American Study

This section reports briefly a study by Laosa of Chicano families in Los Angeles.[31] We include it because it brings a Latin American sample into our comparative perspective and shows that some of the findings (and problems) encountered abroad are also located in the United States. Laosa selected 43 5-year old Chicano children from the kindergartens of two public schools in Los Angeles. The Maternal Teaching Observation Technique (MTOT) was administered at home to each of the mothers with her 5-year-old. In the MTOT the mother is shown an assembled model of a robot and then of an airplane, and asked to teach her child how to make a model like the one already assembled. The observer records the frequency of occurrence of nine categories of maternal behavior as she does so.

[31] Luis Laosa, "Maternal Teaching Strategies in Chicano Families of Varied Educational and Socioeconomic Levels." *Child Development* 49 (1978): 1129–35.

All of the most significant results of this investigation involve parental education. "Modeling," the frequency of the mother's doing part of the task for the child's observation and imitation, is inversely correlated with both mother's (−.68) and father's (−.78) education for boys though not for girls. "Praise," the frequency of the mother's praise or verbal approval for the child's activity or product, is directly correlated with parents' education for both sexes, with correlations of .66 to .72. "Inquiry," the frequency with which the mother asks the child a question, is also correlated with parents' education for both sexes, with correlations of .50 −.65 ($P < .01$). There were hardly any significant correlations with parent's occupation levels.

These are striking results, especially in terms of the magnitude of the relationships and their consistency with other research. The more educated mothers teach through a more conversational style ("Inquiry") rather than motoric demonstration ("Modeling"), and they especially include verbal reinforcement ("Praise") in their method of teaching. One might say they are imitating the academic style of the school classrooms in which they have spent so much of their lives! Conversely, it is very significant that father's education is almost as good at predicting mother's behavior as her own education. This requires a closer look at the background data.

Both parents vary widely in the schooling they have had: the mothers from 1 to 14 years, with a mean of 8.79; the fathers from 2 to 18 years, with a mean of 8.9. In other words, the sample encompasses a range from the barely literate to those with postsecondary education, which is partly responsible for the magnitude of the correlations. The schooling of mother and father are correlated (rho = .66), which helps account for the strong relationship between father's education and maternal behavior. But in only two of the five sets of significant correlations is mother's education appreciably better than father's education in predicting her own teaching behavior. This suggests that husbands exert an influence on their wives that goes beyond mating by level of schooling and that patterns of husband-wife interaction must be involved. Thus these data show that parental education is more important than father's occupation in accounting for maternal teaching strategies, but they do not support the idea that mother's education acts independently of her husband's characteristics even in organizing her own behavior toward their children.

Critique of Studies on Schooling and Mothering

In the set of hypotheses concerning schooling and mothering with which we have been implicitly concerned, schooling involves a process of attitude formation or attitude change. The educated woman brings attitudes acquired in school into the situation of mothering where they affect the way she behaves toward her child, thus influencing the child's behavior in a way that bears on his or her subsequent adaptation. Testing the whole set of hypotheses would not only require studying women in school but also four hypothesized outcomes of schooling: maternal attitudes, maternal behavior (during infancy and early childhood), infant behavior (observed in natural and test situations), and child behavior (assessed through interviews, observations, and tests) —nine categories of data altogether. In the four studies we have reviewed, seven of the categories are covered in at least one study, but only two (maternal attitudes toward infants and children) are found in more than one study. The studies are thus not comparable even though they draw on the same basic theoretical viewpoint in relating woman's education to one or more of its hypothesized outcomes. Furthermore, except for the Gusii and Manila studies, the correlational data do not lend themselves to the causal inferences which the hypotheses require. They do not cover enough points in the hypothesized sequence to constitute even a hypothetical time series let alone an actual one. The conclusions to be reached on the basis of such limited evidence cannot be more than tentative.

The results of these four studies among culturally diverse peoples are remarkably consistent with each other and with the hypothesis that mother's education is a factor in promoting reciprocal verbal interaction in the mother-child relationship and other early relationships, with praise as a reinforcer for child behaviors that lead to improved preschool performance on Western tests. The results are, however, consistent with several alternative theses: That the more educated women had parents who were more educated, sophisticated, or otherwise privileged, from whom they acquired the attitudes attributed to schooling before going to school. That the more educated women married men of greater education, wealth, or distinctive values who made it possible in terms of material conditions and ideological influence for the women to acquire the maternal attitudes attributed to maternal schooling. Other theses may be generated, but these arise directly from the studies reviewed above.

None of the studies we have reviewed was specifically designed to detect the independent effects from those confounding variables, or to eliminate alternative explanations of variations in maternal attitudes and behavior and the performance of infants and children. Our examination of the place of women's education in their results leads to definite guidelines for the design of future research that is intended to focus on the contribution of maternal schooling to child rearing and development. What follows is a minimal set of guidelines:

1. Independent bodies of data should be collected on (*a*) maternal attitudes (interview); (*b*) maternal behavior (observation) of some women,

covering, if possible, both the infancy and early childhood of their children; (c) the behavior of infants and children raised by the same women. Only in this way will it be possible to test the hypothesis that these variables constitute a causal chain leading from mother's schooling.

2. Socioeconomic and educational background data should be collected on (a) the women's parents and other caretakers, (b) the women's husbands, and (c) any other caretakers involved with the child. Furthermore, data should be collected on husband-wife decision making concerning the child's environment and the quantity and quality of father-child interaction. These data are necessary to test some of the rival hypotheses that we have outlined above.

3. Multivariate and causal inference techniques should be applied to the data to identify the contribution of maternal education to its hypothesized outcomes and to test the validity of causal paths that lead from mother's schooling through maternal attitudes and behavior to infant and child behavior. This will often require larger samples than have been used in previous studies.

4. Cross-national collaboration should be worked out so that comparable data can be collected in different countries with different educational and cultural contexts, to make comparisons possible and test the generality of correlational findings within specific regions.

Conclusions and Recommendations

As women's schooling has spread in the Third World, our understanding of its effects on mothering has also moved forward, though unevenly. We know more than we did 15 years ago, but questions have grown as rapidly as answers. Some generalizations can be advanced on the basis of evidence to date: Women's schooling is often associated with lower fertility, lower infant and child mortality, and a style of maternal behavior toward young children that is more pedagogical and conversational than the styles indigenous to many Third World cultures. None of these generalizations can be claimed as universal or uniform across regions, levels of schooling, or age cohorts. Even the fertility relationship, for which there is much evidence, may be reversed in regions of relatively low literacy such as tropical Africa, where the data are less adequate. Nonetheless, the demographic research reviewed in this article includes large-scale studies showing that the schooling of women has effects on fertility and mortality independent of material conditions, husband's education, and other factors attributable to the external situation of the mother. Demographers have been moved to suggest a psychological influence of schooling on the reproductive behavior of women in the Third World.

307

The demographic findings, particularly if confirmed by subsequent research, have important implications for the development of children in the Third World. Insofar as women with more schooling deliberately bear fewer children and take more effective measures for their survival, these children grow up in distinctive environments, with fewer siblings and access to a greater share of family resources. As sons and daughters of the demographic transition, their psychosocial development as well as their life expectancies should differ from the children of less educated women in ways that have not yet been investigated.

The evidence concerning maternal attitudes and behavior, in contrast with the demographic data, is admittedly preliminary and fragmentary, yet it suggests that schooling has an effect on how women in the Third World societies think about and behave toward their infants and young children in ways that might affect their psychological development. A greater pedagogical interest in and conversational approach to the pre-school child is most clearly associated with maternal schooling when mothers with at least a primary education are compared with those who have had little or no school experience. Larger and more comprehensive research, outlined in the preceding section, is needed to tease out the specific contribution of education to this pattern of maternal behavior and to identify its effects on the child's performance. It cannot be claimed that children of more educated mothers necessarily do better in school; indeed, at least one large-scale study shows that they do not.[32] But most of the evidence shows the education of women to be deeply implicated in social change relating to the family and early education and indicates that it will continue to be a factor of central importance, however the pathways of causal influence run from institutional innovation to individual performance.

A major question raised by this review is how the schooling of girls effects a change in their subsequent reproductive and maternal behavior. What happens in school that leaves women who have had more years of it with maternal attitudes and behavioral tendencies differing from those who have had less? This question is particularly important because it involves the issue of what kind of psychological change schooling brings about in women and what kind of social change might be expected from it. Since there is little speculation and less information about this in the literature, an exploration of alternative hypotheses might be useful. We see three plausible models concerning the process of schooling and its impact on reproduction and mothering:

[32] Stephen P. Heyneman, "Why Impoverished Children Do Well in Ugandan Schools" (unpublished report, 1979). Heyneman surveyed more than 2,000 seventh-grade pupils throughout Uganda and found zero correlations between examination results and family status variables, including mother's education.

1. *Cognitive growth:* In this model, schooling endows the girl with an expanded awareness of means-ends relationships in her environment and the capacity to use it in novel contexts as she encounters them. Thus the woman with more education is more likely to see births in relation to future expenditures, diet in relation to health and growth, the speech of infants and young children in relation to school performance, than her unschooled sister. This would account for the fact that schooling fosters birth limitation, reduced infant mortality, and verbal interaction with preschoolers even where schools do not give explicit instruction on these topics. By making girls more reflective about what leads to or causes what and more sensitive to means-ends connections through primary classroom instruction of the usual kind, schooling may be preparing them to understand and accept official advice on family planning, health and hygiene, and a more child-centered ideology of domestic management.

2. *Self-development:* According to this model, participation in school bolsters the self-esteem, sense of personal efficacy, and belief in internal control of a girl whose home environment had cast her into a position of subordination and compliance. This is the "assertiveness training" hypothesis discussed above in relation to the Caldwell study. Although there is a cognitive component in this—belief in one's ability to achieve results—the type of learning envisioned entails social behavior which goes far beyond an improvement in conceptual reasoning or other information-processing abilities.

3. *Imitation or identification:* This model suggests that the classroom introduces a girl to a new kind of interaction between an adult and a child—one in which the adult asks the child to display her knowledge and then praises the child when she is right. In parts of tropical Africa, and perhaps elsewhere in the world, little girls are unlikely to be asked questions with such encouraging intent at home and are rarely if ever praised by adults; for them classroom instruction provides a new style of discourse worthy of imitation. When they become mothers, according to this hypothesis, they take the role of teacher with their infants and engage in reciprocal vocalization, questioning, and praise as their teachers did to them. Unschooled women are unlikely to do this because they have not been exposed to this kind of adult-child interaction. (This model says nothing about fertility or mortality.)

These alternative models of the process by which schooling affects maternal behavior are not necessarily contradictory. They need to be better specified but cannot be, without observations of the learning environments for girls at home and in school, and investigations of the cognitive development, sense of self, and imitative tendencies of school-going and non-school-going girls in diverse communities in the Third World. To resolve the questions raised by this article, investigations of this sort, as well as those suggested in the preceding section, are of the highest priority. These alternative models of educational influence on maternal behavior all assume a discontinuity between the nonschool and school environments of girls —in cognitive style, participation, or interactive exposure. But the discontinuity may be greater in some Third World societies than others and in rural than urban communities everywhere. There is thus no way of answering these questions concerning process without evidence from diverse cultures and educational systems in different parts of the world.

17. Education and Fertility: An Expanded Examination of the Evidence

SUSAN H. COCHRANE

In 1979 a book entitled *Fertility and Education: What Do We Really Know?* was published.[1] Its purpose was to review the evidence on the relationship between education and fertility and to develop a model of the channel through which education operated. Since that book was begun (August 1976), a large number of studies have become available. In particular, the World Fertility Surveys (WFS) have provided far more reliable data on the determinants of fertility in developing countries.[2]

This paper expands on the evidence presented in the earlier book, concentrating in particular on the micro, or household, data rather than looking at the cross-national and cross-regional data. While there may be interactions between aggregate and individual levels of education and fertility that will not be captured by looking at individual studies only, these studies do provide a more reliable method of studying how education affects an individual's behavior than do macro studies.

Therefore, this paper examines individual data (old and new) on the relationship between education and fertility and then presents a model explaining why education may have the variety of effects on fertility that it appears to have. Finally, the evidence (old and new) on the effect of education on the intervening variables in the model is reviewed, particularly on the biological supply of children, since previously data of this kind was scarce.

[1] S. H. Cochrane, *Fertility and Education: What Do We Really Know?* World Bank Staff Occasional Paper No. 26 (Baltimore: Johns Hopkins University Press, 1979).

[2] World Fertility Survey, "The Korea National Fertility Survey, 1974, First Country Report" (Seoul: 1977).

———, "Malaysian Fertility and Family Survey, 1974, First Country Report" (Kuala Lumpur: 1977).

———, "Nepal Fertility Survey, 1976, First Report." (Kathmandu: 1977).

———, "The Survey of Fertility in Thailand, Country Report." (Bangkok: 1977).

———, "Bangladesh Fertility Survey, 1976. First Report" (Government of the People's Republic of Bangladesh: 1979).

———, "Indonesian Fertility Survey, 1976, Principal Report." (Jakarta: 1978).

———, "Sri Lanka, 1975, First Report." (Colombo: 1978).

———, "Republic of the Philippines Fertility Survey, 1978, First Report." (Manila: 1979).

The World Fertility Surveys are available from the Country Statistical Offices or the World Fertility Survey Office, 55–37, Grovenor Gardens, London. SWIW OBS, United Kingdom.

The views and interpretation in this document are those of the author and should not be attributed to the World Bank, to its affiliated organizations, or to any individual acting in their behalf.

Relationship Between Education and Fertility

The cross-individual studies of the relationship in developing countries are of two kinds: (1) studies simply comparing the fertility (adjusted for age) of those of different levels of education, and (2) multiple regression studies in which fertility is the dependent variable, education and income are two of the independent variables, and a control is introduced for age. In the original data reviewed, the first kind of study showed inverse relationships—not necessarily significant—in 49% of the cases (see table 1).

The surprising finding, then, is that in approximately half the cases there was no inverse relationship. The advantage of the cross-tabular evidence is that it can give some insight into the shape of the relationship. In most cases, if the relationship is not inverse, fertility first rises with education and then falls.[3] In the next-to-the-last column of table 1, the level of education at which fertility is at a maximum is shown. In most curvilinear cases, the pattern shows a peak in fertility at lower primary education.

In *Fertility and Education* it was hypothesized that at low levels of aggregate literacy this curvilinear relationship would be observed, but as aggregate literacy rose a uniformly inverse relationship would become more common. For the studies reported in table 1, inverse relations were observed in only 29% of the cases when illiteracy exceeded 60%, but in 52% of the cases when illiteracy was less than 60%.

The data in table 1 also showed variations depending on location and sex. Table 2 shows that education is far more likely to be inversely related to fertility in urban than in rural areas (57% versus 20%) and female education is more likely to be inversely related to fertility than is male education (56% versus 31%).

The logical question that arises is: Do these generalizations remain valid for the more recently published WFS data sets? Table 3 summarizes the relationship between education and fertility, adjusting for marital duration, from 20 WFS surveys.[4]

For the data shown in table 3, we find that there is a relationship between the shape of the curve for female education and the aggregate level of literacy. If illiteracy is less than 60%, 71% of the cases show inverse relations. For male education, an inverse relationship was observed 57% of the time in these countries. For the four countries with illiteracy of 60% or more, no inverse relationship was observed for male

---

[3] The only exceptions are Buenos Aires and urban Thailand.
[4] G. Rodriguez, and J. Cleland, "Socio-Economic Determinants of Marital Fertility in Twenty Countries: A Multivariate Analysis." (Paper delivered at the World Fertility Survey Conference, London, July 7–11, 1980).

or for female education. For all countries the inverse relation was observed for females in 11 of 20 cases, and for males in 8 of 20. Thus the new WFS data tend to confirm that the inverse relation is more likely to be observed in countries where literacy is above 40%, and it is more likely to be observed for female than male education.[5]

The second type of macro studies reviewed in the earlier paper were multiple regression studies that controlled not only for age and education, but also for income or wealth. These studies are summarized in table 4. They confirmed what was found in the cross tabulations: (1) female education was more likely to be inversely related to fertility than male education (78% and 32% of the relations were inverse for females and males, respectively); (2) education in urban areas is more likely to be inversely related than in rural areas (67% versus 41%); and (3) education in countries with literacy rates above 40% is more likely to be inversely related to fertility than in less literate countries (79% and 25% respectively).

A number of other multiple regression studies have been completed since the book was published, and a number of earlier studies have also come to light. These are summarized in table 5.[6]

To what extent do they confirm the earlier patterns? The old multiple regression studies showed inverse relationships in 58% of the cases, while 71% of the 10 new studies show inverse relationships. If one considers only significant coefficients, one finds that in the old group of studies, significantly inverse relations were shown in 31% of the equations. In the new studies, significantly inverse relations were found in

---

[5] The Rodriguez and Cleland paper does not show separate figures for eduational differentials in urban and rural areas. Their analysis shows little interaction between residence and education.

[6] R. Michielutte et al., "Residence and Fertility in Costa Rica," *Rural Sociology* 40, No. 3 (1975): 319–31; K. Banskota, and R. E. Evenson, "Fertility, Schooling and Home Technology in Rural Philippine Households." Unpublished, 1978; E. Navera, "Home Investment in Children in Rural Philippines" (Paper delivered at the International Center for Research on Women Workshop, "Women in Poverty: What Do We Know?" Elkridge, Maryland, April 30–May 2, 1978); D. Chernichovsky, and O. Meesook, "Regional Aspects of Family Planning and Fertility Behavior in Indonesia" (World Bank Report No. 2922-IND, delivered at the meeting of Inter-Governmental Group on Indonesia, Amsterdam, May 7–8, 1980); K. O. Mason and V. T. Palan, "Female Education, Fertility and Family Planning Behavior in Peninsula Malaysia." Unpublished, University of Michigan, 1980; Kathryn H. Anderson, "Determination of Fertility, Child Quality and Child Survival in Guatemala," Yale University Economic Growth Center Discussion Paper No. 332, 1979; A. C. Kelley, and M. N. El-Khorazaty, "Demographic Change and Development in Rural Egypt." (Paper delivered at the seminar, "The Demographic Situation in Egypt," Institute of Statistical Studies and Research, Cairo University, Cairo, December 1980); M. A. Khan, "Relevance of Human Capital Theory to Fertility Research: Comparative Findings for Bangladesh and Pakistan," *Research in Human Capital and Development* 1 (1979): 3–43; R. H. Chaudhury, "Education and Fertility in Bangladesh." *Bangladesh Development Studies* 5, No. 1 (1977): 81–110; S. L. Ketkar, "Female Education and Fertility: Some Evidence from Sierra Leone," *Journal of Developing Areas* 13, No. 1 (1978): 23–33; S. L. Ketkar, "Determinants of Fertility in a Developing Society: The Case of Sierra Leone," *Population Studies* 33, No. 3 (1979): 479–88.

TABLE 1

CROSS-TABULAR STUDIES ON THE RELATION BETWEEN AGE-ADJUSTED FERTILITY AND EDUCATIONAL LEVEL, BY ILLITERACY RATE

Study (date published)	Location	Illiteracy rate (percent)	Data source (sample size)	Characteristics	Shape of Relation	Number of reversals in relation[a]	Percent difference in fertility between educated and not educated
CELADE[b] (1971)	Buenos Aires	(A) 10	1964 survey (2,136)	(F) / (M)	irregular / irregular	3 / 3	ND / ND
CELADE (1972)	San Jose	(A) 14	1964 survey (2,132)	(F) / (M)	curvilinear / inverse	4 + years / 0	+1 / ND
Chung (1972)	Korea	(F) 19	1971 (1,883)	(F)	inverse	0	-20 to -17
Carelton (1965)	Puerto Rico	(F) 22	1960 census	(F)	inverse	0	-15
CELADE (1972)	Panama City	(F) 25	1964 survey (2,222)	(F) / (M)	inverse / inverse	1 / 0	ND / ND
CELADE (1972)	Caracas	(A) 27	1964 survey (2,087)	(F) / (M)	inverse / inverse	1 / 2	-22.9 / -16.6
Knodel and Prachuabmoh (1973)	Thailand	(urban—18; rural—31.7)	1969 survey (1,064 F; 675 M)	(F) urban / (F) rural / (M) urban / (M) rural	curvilinear / curvilinear / irregular / curvilinear	1-3 years / 1-3 years / 3 / 4-6 years	+29 / +29 / +10 / +4
CELADE (1972)	Bogotá	(A) 30.5	1964 survey (2,259)	(F) / (M)	inverse / inverse	1 / 2	-13 / -35
CELADE (1972)	Quito	(A) 34.6	1964 survey (1,082)	(F) / (M)	inverse / inverse	2 / 0	ND / ND
CELADE (1972)	Guayaquil	(A) 34.6	1964 survey (1,243)	(F) / (M)	inverse / inverse	0 / 0	ND / ND
CELADE (1972)	Mexico City	(F) 35	1964 survey (2,353)	(F) / (M)	inverse / inverse	0 / 2	-12.5 / -33
Stycos (1968)	Peru	(A) 39	1960/61 survey (1,078)	(F) Lima / (F) Chimbote / (F) Viru-Huaxlay	inverse / curvilinear / inverse	0 / 1-2 years / 0	-7 / +22 / -16

Study	Country	Fertility measure	Data source	Subgroup	Relationship	Education level	Number
Goldstein (1972)	Thailand	(F) 44	1960 census	(F) Bangkok	inverse	1	− 8
				(F) other urban	inverse	0	− 11
				(F) urban agricultural	inverse	0	+ 3
				(F) rural non-agricultural	curvilinear	1-2 years	+ 0.1
				(F) rural agricultural	inverse	0	− 8
CELADE (1972)	Rio de Janeiro	(F) 40.6	1964 survey (2,512)	(F)	inverse	1	− 22.3
				(M)	inverse	3	− 26.6
Gendell and others (1970)	Guatemala	(A) 45.3	1964 census (urban)	(F) domestics	curvilinear	0	+ 14
				(F) other active	inverse	0	− 55
				(F) inactive	inverse	0	− 8
Palmore (1969)	West Malaysia	(F) 50.4 (urban − 42.1; rural − 54)	1966-67 (5,467)	(F) metropolitan	inverse	0	− 11
				(F) nonmetropolitan urban	curvilinear	1-5 years	+ 7
Hull and Hull (1977)	Indonesia	(F) 51 (urban − 30.2; rural − 55.5)	1971 census	(F) rural	curvilinear	1-5 years	+ 12
				(F) urban	curvilinear	(complete)	+ 15
				(F) rural	curvilinear	(primary)	+ 21
Ewbank (1977)	Tanzania	(F) 85	1967 census	(F)	curvilinear	1-4 years	+ 12
Srinivasan (1967)	India	(F) 87		(M) rural	curvilinear	6-8 years	+ 1
Ohadike (1969)	Lagos, Nigeria	(A) 89	1964 Lagos survey (596)	(F) urban	inverse	0	− 3
				(M) urban	curvilinear	primary	+ 8
El Bady and Rizk (1967)	Cairo, Egypt	(F) 91 (A) 80	1960	(F) upper Egypt	curvilinear	literate	+ 12
				(F) lower Egypt − nonurban	curvilinear	literate	+ 13
				(F) lower Egypt − urban	inverse	0	− 14

SOURCE: Reprinted by permission of the publisher from S. H. Cochrane, *Fertility and Education: What Do We Really Know?* World Bank Staff Occasional Paper No. 26 (Baltimore: The Johns Hopkins University Press, 1979). Tables 1, 2, 4, 6, 7 and 8 are published for The World Bank by The Johns Hopkins University Press.

NOTE: (F) = education of women; (M) = education of men; (A) = education of adults; ND = no data.

[a] Number of reversals in general inverse relations; if the relation is nonlinear, this column reports on the level of education with highest fertility.

[b] United Nations Regional Center for Demographic Training and Research in Latin America.

315

TABLE 2

THE RELATION BETWEEN AGE-ADJUSTED FERTILITY AND THE LEVEL OF
EDUCATION, CLASSIFIED BY GROUP CHARACTERISTICS

Group characteristics		Direction of relation		Percent of cases inverse
		Inverse (number of cases)	Not inverse (number of cases)	
Urban	female	15	7	68
	male	4	7	36
	total	19	14	57
Rural	female	2	6	25
	male	0	2	0
	total	2	8	20
Overall	female	17	13	56
	male	4	9	31
	total	21	22	49

SOURCE: Cochrane, *Fertility and Education*, 1979.
NOTE: Figures generated from cross-tabular studies in Table 1.

38%. In both the old and new groups, more inverse relations were found in urban than in rural areas.

In both old and new data sets, female education was more likely to be significantly inversely related to fertility than was male education (42% versus 7% in the old, and 50% versus 14% in the new). Thus the new multivariate studies do not show major differences from the patterns found in the earlier review. While these new studies verify the earlier patterns, neither set of studies establishes the causal relationship between the variables nor explains why education has different impacts on fertility in different situations. To resolve these problems a causal model is needed.

The Causal Model

In the original book, a model was developed that was based on the premise that education does not directly affect fertility, but acts through a large number of variables which in turn determine fertility. In that model, fertility is determined by three primary factors: the biological supply of children, the demand for children, and the regulation of fertility. Each of these factors is in turn influenced by a large number of variables. Figure 1 presents a simplified version of the model. In that model the current number of living children is compared with demand for children. If that number equals or exceeds demand, then there is a possibility that fertility regulation will be used to limit further fertility. Whether regulation is in fact used, however, also depends on attitudes toward, knowledge of, and access to fertility regulation. In addition, effective use also depends on husband-wife communication. The effect of education on fertility depends on how education affects the demand for children, on the supply of children, and on the use of fertility regulation if another child is not desired, and, in turn, how these variables affect fertility. Table 6 shows the hypothesized effect of the intervening variables on fertility and lists studies that give evidence on these relationships. Table 7 shows the hypotheses set forth on the relationship between education and these intervening variables (columns 1 and 2) and,

TABLE 3

THE RELATIONSHIP BETWEEN EDUCATION AND CHILDREN EVERBORN
ADJUSTED FOR MARITAL DURATION FOR 20 WFS SURVEYS

Location	Illiteracy Rate	Male or Female	Shape of Relation	Education Group with Maximum	Percent Difference between No School and Some School
Bangladesh	74	F	Curvilinear	Upper primary	+ 6
		M	Irregular	Lower primary	+ 15
Fiji	NA	F	Curvilinear	Lower primary	+ 8
		M	Curvilinear	Lower primary	+ 8
Indonesia	38	F	Curvilinear	Upper primary	+ 12
		M	Irregular	Secondary	+ 20
Korea	7	F	Inverse	No school	− 11
		M	Inverse	No school/ Lower primary	0
Malaysia	40	F	Inverse	No school	− 5
		M	Curvilinear	Lower primary	+ 7
Nepal	81	F	Curvilinear	Lower primary	+ 7
		M	Irregular	Upper primary	− 11
Pakistan	79	F	Irregular	Upper primary	− 4
		M	Irregular	Upper primary	− 5
Philippines	13	F	Curvilinear	Lower primary	+ 11
		M	Curvilinear	Lower primary	+ 11
Sri Lanka	22	F	Irregular	No school/ Upper primary	− 4
		M	Inverse	No school	− 2
Thailand	16	F	Curvilinear	Lower primary	+ 4
		M	Curvilinear	Lower primary	+ 33
Colombia	19	F	Inverse	No school	− 12
		M	Inverse	No school	− 9
Costa Rica	10	F	Inverse	No school	− 13
		M	Inverse	No school	− 4
Dominican Republic	33	F	Inverse	No school	− 3
		M	Curvilinear	No school	+ 8
Guyana	NA	F	Inverse	No school	− 15
		M	Curvilinear	Lower primary	+ 15
Jamaica	14	F	Inverse	No school	− 11
		M	Inverse	No school	− 10
Mexico	24	F	Inverse	No school	− 3
		M	Inverse	No school	− 3
Panama	22	F	Inverse	No school	− 7
		M	Inverse	No school	− 8
Peru	28	F	Inverse	No school	− 10
		M	Curvilinear	Lower primary	+ 3
Jordan	30	F	Inverse	No school	− 17
		M	Inverse	No school	− 2
Kenya	60	F	Irregular	Lower primary	+ 9
		M	Irregular	Lower primary	+ 14

SOURCE: Derived from Rodriguez and Cleland, "Marital Fertility," 1980, Table 7, pp. 26, 30, and 41.

TABLE 4

MULTIPLE REGRESSION STUDIES OF AGE-ADJUSTED FERTILITY AND EDUCATIONAL LEVEL, CONTROLLING FOR RESIDENCE AND INCOME

Study (date published)	Location	Illiteracy rate (percent)	Data source (sample size)	Equation	Education Sign	Education Measurement	Income Sign	Income Measurement	Other significant variables
McCabe and Rosenzwieg (1976)	Puerto Rico	(F) 13.4	1970 census	35-44 working women	(F) –	years completed	+	male wage	predicted wage of males and females
Davidson (1973)	Caracas	(G) 27	1963-64, CELADE (2,087)	20-24	(F) –	years completed	– [a]	husband's income	age of marriage
				25-29	(F) –				
				30-34	(F) – [a]				
				35-39	(F) –				
Encarnación (1974)	Philippines	(G) 28	1968 National Fertility Survey (used 3,629 single family households)	total	(F) +	years completed	–	family income	age of and duration of marriage
				urban	(F) +		–		
				rural	(F) + [a]		+		
				lower income	(F) + [a]		+		
				upper income	(F) – [a]		–		
Rosenzweig (1976)	Philippines	(G) 28	1968 National Fertility Survey (1,830)	35-39	(F) – [a]; (M) +	years of schooling	–	predicted income of husband	age of marriage; infant mortality; wage of children
Kogut (1974)	Brazil	(G) 29	1960 census	northeast	(F) – [a]; (M) – [a]	years of schooling	–	household income	locale; age; duration of marriage
				south	(F) – [a]; (M) – [a]		– [a]		
				east	(F) – [a]; (M) – [a]		– [a]		locale; age; duration of marriage; religion
Iutaka (1971)	Brazil	–	1959-60 urban survey (1,280)	total	(F) – [a]; (M) + [a]	years	– [a]	social status	age; age at marriage; city, size; color
				urban natives	(F) – [a]; (M) +		– [a]		
				urban migrants	(F) – [a]; (M) –		– [a]		
Chernichovsky (1976)	Brazil	–	rural (170)	mortality control	(F) –; (M) – [a]	years; literacy	– [a]	land owned or cultivated	age; age at marriage; extended family
				no mortality control	(F) –; (M) –	years; literacy	+ [a]		
Davidson (1973)	Mexico City	(F) 35	1963-64, CELADE (2,353)	20-24	(F) –	years completed	–	husband's occupation	age at marriage
				25-29	(F) –		–		age and work status
				30-34	(F) –		0		age at marriage
				35-39	(F) –				age at marriage

318

Study		Survey	Sample	Education variable	Education sign	Income variable	Income sign	Other variables
Khan and Sirageldin (1975)	Pakistan (G) 61	1968-69 survey 35-49 want no more (2,910)	total	literacy	(F) –ᵃ	family income	–	education desired for child; child deaths; family planning
				years	(M) +		–	
			urban	literacy	(F) –ᵃ		–	
				years	(M) +		–	
			rural	literacy	(F) –		+	
				years	(M) +		+	
Knowles and Anker (1975)	Kenya (G) 70	1974 survey (1,074)	all women	years	(F) +	household income	+	land owned; urban residence; years married
Kelley (1976)	Kenya –	401 urban nuclear households	all women	primary	(F) +	earned household income	+ᵃ	age of wife
				primary	(M) +			
				secondary	(F) –ᵃ			
				secondary	(M) +			
Chernichovsky (1976)	India (G) 71	rural survey (212)	all women	literacy	(F) +	income from agriculture and other occupation	+ᵃ	mother's age; age at marriage; number of child deaths
				years	(M) +			
Kocher (1977)	Tanzania (G) 85	1973 survey northeastern region (800)	20-29		(F) –ᵃ	household crop production imputed farm income plus other income	–	building quality index; no variable significant in demand; equation; all significant in supply
			30-39		(M) –		+	
Cochrane and others (1977)	Nepal (F) 97.4	1976 rural (122)	all women	years	(M) +	income per household member; land area worked per capita has positive coefficient	–	duration of marriage
				literacy	(M) +ᵃ		–	
				literacy score	(M) +ᵃ		–	
				numeracy	(M) +ᵃ		–	
				picture vocabulary	(M) +		–	
				induction of classes	(M) +			

SOURCE: S. H. Cochrane, *Fertility and Education*, 1979; pp. 41-47.
NOTE: (F) = education of women; (M) = education of men.
ᵃStatistically significant.

319

COCHRANE

TABLE 5

New Multiple Regression Studies of Age-Adjusted Fertility Controlling For Income or Wealth and Residence

Study	Location	Illiteracy Rate (1976)%	Data Source	Education — Sign	Education — Measurement	Other Significant Variables
Michielutte et al. (1975)	Costa Rica	10	292 women (35-49) (clinic & control)	(F) $-$ [a]	Years	Residence, church attendance, age at 1st conception
Banskota & Evenson (1978)	Philippines (Laguna)	13	320 Rural	(F) $+$ / (M) $-$	Years completed	Infant deaths, predicted wage (wife, child), home technology, years married, father's farm background
Navera (1979)	Philippines (Laguna)	13	320 Rural	(F) $-$ / (M) $-$	Years completed	Duration of marriage
Chernichovsky & Meesook (1980)	Indonesia	38	60,000 households	(F) $-$ Java-Bali / (F) $+/-$ Outer Islands	Dummies for categories [b]	Age at marriage, age, marital status, work in home, work outside, modern durables, household expenditures, expenditures squared, knows contraception, rural
Mason and Palan (1980)	Malaysia	40		(F) non-linear / (F) $-$ [a] $-$ [a] / (F) $-$ [a] $-$ (urban)(rural)	Malays / Chinese / Others } Years completed [c]	Significance not reported
Anderson (1979)	Guatemala	53	657	(F) $-$ [a] / (M) $-$	Years	Wife's age
Kelley et al. (1980)	Egypt (Rural)	56	3,821 households	(F) $+$ / (M) $+$ [a]	Dummy variables for levels	Wife's age, (age)[c], age at marriage, electricity, child deaths, personal assets
Khan (1979)	Bangladesh (Rural)	74	265 women 35-49	(F)[d] $+$ [a] / (M) $-$	Literacy Years completed	Dead children, monthly income, land owned, income adequacy, age of marriage, education of children
Chaudhury (1977)	Bangladesh (Dacca)	74	1,130 women	(F) $-$ [a] / (M) $-$ [a]	Dummy variables for levels	Significance of other variables not reported
Ketkar (1978/79)	Sierra Leone	85	1,999 women	(F) $-$ / (M) $+$	Years completed	Wife's age, number of adult female, community infant mortality

SOURCES: Full references for the studies in column 1 are given in reference no. 6.

320

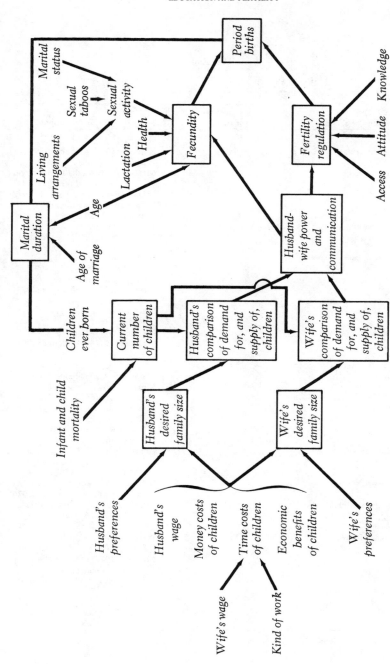

FIG. 1 – Model of the intervening variables determining fertility.

SOURCE: Cochrane, *Fertility and Education*, 1979, p. 60. Published for The World Bank by The Johns Hopkins University Press.

TABLE 6

EVIDENCE OF THE EFFECT OF INTERVENING VARIABLES
ON COMPLETED FERTILITY

Intervening variable	Direction of relation	Empirical support
Supply factors		
Probability of marriage	+	Schultz (1972), Mazur (1973), Maurer (1973)
Wife's age at marriage	−	McGreevey-Birdsall, Encarnación (1968), Kim and others (1974), Davidson (1973), Yaukey (1972), Palmore and Ariffin (1969)
Health	+	Butz (1976), Baird (1965)
Separate location of spouse	−	Williams (1976)
Joint family living	? (−)	United Nations (1973), Williams (1976)
Legal, monogamous marriage	? (+)	Mason and others (1971) (+), Nerlove and Schultz (1969) (+), Miro and Mertens (1968) (mixed), United Nations (1973) (mixed)
Taboos on sexual activity	−	United Nations (1973) (several studies cited)
Infant and child mortality	+	McGreevey-Birdsall (1974), Snyder (1974), Williams (1976)
Demand factors		
Preferences for children	? (+)	
Husband's wage	?	Simon (1974), Williams (1976)
Money cost of children	−	Mueller (1972), Bulatao (1975), Arnold and others (1975)
Wife's wage	−	Mason and others (1971) DaVanzo (1972), Snyder (1974), Rosenzweig and Evenson (forthcoming)
Incompatibility of wife's work	−	Goldstein (1972), United Nations (1973), Bindary and others (1973), Williams (1976)
Cost of child care substitutes	−	Cain and Weinenger (1973), McCabe and Rosenzweig (1976)
Economic benefits of children	+	Mueller (1972), Harmon (1970), McGreevey-Birdsall (1974)
Fertility regulation		
Husband's marital power	? (+)	Weller (1968) (+), Mitchell (1972) (+)
Husband-wife communication	−	Mitchell (1972), Michel (1967), Hill and others (1959), Ramakumar and Gopal (1972)
Knowledge of birth control	−	
Attitude toward birth control	−	
Access to birth control	−	Mason and others (1971), Schultz (1972)

SOURCE: Cochrane, *Fertility and Education*, pp. 66–67.

TABLE 7

EFFECT OF EDUCATION ON FERTILITY
THROUGH INTERVENING VARIABLES

Intervening variable	Effect of education on the intervening variables		Effect of intervening variables on fertility	Effect of education on fertility through intervening variables	
	Male	Female		Male	Female
Supply factors					
Probability of being married	+	−	+	+	−
Wife's age at marriage	?	+	−	?	−
Health	+	+	+	+	+
Separate location of spouse	−	?	−	+	?
Joint family living	−	−	? (−)	? (+)	?
Legal, monogamous marriage	?	+	? (+)	?	? (+)
Taboos on sexual activity	−	−	−	+	+
Infant and child mortality	−	−	+	−	−
Demand factors					
Preferences for children[a]	−	−	? (+)	−	−
Husband's wage	+	0	?	?	0
Money cost of children	+	+	−	−	−
Wife's wage	0	+	−	0	−
Incompatibility of wife's work	0	+	−	0	−
Cost of child care substitutes[b]	0	+	−	0	−
Economic benefits of children	−	−	+	−	−
Fertility regulation					
Husband's marital power	+	−	? (+)	?	?
Husband-wife communication	+	+	−	−	−
Knowledge of birth control	+	+	−	−	−
Attitude toward birth control[a]	+	+	−	−	−
Access to birth control	+	+	−	−	−

SOURCE: Cochrane, *Fertility and Education*, 1979, p. 71.

[a]Depends in part on whether the education is religious or secular.
[b]Depends on community level of female education.

through these intervening variables, its relationship to fertility (column 4).

Not all the variables in tables 6 and 7 have been well studied. Table 7 summarizes the number of studies relating education to these intervening variables that were available at the time of the original review. These studies show that education acts through the demand for children, child mortality, the biological supply of children, and fertility regulation. Table 8 shows that education tends to reduce the demand for children as measured by desired family size, by reducing preferences for children and the perceived benefits of children. However, education also tends to increase the perceived ability to afford children, which counters these negative effects to some extent but does not outweigh them. The relationship between education and perceived or actual costs of children is poorly documented, but existing evidence supports the hypothesis set forth above. Education also reduces the number of births needed to achieve a particular desired family size, by lowering infant and child mortality. The evidence is also very strong that education increases contraceptive use, by improving attitudes toward and knowledge of contraception.

The greatest uncertainty in terms of education's effect on fertility is

TABLE 8

EVIDENCE SUPPORTING THE RELATION BETWEEN EDUCATION
AND FERTILITY THROUGH THE INTERVENING VARIABLES

Variable	Relation of education and variable	Probable relation of education through the variable	Results Supporting (number of cases)	Not supporting (number of cases)
Potential supply of births	?	?	–	–
Probability of marrying	inverse	–	6	5[a]
Age of marriage	direct	–	59	12[a]
Health	direct	+	2	0
Lactation	inverse	+	6	0
Postpartum abstinence	inverse	+	2	0
Infant of child mortality	inverse	–	16	7
Demand for children (desired family size)	inverse	–	17	8[a]
Preference for children	inverse			
Ideal family size		–	20	7[a]
Desired number of sons		–	8	1
Perceived benefits of children	inverse	–	17	2
Perceived costs of children	direct	–	2	0
Perceived ability to afford children	direct	+	9	3
Fertility regulation (contraceptive use)	direct	–	26	11
Attitudes toward birth control	direct	–	28	4
Knowledge of birth control	direct	–	28	1
Husband-wife communication	direct	–	9	0

SOURCE: Cochrane, *Fertility and Education*, 1979, p. 146.

[a]Relation of male education to the variable is much weaker than that of female education.

related to the effect of education on the potential biological supply of births, or fecundity. While female education seems to reduce the years married by raising the age of marriage and, at least in some countries, reducing the probability of marriage, education's effect on the fecundity of married women appears to operate in a different direction. It appears that education improves the health of women sufficiently to improve either their chances of conceiving or their ability to carry births to term. In addition, more educated women tend to give up such traditional behavior as prolonged lactation and postpartum abstinence, which tend to suppress fertility. However, data on educational differences in the biological supply of births was relatively scarce at the time of the original survey.

Increased attention has been given to natural fertility in recent years[7] and therefore more data is now available on the relationship between education and several factors determining the biological supply of births. Consequently, the studies in Table 8 can be supplemented with new data on the relationship between fecundity (or health) and education and between lactation and education.

New Data on Education's Effect on the Biological Supply of Children

Several factors that are related to fecundity can now be examined in greater detail. The two factors most easily studied are the age of menarche and the proportion of women who are fertile (or who perceive themselves as being fertile). For age at menarche, no data are readily available on a woman's education and her age of menarche, but substantial data are available on her parents' socioeconomic status, and her age of menarche and parental SES are closely related to her own education. The evidence reviewed in Cochrane shows a very clear pattern: The higher the socioeconomic status, the younger the average age of menarche.[8] This relationship was significant for six of seven studies from developing countries. The only insignificant result was for a small sample in India. These data show wide differences between countries. Hong Kong, Singapore, and Istanbul have lower ages than do those areas with lower levels of development (ranges of 12–13 years, as opposed to 13–14

[7] See M. Nag, "How Modernization Can Also Increase Fertility" (Working Paper, Population Council, New York, 1979); J. Bongaarts, "Malnutrition and Fecundity: A Summary of Evidence" (Center for Policy Studies Workshop Paper, Population Council, New York, 1979); W. P. Butz, and J.-P. Habicht, "The Effects of Nutrition and Health on Fertility: Hypotheses, Evidence and Intervention," in *Population and Development*, R. Ridker, ed. (Baltimore: Johns Hopkins University Press, 1976).

[8] S. H. Cochrane, "The Effect of Development on Fertility: Education and Residence," mimeographed (Washington, D. C.: Population and Human Resources Division, World Bank, 1981).

in India and Nigeria, and over 15 years among the Bantu of South Africa). The differences in age of menarche by socioeconomic status range from about 5 months to up to 16 months.

The data on age of puberty are suggestive of differences in fecundity, but the effect on fecundity will only be substantial if the age of marriage is close to the age of puberty. When the age of marriage is substantially above menarche, differences in the age of puberty will only be associated with differences in fecundity if the age of puberty is correlated with fecundity at later ages. This seems plausible on a priori grounds.

The age of the menarche, which varies considerably, marks the beginning of the fertile period in a woman. Women also vary substantially in the age at which they cease to be fertile. Do women with more education tend to remain fertile longer as a result of better health? One can examine WFS data on the proportion of women who report that they are still fertile at various ages over 35. For eight WFS countries in Asia, these data are summarized in table 9. The pattern of relationship varies by age. For women 35–44, uniform inverse relationships are observed in Thailand, Indonesia, Sri Lanka, and Bangladesh. For women over 45, uniform inverse relationships are shown in Thailand, Sri Lanka, and Malaysia.

One reason for the lack of uniform inverse relationships might well be the small samples in some educational categories, but there are reverses in the expected pattern even when the samples involved exceed 50. The pattern may therefore not be uniform over the entire educational continuum. The inverse relationship is very clear when comparing those having no schooling with those having a small amount of schooling. In all cases except Nepal and Bangladesh where samples are small, higher proportions are infertile over 35 in the group with no schooling than in the group with some schooling.

For the combined group, we find that for women 35–44, 20% of those with no schooling are infertile, compared with 15% of those with some schooling. For women 45 and over, the percentages are 48 and 47 respectively. If women with no schooling are compared with those having any schooling at all, the contrast is even stronger.[9] A major impact of this factor could only result if fecundity decreases over time prior to infertility.

In addition to these data on the onset and termination of fecundity, which indicate that women with more education have a longer potential childbearing period, there are also more data now indicating that women with more education might have a higher susceptibility to

---

[9] Only 12% of women 35–44 with any schooling are infertile, compared with 20% with no schooling, while for women 45 and older the figures are 45% and 48%.

TABLE 9

PROPORTION OF WOMEN INFERTILE FOR REASONS OTHER THAN CONTRACEPTION
BY AGE AND EDUCATION, SAMPLE SIZE IN PARENTHESIS

Age	Education					
THAILAND	None	1–4	5–10	Over 10		
35–44	22.2 (270)	19.0 (847)	11.1 (27)	9.5 (21)		
35–49	62.7 (153)	57.0 (277)	59.1 (22)	50.0 (4)		
				Junior High	Senior High	
INDONESIA	None	Incomplete	Complete			
35–44	31.2 (1749)	18.3 (671)	15.3 (126)	11.5 (46)	3.1 (47)	
45 +	49.5 (718)	46.0 (185)	43.7 (36)		47.1 (17)	
SRI LANKA	None	1–5	6–9	10–11	Higher	
33–44	20.6 (577)	16.1 (849)	11.3 (472)	6.0 (157)	4.4 (113)	
45 +	48.2 (342)	38.1 (412)	43.2 (181)	41.6 (36)	20.8 (24)	
KOREA	None	Primary	Middle	High	College	
35–44	15.5 (560)	13.4 (986)	11.1 (135)	13.4 (164)	7.7 (39)	
45 +	58.5 (357)	53.3 (242)	33.3 (9)	16.2 (37)	25.0 (24)	
BANGLADESH	No School	Primary	Higher			
35–44	11.9 (1105)	10.5 (165)	4.2 (25)			
45 +	22.5 (437)	28.2 (47)	14.6 (8)			
NEPAL	None	Primary	Secondary			
35–44	18.9 (1434)	17.6 (17)	50.0 (2)			
45 +	48.4 (512)	50.0 (4)	-			
MALAYSIA	None	Less than 7	7–12	Over 12		
35–44	12.2 (942)	9.1 (794)	5.8 (121)	20.0 (15)		
45 +	49.4 (629)	37.2 (223)	34.4 (43)	16.7 (6)		
PHILIPPINES	None	Primary	Intermediate	High	Some College	Degree
35–44	19.6 (197)	13.6 (876)	8.1 (1128)	10.3 (564)	6.8 (77)	3.7 (241)
45 +	66.8 (163)	52.7 (417)	44.8 (299)	45.1 (182)	37.6 (40)	45.4 (99)

SOURCES: World Fertility Surveys: Thailand, Table 1.5.3; Indonesia, Table 1.3.3.; Sri Lanka, Table 1.6.3A; Korea, Table 1.6.3A; Bangladesh, Table 1.6.3A; Nepal, Table 1.6.3A; Malaysia, Table 1.6.3A; Philippines, Table 1.6.3A (see reference 2).

pregnancy because of shorter periods of breast feeding. In the original paper, six studies were cited showing an inverse relationship between maternal education and the duration of breast feeding. Jain and Bongaarts have reviewed data on eight additional countries.[10] These data showed that in all countries there was an inverse relationship. This was also true within the urban and rural sectors considered separately, with one minor exception (see table 10). These data indicate that on average women with no schooling breast feed their children 2 1/2 months longer than do women with primary schooling, but the big difference is between those with secondary schooling and those with no schooling—a difference of almost 8 months.

[10] A. K. Jain and J. Bongaarts, "Socio-biological Factors in Exposure to Childbearing: Breastfeeding and Its Fertility Effect" (Paper presented at the World Fertility Survey Conference, London, July 7–11, 1980).

TABLE 10

AVERAGE DURATION OF BREAST FEEDING (MONTHS) BY WIFE'S
EDUCATION AND PLACE OF RESIDENCE FOR ALL WOMEN

Place of Residence	Education	Bangladesh	Indonesia	Sri Lanka	Jordan	Peru	Guyana	Columbia	Panama
	Total	24.4	21.4	16.7	15.5	15.6	11.1	10.6	11.0
Rural	None	24.5	21.8	17.6	15.9	16.8	14.4	12.1	15.1
	Primary	24.2	21.0	18.1	14.9	13.8	11.2	10.1	11.0
	Secondary	20.7*	15.8	13.8	0.0	10.7	9.3	8.9	5.2
	Total	20.9	13.8	12.8	11.2	9.5	7.4	7.5	5.8
Urban	None	21.9	16.3	15.7	13.2	13.2	15.8*	11.2	10.3*
	Primary	21.2	13.8	13.7	10.4	10.3	7.9	7.8	7.9
	Secondary*	15.8	9.5	11.7	6.4	5.5	6.0	4.4	4.1
	Total	23.6	19.0	15.7	12.5	11.7	10.0	8.6	8.3
Total	None	24.0	20.5	17.3	14.2	15.5	14.3	11.7	14.3
	Primary	23.4	18.6	17.2	10.8	11.3	10.4	8.7	9.8
	Secondary*	16.9	10.7	13.0	6.5	5.6	7.4	4.7	4.3

SOURCE: Jain and Bongaarts, "Factors in Exposure to Childbearing," 1980.
*Less than 25 cases.

These new data on the age of the menarche, perceived fertility, and breast feeding indicate that fecundity may be higher among women who have more education. It is also possible that the rate of fetal loss is lower among more educated women, but retrospective data on fetal loss is notoriously subject to reporting bias. Therefore, this point cannot be verified with readily available data.

In addition to higher potential fertility among the more educated, there are, of course, higher survival rates for offspring.[11] A considerable amount of data is now available on educational differences in child survival. These data show a very clear, direct relationship between child survival and maternal education. A review of the evidence indicates that an additional year of maternal education reduces the death rate for infants and young children in developing countries by about 9 per 1,000 on average.[12] The father's education appears to have about half the effect of the mother's education, but this is based on far weaker data.

If there is a higher potential supply of children among more educated women, this potential may or may not be realized, depending on the age at which these women marry and their use of contraception. Education has been shown in the earlier study to reduce fertility because of its effect on both of these variables. Since most studies of fertility are restricted to ever married women, there is a tendency for education's

[11] This could have a countereffect on fecundity to the extent that breast feeding is prolonged by child survival.
[12] See S. H. Cochrane, J. Leslie, and D. O'Hara, "Parental Eduation and Child Health: Intra-Country Evidence," in Cochrane et al., "The Effects of Education on Health" (World Bank Staff Working Paper No. 405, 1980).

positive effect on children ever born to be somewhat exaggerated. To explore this possibility, Rodriguez and Cleland compared TFR's for women of every marital status with children ever born, adjusted for marital status for 15 WFS surveys. The unweighted averages showed that for all women fertility decreased by 1/2 a child between the categories of no school and lower primary. If one looks at married women, the decrease was only 1/5.

To understand fully education's effect on fertility, it will be necessary to understand better education's effect on the age of marriage, as well as its effect on the potential supply of births per year married. The curvilinear relationships observed may arise as a result of differential effects of education levels on these two factors affecting fertility. If low levels of education are sufficient to improve maternal health,[13] and thus fecundity, but are insufficient to alter age at marriage, then a curvilinear pattern may be observed. This is a point that can be further explored with WFS data, and a resolution should be expected in the near future.

Summary and Conclusions

This review of new evidence confirms earlier evidence on the relationship between education and adjusted fertility: (1) In many cases education and fertility are not inversely related, but the higher the literacy rate of a country, the more likely there is to be an inverse relationship between education and fertility; (2) female education is more likely to be inversely related to fertility than is male education. The interaction between education and residence has not been directly clarified by new evidence, and more work needs to be done.[14]

The causal mechanisms through which education affects fertility suggest that education has its positive effects through the increased biological supply of children, as well as possibly through an increased ability to afford children that results from a positive income. There are no new data on the relationship between education and the perceived ability to afford children, but there is new evidence on the relationship between education and the biological supply of children. There are three types of evidence related to this variable: age of menarche, perceived infertility, and duration of lactation.

Whereas there were only two studies reviewed in the original survey on the relationship between education and fecundity, there are

---

[13] Cochrane, Leslie, and O'Hara, "Parental Education," showed that small amounts of maternal education were sufficient to improve child health.

[14] See S. H. Cochrane, "The Economics of Fertility with Examples from Asia." (Washington, D.C.: Discussion Paper No. 2, Population and Human Resources Division, World Bank, 1981).

now an additional seven studies showing that women from families with high SES have earlier ages of menarche and eight studies from Asia showing that women who have attended school are less likely to report themselves as being infertile at ages over 35 than are women who have not attended school. Likewise, new evidence shows that more educated women breast feed for shorter periods and are thus likely to have shorter periods of postpartum amenorrhea. This evidence is suggestive, but it does not definitely prove that women with a higher education are likely to have a greater ability to conceive. More work is needed on the length of time it takes to conceive and on fetal loss, in order to verify this relationship. More work is also needed to determine the extent to which improved fecundity results from the higher incomes associated with more education or from improved health practices resulting in better knowledge of hygiene, preventative health practices, and nutrition. Finally, education's total effect on the potential supply of children depends on its effect on the age of marriage, as well as on fecundity. Samples that are restricted to ever married women tend to underestimate this negative effect of education. Therefore, research is needed on the positive and negative effects of education on the supply of births, to determine in which circumstances the negative effects on fertility might be expected to counteract the positive effects.

18. New Directions for Research

CAROLYN M. ELLIOTT AND GAIL P. KELLY

What has research to tell us about the existing patterns of education of women and the possibilities of improving them? We know most at the descriptive level. As Bowman and Anderson underscore in their review essay, fewer girls than boys go to school, but there is considerable variation among Third World countries in their participation and educational attainment. A UNESCO study cited by Isabelle Deblé in her comparable review of women's educational patterns states it even more strongly, that there is no relation between the intensity of enrollment and the percentage of students who are girls. Numerical equality among boys and girls is found in countries with low total enrollment, and girls may form a low percentage of pupils in countries with comparatively high enrollments.[1] The differences within countries are as great, making it very difficult to use broad national averages as the basis for hypothesis building regarding the reasons for sex differences. One finding does appear firm: Girls in school tend to be from families of higher socioeconomic status than boys, and this difference is compounded at higher levels of education. Thus girls from less privileged families are less likely to be in school than their brothers. Smith and Cheung demonstrate how persistent this pattern is by showing it to be true even in the Philippines where sex equality in education is widely thought to have been achieved. Fathers with little schooling are found to provide more education to sons than to daughters. Equal allocation of education to sons and daughters is a recent phenomenon among relatively well-educated urban families.

Efforts to explain these variations among and within countries start with relating education to levels of economic development. Bowman and Anderson explore whether, as economic development proceeds, women tend to receive educational parity with men. They find that this is sometimes true, but they also cite many cases where development has so far produced even greater disparities. Whether this is a transitional phenomenon, whereby boys' education levels lead that of girls' but girls later catch up, or whether modernization is producing long-term relative disabilities for girls, is a question that has concerned many students of modernization. Bowman and Anderson see girls approaching parity with boys in pretertiary schooling in an impressive number of poor countries. Deblé's analysis for UNESCO is, however,

---

[1] Isabelle Deblé, *The School Education of Girls* (New York: UNESCO, 1980) p. 29.

more pessimistic. While acknowledging that relative sex disparities in primary education are decreasing somewhat, she emphasizes that in absolute numbers the gap between the number of boys and girls in school is widening at all age groups and levels of instruction.[2] The Philippine data on the persistence of the fathers education as a determinant of educational attainment despite the progress of modernization is a case in point. It reflects a rigidity in that society's valuation of girls is unaffected by general patterns of social change.

Tracing the effects of broad cultural patterns on women's access to education represents another important attempt to account for sex differences in education. Some scholars have argued that women's access to institutions like schools depends on the extent to which cultural and religious beliefs accord women a role in life outside the family. Thus we should expect to find that, in cultures where female seclusion is widespread (e.g., in Islamic societies), women would have less access to schools than elsewhere. Similarly, we would expect to find that in Latin America, where constraints on women's equality appear to be embedded in core cultural values, women's participation in education would be lower than it is, for example, in non-Islamic African cultures where values differ.

Such hypotheses do not hold when taken against the broad array of data Bowman and Anderson present. While in some Islamic nations women's participation in education lags considerably behind that of women in societies that do not practice female seclusion, this pattern is not evident in all Muslim nations, nor is Islam always a barrier to women's schooling. Jones's article in this volume shows that in Tunisia women's access to schools has grown appreciably over the past decades. Similarly, Schiefelbein and Farrell's contribution in this volume demonstrates that in Chile, women's rates of participation in education at all levels is nearly equal to that of man, the tradition of machismo notwithstanding. Their rates of participation transcend many of those in Western Europe and, in higher education, the more industrialized United States. Farrell and Schiefelbein explain these high rates as a function of the peculiar historical development of Chile. Whether one could identify in the Chilean experience factors that could serve as a basis for broader generalization must await further research.

Even if one could establish clear correlations between girls' education and levels of development or cultural patterns, little would be known about causation. A basic issue is how the provision of schools relates to utilization. Do wealthier countries generally get higher female participation rates because they provide more schools for girls, or are

[2] Deblé, *School Education of Girls.*

families in these countries more willing to send daughters to school? Alternatively, should we attribute low rates of female education to lack of school places for girls or to cultural and other factors making parents withhold their daughters from school?

The authors in this volume explore several dimensions of this argument. Marie Thourson Jones's work on educational policy in Tunisia emphasizes the importance of the supply side of the equation. She attributes the slackening of female enrollment to the low quality and poor accessibility of schools and to the government's growing disinclination to make schooling attractive to the reluctant portions of the population. Effectively supplying schooling to families who do not readily come forward to place daughters in schools requires a different and more expensive kind of investment in education.

The findings of this case study are supported by a survey of 62 governments made by UNESCO. These governments readily admitted to difficulties in providing even primary education to all children. Lack of transportation, lack of teachers, and lack of canteens were mentioned most frequently as critical constraints on the supply of education opportunity.[3] Except for Latin America, where enrollments are comparatively equal for boys and girls, the governments expressed particular concern about the wastage among girls. However, many saw no need for government attention to girls dropping out of school. They were inclined to see unsatisfactory levels of girls' enrollment as a result of cultural norms and parental decisions, rather than a result of omissions in educational planning. Such attitudes do not promise a willingness to look for, and pay for, the innovations needed to make schooling effectively available to girls, for example, child care, continuing education for married women, night classes for working children, and so on.

To understand the demand for education, we need to know why girls go to school and why they are prevented from doing so. Research in this area has so far concentrated largely on parental and daughters' aspirations for marriage and careers. Although none of these studies is included in this volume, surveys in Latin America and Africa have shown that a principal motivation among girls to remain in school is to have more say in the choice of a husband. Girls' education is now valued in many circles as a positive factor in the securing of husbands of high status, as reported by 65 percent of persons interviewed in an Indian study, or of high marriage settlements, as in Africa.[4] Bowman and Anderson review a number of other factors that must also be considered:

[3] Deblé, *School Education of Girls*, p. 83.
[4] Government of India, *Towards Equality: Report of the Committee on the Status of Women* (New Dehli, 1976).

early marriage, seclusion of girls at puberty, and the opportunity costs of schooling relative to more traditional forms of training for adulthood at home.

Studies in this volume concentrate on two key factors that have been widely discussed but not previously submitted to systematic examination: the time constraints on women's capacity to pursue schooling and the perceived economic rewards that influence family desires to invest in the education of daughters. McSweeney and Freedman show us that the work load of women and girls in rural communities, such as those they studied in Upper Volta, allows females of all ages little time to pursue education. Both school-age boys and adult men have spare time that can be used to go to school or participate in nonformal educational programs. But, as McSweeney and Freedman point out, time alone is not the only barrier between women and an education. In the United Nations project they describe, which was designed to lighten female work loads, adult women did not use the time they gained to attend literacy and other nonformal educational programs. Rather, they chose to use the free time to increase their families' well-being, ignoring educational programs unless there was a tangible economic or health benefit for their families. The lightening of women's work, however, did result in greater participation of school-aged girls in the educational system.

Naik's experience with night classes for working children in India bears this out. She has found that adjusting school hours to the time available to these children elicited a broad interest in girls' education. This is a fine example of how a policy innovation negated common assumptions about families' reluctance to educate girls and their unwillingness to allow girls out at night.

Perception of rewards for education is the second major factor explored here. Scholars of education have frequently speculated on how the labor market's inequalities may depress girls' interest in education, or families' willingness to invest less in their daughters' education than in their sons'. Since sex-role socialization and family background are such strong factors in occupational choice, however, it has been difficult for researchers to get clear evidence for the independent effect of occupational irregularity.

Bee-Lan Chan Wang utilizes the opportunity of the government's preferential hiring policies in Malaysia to sort out these variables. In a situation where the government is skewing employment opportunities toward groups with less advantaged backgrounds, students from these groups express higher eduational aspirations than do students of advantaged backgrounds. Because women in the now favored groups continue to experience more job discrimination, however, they are less likely than their brothers to invest in further education. In Chile, on the other hand, women were motivated by job discrimination to continue education in order to compete effectively. Thus, an understanding of rewards and incentive structures can tell us much about sex differences in educational attainment.

Process of Education

From access and utilization we turn to the equality of women's participation in education. Finn, Reis, and Dulberg pose the question most directly: What is the role of the schooling process in creating or exacerbating sex differences? They argue that it is a denial of equal opportunity in education to fail to expose both sexes not only to the full range of course contents and adult sex-role models, but also to the highest expectations and support for their performance. Their review argues that formal schooling is not equal for girls and boys. Differential interaction patterns between teachers and students by gender, "messages" implicit in curricular materials, lack of role models within the schools, schools' authority structures, and the like may all teach girls that to achieve is "unfeminine" or imply that girls will receive little reward for superior academic performance. Finn, Reis, and Dulberg's article is suggestive and can be nothing more, for most of the studies they cite were carried out in Western Europe and the United States. But three studies in this volume suggest much that is similar in the Third World.

Historically, equal participation was often not a goal of educators. Yates's study of the Belgian Congo describes the interest of colonial and mission educators there to train good Christian wives and mothers, requiring a very different curriculum for girls than boys. Guided by Western conceptions of the proper woman's role, educators discouraged Congolese girls from pursuits outside the home, particularly their traditional role in agriculture, and denied them skills for effective participation in any but the most stereotypically female among modern occupations. A parallel study in India by Gail Minault shows how indigenous groups often had a similar view of women's education. Minault chronicles the movement for education of aristocratic Muslim girls at the major center of modern Muslim education in nineteenth century India, Aligarh University. This movement was explicitly devoted to educating wives for the male university graduates, a continuation of traditional women's roles in new circumstances. In this case, the school even rigidified such customs as *purdah* by codifying and sanctioning it for modern families.[5]

[5] Gail Minault, "Shaikh Abdullah, Begum Abdullah, and *Sharef* Education for girls at Aligarh," unpublished manuscript, 1981.

The sobering fact of these historical experiences is the shadow they cast on the life chances for contemporary women. As Yates argues, it is difficult to equalize opportunity once some groups have established an initial lead, and even more so with current constraints on increasing educational investment and government employment. After actively discriminatory policies have set inequalities in motion, sex-neutral policies are sufficient to maintain established patterns. Thus the educational gap continues, as does the clustering of women in low-paid service occupations.

Two studies in this volume reveal how the legacy is passed along. In a study of school textbooks, Kalia shows that instructional materials in India differentiate male from female. They praise the female for passivity, unscholarly attributes, and her dependence on others, while they show males as active agents and achievers. Kalia's study is important in beginning to demonstrate that "school knowledge" may be differentially imparted and directed at one sex rather than both sexes. We do not know whether the sex stereotypes presented in Indian primers are derived from Indian culture and colonial experience, or pervade curricula of all Third World countries. Finn, Reis, and Dulberg imply they do, and several unpublished studies of Latin American school texts would support their contention, with some minor variations. The extent to which Kalia's findings replicate analyses of texts carried out in the United States is striking.

It is important to know how the messages implicit in the formal curriculum of textbooks may be reinforced by other messages in the "hidden" curriculum of schools—authority structures, staffing patterns, and regularities in classroom interactions by gender. This hidden cirriculum of a school may be as significant, or even more so, than the formal curriculum in molding educational outcomes. Biraimah's research on a coeducational secondary school in Togo, reported in this volume, is an important step in tracing such impacts. She suggests that the schools reproduce, in their authority, staffing, and classroom interaction patterns, the sex differentiation Kalia found in Indian texts. Furthermore, Biraimah found that teachers themselves shared such stereotypical notions, regardless of actual student performance.

How the school environment affects what children learn remains a question. At the most extreme, it may prevent them even from going to school. One doesn't know whether the reluctance of Congolese families to send girls to school, as reported by Yates, was because they disapproved of the curriculum or for other reasons. But Chitra Naik, in her report on alternative schooling in India, reveals her conviction that the curriculum and the process of teaching have a major impact in children's attending school. Many drop out, she finds, because of bad experiences with teachers, or boredom. Thus, her project to universalize primary education involves not only altering time schedules, but making fundamental changes in the recruitment of teachers, the conduct of classes, and the content of materials. Early results show a marked change in girls' self-presentation, as well as their school attendance and achievement.

Where the classroom experience differed for boys and girls, however, Biraimah found no sex differences in achievement. Girls did as well as boys on tests and did not share teachers' attitudes about their personal and career goals. Thus we cannot assume that students internalize the messages of their textbooks and teachers; under the worst conditions, they resist internalization of sex-stereotyped attitudes. To explain her Togo findings, Biraimah provides several speculations, which may be generalizable. She suggests that where school teachings diverge from the actual roles of women in the society, girls may understand full well the schools' messages and "tune out," choosing neither to interact with their teachers nor to take them as significant role models. The relative absence of female teachers in the classroom may decrease the girls' identification with their teachers. Finally, where the organization of the classroom favors lectures, this may limit the transmittal of teachers' personal attitudes.

These exploratory studies raise more questions than they answer, for research on the process and impact of different kinds of educational experiences is only beginning. Traditionally scholars have turned to such out-of-school variables as class, gender, or race to explain educational outcomes. Or they have reduced school variables to quantifiable but relatively indirect factors, such as class size, level of teachers' education, amount of time spent in subject-matter instruction, and expenditures per student. None of these help us to see factors that directly determine a student's experience in school and her performance. All too often scholars have led us to conclude that "schools make no difference," an unwarranted conclusion given the present state of our knowledge about what goes on within schools.

Women's Education and the Work Force

Research on the outcomes of women's education has concentrated on women's participation in the labor force. Does such participation rise with educational level? Does education yield similar occupational rewards for both women and men? For the most part, education does not correlate with labor force participation in Third World countries in the same way for women as it does for men. Rati Ram's review essay shows us that there is great variation in women's labor force participation in the Third World. Part of the variation may be explained by inconsistencies in how work force participation is measured—counting women employed in the traditional sectors of the economy or solely in the modern industrial and service sectors. Nevertheless, it appears clear that women's participation in the modern sector of the labor force is less than males' and that women are, for the most part, in the lower-status, lower-paying jobs. Increases in women's educational levels have not altered this pattern.

Ram explores two explanations for this phenomenon: Either discrimination in hiring precludes women from using their education to full advantage, or women, by virtue of their roles as wives and mothers, are constrained from maximum work force participation because they have a "comparative advantage" in child rearing. While Ram believes the two interpretations are not mutually exclusive, he follows the human capital approach. He posits that childbearing and marriage, rather than discrimination, are the primary sources of differential labor force participation rates among educated men and women. Ram's analysis is controversial, for many would argue that women's decision to stay at home to rear children rests on an assessment of how much they might earn in the labor force relative to their husbands, rather than on a natural advantage in child raising. Ram emphasizes, however, that data to support either theory are weak for Third World countries and that much more research is needed to discern patterns.

Three studies in this volume bear on this problem. By introducing new types of data and modes of analysis, these studies may serve to break the stalemate between interpretations of women's labor market behavior.

Schiefelbein and Farrell examine how women's education relates to labor force participation in Chile, an unusual case because female participation there is very high in comparison to other societies. They examine whether the differences between women's and men's participation in the labor force are connected to the quality of education or the status of schools, and they reach a conclusion quite opposite from patterns prevailing elsewhere. Women in Chile attend schools of higher quality than do men, achieve equally by national measures, and show no evidence of experiencing educational discrimination. But, because they anticipate discrimination in the labor market, they tend to remain in school longer than men in order to compete for the same jobs. Thus, their answer to Ram's question is that labor market practices do affect decisions in education, for women as well as for men. Where women have access to nondiscriminatory education, they prepare themselves to compete in the labor market, even to the extent of enduring longer preparation time despite cultural anticipation of their future roles as wives and mothers. While it is too much to conclude that adoption of truly nondiscriminatory education would have such an impact elsewhere, the Chilean experience attests to the strength of women's chances for equal labor force participation in that country.

A contrasting case of countries with low labor force participation for women is presented by Wainerman. Through a careful study of women in Argentina and Paraguay, in which levels of economic and educational development differ considerably, she shows that marriage, childbearing, and child rearing drive women from the work force. However, education reverses this trend. In both countries, educated women tended to maintain their labor force participation rates: They did not leave the work force upon marriage or raising a family, which their uneducated peers with children did. This also modifies Ram's argument regarding a natural advantage of women in childbearing. It shows that marriage and child rearing are social facts, rather than natural ones, which have varying impacts on women, depending on educational and class status.

Raj's study of well-educated women in India deepens this analysis by probing into the quality of the impacts. In her interviews of women scientists, she finds that their career aspirations are mitigated by involvement in family life. Becaue they derive much satisfaction from contributions to the family, they accept lack of career advancement and fail to detect discrimination. She points as well to the impact of generational change (complementing the report of Smith and Cheung) whereby first-generation employed women may respond differently to job discrimination than others. Her conclusion echoes the theme announced in the introduction, that educational outcomes for women must be seen in terms of women's lives, not only in comparison to men. The women she studied compare themselves, not with men, but with the women in their families who preceded them, and they assess their work advancement as just one component of the full range of the daily reality they experience.

Education and the Family

The impact of education on the private sphere of marriage, family, and self is the subject of the final three papers. The effect on fertility has attracted the greatest attention of scholars, making possible several somewhat firm conclusions. It is now quite clear that women's education does reduce fertility in the majority of cases, but the number of instances where it does not is large and suggestive. Countries and rural groups within contries where low literacy prevails are the populations in which women's education increases fertility.

Efforts to explain the causal relationship have identified a large number of intermediate mechanisms by which education might affect fertility. Cochrane provides a model that shows how the effects of education in reducing both infant mortality and the demand for children may be countered by its increasing not only the ability to afford children but also women's ability to conceive. Countries where education does not decrease fertility are those where poor health and traditional practices limit births, these being factors that education is likely to remove.

LeVine takes us from fertility to mothering, with the question whether educated women make better mothers. This is clearly one of the most important concerns motivating the education of women, but it is so value-laden that few scholars have dared to address it directly. LeVine brings a very useful orientation, which enables him to set aside ideology and examine research evidence. He begins with the assumption that in-digenous patterns of infant and child care represent largely successful adaptations to the conditions of life in different societies, and that nonliterate women have been very effective transmitters of these pat-terns. The question he poses is whether educated mothers are better able to prepare children for participation in a new socioeconomic order that involves schooling and employment. In effect, are educated mothers better able to prepare their children to be successful in school and the modern labor market?

As we have tried to do throughout this volume, LeVine attempts to distinguish the independent effects of education. This means sorting out the impact of education from confounding factors usually associated with education, such as family income, urban residence, and media ex-posure. He finds that one cannot make clear statements because the available research was not designed to answer this question. There is substantial evidence, however, that mothering behavior does change among educated women, so that their children perform better on Western preschool tests. Just how schooling causes this change in mothering behavior remains an unanswered question. LeVine provides interesting speculations, but answers must await investigation of the many linkages in the complex path of schooling to motherhood. Raj pro-vides partial answers from her Indian interviews, which indicate that educated women utilize modern knowledge more effectively for family health and nutrition.

Perhaps the most difficult problem is the one with which this volume began, namely the impact of education on a woman's view of herself and her world. This has not been a fashionable question recently, for world interest in education has shifted from a humanitarian interest in enlightenment to more practical concerns with jobs and national development. Yet one cannot ignore the testimony of individuals from all parts of the world to the intellectual and personal liberation that education has brought to their lives. Ultimately these issues are philosophical ones, which is perhaps why researchers have shied away.

Raj reminds us, however, that one must come to terms with these hopes for education in order to assess whether educational goals are being accomplished. As a member of a poor country where customary practices act as a severe drag on urgently needed progress in many areas affecting human welfare, she holds high expectations of scientific education to overcome them. Although her expectations are largely disappointed, they cannot be dismissed, for they serve as a strong critique of the educational systems we have settled for, and a goal toward which we must strive in the education of both women and men.

Reflections from India

Since beginning work on this volume, one of the editors, Carolyn Elliott, has moved to India with the Ford Foundation. There one senses several attitudes affecting women's eduation which, if true elsewhere, suggest the need for a rededication to education.

Early naive faith in education as the key to national progress has been belied. Growing numbers of unemployed graduates emphasize the need for creating employment before skills can be utilized. It is also widely recognized that India's system of formal education does not impart the skills and attitudes needed for development, and that it is ineffective—and certainly inefficient—even in teaching basic literacy. Educators over the years have proposed many schemes to reshape the educational system, but these have yielded largely mechanistic exercises, such as juggling the years assigned to each level of schooling. Meanwhile the very visible success of other approaches to development, most notably the green revolution, have turned attention away from education to more promising avenues to progress. One senses the nation's intellectuals are bored with trying to reform education.

Without a more adequately financed and stronger political commitment to education, efforts to change it are likely to come to nought in any case. India currently invests just 2.2% of its budget on education, low compared to the U.S. and even compared to developing countries. Within the educational spending pattern is a very top-heavy investment in higher education, 20 times the expenditure per student in primary and secondary schooling, compared to a ratio of 3 to 1 in the U.S.[6] This pattern suits local rural power structures well, for it draws ambitious youth out of the countryside to urban colleges and does little to raise the aspirations of those left behind. Efforts under a recent populist government to change this power equation by a significant investment in adult education have now been withdrawn, as the potential

[6] Calculated for 1977–8 from figures provided in The Planning Commission, Government of India, "Draft Sixth Five-Year Plan, 1978–83," rev., pp. 423, 429.

of adult education for social mobilization and partisan political activity have become apparent.

Despite clearly established relationships between women's education and India's national policy goals in health and family planning, there appears to be little political will behind women's education. Although the new national plan cites the need for special measures to increase the enrollment and retention of girls in school—child care centers at schools, women teachers, and night classes—there is no national program for women's education. In school there is a widespread recourse to cultural explanations for the lack of activity. One finds in talking with educational administrators a full circle of explanations accounting for low enrollment rates of girls—sibling care, early marriage, parental unwillingness to invest in girls, women teachers' reluctance to work in villages, parental reluctance to allow girls to attend classes at night—which makes improvement seem impossible without long-term evolutionary social change. This proclivity to attribute women's lack of participation in education, and in all development programs, to family and culture is a major obstacle to creative thinking about policy innovations that would increase women's participation. And they mask the reluctance of policy makers to make the required financial investments in the levels of both primary and adult education that would reach the large proportion (75%) of Indian women who remain illiterate.

In higher education, India has a relatively strong ratio of girls to boys and a good stock of well-educated women, as the Raj paper demonstrates. However, the sex stereotyping of fields is marked, with consequences both for individual career choices and for development programs. Women's enrollment for an agricultural degree are still miniscule, and nonexistant in forestry. This means that development programs in critical areas of women's work—agriculture, fuel, and fodder—are designed, directed, and evaluated by male experts who, because of customary practices prevalent in most of India, can have no direct access to village women. There is some official reluctance to encourage women to enter agricultural colleges, because home economics is seen as a more suitable course and because there is unemployment among male agricultural graduates. Medicine is another critical area in which trained women are needed because of the reluctance of women patients to consult male doctors. India has a large stock of women doctors, but enrollments in medical colleges are declining, a worrisome trend. The probable reason is the rise of private medical colleges with capitation fees that parents are unwilling to pay for a daughter's education.

Persons concerned with women and development have not largely been a source of thinking or energy on behalf of women's education.

Because the income needs of poor women are so obvious and urgent, they have emphasized income-generating programs. No one can question the need for these programs, nor the importance of integrating literacy with economic and health improvement. Without such linkages, previous literacy schemes have often failed to sustain participation. It is a matter of concern, however, that educational needs are often neglected. All too many income schemes stabilize or marginally improve the economic position of participants, but do not provide the skills and knowledge that would enable poor women to manage their own organizations or secure further mobility.

How might research help to develop a renewed zeal for women's education? The various studies in this volume show many possibilities—by documenting improvement and identifying groups falling behind, by clarifying motivations and effective incentives, and by demonstrating social pay-offs to investment in education. Perhaps most important, however, is to put cultural stereotypes in their place and demonstrate how improvement can be made.

Studies focusing on what can be changed, such as the distribution of schools, rather than on cultural values, such as religion or early marriage, that are difficult to affect, may raise the sense of possibility, and thus the commitment to education. Chitra Naik's description of night classes for working children may be the most important piece in the volume.

Women and Schooling in the Third World:
A Bibliography

DAVID H. KELLY AND GAIL P. KELLY

Introduction

The education of women in the Third World is a relatively new and growing area of research. Before 1970, studies of women's schooling were confined to histories of specific institutions or descriptive summaries of the amount of education women and girls received. The early literature was relatively scant and lacking in analytic perspective. It rarely focused on the determinants of women's education, the differences in the type of eduacation females as compared to males received, or the personal, social, or political outcomes of women's education. Since 1970, studies of women's schooling focusing on such topics have proliferated, especially in such Western industrialized societies as the United States and Great Britain. There is now a substantial literature for these countries on access to education, the formal and "hidden" curriculums of the schools, counseling practices, educational outcomes, and the relation between schooling and women's roles and status in society and family life. Such research, conducted in the Third World, remains far less extensive, although since 1975 there has been a noticeable increase. This bibliography reflects the earlier work, but concentrates on the state of research on women's education in the Third World since 1975.

In compiling the bibliography we were faced with some difficult choices about what to include. We focus exclusively on women's education in the Third World. We define the "Third World" in terms of the relatively unindustrialized nations of Asia, Latin America, Africa, and the Middle East. The bibliography does not contain studies of women's education in highly industrialized countries of Asia and Africa, notably Japan and Israel. Nor does it cover studies of the education of African, Asian, Middle Eastern, and Latin American women living in the industrialized West.

The bibliography focuses on education. Studies of women's roles in the family, their relationships to men, their participation in both preindustrial and industrial sectors of the economy, the women's movement, women's political participation, and women's contribution to development are included only if they make a direct link to education. While

Tereffe Asrat, Saraswati Balasubramanian, Younus Lulat, Eva Rathgeber, and Cristina Vergel assisted in the preparation of this bibliography.

many of these studies are important in analyzing educational patterns, barriers to women's education, or the broad implications of education, we have chosen not to include them in this bibliography because numerous guides to that research, many of which are listed in the pages that follow, are readily available. Our task is to provide a guide to the education literature.

The studies contained in the bibliography are either directly on women's education or use sex differences or gender as analytical categories. For example, we have selected studies on the relation of education to sex-role divisions of labor in the society, changes in women's social status, women's participation and status in the work force, fertility, marriage, child rearing and nutrition, and equality between males and females.

Women's education in the nations of Africa, Asia, Latin America, and the Middle East defines the scope of this bibliography. It contains research on the history of women's education, the status of women's schooling (how many females are educated, literate, currently attend school, and the level of their educational attainment); access of women to educational institutions and the factors that affect access; the process of education, including formal as well as "hidden" curriculums, guidance practices, and textbook analyses; achievement patterns of females relative to males; social, personal, and career aspirations of female students; nonformal education; and the outcomes of women's education as they affect development, women's labor force participation, the professions, changes in women's social status, and family life.

The bibliography is organized topically rather than geographically. Much of the research deals with more than one country and region. In addition, there is considerable imbalance in the types of studies conducted among regions. For example, the literature we report on women's educational achievement often gives general trends, not those of a particular nation. Not only does much of the research defy geographical categorization, the topic of research conducted varies considerably by region. There are, for example, very few studies on women's education and its relation to the work force participation that have been conducted outside of Latin America. Additionally, the literature on nonformal education is predominantly about Asia and Latin America. The geographical variation in the type of scholarship on women's education is in itself an interesting phenomenon. However, we have not chosen to highlight that variation. We believe that, while there are many distinctions to be made between nations, regions, and cultures on the significance of education, research on a given topic, such as the expansion of education and its effect on women's entry into the labor force, has vast implications for all the Third World, regardless of the geographical base of that research. In short, a topically arranged bibliography provides a more useful guide about both the state of scholarship on women's education in the Third World and areas in need of further investigation.

While we have arranged the bibliography topically, the categories we have used are not always discrete. Much of the literature on nonformal education, for example, relates to development; similarly, the many studies of the status of women's education contain information on both female social status and access to education.

Our intent in compiling this bibliography is to provide a guide to readily available materials. We have included published materials, such as books, book chapters, and journal articles. We have also provided a comprehensive listing of UNESCO reports and have included government and private agency reports that can be obtained. Doctoral and master's dissertations in the U.S. and some other nations are included. We have avoided references to unpublished materials to which the user cannot gain access.

The bibliography contains works in English, French, and Spanish. While this somewhat limits the materials, that limitation is not as serious as it might seem. Most contemporary scholarly research on the topic has been published in the languages we cover.

One of the most important contributions of this bibliography is what it reveals about the strengths and weaknesses in research coverage about women's education in the Third World. The type of research conducted tells us as much about what we know about women's education in the Third World as it does about what we have yet to learn. By far, the most research that has been generated since 1975 has been general descriptions of the status of women's education, detailing the number of women attending school, literacy, and attainment levels. Many of the items we list, half of which are books, simply provide enrollment and literacy statistics. This charting of women's educational status, as the bibliography shows, is far from comprehensive. Much of it presents fragmentary data, often based on incomplete government reportage. Noticeable in the literature is an almost complete absence of such studies for sub-Sarharan Africa.

While research has tended to focus on women's educational status, and to a lesser extent on the factors affecting access to schooling, it has been extremely sparse when it comes to studying the processes of education and educational outcomes (male versus female achievement patterns). It is clear that women throughout most of the Third World do not enter school at the same rate as men, are less educated than men, and have not achieved social status equal to men even when obtaining the same amount of education; research has not inquired whether the type of education offered women relates to these patterns. There are but a handful of studies of school practices, formal and informal curriculums, or the interaction patterns within the classroom and how they relate to differences in male/female attendance and attrition rates or educatonal, social, and economic outcomes of schooling, or how they affect girls' occupatonal and social aspirations. Such research, as the few studies we have been able to locate underscore, may begin to explain persistence in women's undereducation.

Not only are there few studies of educational processes, even sparser are studies of women's educational achievement patterns, especially in the last five years. While research has neglected personal educational outcomes, it has focused heavily on a variety of social and economic outcomes of education. Most of this literature concerns women and economic development, work force participation rates, entry into the professions, and social status. By far the greatest concentration is on the work force. The vast majority of these studies are based in Latin America. Three deal with Africa, three the Middle-East and eight on Asia. The studies generated on women and the professions similarly are based heavily in Latin America. It is interesting to note that since 1975 we have been able to identify 18 studies of women in the professions. However, in the same time period, there have been very few studies of women's higher education, which is preparatory for the professions. A good bit of work on these topics from the 1960's and early 1970's is listed, and nursing education and its professional outcome, generally, is better covered, especially in dissertation research.

The literature that has evolved over the past five years on women and development has not focused on the relation of education to women's participation in the modern sector of the economy, as does the literature on women and the work force and professions. Rather, as the studies we have listed indicate, the emphasis has been on how or whether education has increased women's productivity in the traditional agricultural sector of the economy. Much of this literature is not interested in whether education changes women's status, its concern is the relation of women's education to meeting basic community needs. A similar focus is evident in the literature on nonformal education.

While research has intensified on the public, social outcomes of education, it has left virtually untouched the effect of education on women's lives in the family or as mothers. While we have located 70 items broadly classified as "Education and the Family," the vast majority of these studies focus on education and fertility, dealing heavily with Asia. There are very few studies on the effect of education on women's marriage choices, child nutrition, child health, children's achievement, or women's roles in the family.

The imbalances in the research on women's education generated since 1975 are recorded in this bibliography. They should give little surprise. It is but 10 years since research on women's education in the Third World has re-emerged both as a scholarly interest and as a concern of most governments. The literature is still in the process of documenting imbalances between male and female education, and defining its dimensions, and its significance. In the future, research will become more analytic and begin to focus on areas where little is known. We see this bibliography as a guide to the literature produced since 1975, and as a means for highlighting those areas in which more research is needed.

Overview

Books

African Bibliographic Center. *Contemporary African Women: An Introductory Bibliographical Overview and a Guide to Women's Organizations, 1960–1967.* Washington, D.C.: African Bibliographic Center, 1968.

Bereaud, Susan. *Women in Education: A Bibliography.* Ithaca, N.Y.: Cornell University, Women's Studies Program, 1971.

Bickner, Mei Liang. *Women at Work: An Annotated Bibliography.* Los Angeles: University of California, Los Angeles, Manpower Research Center, 1974.

Buvinic, Myara. *Women and World Development: An Annotated Bibliography.* Washington, D.C.: Overseas Development Council, 1976.

Cabana, Alfredo; Jaramillo, Luz; and Silva, Renán. *Guía bibliografica de estuidios sobre la mujer y la educación.* Bogata: Universidad Pedagógica Nacional, Centre de Investigaciones, 1979.

Chandler, Dale, and Thairu, R. W. *Women of Kenya: An Annotated Bibliography.* Nairobi: Women's Bureau of the Ministry of Housing and Social Services and the United Nations, 1977.

Chung, Betty Jamie. *The Status of Women and Fertility in Southeast and East Asia: A Bibliography.* Singapore: Institute of Southeast Asian Studies, 1977.

Cismaresco, Françoise. *Education and Training of Women.* Paris: Unesco and International Bureau of Education, 1975.

Cohen Stuart, Bertie A. *Women in the Caribbean: a Bibliography.* Leiden: Department of Caribbean Studies, Royal Institute of Linguistics and Anthropology, 1979.

Commonwealth Bureau of Agricultural Economics. *Women in Rural Society: An Annotated Bibliography.* Oxford: Commonwealth Bureau of Agricultural Economics, 1972.

Dasgupta, Kalpana, ed. *Women on the Indian Scene: An Annotated Bibliography.* New Delhi: Abhinav Publications, 1977.

Een, Jo Ann Delores, and Rosenberg-Dishman, Marie B. *Women and Society— Citations 3601 to 6000: An Annotated Bibliography.* Beverly Hills, Calif.: Sage Publications, 1978.

Epskamp, C. *Inequality in Female Access to Education in Developing Countries: A Bibliography.* The Hague: Centre for the Study of Education in Developing Countries, NUFFIC/CESO, 1979.

International Institute for Adult Literacy Methods. *Literacy Programmes for Women.* Tehran: International Institute for Adult Literacy Methods, 1977.

Jacobs, Sue-Ellen. *Women in Perspective: A Guide for Cross-cultural Studies.* Urbana: University of Illinois Press, 1974.

Kohen, A. I.; Breinich, S. C.; and Shields, P. *Women and the Economy: A Bibliography and a Review of the Literature on Sex Differentiation in the Labor Market.* Columbus: Ohio State University Center for Human Resource Research, March 1975 (suppl., July 1977).

Knaster, Meri. *Women in Spanish America: An Annotated Bibliography from Preconquest to Contemporary Times.* Boston: G. K. Hall & Co., 1977.

Kratochvil, Laura, and Shaw, Shauna. *African Women: A Select Bibliography.* Cambridge: Cambridge University, African Studies Centre, 1974.

Misra, L. *Education of Women in India, 1921–1966.* Bombay: Macmillan Co., 1966.

Mukerjee, A. K.; and Katyal, F. C. *Education of Indian Women: a Bibliography.* New Delhi: Documentation Cell, Library and Documentation Unit, National Council of Educational Research and Training, 1979.

Muway, J. *Preliminary Bibliography on Women in Africa.* Los Angeles: University of California, Los Angeles, African Studies Center, 1974.

Parker, Franklin; and Parker, Betty June. *Women's Education, a World View: Annotated Bibliography of Doctoral Dissertations.* Westport, Conn.: Greenwood Press, 1979.

Plisnier-Ladame, F. *Bibliographie de la condition de l'africaine en Afrique noire.* Brussels: LEDFSA, 1961.

Qazzar, al-, Ayad. *Women in the Middle East and North Africa: An Annotated Bibliography.* Austin: University of Texas Center for Middle Eastern Studies, 1977.

Raccagni, Michelle. *The Modern Arab Woman: A Bibliography.* Metuchen, N.J.: Scarecrow Press, 1978.

Research Unit on Women's Studies of Shreemati Nathibai Damodar Thackersey University, Bombay. *A Select Bibliography on Women in India.* New Delhi: Allied Publishers, 1977.

Rihani, May. *Development as If Women Mattered: An Annotated Bibliography with a Third World Focus.* Washington, D.C.: Overseas Development Council, 1978.

Rosenberg, Marie Barovic, and Bergstrom, Len V. *Women and Society: A Critical Review of the Literature with a Selected Annotated Bibliography.* Beverly Hills, Calif.: Sage Publications, 1975.

Saulniers, Suzanne, and Rakowski, Cathy. *Women in the Development Process: A Select Bibliography on Women in Sub-Saharan Africa and Latin America.* Austin: Institute of Latin American Studies, University of Texas Press, 1978.

Sharma, Prakash C. *Female Working Role and Economic Development: A Selected Research Bibliography.* Monticello, Ill.: Council of Planning Librarians, 1974.

Technical Assistance Information Clearing House of the American Council of Voluntary Agencies for Foreign Service, Inc. *Women: A Bibliography.* New York: Technical Assistance Information Clearing House of the American Council of Voluntary Agencies for Foreign Service, Inc., 1975.

Tejeira, Otilia Arosemena de. *La jaula invisible: la mujer en América Latina.* Mexico: B. Costa-Amic, 1977.

Tinker, Irene, and Bramsen, Michele Bo, eds. *Women and World Development (with an Annotated Bibliography).* New York: Praeger Publishers, 1976.

Unesco. *Documents on Women's Education and Women in Public Life.* Bangkok: Unesco Regional Office for Education in Asia, 1970.

Unesco. Oficina regional de educación para América Latina y el Caribe, Services de biblioteca y documentación. *Bibliografía sobre education de la mujer en areas rurales.* Santiago, Chile: 1979.

Articles

Ananda, Peter. "Women in the Philippines: A Preliminary Bibliography." *Cormosea Newsletter* 7 (1973–74): 18–21.

Bay, E., et al., eds. "Women in Africa, (Symposium)" *African Studies Review* 18 (December 1975): 1–200.

Beoku-Betts, J. A. "Published and Unpublished Sources on Sierra Leonean Women." *African Research Bulletin* 6 (1975–76): 114–25.

Colina, Lydia, comp. "Women in the Philippines: A Preliminary Bibliography." *Cormosea Newsletter* 8 (September 1975): 10–11.

Feinberg, R. "Select Bibliography on Women: Their Education and Employment Both National and International, 1973–1976." *Journal of Research and Development in Education* 10, no. 4 (1977): 77–87.

Kelly, A. "Women in Science: a Bibliographic Review." *Durham Research Review* 7, no. 36 (1976): 1092–1108.

Kerina, J. M. "Women in Africa: A Select Bibliography." *Africa Report* 22, no. 1 (1977): 44–50.

Knaster, Meri. "Women in Latin America, the State of Research." *Latin American Research Review* 11, no. 1 (1976): 3–74.

León de Leal, M. "Personas interisados en la problemática feminina en Perú, Argentina, Brasil y Venezuela." *Latin American Research Review* 14, no. 1 (1979): 134–44.

Leonard, K. "Women in India: Some Recent Perspectives." *Pacific Affairs* 52 (Spring 1979): 95–107.

Quazzaz, al-, A. "Current Status of Research on Women in the Arab World." *Middle Eastern Studies* 14 (October 1978): 372–80.

Salmon, Claudine. "Essai de bibliographie sur la question féminin en Indonésie." *Revue Archipel* 13 (1977): 23–36.

Soeiro, Susan A. "Recent Work on Latin American Women: A Review Essay." *Journal of Foster-American Studies and World Affairs* 17 (November 1975): 497–516.

Westfall, G. D. "Nigerian Women: a Bibliographical Essay." *Africana Journal* 5, no. 2 (1974): 99–138.

Histories of Women's Education

Books

Abu Zayd, Hikmat, et al. *The Education of Women in the U.A.R. during the Nineteenth and Twentieth Centuries.* Cairo: National Commission for Unesco, 1970.

Alzona, Encarnacion. *Education of Women.* Manila: University of the Philippines Press, 1939.

Goldstein, Rhoda L. *Women in Transition: Bangalore Case Study.* Metuchen, N.J.: Scarecrow Press, 1972.

Gedge, Evelyn Clara, ed. *Women in Modern India: Fifteen papers by Indian Women.* Westport, Conn: Hyperion Press, 1976.

Hahner, June, ed. *Women in Latin American History, Their Lives and Views.* Los Angeles: UCLA Latin American Center Publications, University of California, 1976.

Lewis, Ida Belle. *The Education of Girls in China.* 1919. Reprint. New York: AMS Press, 1972.

Naik, J. P. *Equality, Quality, and Quantity: The Elusive Triangle of Indian Education.* Bombay: Allied, 1975.

Nanda, B. R., ed. *Indian Women: From Purdah to Modernity.* New Delhi: Vikas Publishing House, 1976.

Osei, Gabriel Kingsley. *Caribbean Women: Their History and Habits.* London: African Publication Society, 1979.

Rahman, S. A. *Education of Women in Modern Indian Society: A Historical Study with a Critique of Contemporary Educational Thought.* Columbus: Ohio State University, 1963.

Articles

Chan, Itty. "Women of China: From the Three Obediences to Half-the-Sky." *Journal of Research and Development in Education* 10 (Summer 1977): 38–52.

Gálvez Berrera, A. M. "Historical Status of Women in Peru." *Impact of Science on Society* 30 (January 1980): 7–9.

Hahner, J. E. "Feminism, Women's Rights and the Sufferage Movement in Brazil, 1850–1932." *Latin American Research Review* 15, no. 1 (1980): 65–111.

Hironaka, K. "Education for Girls and Women in India. Progress and Problems." *Research Bulletin of the National Institute for Educational Research*, no. 13 (1975): 53–60.

Kartini, Raden Ajeng. "Educate the Javanese! [Geef den Javaan Øpvoeding!]: A Memorial Addressed to the Dutch Government in January 1903 by Raden Ajeng Kartini." Translated by Jean Taylor. *Indonesia* 17 (April 1974): 83–98.

"L'Enseignement féminin en Tunisie." *Ferida* 1 (May 1975): 34–35.

Liman, Daniel le. "L'Education de la femme en Tunisie: Son évolution." *Convergence* 2, no. 2 (1969): 70–72.

Moorman, Paul. "The Golden Age of Islamic Education." *Change* 10 (March, 1978): 13–14, 16–17.

Parker, Franklin. "Women's Education: Historical and International View." *Contemporary Education* 43 (February 1972): 198–201.

Penders, L. M. "Kartini: Indonesian Patriot and Reformer." In *Indonesian Women: Some Past and Current Perspectives*, edited by B. B. Hering. Brussels: Centre d'étude du Sud-Est Asiatique et de l'Extrême Orient, 1976.

Perez Venero, Mirna M. "The Education of Women on the Isthmus of Panama." *Journal of the West* 12, no. 2 (1973): 225–34.

Russel-Wood, A.J.R. "Women and Society in Colonial Brazil." *Journal of Latin American Studies* 9 (May 1977): 1–34.

Sanderson, Lilian M. "Some Aspects of the Development of Girls' Education in the Northern Sudan." *Sudan Notes and Records* 42 (1961) 91–101.

Shridevi, S. "Women's Higher Education in India since Independence." *Improving College and University Teaching* 20 (Winter 1972): 71–72.

Spade, B. "Education of Women in China during the Southern Dynasties." *Journal of Asian History* 13, no. 1 (1979): 15–41.

Tennant, Margaret. "Natural Directions: The New Zealand Movement for Sexual Differentiation in Education during the Early Twentieth Century." *New Zealand Journal of Educational Studies* 12 (November 1977): 142–153.

Vaughan, Mary K. "Women, Class and Education in Mexico, 1880–1928." *Latin American Perspectives* 4 (Winter-Spring 1977): 135–42.

Unpublished Materials

Bouche, D. "L'enseignement dans les territories français de L'Afrique Occidentale de 1817 à 1920: Mission civilisatrice ou formation d'une elite?" Ph.D. dissertation, l'Universite de Paris, 1974.

Hammam, Mona. "Women Workers and the Practice of Freedom as Education: The Egyptian Experience." Ph.D. dissertation, University of Kansas, 1977.

Lahiri, Krishna. "Education of Women in Bengal, 1849–1882, with Special Reference to Missionary Contributions." Ph.D. dissertation, University of Pennsylvania, 1979.

Lombardi, Mary. "Women in the Modern Art Movement in Brazil: Salon Leaders, Artists, and Musicians, 1917–1930." Ph.D. dissertation, University of California, Los Angeles, 1977.

Maskiell, Michelle Gibson. "Women's Higher Education and Family Networks in South Asia: Kinnaird College, Lahore, 1913–60." Ph.D. dissertation, University of Pennsylvania, 1979.

Paul, Glendora B. "Emancipation and Education of Indian Women since 1829." Ph.D. dissertation, University of Pittsburgh, 1970.

Peacock, M. G. P. "The History of the Freetown Secondary School for Girls." Ph.D. dissertation, Fourah Bay College, 1960.

Robinson, Betty Sue. "The Ramakrishna Sarada Math: A Study of a Women's Movement in Bengal." Ph.D. dissertation, Columbia University, 1978.

Senalak, Thatchanaphin. "Development of Education and Vocations for Thai Women in Raltanaksin Bangkok Period." Master's thesis, Chulalongkorn University, Bangkok, 1963.

Staelin, Charlotte Dennett. "The Influence of Missions on Women's Education in India: The American Marathi Mission in Ahmadnagar, 1830–1930." Ph.D. dissertation, University of Michigan, 1977.

Thomas, Ethel Nichols. "Mary Mills Patrick and the American College for Girls at Istanbul in Turkey." Ed.D. dissertation, Rutgers University, 1979.

Wichakorakom, Phanii. "Development of Education for Thai Women." Ph.D. dissertation, Chulalongkorn University, Bangkok, 1957.

Witke, Roxane Heater. "Transformation of Attitude towards Women during the May Fourth Era of Modern China." Ph.D. dissertation, University of California, Berkeley, 1970.

Status of Women's Education (General)

Books

Aggarwal, J. C. *Indian Women: Education and Status (Including Major Recommen-*

dations of the Report of Women in India, 1917–74). New Delhi: Arya Book Depot, 1976.

Bahrain. Ministry of Education, Directorate of Planning, Unit of Documentation and Research. *Development of Education in Bahrain (1975–1976)*. Manama: 1977.

Bangladesh. Ministry of Education. *Development in Education to Bangladesh, 1975–1977. A Country Report*, Dacca: 1977.

Centro de Estudios Sociales con la Cooperación AITEC. *La participación feminina en el sistema educacional Venezolano*. Documento Tecnico no. 2. Caracas: Centro de Estudios Sociales con la Cooperación AITEC, 1975.

Chabaud, Jacqueline. *The Education and Advancement of Women*. Paris: Unesco, 1970.

Cheng, Siok Hwa. *Women in Singapore: Legal, Educational and Economic Aspects*. Institute of Humanities and Social Sciences Occasional Paper Series, no. 22. Singapore: Nanyang University, 1976.

Cordell, Magda, et al. *Women in World Terms: Facts and Trends*. Binghamton: State University of New York at Binghamton, Center for Integrative Studies, 1975.

Covarrubias, Paz; and Franco, Rolando, eds. *Chile mujer y sociedad*. Santiago: Unicef, l979.

Deblé, Isabelle. *The School Education of Girls: An International Comparative Study of School Wastage among Girls and Boys at First and Second Levels of Education*. Paris: Unesco, 1980.

Education and Veil. Karachi: Peermahomed Ebrahim Trust, 1975.

Gerard, R. *Education des femmes en Iran, Septembre 1969–juin 1972*. Paris: Unesco, 1972.

Harby, M. K., and Mehrez, Z. M. *Education for Women in the U.A.R.* Cairo: Educational Documentation Centre of U.A.R., 1961.

Hussein, A. *The Arab Republic of Egypt: Survey of Women Development and Educational Opportunities*. Cairo: Arab Republic of Egypt, Ministry of Education, 1973.

Indian Council of Social Science Research. Advisory Committee on Women's Studies. *Critical Issues on the Status of Women: Suggested Priorities for Action*. Publication, no. 107. New Delhi: Indian Council of Social Science Research, 1977.

International Institute for Adult Literacy Methods. *Literacy Programmes for Women*. Tehran: International Institute for Adult Literacy Methods. 1977.

Islam, S. *Women's Education in Bangladesh: Needs and Issues*. Dacca: Foundation of Research on Educational Planning and Development, 1977.

McGrath, Patricia L. *The Unfinished Assignment: Equal Education for Women*. Worldwatch Paper no. 7. Washington, D.C.: Worldwatch Institute, 1976.

Mblinyi, Marjorie. *The Education of Girls in Tanzania*. Dar es Salaam: University College, 1969.

Melo de Cardona, Ligia A. *Participación de la mujer en la educación sistemática en la Republica Dominican*. Colección UASD crítica, vol. 238, no. 19. Santo Domingo, R.D.: Universidad Autonoma Santo Domingo, 1977.

Movimento brasilerio de alfabetização. *The Development of Educational Programs for the Social and Economic Advancement of Women in the Rural Areas*. Rio de Janiero: 1975.

Muckenhirn, Erma F. *Secondary Education and Girls in Western Nigeria*. Comparative Education Dissertation Series 9. Ann Arbor: University of Michigan, 1966.

Mustaffa-Kedah, O. *Towards a Rational Education for Women in the Arab World*. Tehran: International Institute for Adult Literacy Methods, 1976.

National Seminar on the Role of Women in Education in India, Madras, 1975. *The Role of Women in Education in India: A Report*. Madras: Society for the Promotion of Education in India, 1976.

Oman. Ministry of Education. *Development of Education in the Sultanate of Oman during the school year 1974–1975 — 1975–1976*. Muscat: 1977.

Organization of American States. *Women and the System of Formal Education in Latin America*. Washington, D.C.: Inter-American Commission of Women, Organization of American States, 1975.

Palmer, Penny. *Girls in High School in Papua, New Guinea*. Report no. 23. Port Moresby: University of Papua, New Guinea, Educational Research Unit, 1978.

Saudi Arabia. Ministry of Education. *The Bi-Annual Report of the Ministry of Education, 1975 and 1976*. Riyadh: 1977.

Slama, Saida; and Sauvageot, C. *Comparative Analysis of Male and Female Enrollment and Illiteracy*. Paris: Unesco, 1980.

Thibert, Marguerite. *Rapport au gouvernement de la Tunisie sur la preparation professionnelle des jeunes filles en Tunisie*. Geneva: UNICEF, 1966.

Unesco. *Women, Education, Equality: A Decade of Experiment*. Paris: Unesco, 1975.

——. *A Summary Statistical Review of Education in the World, 1960–75*. Paris: Unesco, 1977.

University of Delhi, Agriculture Economics Research Centre. *Primary Education in Rural India*. Delhi: Tata Institute, 1971.

Wahjudi, M. *Statistics on Women in Formal Education in Indonesia*. Jakarta: Office of Educational Development, National Commission on the Status of Women, 1973.

World Education. *Special Report on BRAC*. New York: World Education, 1976.

Articles

Advani, L. "Women and the Widening Horizons in Education." In *The Position of Women in India: Proceedings of a Seminar Held in Srinagar, September, 1972*, edited by K. Bhasin. Bombay: Shakuntala Publishing House, 1972.

Anderson, G. M. "Women and Literacy in Developing Nations." *America* 141 (July 21, 1979): 27–29.

Bell, Jane. "Further Education for the Women of Uganda." *African Women* 4 (June 1962): 73–77.

Bhansali, K. "Education of Women in Modern India: Some Achievements and Problems." *Education Quarterly* 21 (Spring 1969): 36–43.

Bugnicourt, Jacques. "Disparités scolaires en Afrique." *Tiers monde* 48 (1971): 751–86.

Calixto, J. "Education of Women in Developing Countries." *Science Review* 10 (February 1969): 20–26.

Cornell, M. L. "The Development of Education for Women in Kuwait." *Canadian and International Education* 5, no. 2 (1976): 73–83.

"Democratic India and Women's Education.' *Education Quarterly* 13 (1961) 117–220.

Dodd, Peter C. "Youth and Women's Emancipation in the United Arab Republic," *Middle East Journal* 22, no. 2 (1968): 159–72.

"The Education of Women and Girls in Uganda." *Women Today* 6 (June 1964): 42–44.

Eliou, Marie. "The Education and Advancement of Women in Africa: Ivory Coast, Upper Volta, Senegal." *International Review of Education* 19, no. 1 (1973): 30–46.

"Femmes, Educations, Avenir." *Recherches Pédagogie et Culture* 4, no. 19 (1975): 1–72.

Franco, Zoila. "Women in the Transformation of Cuban Education." *Prospects* 5, no. 3 (1975): 387–90.

Glazer, Daphne. "Problems of the Education of Girls in Nigeria." *Aspects of Education*, no. 19 (1977): 33–42.

Hwang Kyung, Ko. "Korean Women and Education." *Korea Journal* 4 (February 1964): 10–13.

"Invisible Women: Special Issue." *Unesco Courier* 33 (July 1980): 3–34.

Jalón, Ana María. "La Mujer y su papel de ecucadora." *Revista de la Universidad Nacional de Cordobaoi*, nos. 1 and 2 (1961): 305–18.

Kelly, Gail Paradise. "Research on the Education of Women in the Third World: Problems and Perspectives." *Women's Studies: International Quarterly* 1, no. 4 (1978): 365–73.

Labarca, Amanda H. "Women and Education in Chile." In *Problems in Education V: Women and Education*, edited by Unesco. Paris: Unesco, 1953.

357

Laurin, Geneviève. "The Status of Women in Niger." *International Journal of Adult and Youth Education* 15, no. 3 (1963): 120–24.

Lipeovich de Querd, Tamara, and San Martin, Ester Romero. "A View of Women's Education in Peru." *Convergence* 2, no. 2 (1969): 37–48. (Text Spanish, abstract English).

Mandl, P.-E., et al. "Introduction: Some Facts and Figures, Time, Health, Nutrition, Education and Training . . . ." *Assignment Children/Les Carnets de l'enfrance*, no. 49–50 (Spring 1980): 17–41.

Manea, Lucian. "Education des filles, dot et société feminine chez les bati." *Revue de l'action populaire*, no. 180 (July–August 1964), pp. 822–32.

Metzger, L. "The Role of Women in Education: the Sierra Leone Experience." In *La Civilisation de la femme dans la tradition africaine*. Abidjan: Colloque d'Abidjan, 1972.

Minces, Juliette. "Women in Algeria." In *Women in the Muslim World*, edited by Lois Beck and Nikki Keddie. Cambridge: Harvard University Press, 1978.

Moretta, Clavijo Fabiola. "Ecuador: Falta la investigación sobre la situación actual de la mujer." *Boletin documental sobre la mujer* 1, no. 1 (1971): 52–56.

Mustoffa, Kedah Omar. "The Education of Women in the Arab States." *Literacy Discussion* 6 (Winter 1975/76): 119–39.

Ochoa Nuñez, H. "La mujer en el sistem educativo." In *La mujer y el desarrollo en Colombia*, edited by Magdalena Leon de Leal. Bogota: Asociación Colombiana para el Estudio de la Población, 1977.

O'Shaughnessy, T. J. "Growth of Education Opportunity for Muslim Women, 1950 to 1973." *Anthropos* 73, no. 5–6 (1978): 887–901.

Ramachandran, P. "Women and Education." *Indian Journal of Social Work* 23, no. 4 (1963): 331–41.

Sanderson, Lillian M. "Girls' Education in the Northern Sudan, 1898–1956." In *Conflict and Harmony in Education in Tropical Africa*, edited by Godfrey N. Brown and Mervyn Hiskett. Cranbury, N.J.: Fairleigh Dickinson University Press, 1975.

Schiefelbien, E. "La mujer en la educación primaria y media." In *Chile mujer y sociedad*, edited by P. Covarrubias, and R. Franco. Santiago: UNICEF, 1978.

"Scolarisation des jeunes filles en Algerie." *El Djeich* (September 1968): 17–19.

Siriwardena, Subadra. "The Education of Girls and Women in Ceylon." *International Review of Education* 19, no. 1 (1973): 115–20.

Soriano, Liceria Brillantes. "Women and Education." *Phillippine Law Journal* 50 (February 1975): 88–102.

Souad, Khalil Ismail. "Women's Education in the Arab Countries." In *L'Educat nouvelle*. Beirut: Unesco Regional Office for Education in the Arab Countries, 1975.

Vaughan, Mary K. "Women, Class and Education in Mexico, 1880-1928." *Latin American Perspectives* 4 (Winter-Spring 1977): 135-52.

Visitsurakarn, Khunying Suparb. "The Asian Experience: The Education of Women in Thailand." In *The Educational Dilemma of Women in Asia*, edited by Alma de Jesus-Viardo. Manila: Philippine Women's University, 1969.

Weis, Lois. "Women and Education in Ghana: Some Problems in Assessing Change." *International Journal of Women's Studies* 3, no. 5 (September–October 1980): 431-53.

Wickramsinghe, Shanti, and Radcliffe, David. "Women and Education in South Asia." *Canadian and International Journal of Education* 8, no. 2 (1979): 117-25.

"Women's Education in Upper Volta: An Interview with Mrs. Sira Diop." *Unesco Chronicle* 21 (December 1975): 353-59.

"Women's Education in Western Nigeria." *African Survey* (February–March 1964): 11-15.

Yeld, E. R. "Educational Problems among Women and Girls in Sokoto Province of Northern Nigeria." *Sociologus* 7 (1962): 160-73.

Youssef, N. H. "Education and Female Modernization in the Muslim World." *Journal of International Affairs* 30 (Fall/Winter 1976-1977): 191-209.

Unpublished Materials

Keino, Esther Rose Cherno. "The Contribution of Harambee (Self-Help) to the Development of Post-Primary Education in Kenya: The Case of Sosiot Girls' High School, 1969-1978." Ed.D. dissertation, Harvard University, 1980.

Kim, Chung Han. "Changing Functions of Women's Higher Education in the Republic of Korea: A Study of Educational Equality between Men and Women." Ph.D. dissertation, George Peabody College for Teachers, 1975.

Nuckols, Margaret Lynn. "A Comparative Analysis of Selected United Nations Documents Related to Educational Opportunities for Women during the First Development Decade (1960-1970)." Ph.D. dissertation, Florida State University, 1975.

Access to Education

Books

Access of Girls and Women to Education in Rural Areas in Indonesia: A Contribution to the UNESCO Asian Conference Bangkok, 1962. Jakarta: Ministry of Education, 1962.

Argentine Republic, Ministerio de Cultura y Educación. *Encuesta: Conferencia interamericana especializada sobre educación integral de la mujer.* Buenos Aires: Centro Nacional de Documentación e Información Educative, 1972.

Asian Regional Seminar on Access of Girls to Primary Education in Rural Areas. *Experimental Project for Equal Access of Girls and Women to Education in Nepal: Background Paper.* Kathmandu: 1978.

———. *Experimental Project for Equal Access of Girls and Women in Nepal: Final Report.* Kathmandu: Tribhuvan University, 1979.

———. *Status of Girls in Primary Education in Some Asian Countries.* Kathmandu: 1978.

Bremer, M. A., and Pauli, L. *Wastage in Education: A World Problem.* Geneva: Unesco, 1971.

Consultative Panel for Asia and Oceania for Equality of Educational Opportunities for Girls and Women. *Educational Opportunity for Girls and Women: A Review of Problems and Some Suggestions for Action.* Bangkok: Unesco Regional Office for Education in Asia and Oceania, 1979.

Fall-Ba, O. *Projet expérimental d'égalité d'accès des femmes et des jeunes filles à l'éducation: Juin 1967–Juillet 1971.* Paris: Unesco, 1978.

Fonseca, C. *Projet expérimental d'égalité d'accès des jeunes femmes à l'éducation.* Paris: Unesco, 1972.

McGrath, Patricia L. *The Unfinished Assignment: Equal Education for Women.* Worldwatch Paper no. 7. Washington: Worldwatch Institute, 1976.

Roques, Elaine. *L'Access equalitaire des jeunes Ivoriens et Ivoriennes al l'enseignement technique et professionel: Republique de Cote d'Ivorie-Mission 8 juin-11 juillet 1976.* Paris: Unesco, 1976.

Salas, Irma. *Education of Women in Pakistan: Preliminary Report of the Unesco Mission on the Access of Women to Education.* Mexico City: Unesco, 1954.

Saran, Raksha. *Education of Girls and Women in Rural Areas in India.* New Delhi: Ministry of Education, 1962.

Shrestka, Bihar K., and Gurung, S. B. *Equality of Access of Women to Education in Pokhara, Nepal.* Paris: Unesco, 1973.

Sock, B. Projet expérimental d'égalité d'accès des jeunes femmes à l'éducation. Paris: Unesco, 1972.

Unesco. *Meeting of Experts on the Access of Girls and Women to Education in Rural Areas in Asia. Bangkok, February 26–March 8, 1962.* Paris: Unesco, 1962.

———. *Access of Women and Girls to Education in Rural Areas: A Comparative Study.* Paris: Unesco, 1964.

———. *Access of Girls and Women to Secondary Education.* Paris: Unesco, 1966.

———. *Equality of Access of Women to Literacy: A Comparative Study.* Paris: Unesco, 1970.

———. *Study on the Equality of Access of Girls and Women to Education in the Context of Rural Development*. Paris: Unesco, 1973.

———. *Report of the Research Team Appointed by the Sierra Leone Commission for Education, Training and Employment Opportunities for Women in Sierra Leone*. Commissioned by Unesco in collaboration with the International Labour Organisation. Freetown, Sierra Leone: Unesco, 1974.

———. *Women, Education, Equality: A Decade of Experiment*. Paris: Unesco, 1975.

United Nations Commission on the Status of Women. *Study on the Equality of Access of Girls and Women to Education in the Context of Rural Development*. New York: United Nations Economic and Social Council, 1972.

United Nations Economic Commission for Africa. *Education and Training of Women—Special Reference to Africa*. Addis Ababa: UN Economic Commission for Africa, 1969.

United Nations Economic Commission for Africa, and German Foundation for Developing Countries. *Report of the Regional Conference on Education, Vocational Training and Work Opportunities for Girls and Women in African Countries, Rabat, Morocco, May 20–29, 1971*. New York: UN Economic Commission for Africa, 1971.

Upper Volta. Ministere de l'éducation nationale et de la culture. *Project Haute-Volta—Unesco d'accès des femmes et des jeunes filles à l'éducation: phase expérimentale, 1967–1976*. Ouagadougou: 1976.

Articles

"Access of Girls to Secondary Education." *Unesco Information Bulletin* 26 (June 1, 1966): 8–10.

Benitez, Helena Z. "Cultural Educational Differentials: A Challenge." *South-East Asia Quarterly* 4 (July 1969): 1–12.

Castellanos, Rosario. "La participación de la mujer en la educación formal." *Colegio de Mexico* 44 (1972): 4–10.

Collazo-Collazo, Jénaro. "Participación de la mujer en la fase educativa de vida Puertorriqueñe." *Departamento de instruccion de Puerto Rico* 22, no. 27 (1969): 41–53.

Comhaire-Sylvain, S. "L'Instruction des filles à Lomé." *Problemes sociaux congolais*, no. 82 (1968): 93–122.

Doeriat, F. "Overpopulation, Population Growth and the Status of Indonesian Women." In *Indonesian Women: Some Past and Current Perspectives*, edited by B. B. Hering. Brussels: Centre d'etude du Sud-Est Asiatique et de l'Extrême Orient, 1976.

"Le droit de la femme a l'education." *Literacy Work* 5, no. 4 (1976–77): 27–34.

Eberstadt, N. "Women and Education in China: How Much Progress?" *New York Review of Books* 26 (April 19, 1979): 41–45.

Eliou, Marie. "Scolarisation et promotion féminines en Afrique." *International Review of Education* 19, no. 1 (1973): 30–46.

Hirschman, Charles. "Political Independence and Educational Opportunity in Peninsular Malaysia. *Sociology of Education* 52 (April 1979): 67–83.

Jiagge, Annie. "The Role of Non-governmental Organisations in the Education of Women in African States." *Convergence* 2, no. 2 (1969): 70–72.

Kotwal, M. "Inequalities in the Distribution of Education between Countries, Sexes, Generations, and Individuals." In *Education, Inequality and Life Chances*. vol. 1. Paris: Organization for Economic Cooperation and Development, 1975.

Kutner, Nancy G., and Brogan, D. "Sources of Sex Discrimination in Educational Systems: A Conceptual Model." *Psychology of Women Quarterly* 1, no. 1 (1976): 50–69.

Robertson, C. L. "The Nature and Effects of Differential Access to Education in a Society." *Africa* 47, no. 2 (1977): 208–19.

Shafii, Forough; Mohseni, Manouchr; and Motabar, Mansour. "Formal Education in a Tribal Society, Iran." *Sociologia Rurales* 17, no. 1–2 (1977): 151–57.

Tardits, C. "Réflexions sur le problème de la scolarisation des filles au Dahomey." *Cahiers d'etudes africaines* 3, no. 10 (1962): 226–81.

Unesco, "Access of Girls to Education in the Arab States." *Unesco Chronicle* 10 (May 1964): 173.

Vernier, Pierre. "Education for Arab Girls, Economic Expansion, Changing Attitudes Favour Progress." *Unesco Features* 437 (April 1964): 14–17.

"Women: Their Access to Education and Employment." *Literacy Discussion* 6 (Winter 1975–76): 35–40.

Unpublished Materials

El-Sanabary, Nagat Morsi. "A Comparative Study of the Disparities of Educational Opportunities for Girls in the Arab States." Ph.D. dissertation, University of California, Berkeley, 1973.

Gerhold, Caroline Rose. "Factors Relating to Educational Opportunity for Women Residents of the Malay Peninsula." Ph.D. dissertation, Cornell University, 1971.

Process of Education (Curriculum, Guidance, Classroom Interaction)

Books
Expert Meeting on Educational and Vocational Guidance for Girls and

Women, Paris, 1976. *Organization de l'orientation scolaire et professionelle a Cuba.* n.p.: 1976.

Hasan, P. *Educational and Vocational Guidance for Girls and Women in Pakistan.* Expert Meeting on Educational and Vocational Guidance for Girls and Women, Paris, 1976. Karachi: Board of Secondary Education, 1976.

International Labour Organisation. *Vocational Guidance and Training of Girls and Women: Meeting of Consultants on Women Workers' Problems, Geneva, 1961.* Geneva: ILO, 1965.

Karim, N. H. A. *Report on the Educational and Vocational Guidance for Girls and Women in Iraq.* Expert Meeting on Educational and Vocational Guidance for Girls and Women, Paris, 1976. Baghdad: Ministry of Education, 1976.

Pakistan. National Commission for Unesco. *Improvement of the Organization and Management of Education Systems as a Means of Raising Efficiency in Order to Extend the Right to Education.* Islamabad: 1978.

Ramtu, J. K. *Country Report to be Presented to the Expert Meeting on Educational and Vocational Guidance for Girls, Unesco, Paris, 6-10 Sept., 1976.* Nairobi: Kenyatta University College, 1976.

Unesco. *Educational and Vocational Guidance for Girls and Women: Country Paper, Indonesia.* Expert meeting on educational and vocational guidance for girls and women, Paris, 1976. Jakarta: Department of Education and Culture, Directorate General of Nonformal Education and Sport, 1976.

——. *Expert Meeting on Educational and Vocational Guidance for Girls and Women.* Paris: Unesco, 1976.

——. *Expert Meeting on Educational and Vocational Guidance for Girls and Women. Final Report.* Paris: Unesco, 1976.

United Nations. *Civic and Political Education of Women.* New York: UN Department of Economic and Social Affairs, 1964.

United Nations Economic Commission for Africa. *ECA Five Year Programme on Pre-Vocational and Vocational Training of Girls and Women, toward their Full Participation in Development (1972-1976).* New York: UN Economic Commission for Africa, 1976.

Venezuela. Ministerio de educación. Oficina ministerial de asuntos internacionales. Expert Meeting on Educational and Vocational Guidance for girls and Women, Paris, 1976. *L'orientation scolaire et professionelle au Venezuela tant au neveau primaire que secondaire.* Caracas: 1976.

Articles

Baan, Janice Ann. "Growth and Development of Physical Education for for Women in the Philippines." *Silliman Journal* 15 (1968): 427-38.

Chodorow, Nancy. "Being and Doing: A Cross-cultural Examination of the Socialization of Males and Females." In *Women in Sexist Society*, edited by V. Gornick and B. K. Moran. New York: Basic Books, 1971.

Coutrot, A. M., and Thiriet, M. "L'Education aux Isles pour parents et enfants de Guadeloupe." *L'Ecole des Parents*, no. 7 (1976): 50–59.

"Education for Womanhood in East Africa." *Convergence* 2, no. 2 (1969): 32–36.

Elu de Lenero, Carmen. "Educación y participación de la mujer en la P.E.A. de Mexico." *Revista del centro de estudios educativos* 7, no. 1 (1977): 71–83.

Hawkins, John. "Family Planning, Education and Health Care Delivery in the People's Republic of China: Implications for Educational Alternatives." *Comparative Education Review* 20 (June 1976): 151–64.

Heritier, F. "Adolescence et sexualité." *Le Groupe Familial*, no. 73 (1976): 3–12.

Masemann, Vandra Lea. "The Hidden Curriculum of a West African Girls' Boarding School." *Canadian Journal of African Studies* 8 (February 1974): 479–94.

Ng, See Ngean. "The Effect of Race, Sex, Age and S.E.S. on School Anxiety and Coping Style." *Malaysian Journal of Education* 12, nos. 1–2 (1975): 1–7.

Nischol, K. "The Invisible Woman: Images of Women and Girls in School Textbooks." *Social Action*, 26 (July–September 1976): 267–81.

Okorie, John U. "Hunger Solution in a Nigerian Girls' School." *Agricultural Education Magazine* 48 (October 1975): 89, 94–95.

Peerbhoy, Homai. "Civic Education for Women." In *Long-Term Educational and Training Programmes for Advancement of Women in Asia*. Bombay: International Seminar, 1967.

Rivero, Eneida, B. "Educación sexual in Puerto Rico." *Revista de Ciencias Sociale* 19 (June 1975): 167–91.

Saunders, Fay E. "Sex Roles and the School." *Prospects* 5, no. 3 (1975): 362–71.

Sharma, Prabhu Datta. "Women's Education: A Curricula Model for India." *Education Quarterly* 25 (July 1973): 5–12.

Spender, Dale. "Learning to Create our Own Knowledge." *Convergence* 13, no. 1–2 (1980): 14–24.

Wang, V. L. "Application of Social Science Theories to Family Planning Health Education in the People's Republic of China." *American Journal of Public Health* 66 (May 1976): 440–45.

Za'Rour, George I. and Nashif, Rawdah Z. "Attitudes toward the Language of Science Teaching at the Secondary Level in Jordan." *International Journal of the Sociology of Language* 14 (1977): 109–18.

Zouabi, Mustafa. "Physical Education and Sport in Tunisia." *International Review of Sport Sociology* 10, nos. 3–4 (1975): 109–14.

Unpublished Material

Alkadhi, Ann Louise Bragdon. "Schools as Mediators in Female Role Formation: An Ethnography of a Grils' School in Baghdad." Ph.D. dissertation, State University of New York at Buffalo, 1979.

Barber, H. E. "The Relative Popularity of Secondary School Subjects among Girls." Master's thesis, Fourah Bay College, 1969.

Fouda, Soheir Zakaria. "Effectiveness of Two Instructional Designs Based on Gagne's Learning Hierarchy and Ausubel's Subsumption Theory and Two Modes of Presentation in Teaching the Concept of 'Mutualism in Nature' to Tenth Grade Girls in the Egyptian High Schools." Ed.D. dissertation, Temple University, 1980.

Jolly, Laura E. "Visual Aids in Education in the Girls' Secondary Schools in the Colony of Sierra Leone." Master's thesis, Fourah Bay College, 1954.

Pratt, A. "The Problem of Discipline in Girls Secondary Schools in Freetown." Master's thesis, Fourah Bay College, 1965.

Pratt, Philomena. "Some Problems in the Education of Girls with Particular Reference to Queen of the Holy Rosary School, Bo." Master's thesis, Fourah Bay College, 1972.

Salib, Tahany Migally Abdallah. "The Effect of Discovery and Expository Methods of Teaching Selected Physical Science Concepts on Science Achievement and Attitude of Students in an Egyptian General Preparatory School for Girls." Ph.D. dissertation, Pennsylvania State University, 1978.

Youssef, Zeinab Abdel Hamid. "An Experimental Study Comparing Effects of Biological Science Curriculum Study (BSCS) and Traditional Biology Instruction in an Egyptian Public Secondary School for Girls." Ph.D. dissertation, Pennsylvania State University, 1979.

Wang, Yu Jung. "An Analysis of Male and Female Roles in Chinese Children's Reading Material Published in Taiwan, China." Ph.D. dissertation, New York University, 1980.

Achievement

Books

Carroll, J. B. *The Teaching of French as a Foreign Language in Eight Countries.* International Studies in Evaluation, vol. 5. New York: Halsted Press, 1975.

Comber, L. C., and Keeves, J. P. *Science Education in Nineteen Countries.* International Studies in Evaluation, vol. 1. New York: Halsted Press, 1973.

Downing, J. *Comparative Reading: Cross-national Studies of Behavior and Processes in Reading and Writing.* New York: Macmillan Co., 1973.

Husen, T., ed. *International Study of Achievement in Mathematics: A Comparison of Twelve Countries.* 2 vols. New York: John Wiley & Sons, 1967.

Lewis, E. G., and Massad, C. E. *The Teaching of English as a Foreign Language in Ten Countries.* International Studies in Evaluation, vol. 4. New York: Halsted Press, 1975.

Passow, A. H., et. al. *The National Case Study: An Empirical Comparative Study of Twenty-One Educational Systems.* International Studies in Evaluation, vol. 7. New York: Halsted Press, 1976.

Purves, A. C. *Literature Education in Ten Countries.* International Studies in Evaluation, vol. 2. New York: Halsted Press, 1973.

Purves, A. C., and Levine, D. U., eds. *Educational Policy and International Assessment: Implications of the IEA Surveys of Achievement.* Berkeley: McCutchan Publishing, 1975.

Thorndike, R. L. *Reading Comprehension Education in Fifteen Countries.* International Studies in Evaluation, vol. 3. New York: Halsted Press, 1973.

Tittle, C. K.; McCarthy, K.; and Steckler, J. F. *Women and Educational Testing: A Selective Review of the Research Literature and Testing Practices.* Princeton, N.J.: Educational Testing Services, 1974.

Torney, J. V.; Oppenheim, A. N.; and Farnen, R. F. *Civic Education in Ten Countries.* International Studies in Evaluation, vol. 6. New York: Halsted Press, 1975.

Articles

Alexander, Karl, and Eckland, Bruce K. "Sex Differences in the Educational Attainment Process." *American Sociology Review* 39 (1974): 668–82.

Barber, Elinor G. "Some International Perspectives on Sex Differences in Education." *Signs: Journal of Women in Culture and Society* 4 (Spring 1979): 584–92.

Finn, Jeremy D.; Dulberg, Loretta; and Reis, Janet. "Sex Differences in Educational Attainment: A Cross-national Perspective." *Harvard Educational Review* 49 (November 1979): 477–503.

Johnson, Dale D. "Sex Differences in Reading across Cultures." *Reading Research Quarterly* 9, no. 1 (1973–74): 67–86.

Keeves, J. "Differences between the Sexes in Mathematics and Science Courses." *International Review of Education* 19 (1973): 47–74.

Salili, F. "Determinants of Achievement Motivation for Women in Developing Countries." *Journal of Vocational Behavior* 14 (June 1979): 297–305.

Sara-Lafosse, Violeta. "Le condición femenina en el Perú." *Rikchay* 2 (1972): 32-35.

Simmons, John, and Alexander, Leigh. "The Determinants of School Achievement in Developing Countries: A Review of the Research." *Economic Development and Cultural Change* 26 (January 1978): 341-57.

Watkins, D., and Astilla, E. "Field Dependence and Self-esteem in Filipino Girls." *Psychological Reports* 44 (April 1979): 574.

Youngblood, R. L. "Female Dominance and Adolescent Filipino Attitude Orientations and School Achievement." *Journal of Asian and African Studies* 13, nos. 1-2 (1978): 65-80.

Unpublished Materials

Hodd, F. "The Attitude of Girls in Sierra Leone Schools towards Learning Mathematics." Master's thesis, Fourah Bay College, 1964.

Lawson, Omojowo. "The Social Problems of Secondary School Girls in the Colony of Sierra Leone and the Effect of These on School Achievement." Master's thesis, Fourah Bay College, 1954.

Raval, Bina Dinker. "Comparing the Factor Patterns of Intelligence of High School Boys and Girls in India." Ph.D. dissertation, Catholic University of America, 1972.

Salvador-Burris, J. "Modernization, Social Class, Child Bearing and Cognitive Performance: Their Inter-Relationships in an Urban Community in the Philippines." Ph.D. dissertation, Univeristy of Chicago, 1977.

Wang, Bee-Lan Chang. "An Inter-ethnic Comparison of Educational Selection, Achievement and Decision-making among Fifth-Form Students in West Malaysia." Ph.D. dissertation, Univeristy of Chicago, 1975.

Higher Education

Books

Kotb, Issac. *Social and Academic Adjustment of University Women of the Arab Gulf States.* Kuwait: Kuwait University, 1975.

Melo Rodriguez, S. *La participación de la mujer en el proceso de la educación superior en Colombia.* Bogotá: Universidad Juveriosa, 1974.

Still, K., and Shea, J. *Something's Got to Be Done So We Can Survive in This Place: The Problems of Women Students at U.P.N.G.* Research Report no. 20. Papua New Guinea: University of Papua New Guinea, 1976.

Unesco. *Comparative Study on Access of Girls and Women to Higher Education.* Paris: Unesco, 1967.

Wahjudi, M. *Statistics on Women in Higher Education in Indonesia.* Jakarta: Office of Educational Development, National Commission on the Status of Women, 1973.

Articles

"A Hit with the Misses: Inside the University College for Women." *Kuwaiti Digest* 2 (April–June 1977): 22–24.

Anderson, C. A. "Social Class as a Factor in the Assimilation of Women into Higher Education." *Acta Sociologica* 4, no. 3 (1959): 27–32.

Aragonés, María. "La mujer y los estudios universitarios in Chile: 1957–1974." In *Chile: mujer y sociedad*, edited by P. Covarrubias and R. Franco. Santiago: Unicef, 1978.

Atienza, Maria Feg. "The Philippine Women's University and Extra-Mural Education for Women." *Indian Journal of Education* 27 (July 1976): 11–16.

Beckett, Paul A., and O'Connell, James. "Education and the Situation of Women: Background and Attitudes of Christian and Muslim Female Students at a Nigerian University." *Cultures et développement* 8, no. 2 (1976): 242–65.

Blat, R. V., et al. "Performance of Women Medical Graduates from Medical College, Barsda 1969–78." *Medical Education* 10 (July 1976): 293–96.

Bonnell, Susanne. "Women at Vudal Agricultural College." *Administration for Development* 5 (October 1975): 26–31.

Comhaire-Sylvain, S. "Higher Education and Professional Training of Women in Ethiopia." *Women Today* 6, no. 3 (1964): 58–59.

D'Brot, Carmela. "La mujer triunfa en las universidades." *Siete dias* 23, no. 782 (1973): 60–61.

Fisher, M. J. "Higher Education of Women and National Development in Asia." *Asia Survey* 8, no. 4 (1968): 263–69.

Goldstein, R. L. "Students in Saris: College Education in the Lives of Young Indian Women." *Joint Asian Studies* 5 (July 1970): 193–201.

Gould, Terri F. "The Educated Women and Social Change: A Sociological Study of Women Students at the National University of Zaire." In *Papers in Education and Development*. Dar es Salaam: 1976.

Gregory, Sister Mary. "Chinese College Women." *Contemporary Education* 45 (Spring 1974): 187–89.

Hecker, M. "Access of Girls to Higher Education." *Unesco Chronicle* (April 1967): 157–62.

Hoffer, Stefan N. "Private Rates of Return to Higher Education of Women." *Review of Economics and Statistics* 55 (November 1973): 482–86.

Jurado, L. M. "Planning Higher Education Programmes for Women in Agriculture and Home Economics in Africa." In *Food and Agricultural Organisation of the United Nations*. Agricultural education and training, annual review of selected developments. Rome: FAO, 1968–69.

Kim, Okgill. "The Place of Women's Colleges—The Korean Experience:

Ewha University." *New Frontiers in Education* 8 (January–March, 1978): 47–56.

Korson, J. Henry. "Career Constraints among Women Graduate Students in a Developing Society: West Pakistan." *Journal of Comparative Family Studies* 1 (Autumn 1970): 83–100.

Obi, Margaret. "Young Women Pursuing Higher Education and a Career." *Administration for Development* 3 (October 1975): 32–35.

Saad, Mahasin. "Notes on Higher Education for Women in the Sudan." *Sudan Notes and Records* 53 (1972): 174–81.

Shridevi, S. "Women's Higher Education in India since Independence." *Improving College and University Teaching* 20 (Winter 1972): 71–72.

Strauss, M. "Family Characteristics and Occupational Choice of Univeristy Entrants as Clues to the Social Structure of Ceylon." *University of Ceylon Review* 10, no. 2 (1951): 125–35.

Unesco. "Access of Girls to Higher Education." *Unesco Information Bulletin* 38 (June 1967): 7–13.

Unpublished Material

Adedoyin, Cecilia Olufunmilayo. "The Analysis of the Curricular Content of the Nursing Education Program of the Lagos University Teaching Hospital." Ed.D. dissertation, Columbia University, Teachers College, 1980.

Herrmann, Eleanor Krohn. "The Development of Nursing Education in Belize (British Honduras), Central America, 1920 to 1970." Ed.D. dissertation, Columbia University, Teachers College, 1979.

Kim, Chung Han. "Changing Functions of Women's Higher Education in the Republic of Korea: A Study of Educational Equality between Man and Woman." Ph.D. dissertation, George Peabody College for Teachers, 1975.

Lee, Dong Wook. "Proposed Programs in the Christian Women's Two Year College in Korea." Ed. D. dissertation, University of Tulsa, 1974.

Lee, Soo Duk. "An Analysis of Institutional Goals Perceived and Preferred by Students, Assistants, Faculty, and Administrators at Seoul Woman's College in Korea." Ph.D. dissertation, George Peabody College for Teachers, 1977.

Sabri, Marie Azia. "Beirut College for Women and Ten of Its Distinguished Pioneering Alumnae." Ph.D. dissertation, Columbia University, 1965.

Wolle, Helen Osbey. "A Descriptive Study of the Status of Women Students in Continuing Education Programs in University Settings in New Zealand." Ed.D. dissertation, George Washington University, 1979.

Female Students Aspirations and Attitudes

Books

Centro de Estudios de Participación Popular. *Como vive la mujer trabajadora en el Perú? Situación y aspiraciones de la mujer en el Perú.* Lima: SINAMOS, 1974.

Gorwaney, Naintara. *Self-Image and Social Change: A Study of Female Students.* New Delhi: Sterling Publishers, 1977.

Articles

Abu-Laban, Baha. "Sources of College Aspirations of Lebanese Youth." *Journal of Developing Areas* 2 (January 1968): 225–40.

Baali, Fuad. "Educational Aspirations among College Girls in Iraq." *Sociology and Social Research* 51 (July 1967): 485–93.

Beckett, Paul, and O'Connell, James. "Education and the Situation of Women: Background and Attitudes of Christian and Muslim Female Students at a Nigerian University." *Culture et développement* 8, no. 2 (1976) 242–65.

Brown, M., and Amoroso, D. M. "Attitudes toward Homosexuality among West Indian Male and Female College Students." *Journal of Social Psychology* 97 (December 1975): 163–8.

Castillo, Gelia Tagumpay. "Occupational Sex Roles as Perceived by Filipino Adolescents." *Philippine Sociological Review* 9 (January–April 1961): 2–11.

Evans, D. R. "Image and Reality: Career Goals of Educated Ugandan Women." *Canadian Journal of African Studies* 6, no. 1 (1972): 213–32.

Garison, H. H. "Education and Friendship Choice in Urban Zambia." *Social Forces* 57 (June 1979): 1310–24.

Hochschild, Arlie. "Women at Work in Modernizing Tunisia: Attitudes of Urban Adolescent Schoolgirls." *Berkeley Journal of Sociology* 11 (1966): 32–53.

Kathuria, M., and Sinha, S. N. "Relationship between Vocational Maturity, Aspirations and Prestige among Female Undergraduate Students." *Indian Journal of Psychology* 47, pt. 4 (1972): 383–91.

Klineberg, Stephen L., "Parents, Schooling and Modernity: An Exploratory Investigation of Sex Differences in the Attitudinal Development of Tunisian Adolescents." *International Journal of Comparative Sociology* 14 (1973): 221–43.

Levine, R. L., and West, L. "Attitudes toward Women in the United States and Brazil." *Journal of Social Psychology* 108 (August 1979): 265–66.

Lindsay, B. "Career Aspirations of Kenyan Women." *Journal of Negro Education* 49 (Fall 1980): 432–40.

Mamaril, A. P., and Castillo, Geila T. "Parental Authority and Job

Choices: Sex Differences in Three Cultures." *American Journal of Sociology* 69 (September 1963): 143-49.

Mehryar, A. H., and Tashakkori, G. A. "Sex and Parental Education as Determinants of Marital Aspirations and Attitudes of a Group of Irani Youth." *Journal of Marriage and the Family* 40 (August 1978): 629-37.

Moracco, John C., and Movses, Arpy. "Relationship of Armenian School Children's Attitudes toward School, Their Sex, Age, and Mother's Authoritarianism." *International Journal of Sociology of the Family* 7 (July-December 1977): 135-41.

Ngean, N. G. "The Effects of Race, Sex, Age and SES on School Anxiety and Coping Style. *Malaysian Journal of Education* 12, no. 1-2 (1975): 1-7.

Nouri, al-, Q. N. "Modern Professionalism in Lybia: Attitudes of Univeristy Students," *International Social Science Journal* 27, no. 4 (1975): 691-702.

Prasad, M. B., et. al. "Perception of Parental Expectations and Need Achievements." *Journal of Social Psychology* 109 (December 1979) 301-2.

Rosen, Bernard C., and La Raia, Anita. "Modernity in Women: An Index of Social Change in Brazil." *Journal of Marriage and the Family* 34 (May 1972): 353-60.

Seward, Georgene H., and Williamson, Robert C. "A Cross-national Study of Adolescent Professional Goals." *Human Development* 12, no. 4 (1969): 248-54.

Tan-Willman, C. "Prospective Teachers' Attitudes toward the Rights and Roles of Contemporary Women in Two Cultures." *Psychological Reports* 45 (December 1979): 741-2.

Tomeh, A. K. "Birth Order, Club Membership and Mass Media Exposure." *Journal of Marriage and Family* 38 (February 1976): 151-64.

Ugwuegbu, D. C. E. "Educational Orientation and the Nigerian Students' Attitudes to Husband-Wife Relations." *Journal of Social Psychology* 106 (December 1978): 167-71.

Vlassof, C. "Unmarried Adolescent Females in Rural India: A Study of the Social Impact of Education." *Journal of Marriage and the Family* 42 (May 1980), 427-36.

Unpublished Materials

Amiri, Soudabeh. "Career Motivation of Iranian High School Females with an Emphasis on Social Class, Parents, and Peers." Ph.D. dissertation, University of Illinois, Urbana-Champaign, 1979.

Christy, Lai Chu Tsui. "Culture and Control Orientation: A Study of

Internal-External Locus of Control in Chinese and American-Chinese Women." Ph.D. dissertation, University of California, Berkeley, 1977.

Conroy, Patricia Agnes. "A Study of Selected Value Orientations of Korean Nursing Eduation." Ph.D. dissertation, Columbia University, 1970.

Espín, Oliva María. "Critical Incidents in the Lives of Female College Students: A Comparison between Women of Latin America and the United States." Ph.D. dissertation, University of Florida, 1974.

Johnson, Felicia G. E. "The Prospect of Marriage: A Study of the Attitudes towards Further Education of a Sample Group of Secondary School Leavers." Master's thesis, Fourah Bay College, 1959.

Longres, John Frank. "Social Conditions Related to the Acceptance of Modern Medicine among Puerto Rican Women." Ph.D. dissertation, University of Michigan, 1970.

Montsi, Mercy Rapelesega. "A Study of the Self-Concept of Basotho Male and Female Adolescents in Secondary Schools." Ed.D. dissertation, University of Massachusetts, 1978.

Nelson, James Franklin. "Some Causes and Consequences of Female Liberation Attitudes in Two Latin American Metropolises: A Causal Analysis of Non-Interval Data." Ph.D. dissertation, University of Chicago, 1975.

Pratt, Selina Lani. "Occupational Social Aspirations and Attitudes of Educated Women in a Developing Country: A Review of the Literature and a Study amongst Fourah Bay College Students." Master's thesis, Fourah Bay College, 1970.

Randeri, Kalindi Jaswant. "The Relevance of Liberal Arts Education in Terms of the Role of the Educated Indian Woman as Perceived by Students, Parents, Alumnae and Administrators." Ph.D. dissetation, Southern Illinois University, 1974.

Saidian, Mehdi. "A Study of Job Satisfaction as Measured by the Minnesota Satisfaction Questionnaire as Applied to Selected Male and Female Vocational and Technical Teachers of Esfahan, Iran." Ph.D. dissertation, University of Kansas, 1980.

Sallam, Azza Mohamed Ahmed. "The Return to the Veil among Undergraduate Females at Minya University, Egypt." Ph.D. dissertation, Purdue University, 1980.

Sitthiphong, Bularat Suvarnabriksha. "A Comparative Study of Work Values between Selected Tenth-Grade Thai Girls in Bangkok and Chiangmai, Thailand." Ed.D. dissertation, Oregon State University, 1981.

Talbot, Dorothy McComb. "Professionalization among Student Nurses in Peru: A Sociological Analysis." Ph.D. dissertation, Tulane University, 1970.

Turay, Badiatu, J. "Factors Influencing Choice of Career among Boys and Girls." Master's thesis, Fourah Bay College, 1973.

Nonformal Education

Books

Ahmed, M., and Coombs, P. H. *Education for Rural Development.* New York: Praeger, 1975.

Bordia, A.; Kidd, J. R.; and Draper, J. A., eds. *Adult Education in India: A Book of Readings.* Bombay: Indian Adult Education Association, 1973.

Chemli, M. *L'éducation permanente: l'exemple tunisien.* Tunis: Institut national des sciences de l'éducation, 1978.

Crone, C. D. *Research on Innovative Nonformal Education for Rural Adults: Implications for Literacy.* New York: World Education, 1978.

——. *Research on Innovative Non-formal Education for Rural Women.* New York: World Education, 1977.

Derryck, Vivian Lowery. *The Comparative Functionality of Formal and Non-formal Education for Women: Final Report.* Washington, D.C.: Agency for International Development, Office of Women in Development, 1979.

Einsiedel, L. A. *The Impact of the Community Development Women and Youth and Lay Leadership Institutes of the P.A.C.D.* Quezon City: University of the Philippines, Development Research Council, 1967.

Fougeyrollas, Pierre. *Television and the Social Education of Women: A First Report on the Unesco-Senegal Pilot Project at Dakar.* Paris: Unesco, n.d.

Ghassemi, A. *Projet expérimental d'accés des femmes à l'éducation: Alphabétisation fonctionelle; Novembre 1971–Septembre 1973.* Paris: Unesco, 1974

Government of India. *Misconceptions Influencing Nonformal Education for Women.* Question ser. 5. New Delhi: Directorate of Nonformal (Adult) Education, Ministry of Education and Social Welfare, 1975.

Hoque, Naseem. *Non-formal Education for Women in Bangladesh.* Supplementary Paper, Program of Studies in Non-formal Education, no. 5. East Lansing, Mich.: Agency for International Development, 1976.

Homayounpour, P. *The Experimental Functional Literacy Project for the Social and Economic Promotion of Rural Women: The Final Report.* Tehran: National Centre for Adult Education and Training, 1977.

India. Committee on Adult Education. Programmes for Women. *Adult Education Programmes for Women.* New Delhi: Ministry of Education and Social Welfare, 1978.

Indian Adult Education Association. *Adult Education of Women in the Changing Pattern of Society.* New Delhi: Indian Adult Education Association, 1973.

Innovative Education for Preliterate Rural Women: A Project Proposal. New York: World Education, 1974.

International Congress on the Situation of Women in Technical and Vocational Education. Bonn, June 9–12, 1980. *Final Report.* Paris: Unesco, 1980.

International Labour Organisation. *The Employment and Vocational Preparation of Girls and Women in Africa, Regional Meeting, Addis Ababa, March 1969.* Geneva: International Labour Organisation, 1969.

International Labour Organisation. *The Vocational Preparation of Girls and Women.* Geneva: International Labour Organisation, 1970.

Kleis, R. *Case Studies in Non-formal Education: Study Team Report.* East Lansing: Michigan State University, 1974.

Learning from Rural Women: Village-level Cases of Rural Women's Groups' Income Raising activities. Bangkok: UN Economic and Social Commission for Asia and the Pacific; Food and Agriculture Organization, 1979.

Padmodisastro, S. *The Women's Movement: Non-formal Education in Indonesia.* Jakarta: Indonesian Ministry of Education and Culture, Office of Education Development, 1975.

Paolucci, B., et al. *Women, Families and Non-formal Learning Programs.* East Lansing, Mich.: Michigan State University, 1976.

Prawirodihandjo, T., and Krishna, T. *Community Education in India.* Jakarta: Indonesian Ministry of Education, 1974.

Transfer of Knowledge and Skills among Peer Groups: A Manual of Methodology. Bangkok: UN Economic and Social Commission for Asia and the Pacific; Food and Agriculture Organization, 1979.

Trivedi, Sheela. *Nonformal Education for Women Officers, Education Department. U.P. Report of the State Level Orientation Seminars on Nonformal Education.* Lucknow: Literacy House, 1977.

United Nations Economic Commission for Africa. *Country Report for Lesotho on Vocational Training Opportunities for Girls and Women.* Addis Ababa: Economic Commission for Africa, 1972.

———. *Country Report for Nigeria on Vocational Training Opportunities for Girls and Women.* Addis Ababa: Economic Commission for Africa. 1973.

———. *Country Report for Ghana on Vocational Training Opportunities for Girls and Women.* Addis Ababa: Economic Commission for Africa, 1974.

United National Economic Commission for Africa and German Foundation for Developing Countries. *Education, Vocational Training and Work Opportunities for Girls and Women in African Countries.* Rabat: May 1971.

United Nations Food and Agricultural Organisation. *Workshops for Trainers in Home Economics and Other Family-oriented Fields.* Rome: Home Economics and Social Programmes Service, 1974.

———. *Integrated Functional Education: An Approach for Rural Education.* Rome: Home Economics and Social Programmes Service, 1974.

Weisinger, R. J. *Light Me a Candle: Two Years of Literacy and Adult Education Work among the Women of Khuzistan, Iran.* Bombay: Shakuntala Publishing House, 1973.

Youssef, N.; Sadka, N.; and Murphy E. *An Evaluation of Non-formal Educational Programmes for Women in Morocco: Report to USAID.* Washington, D.C.: U.S. Agency for International Development, 1976.

Articles

African Training and Research Center for Women. "Taches excessives des femmes et accés aux techniques." *Carnets de l'Enfance,* no. 36 (1976): 38-52.

Bird, Edris. "Adult Education and the Advancement of Women in the West Indies." *Convergence* 8, no. 1 (1975): 57-64.

Blake, Myrna. "Education—Research Mobilization Needs of Women's Employment Trends in Asia." *Convergence* 13, nos. 1-2 (1980): 65-78.

Brown, Lalage. "Adult Education and Its Role in National and Sectional Development." *Literacy Work* 4 (July–September 1974): 67-89.

Callaway, H. "The Voices and Silences of Women." *Literary Discussion* 6 (Winter 1975-76): 17-34.

Cebotarev, E. A. "Non-Oppressive Framework for Adult Education Programs for Rural Women in Latin America." *Convergence* 13, nos. 1-2 (1980): 34-49.

Clason, C. "La campesina: Acción Cultural Popular Reaches Rural Women with Mixed-Media Programs in Colombia." *World Education Reports,* no. 10 (1975).

Cole, J. "Providing Access to New Skills and Modern Techniques: the Ghana National Council on Women and Development." *Carnets de l'Enfance,* no. 38 (1977): 71-79.

Dawit, T. "Media et femmes rurales en Afrique." *Carnets de l'Enfance,* no. 38 (1977): 64-70.

Decker, H. De. "L'Animation rurales féminine á Kukavu." *Congo-Afrique* 10, no. 48 (1970): 441-53.

Fonseca, C. "Functional Literacy for Village Women: An Experiment in Upper Volta." *Prospects* 5, no. 3 (1975): 380-86.

Gayfer, Margaret. "Women: Speaking and Learning for Ourselves." *Convergence* 13, nos. 1-2 (1980): 1-13.

Haukaa, R. "Competence-building Adult Education for Women." *Convergence* 8, no. 1 (1975): 68-81.

Homayounpour, P. "The Experimental Functional Literacy Project of the Women's Organization in Iran." In *The Design of Educational Programmes for the Promotion of Rural Women.* Tehran: International Institute for Adult Literacy Methods, 1975.

Hussain, Ghulam. "Pakistan: The Role of the Agricultural University in Promoting Adult Literacy." *Literacy Work* 4 (April–June 1975): 69–82.

Igoche, M. H. G. "Integrating Conscientization into a Program for Illiteracy, Women in Nigeria." *Convergence* 13, nos. 1–2 (1980): 110–17.

Jenkins, Janet. "Non-formal Education for Women: What Use is it?" *Educational Broadcasting International* 12 (December 1979): 158–61.

Jiagge, Annie. "The Role of Non-governmental Organization in the Education of Women in African States." *Convergence* 2, no. 2 (1969): 73–78.

Koshy, T. A. "Non-formal Education for Rural Women: An Experimental Project for the Development of the Young Child." *Indian Journal of Adult Education* 36 (January–February 1975): 1–2, 17–19.

Kumar, K., and Snehlata Mago. "Training Needs of Farm Women in Haryana." In *Farmers Training and Functional Literacy*, edited by A. Bordia. New Delhi: Indian Adult Education Association, 1975.

Loring, R. "Women in the Profession of Adult Education." *Convergence* 8, no. 1 (1975): 49–56.

McSweeney, Brenda G. "Time to Learn, Time for a Better Life: The Women's Education Project in Upper Volta." *Carnets de l'Enfance*, nos. 49/50 (Spring 1980): 109–26.

Osborne, R. J. "Out-of-school Education for Women in African Countries." *Convergence* 6 (1973): 7–19.

"Plan for Action in Rural Areas." *Literacy Discussion* 6 (Winter 1975–76): 152–62.

Rai, S. "Female Education in Villages." *Social Welfare* 16 (September 1969): 12–21.

"Resolutions from the 2nd Conference of the Organization of Mozambican Women." *Race and Class* 18 (Spring 1977): 397–*404*.

Ruddle, Kenneth, and Chesterfield, Ray. "Venezuelan 'Demonstradora del Hogar': An Example of Woman in Nonformal Rural Education." *Community Development Journal* 9 (April 1974): 140–44.

Sayogyo, P. "Les centres de rehabilitation nutritionnelle en Indonésie." *Carnets de l'Enfance*, no. 38 (1977): 57–63.

Shaw, K. "Pattern for Change. (Human Development Project of the Costa Rican Federation of Voluntary Organizations)." *Americas* 32 (March 1980): 49–51.

Shelley, N. "An Approach to Innumeracy in Our Society and the Place of Women Vis-a-vis Mathematics." *Literacy Discussion* 7, no. 3 (Autumn 1976): 17–31.

Smith, Mary Ann. "An Adult Education Programme for the Igorof Women of Northern Philippines." *Convergence* 8, no. 1 (1975): 16–24.

Suleiman, Michael W. "Changing Attitudes toward Women in Egypt: The Role of Fiction in Women's Magazine." *Middle Eastern Studies* 14 (October 1979): 352–71.

Tandon, K., and Rao, V. R. "Learning from and about Women's Organization: An Exploratory Analysis in the Indian Context." *Convergence* 13, nos. 1–2 (1980): 124–35.

United Nations Economic Commission for Africa: "Out of School Education for Women in African Countries." *Convergence* 6, nos. 3–4 (1973): 7–19.

Vyas, V. S. "Factors Influencing the Level of Literacy in Rural Areas." *Artha-Vilnas* 3, no. 1 (1967): 15–23.

Wiesinger, R. "Economic Development and Functional Literacy for Women: A Pilot Project in Iran." *International Review of Education* 19, no. 1 (1973): 99–106.

Unpublished Materials

Alauddin, Fatema Banu. "Need for Development Education as Expressed by the Rural Women of Bangladesh." Ph.D. dissertation, University of Michigan, 1979.

Khalidi, Muhammad Zohair Ibrahim. "The Uses of Technology-Based Adult Education in Developing the Social Roles of Arab-Muslim Women: Towards a Policy Prescription." Ph.D. dissertation, Indiana Univeristy, 1977.

King, L. U. "The Education of Women in the Highland Communities of Chiapas, Mexico." B. Litt. thesis, Oxford University, 1978.

Odu, Dorcas Bola. "A Conceptual Programme Planning Model for Adult Education Programmes for Women in Rural Areas of Nigeria through Extension Home Economics." Ph.D. dissertation, University of Nebraska, Lincoln, 1978.

Sagasti, H. de. "Social Implications of Adult Literacy: A Study among Migrant Women in Peru." Ph.D. dissertation, University of Pennsylvania, 1972.

Shrivastava, Virginia Ann. "Nonformal Education Programmes for Women in Indian Villages: A Study of Social Change and Leadership Patterns." Ed.D. dissertation, University of Toronto, 1980.

Education, Women, and Development

Books

Boserup, Esther. *Women's Role in Economic Development.* New York: St. Martin's Press, 1970.

Boriboonsack, Pindip. *The Role of Women in Rural Development in Education in Thailand.* Bangkok: Thai Ministry of Education, n.d.

Clark, N. *Education for Development and the Rural Women.* Vol. 1. Washington, D.C.: World Education, 1979.

Development Alternatives, Inc. *A Seven Country Survey of the Roles of Women in Rural Development*, Washington, D.C.: U.S. Agency for International Development, 1974.

Droegkamp, Janis, and Munger, Fredi. *Women Centered Training: Responding to Issues and Ideas for Women in Development*. Amherst, Mass.: Center for International Development, University of Massachusetts, 1979.

Educational Advancement and Socioeconomic Participation of Women in India. Saveh: Indian Ministry of Education and Social Welfare, 1975.

Hamamsy, el-, Laila Shukay. *Assessment of Unicef Assisted Projects for the Preparation and Training of Women and Girls for Community Development in Tunisia*. Geneva: Unicef, 1969.

Henriquez, de Paredes, et al. *Participación de la mujer in el desarrollo de America Latina y del Caribe*. Santiago: United Nations Children's Fund, 1975.

Hesse, M. C. *Ghana: Survey of Women, Development and Educational Opportunities*. Accra: n.p., 1973.

Hossain, Monowar; Sharif, Raihan; and Huq, Jahanara, eds. *Seminar on the Role of Women in Socio-Economic Development in Bangladesh, May 9–10, 1976*. Dacca: Bangladesh Books International, 1977.

Huston, Perdita. *Third World Women Speak Out; Interviews in Six Countries on Change, Development and Basic Needs*. New York: Praeger, 1979.

Lambert, S. *United Republic of Cameroon: Survey of Women, Development and Educational Opportunities*. Yaounde: n.p., 1973.

León de Leal, Magdelena. *La Mujer y el desarrollo en Colombia*. Bogatá: Asociación Colombiana para el Estudio de la Población, 1977.

Magala, S. *Uganda: Survey of Women, Development and Educational Opportunities*. Kampala: Makarere University, 1973.

Mbilinyi, M. J. *The United Republic of Tanzania: Survey of Women, Development and Educational Opportunities*. Dar es Salaam: University of Dar es Salaam, 1973.

——. *Barriers to the Full Participation of Women in the Socialist Transformation of Tanzania*. Dar es Salaam: University of Dar es Salaam, 1974.

Meharo,N. E. *Literacy: A Tool for the Development of Rural Women in Tanzania*. Studies in Adult Education, no. 27. Dar es Salaam: Institute of Adult Education, 1977.

Mutiso, C. G. *Kenya: Survey of Women, Development and Educational Opportunities*, Nairobi: University of Nairobi, 1973.

Regional Seminar on Education of Women for Involvement in National Development, Sri Lanka Foundation Institute, 1975. Regional Seminar, S. E. Asia: Education of Women for Involvement in National Development. Colombo, November 6–11, 1975. Colombo: Sri Lanka Foundation Institute, 1975.

Séminaire opérationnel régional d'alphbétisation fonctionelle, Banfora, Haute-Volta, 1975. *La place et le rôle de la femme dans le developpement économique et social d l'Afrique: rapport du Séminaire.* Dakar: Bureau regional de l'Unesco pour l'éducation en Afrique, 1976.

Servicios de apoyo: Mechanismos para la incorporación de la mujer al desarrollo. Santiago: United Nations Children's Fund, Regional Office for Latin America, 1975.

Unesco. *The Influence of Educational Programmes for Women on Agriculture and on Economic and Social Development in Africa.* Paris: Unesco, 1966.

United Nations. *Participación de las mujeres en el desarollo económico y social de suspaises.* Geneva: United Nations, 1970.

UN Economic Commission for Africa. *ECA Five Year Programme on Pre-Vocational and Vocational Training of Girls and Women, toward Their Full Participation in Development. (1972–1976). New York: UN Economic Commission for Africa, 1976.*

Wellesley Editorial Committee, ed. *Women and National Development: The Complexities of Change.* Chicago: University of Chicago Press, 1977.

Yusef, Sal El-Din Kotb, ed. *Education and Modernization in Egypt.* Cairo: Ain Shams University Press (for American Association of Colleges for Teacher Education), 1973.

Articles

Abbot, Susan. "Woman's Importance for Kenyan Rural Development." *Community Development Journal* 10 (October 1975): 179–82.

Antrobus, P. "Women in Development: The Issues for the Caribbean." *Convergence* 13 nos. 1–2 (1980): 60–64.

Boulding, Elsie. "Integration into What? Reflections on Development Planning for Women." *Convergence* 13, nos. 1–2 (1980): 50–59.

Clason, C. "Women and Development: Three Experimental Projects." *Literacy Discussion* 6, no. 4 (1975–76): 77–95.

Cruiziat, A. "La jeunesse africaine et les problèmes de son insertation dans le développement." *Cahiers d l'Animation,* no. 18 (1977): 5–30.

Dodge, Norton T. "Women in Economic Development: A Review Essay." *International Review of Education* 19, no. 1 (1973): 161–66.

Feldman, R. H. L. "The Relationship of School, Grade and Sex to Traditional-Modern Attitudes among Gusii Students in Kenya." *Journal of Social Psychology* 96 (June 1975): 135–36.

Fox, Greer L. "Some Determinants of Modernism among Women in Ankara, Turkey." *Journal of Marriage and the Family* 35, no. 3 (1973): 520–59.

"Integration of Women in Rural Development. FAO World Conference Report." *Convergence* 12, no. 4 (1979): 72–73.

Jacobson, D. "Indian Women in Processes of Development." *Journal of International Affairs* 30 (Fall/Winter 1976/1977): 211–42.

Joyner, Christopher, and Joyner, Nancy D. "Women, Development, and the Challenge of Global Education." *Journal of the Nawdac* 41 (Summer 1978): 157–60.

Kokuhirwa, Hilda. "Toward the Social and Economic Promotion of Rural Women in Tanzania." *Literacy Discussion* 6 (Winter 1976/75): 47–64.

Maher, Venessa. "Women and Social Change in Morocco." In *Women in the Muslim World*, edited by Lois Beck and Nikki Keddie. Cambridge: Harvard University Press, 1978.

Mair, Lucille. "Adult Learning, Women and Development." *Prospects* 7, no. 2 (1977): 238–443.

———. "Meaning and Implications of the Expanded Concepts of Development for Action." *Literacy Discussion* 7, no. 4 (1976–1977): 85–96.

Meleis, A. I.; El-Sanabary, N.; and Beeson, Diane. "Women, Modernization and Education in Kuwait." *Comparative Education Review* 23, no. 1 (February 1979): 115–24.

Noor, Yetty Rizali. "Indonesian Women's Participation in Development." In *Indonesian Women: Some Past and Current Perspectives*, edited by B. B. Hering. Brussels: Centre d'etude du Sud-Est Asiatique et de l'Extrême Orient, 1976.

Palmer, Ingrid. "Rural Women and the Basic Needs Approach to Development." *International Labour Review* 115, no. 1 (1977): 97–107.

Rigalt, Francisco. "La mujer rural y el Instituto Nacional de Technologia Agropecuaria." *Revista de la Universidad de Cordoba* 10, nos. 1–2 (1969): 217–20.

See, Yvonne. "The Importance of the Education of Women in the Sphere of Development." *ASPBAE Journal* 5 (February–May 1971) 15–20.

United Nations Economic Commission for Africa, Human Resources Development Division. "Women: The Neglected Human Resource for African Development." *Canadian Journal of African Studies* 6, no. 2 (1972): 359–70.

United Nations Economic Commission for Africa, Women's Research and Training Center. "Women and National Development in African Countries: Some Profound Contradictions." *African Studies Review* 18, no. 3 (1975): 47–69.

Weisinger, Rita. "Economic Development and Functional Literacy for Women." *International Review of Education* 19, no. 1 (1973): 96–100.

"Women and Development: Symposium." *Educational Broadcasting International* 12 (December 1979): 146–91.

"Women, Literacy and Development." *Literacy Discussion* 4, no. 4 (Winter 1975–1976) 1–172.

Zeidenstein, George. "Including Women in Development Efforts." *World Development* 6, no. 7/8 (July–August 1978): 971–8.

Zeidenstein, Sondra. "A Regional Approach to Women's Needs: The Women and Development Unit in the Caribbean." *Carnets de l'Enfance*, nos. 49/50 (Spring 1980): 155–71.

Unpublished Materials

Arias, Sister María Cecilia. "A Case Study of the Program of the Overseas Education Fund Institute in Leadership Development for Latin American Women in the United States from 1963 to 1970." Ed.D. dissertation, Boston University School of Education, 1972.
Arntsen, Andrea. "Women and Social Change in Tunesia." Ph.D. dissertation, Georgetown University, 1977.
Chipp, Sylvia A. "The Role of Women Elites in a Modernizing Country: The All Pakistan Women's Association." Ph.D. dissertation, Syracuse University, 1970.

Education and the Work Force

Books

Acosta-Belén, Edna, ed. *The Puerto Rican Woman*. New York: Praeger, 1979.
Blaug, Mark. *Education and the Employment Problem in Developing Countries*. Geneva: International Labour Office, 1974.
Conférence régionale sur l'éducation. *Le Formation professionelle et les possibilitiés d'emploi des jeunes filles et des femmes dans les pays africains, Rabat, May 20–29, 1971.* Bonn: Fondation allemande pour les pays en voie de développement, 1972.
Davin, Delia. *Woman-Work: Women and the Party in Revolutionary China*. Oxford: Clarendon Press, 1976.
Enquête sur les possibilités d'éducation, de formation et d'emploi offerts aux femmes en Cote-d'Ivoire. Abidjan: Ministère de l'éducation nationale, 1974.
Jayaweera, S., ed. *A Study of Educational Opportunities and Employment Opportunities Open to Women in Sri Lanka: A Report on an Investigation Conducted for UNESCO*. Paris: Unesco, 1974.
Kapur, Promilla. *The Changing Status of the Working Woman in India*. New Delhi: Vikas Publications, 1974.
Lloyd, Cynthia, ed. *Sex, Discrimination, and the Division of Labor*. New York: Columbia University Press, 1975.
Mbilinyi, Margorie J. *The Participation of Women in African Economies*. Dar es Salaam: Economic Research Bureau, University of Dar es Salaam, 1971.

Mitchnik, D. A. *Education and Employment Research Project: Improving Ways of Skill Acquisition of Women for Rural Employment in Some African Countries.* Geneva: International Labour Organization, 1977.

Rani, Kala. *Role Conflict in Working Women.* New Delhi: Chetana Publications, 1976.

Rodriguez, Aida, and Schkolnik, Susana. *Chile y Guatemala: Factores que afectan la participación feminina en la actividad económica.* Santiago: Centro Latinoamericano de Demografía, 1974.

Sethi, R. M. *Modernisation of Working Women in Developing Countries.* New Delhi: National Publishing House, 1976.

Srivastava, Vinita. *Employment of Educated Married Women in India: Its Causes and Consequences.* New Delhi: National, 1978.

Standing, Guy, and Sheehan, Glen, eds. *Labor Force Participation in Low-Income Countries.* Geneva: International Labour Organisation, 1978.

Taiana, A. A. *Posibilites d'education, de formation et d'emploi offertes aux femmes.* Paris: Commission nationale Argentine pour l'Unesco, 1974.

Unesco, *Posibilidades de educación, de formación y de empleo ofrecidas a las mujeres.* Paris: Unesco, 1974.

———. *Report on the Relationship between Educational Opportunities and Employment Opportunities for Women.* Paris: Unesco, 1974.

———. *Report on the Relationship between Educational Opportunities and Employment Opportunities for Women.* Paris: Unesco, 1975.

Wadhera, Kiron. *The New Bread Winners: A Study of the Situation of Young Working Women.* New Delhi: Vishwa Yuvak Kendra, 1976.

Youssef, Nadia H. *Women and Work in Developing Societies.* Population monograph ser. no. 15. Berkeley: University of California, Institute of International Studies, 1974.

Articles

Almquist, Elizabeth M. "Review Essay: Women in the Labor Force." *Signs: Journal of Women in Culture and Society* 2 (Summer 1977): 843–55.

Barrera, Manuel. "Estructura educativa de la fuerza de trabajo chilene." *Revista Paraguaya de Sociologia* 15 (January–April 1978): 57–75.

Barrera, Manuel. "La mujer Chilena en la educación y el trabajo." *Revista del centro de estudios educativos* 7, no. 4 (1977): 1–20.

Bean, Lee L. "Utilisation of Human Resources: The Case of Women in Pakistan." *International Labour Review* 97 (April 1968): 391–410.

Bengelsdorf, Carollee, and Hageman, Alice. "Emerging from Underdevelopment: Women and Work in Cuba." *Race and Class* 19, no. 4 (Spring 1978): 361–78.

Blau, Francine D., and Jusenius, Carol L. "Economists' Approaches to Sex

Segregation in the Labor Market: An Appraisal." *Signs: Journal of Women in Culture and Society* 1, pt. 2 (Spring 1976): 181–99.

Blaug, Mark. "Employment and Unemployment in Ethiopia." *International Labor Review* 110 (August 1974): 117–43.

Boserup, Ester. "Employment of Women in Developing Countries." In *Proceedings of the International Population Conference*. Vol. 1. Liege: International Union for the Scientific Study of Population, 1973.

Clignet, Remi. "Social Change and Sexual Differentiation in the Cameroun and the Ivory Coast." *Signs: Journal of Women in Culture and Society* 3, no. 1 (Autumn 1977): 244–60.

Durand, John D. "Changes in Women's Participation in the Labor Force in the Process of Economic Development." In *The Labor Force in Economic Development: A Comparison of International Census Data*. Princeton, N.J.: Princeton University Press, 1975.

Elizaga, Juan C. Participación de la mujer en la mano de obra en America Latina: La fecundidad y otros determinates." *Revista Internacional del trabajo* 89, nos. 5–6 (1974): 569–88.

———. "The Participation of Women in the Labour Force of Latin America: Fertility and Other Factors." *International Labour Review* 109 (May–June 1974): 519–38.

Fucaraccio, A. "El trabajo feminina en Chile: un estudio de caso de las áreas urbanas." In *Chile: mujer y sociedad*, edited by P. Covarrubias and R. Franco. Santiago: Unicef, 1978.

Goldblatt, Phyllis. "The Geography of Youth Employment and School Enrollment Rates in Mexico." *Schools in Transition* (1968): 280–93.

Gonzalez Zalazar, Gloria. "Participación laboral y educativa de la mujer en Mexico." *Boletin documental sobre la mujer* 4, no. 3 (1974): 14–22.

Gubbles, Robert. "Characteristics of Supply and Demand for Women Workers in the Labor Market." In *Employment of Women*. Paris: Organization for Economic Cooperation and Development, 1970.

Hansen, K. T. "Married Women and Work: Explorations from an Urban Case Study." *African Social Research* (Zambia) 20 (1975): 777–99.

Hirschman, C., and Aghajanian, A. "Women's Labor Force Participation and Socio-economic Development: The Case of Peninsular Malaysia, 1957–1970." *Journal of Southeast Asian Studies* 11 (March 1980): 30–49.

Jusenius, C. L. "The Influence of Work Experience, Skill Requirement, and Occupational Segregation on Women's Earnings." *Journal of Economics and Business* 29 (Winter 1977): 107–15.

Leibowitz, Arleen. "Education Allocation of Women's Time." In *Education Income, and Human Behavior*, edited by F. Thomas Justen. New York: McGraw-Hill Book Co., 1975.

Lewis, Barbara C. "Economic Activity and Marriage among Ivorian Urban Women." In *Sexual Stratification: A Cross-Cultural View*, edited by Alice Schlegal. New York: Columbia University Press, 1977.

MacDonald, John Stuart, and MacDonald, Leatrice. "Women at Work in Britain and the Third World." *New Community* 5 (Summer 1976): 76–84.

Mincer, J., and Polachek, S. "Family Investments in Human Capital: Earnings of Women." *Journal of Political Economy* 92 (March, pt. 2, 1974): S76–110 and "Discussion." *Journal of Human Resources* 13 (Winter 1978): 103–34.

Munoz, Izquierdo Carlos, and Lobo, Jose. "Expansion escolar, mercado de trabajo y distribución del ingreso en Mexico." *Revista del Centro de Estudios Educativos* 4, no. 1 (1974): 9–30.

Nath, Kamla. "Education and Employment among Kuwaiti Women." In *Women in the Muslim World*, edited by Lois Beck and Nikki Keddie. Cambridge: Harvard University Press, 1978.

Nelson, Cynthia. "Women, Education, and Labor Force Participation: Introduction." *Signs: Journal of Women in Culture and Society* (Special Issue: Women and National Development) 3, no. 1 (Autumn 1977): 241–3.

Nouacer, Khadija. "The Changing Status of Women and the Employment of Women in Morocco." *International Social Science Journal* 14, no. 1 (1962): 124–37.

Oppenheimer, Valerie K. "Demographic Influence on Female Employment and the Status of Women." In *Changing Women in a Changing Society*, edited by Joan Huber. Chicago: University of Chicago Press, 1973.

Papanek, H. "Purdah in Pakistan: Seclusion and Modern Occupations for Women." *Journal of Marriage and the Family* 33, no. 3 (1971): 517–30.

———. "Men, Women and Work: Reflections on the Two-Person Career." In *Changing Women in a Changing Society*, edited by Joan Huber. Chicago: University of Chicago Press, 1973.

Paul, Radha. "Equipping Women for Participation in Economic Life." In *Long-Term Educational and Training Programmes for the Advancement of Women in Asia*. Bombay: International Seminar, 1967.

Pecht, Waldomiro. "La mujer casada y el mercado de trabajo: grado de participación en las áreas urbanas. In *Chile:mujer y sociedad*, edited by P. Covarrubias and R. Franco. Santiago: Unicef, 1978.

Rosenberg, T. J. "Individual and Regional Influences on the Employment of Colombian Women." *Journal of Marriage and Family* 38 (May 1976): 339–53.

Saavedra, Wilna. "Los jardines infantiles y el trabajo de la mujer." In *Chile: mujer y sociedad*, edited by P. Covarrubias and R. Franco. Santiago: Unicef, 1978.

Safilios-Rothschild, Constantina. "A Cross-Cultural Examination of Women's

Marital, Educational and Occupational Options." *Acta Sociologica* 14 (1971): 96–113.

Santu, R. "Female Labor Force in Argentina, Bolivia, and Paraguay." *Latin American Research Review* 15, no. 2 (1980): 152–61.

Shapiro, D., and Carr, T. J. "Investments in Human Capital and the Earnings of Young Women." In *Years for Decision: A Longitudinal Study of the Educational and Labor Market Experience of Young Women*, Vol. 4. Columbus: Ohio State University Center for Human Resource Research, 1977.

Standing, Guy. "Education and Female Participation in the Labor Force." *International Labor Review* 114 (November–December 1976): 281–97.

Strange, Heather. "Education and Employment Patterns of Rural Malay Women, 1965–1975." *Journal of Asian and African Studies* 13 (January–April 1978): 50–64.

Sundaram, K. "Working Life Span in the Indian Labour Force by Sex and Level of Education." *World Development* 4 (February 1976): 111–20.

Valdemar, Emilia. "Mujeres Panamenas participando en el trabajo." *Boletin documental sobre la mujer* 4, no. 3 (1974): 60–61.

Vasques de Miranda, Glaura. "Women's Labor Force Participation in a Developing Society: The Case of Brazil." *Signs: Journal of Women in Culture and Society* 3, no. 1 (Autumn 1977): 261–74.

Viseria, P. "Labour Force Participation by Age, Sex and Education Level in India." *Journal of the University of Bombay*, no. 40 (1971): 178–204.

Wainerman, C. H., et al. "Participation of Women in Economic Activity in Argentina, Bolivia and Paraquay: A Comparative Study." *Latin American Research Review* 15, no. 2 (1980): 143–51.

Ward, Barbara E. "Women and Technology in Developing Countries." *Impact of Science on Society* 20 (January–March 1970): 93–101.

Wirtenberg, T. J. "Education: Barrier or Boon to Changing Occupational Roles of Women?" *Journal of Social Issues* 32, no. 3 (1976): 165–80.

Woodhall, Maureen. "Investment in Women: A Reappraisal of the Concept of Human Capital." *International Review of Education* (Special Issue: The Education of Women) 19, no. 1 (1973): 9–29.

Young, Anne. "Employment of High School Graduates and Drop-outs (from Caracas to Kuala Lumpur)." *Monthly Labor Review* 94 (January 1971): 9–15.

Youssef, Nadia H. "Social Structure and the Female Labour Force: The Case of Women Workers in Muslim Middle Eastern Countries." *Demography* 8 (November 1971): 427–39.

——. "Differential Labor Force Participation of Women in Latin America and Middle Eastern Countries: The Influence of Family Characteristics." *Social Forces* 51 (December 1972): 135–53.

"Youth and Work in Latin America." *International Labour Review* 90, no. 61 (1964): 1–23.

Unpublished Materials

Arenas de Acosta, Dulce Maria. "The Female Labor Force in Venezuela: Factors Determining Labor Force Participation Rates." Ph.D. dissertation, Ohio State University, 1980.

El-Huni, Ali Mohamed. "Determinants of Female Labor Force Participation: The Case of Libya." Ph.D. dissertation, Oklahoma State University, 1978.

Fong, Monica Skantze. "Social and Economic Correlates of Female Labor Force Participation in West Malaysia." Ph.D. dissertation, University of Hawaii, 1974.

Miranda, Glaura Vasque de. "Education and other Determinant Factors of Female Labor Force Participation in Brazil." Ph.D. dissertation, Stanford University, 1979.

Moore, Brian E. A. "Some Working Women in Mexico City: Traditionalists and Modernists." Ph.D. dissertation, Washington University, 1970.

Tanfer, Koray. "Working Women: A Study of Female Labor Force and Determinants of Participation in Six Large Cities of Turkey, 1970." Ph.D. dissertation, Univeristy of Pennsylvania, 1975.

Women and the Professions

Books

Agnew, Vijay. *Elite Women in Indian Politics*. New Delhi: Vikas, 1979.

Argentine Republic, Ministerio de Trabajo y Seguridad Social. *Evolución de la mujer en las professiones liberales en Argentian: Anos 1900–1960*. Buenos Aires: Ministerio de Trabajo y Seguridad Social, 1965.

Argentine Republic, Secretaria de Estado de Trabajo. Dirección Nacional de Recursos Humanos. Oficina Nacional de la Mujer. *Evolución de la mujer en las professiones liberales en Argentina: Anos 1900–1965*. 2d ed. Boletin de la Oficina Nacional de la Mujer, ser. A. (suppl.). Buenos Aires: Oficina Nacional de la Mujer, 1970.

Barbieri, M. Teresita de. *Acceso de la mujer a las carreras y ocupaciones tecnológicas de nivel medio*. Santiago: ELAS-Unesco, 1972.

Chang, Ligia, and Ducci, Maria Angelica. *Realidad del empleo y la formacion profesional de la mujer en America Latina*. Estudios y monografias, no. 24. Montevideo: CINTEFOR, 1977.

Guy, Henry, and Bailey, Lavern, eds. *Women of Distinction in Jamaica: A Record of Career Women in Jamaica, Their Background, Service and Achievements*. Kingston: Caribbean Herald, 1977.

National Conference on Women Doctors in India. New Delhi, Sept. 19–20, 1975. Proceedings. New Delhi: Indian Medical Association, 1975.

Ramanamma, A. *Graduate Employed Women in an Urban Setting.* Poona: Dastane Ramchandra, 1979.

Articles

Barthel, Diane. "The Rise of a Female Professional Elite: The Case of Senegal." *African Studies Review* 18, no. 3 (1975): 1–17.

Bhat, R. V., et al. "Performance of Women Medical Graduates from Medical College, Barsda, 1969–75." *Medical Education* 10 (July 1976): 293–296.

Blitz, Rudolph C. "An International Comparison of Women's Participation in the Professions." *Journal of Developing Areas* 9 (July 1975): 203–7.

Brendel, M. "The African Career Woman in South Africa." *African Women* 2, no. 2 (1957): 36–38.

Cohen, Lucy M. "Woman's Entry into the Professions in Columbia: Selected Characteristics." *Journal of Marriage and the Family* 35 (May 1973): 322–30.

Fani, al-, Ahmad. "Mademoiselle, enseigner n'est pas un métier ingrat." *Faiza* 22 (February 1962): 20–23.

Gould, T. F. "Value Conflict and Development: The Struggle of Professional Zairian Women." *Journal of Modern African Studies* 16 (March 1978): 133–9.

Guerrero, S. H. "An Analysis of Husband-Wife Roles among Filipino Professionals at University of the Philippnes, Los Banos Campus." *Philippine Sociology Review* 13, no. 4 (1965): 275–81.

Howard, Merriam K. "Women, Education, and the Professions in Egypt." *Comparative Education Review* 23 (June 1979): 256–70.

Khor, Thomas. "Woman Teachers and Equal Pay." *Malayan Educator* 8 (April 1962): 6–19.

Kinzer, Nora Scott. "Women Professionals in Buenos Aires." In *Female and Male in Latin America*, edited by Ann Pescatello. Pittsburgh: University of Pittsburgh Press, 1973.

———. "Sociocultural Factors Mitigating Role Conflict of Buenos Aires Professional Women." In *Women Cross-culturally: Change and Challenge*, edited by Ruby Rohrlich-Leavitt. The Hague: Mouton, 1975.

Lodge, Juliet. "New Zealand Women Academics: Some Observations on Their Status, Aspirations and Professional Advancement. *Political Science* (Wellington) 28 (July 1976): 23–40.

Meleis, A. I., and Hassan, S. H. "Oil Rich, Nurse Poor: The Nursing Crisis in the Persian Gulf." *Nursing Outlook* 28 (April 1980): 238–43.

Mills, S., ed. "Interview with an African Woman, L. N. Kanza." *Essence* 9 (July 1978): 60–61.

Mitchell, E. M. "Women Leaders in Nepal: A Generation Gap." *Delta Kappa Gamma Bulletin* 44 (Fall 1977): 40–51.
Prete, Rogues. "Education et formation professionelle féminines dans les etats africaine et malgache d'expression francaise." *L'Afrique contemporaine* 4 (November-December 1965): 18–20.
Rahal, K. "In Face of the Bacterial Menace, Sex Inequality is Forgotten in Research." *Impact of Science on Society* 30 (January 1980): 43–45.
Simone, J. A. de, and Mora, A. "En favor del acceso de la mujer a carreras técnicas." *Revista de educación* (Santiago de Chile), no. 24–25. (March-April 1970), pp. 72–75.
"Some Ideas from Women Technicians in Small Countries." *Impact of Science on Society* 30 (January 1980): 3–66. [Symposium]
Thein, M. M. "Women Scientists and Engineers in Burma." *Impact of Science on Society* 30 (January 1980): 15–22.
Whiting, Beatrice B. "The Kenyan Career Woman: Traditional and Modern." In *The Anatomy of Advancement*, edited by Ruth B. Kerndsin. New York: William Morrow & Co., 1974.

Unpublished Materials

Ahad, Mohammed Abdul. "Innovations in Indian Nursing: A Study of Foreign Returned Indian Nurses as Innovators.' Ed.D. dissertation, Columbia University, 1973.
Asomani, Carol Ann Garrison. "A Descriptive Survey of the University Women of Ghana and Their Attitudes toward the Women's Liberation Movement." Ed.D. dissertation, George Washington University, 1977.
Asperilla, Purita Falgui. "The Mobility of Filipino Nurses." Ed.D. dissertation, Columbia University, 1971.
Bhargava, Guruadhari. "Becoming a Doctor: A Study in the Professional Identification of Women Medical Students in India." Ph.D. dissertation, York University, 1978.
Gould, Terri F. "The Educated Woman in a Developing Country: Professional Zairian Women in Lubumbashi." Ph.D. dissertation, Union Graduate School, 1976.
Green, Justin Jay. "Women Leaders of the Philippines: Social Backgrounds and Political Attitudes." Ph.D. dissertation, Syracuse University, 1970.
Giffin, Karen Mary. "Opportunities and Ideologies: Women in High-Status Professions in Bahia, Brazil." Ph.D. dissertation, University of Toronto, 1979.
Motamedi, Iran. "Women Administrators in Higher and Secondary Education in Iran." Ph.D. dissertation, Southern Illinois University, 1978.
Park, Kyung-Nan Choo. "Labor Force Participation of Professional Women

in Korea." Ed.D. dissertation, Boston University School of Education, 1979.

Education and Women's Social Status

Books

Baqai, Mohammad Sabihuddin. *Changes in the Status and Roles of Women in Pakistan: An Empirical Study in Karachi Metropolitan Area.* Karachi: Department of Sociology, University of Karachi, 1976.

Barrig, Maruja. *Cinturón de castidad: La mujer de clase media en el Perú.* Lima: Mosca Azul, 1979.

Desai, Chitra. *Girls' School Education and Social Change.* Bombay: A. R. Sheth, 1976.

Documents of the Afro-Asian Symposium on Social Development of Women, Alexandria, 8–10 March 1975. Afro-Asian Publications 66. Cairo: Permanent Secretariat of Afro-Asian Peoples' Solidarity Organisation, 1975.

Everett, Jana Matson. *Women and Social Change in India.* New York: St. Martin's Press, 1979.

Hussaini, Asaf. *The Educated Pakistani Girl: A Sociological Study.* Karachi: Ima, 1963.

Giole, Janet Z., and Smock, Audrey C., eds. *Women and Society: In International and Comparative Perspective.* New York: Wiley-Interscience, 1976.

Government of India. *Toward Equality.* Report of the Committee on the Status of Women in India. New Delhi: Ministry of Education and Social Welfare, 1974.

India, National Committee on the Status of Women. *Status of Women in India.* New Delhi: Allied, 1975.

Kokuhirwa, Hilda. *Toward the Social and Economic Promotion of Rural Women in Tanzania.* Dar es Salaam: Institute for Adult Education, 1975.

Mattielli, Sandra, ed. *Virtues in Conflict: Tradition and the Korean Women Today.* Seoul: For the Royal Asiatic Society, Lorea Branch by Samhwa Pub. Co., 1977.

Mehta, R. *The Western Educated Hindu Woman.* London: Asia Publishing House, 1970.

Nash, June, and Safa, Helen Icken, eds. *Sex and Class in Latin America.* New York: Praeger, 1976.

Newland, Kathleen. *The Sisterhood of Man — The Impact of Women's Changing Roles on Social and Economic Life around the World.* A World Watch Book. New York: W. W. Norton & Co., 1979.

Pellow, Deborah. *Women in Accra: Options for Autonomy.* Algonac, Michigan: Reference Publications, 1977.

Proceedings of the Conference Held on 15th and 16th January 1979 in Connection with UN Decade for Women, 1976-85. Jammu: Government of Jammu and Kishmir, Labour and Social Welfare Department, 1979.

Rojas-Aleta, Isabel; Silva, Teresita; and Eleasar, Christine. *A Profile of Filipino Women: Their Status and Role*. Manila: Philippine Business for Social Progress, 1977.

Saxena, Rajendra Kumar. *Education and Social Amelioration of Women: A Study of Rajasthan*. Jaipur: Saghi Prakashan, 1978.

Schlegel, A., ed. *Sexual Stratification: A Cross-Cultural View*. New York: Columbia University Press, 1977.

Smock, Audrey C. *Women's Education and Roles*. Chicago: University of Chicago Press, 1980.

Unesco. *Women, Education, Equality*. Paris: Unesco, 1975.

United Nations. *Report of the World Conference of the International Women's Year (Mexico City, 19 June-2 July 1975)*. New York: United Nations, 1976.

Villalobos de Urrutia, Gabriela. *Diagnóstico de la situación social y ecónomica de la mujer Peruana*. Lima: Centro de Estudios de Población y Desarrollo, 1975.

Wasi, Muriel. *Educated Woman in India Today*. New York: McGraw-Hill Book Co., 1973.

Articles

Bhely-Quenum, O. "Unesco and the Advancement of Women in Africa." *Unesco Chronicle* 18, no. 2 (1972): 56-60.

Carrasco, V. M. "L'enseignante dans la lutte pour la liberation de la femme—lutte opiniâtre contre la discrimination." *Revue Internationale Enseignants* (Prague), no. 4 (1975): 8-10.

Cheng, Siok-Hwa. "Singapore Women: Legal Status, Educational Attainment, and Employment Patterns." *Asian Survey* 17 (April 1977): 358-74.

Clignet, Remi. "Social Change and Sexual Differentiation in the Cameroun and the Ivory Coast." *Signs: Journal of Women in Culture and Society* (Special Issue: Women and National Development) 3, no. 1 (Autumn 1977): 244-60.

Croll, Elizabeth J. "Social Production and Female Status: Women in China." *Race and Class* 18 (Summer 1976): 39-52.

Damico, Sandra, and Nevill, Dorothy. "The Highly Educated Women: A Study in Role Conflict." *Council on Anthropology and Education Quarterly* 6 (August 1975): 16-19.

Dilley, Lynton. "Education and the Role of Women in Africa." *Delta Kappa Gamma Bulletin* 40 (Summer 1974): 21-35.

Fischer, Carmen, et al. "El desarrollo de la educación parvularia en Chile y su influencia en desarrollo de la mujer." In *Chile: mujer y sociedad*, edited by P. Covarrubias and R. Franco. Santiago: Unicef, 1978.

Giole, Janet Z. "Introduction: Comparative Perspective on Women," In *Women: Roles and Status in Eight Countries*, edited by Janet Giole and Audrey Smock. New York: John Wiley & Sons, 1977.

Hanks, Lucien M., and Hanks, Jane Richardson. "Thailand: Equality between the Sexes." In *Women in the New Asia*, edited by Barbara E. Ward. Paris: Unesco, 1963.

Hannot, Tamara. "La mujer en Venezuela: Nueva imagen o nueva mujer? Valores, estructura y sociedad." *Oficina de estudios socioeconomicos* (Caracas), Fondo Editorial Común (1974): 79–113.

Harper, J. "Educated Women in Niugini." *Australian and New Zealand Journal of Sociology* 10 (1974): 90–95.

Hayani, Ibrahim. "The Changing Role of Arab Women." *Convergence* 13, nos. 1–2 (1980): 136–9.

Ihromi, T. O. "Social and Cultural Background of Concepts of Roles of Women, Reflections on the Indonesian Scene." *Ecumenical Review* (Geneva) 27 (October 1975): 357–65.

Jamurabai, J. "Women's Education: The Roles and Content of Education in the Changing Social Pattern with Special Reference to Women's Education." *Indian Journal of Adult Education* 23 (February 1962): 15–16.

Jaynes, G. "Iranian Women: Looking beyond the Chador." *New York Times Magazine* (April 22, 1979): 36–38.

Kankalil, M. S. "The Odds are Changing for Women in Nepal." Unicef *News* 76 (1973): 18–22.

Lee, Mary S. "The Korean Women and the Quest for Educational, Social, Economic and Cultural Advancement." *Philippine Educational Forum* 16 (June 1967): 48–59.

Link, B. M. "Holding Up the Sky is a Shared Responsibility." *Delta Kappa Gamma Bulletin* 47 (Fall 1980): 14–19.

Luseno, D. "Education and the Social Status of Women in Africa." *Kenya Journal of Adult Education* 2, no. 2 (1972): 17–22.

Mani, R. S. "Women's Education in India and Social Change." *Social Welfare* (Delhi) 11, no. 5 (1964): 1–4.

Meyer, V. J. "Women in Mexican Society." *Current History* 72 (March 1977): 120–23.

Nontawassee, P. "Towards Identity and Self Respect among Thai Women." *Ecumenical Review* (Geneva) 28 (January 1976): 39–41.

Orr, I. C. "The Educated Woman in Modern India." *United Asia* (Bombay) 14, no. 2 (1962): 239–42.

Pakizegi, Behnaz. "Legal and Social Position of Iranian Women." In *Women in the Muslim World*, edited by Lois Beck and Nikki Keddie. Cambridge: Harvard University Press, 1978.

391

Rogers, B. "Well, um, I Suppose We Never Thought of it Like That . . . ."
Development (Enugu, Nigeria) 20, nos. 3–4 (1978): 61–64.

Rojas, A. "La femme en Argentine." *Revue Internationale des Enseignants* (Prague), no. 1 (1977): 29.

Rousseau, Ida F. "Education and the Changing Role of Women in Sierra Leone and Zaire." In *Women Cross-culturally: Change and Challenge*, edited by Ruby Rohlich-Leavitt. The Hague: Mouton, 1975.

Shals, Madhuri R. "Status and Education of Women in India." *Journal of the Gujarat Research Society* 38 and 39 (October 1976 and January 1977): 15–24, 48–57.

Smith, J. I. "Women in Islam: Equity, Equality and the Search for the Natural Order." *American Academy of Religion Journal* 47, no. 4 (December 1979): 517–37.

Smock, A. C., and Youssef, Nadia H. "Egypt, from Seclusion to Limited Participation." In *Women: Roles and Status in Eight Countries*, edited by J. Z. Giole and A. C. Smock. New York: John Wiley & Sons, 1977.

Srinivas, M. N. "Changing Position of Indian Women." *Man* 12 (August 1977): 221–38.

Stiehm, Judith. "Algerian Women: Honor, Survival, and Islamic Socialism." In *Women in the World*, edited by Lynn Iglitzin and Ruth Ross. Santa Barbara, Calif.: American Bibliographical Center—Clio Press, 1976.

Treudy, Jean. "Western Education and Muslim Fulani, Hausa Women in Sokoto, Northern Nigeria." In *Conflict and Harmony in Tropical Africa*, edited by Godfrey N. Brown and Mervyn Hisket. Cranbury, N.J.: Fairleigh Dickinson University Press, 1975.

Van Allen, Judith. "African Women, 'Modernization' and National Liberation." In *Women in the World*, edited by Lynn Iglitzin and Ruth Ross. Santa Barbara, Calif.: American Bibliographical Center—Clio Press, 1976.

Unpublished Materials

Heyman, Barry Neal. "Urbanization and the Status of Women in Peru." Ph.D. dissertation, University of Wisconsin, Madison, 1974.

Johnson, Allan Griswold. "Modernization and Social Change: Attitudes toward Women's Roles in Mexico City." Ph.D. dissertation, University of Michigan, 1972.

Marei, Wafaa Abou-Negm. "Female Emancipation and Changing Political Leadership: A Study of Five Arab Countries." Ph.D. dissertation, Rutgers University, 1978.

Selby, Robert Leon. "Women, Industrialization and Change in Queretaro, Mexico." Ph.D. dissertation, University of Utah, 1979.

Thomas, Sandra Carol. "The Women of Chile and Education for a Contemporary Society: A Study of Chilean Women, Their History and Present Status and the New Demand of a Society in Transition." Ph.D. dissertation, St. Louis University, 1973.

Wahaib, Abdul Amir. "Education and Status of Women in the Middle East with Special Reference to Egypt, Tunesia and Iraq." Ph.D. dissertation, Southern Illinois University, 1970.

Education and the Family

Books

Allman, James. ed. *Women's Status and Fertility in the Muslim World.* New York: Praeger, 1978.

Arnold, F., et al. *The Value of Children: A Cross-national Survey.* Vol. 1 *Introduction.* Honolulu: East-West Populatoin Institute, 1975.

Arnold, F., and Fawcett, J. *The Value of Children: A Cross-national Survey.* Vol. 3, *Hawaii.* Honolulu: East-West Population Institute, 1975.

Bulatao, Rudolfo. *The Value of Children: A Cross-national Survey.* Vol. 2, *The Philippines.* Honolulu: East-West Population Institute, 1975.

Buripakdi, C. *The Value of Children: A Cross-national Survey.* Vol. 4, *Thailand.* Honolulu: East-West Population Institute, 1977.

Cochrane, S. H. *Education and Fertility: What Do We Know?* Baltimore: Johns Hopkins Univeristy Press, 1979.

Encarnacion, Jose, Jr. *Fertility and Labour Force Participation: Philippines 1968.* Population and Employment Working Paper No. 2. Geneva: International Labour Office, 1974.

Fogarty, M. P.; Rapoport, R.; and Rapoport, R. N. *Sex, Career and Family: Including an International Review of Women's Roles.* London: George Allen & Unwin, 1971.

Minturn, L., et al. *Mothers of Six Cultures.* New York: John Wiley & Sons, 1964.

Pettit, J. *Integrated Family Life Education Project: A Project of the Ethiopian Women's Association. Project Assessment,* Washington, D.C.: World Education, 1977.

Roberts, George W.,and Sinclair, Sonja. *Women in Jamaica: Patterns of Reproduction and Family.* Millwood, N.Y.: KTO Press, 1978.

Singh, Kulwant Pritam. *Status of Women and Population Growth in India.* New Delhi: Munshiram Manoharlal, 1979.

Sussman, Marvin B., and Cogswell, Betty E., eds. *Cross National Family Research.* Leiden: E. J. Drill, 1972.

Unicef. *Assessments of Projects for the Education and Training of Women and Girls for Family and Community Life.* New York: Unicef, 1970.

Vaughn, G. G., ed. *Women's Roles and Education: Changing Traditions in Population Planning.* Washington, D.C.: International Family Planning Project, American Home Economics Association, n.d.

Wu, T. S. *The Value of Children: A Cross-national Survey.* Vol. 5 *Taiwan.* Honolulu: East-West Population Institute, 1977.

Articles

Barretto, Felisa R. "Knowledge, Attitudes and Practices of Family Planning in the Philippines." *Studies in Family Planning* 5 (September 1974): 294-9.

Becker, Gary S., and Lewis, H. Gregg. "Interaction between Quantity and Quality of Children." In *Economics of the Family: Marriage, Children and Human Capital,* edited by Theodore W. Schultz. Chicago: University of Chicago Press, 1974.

Benham, Lee. "Benefits of Women's Education within Marriage." In *Economics of the Family,* edited by T. W. Schultz. Chicago: University of Chicago Press, 1974.

Boserup, Ester. "Employment and Education: Keys to Smaller Families." *Victor Bostrum Fund Report,* vol. 18 (Spring 1974).

Brody, E. B., et al. "Early Sex Education in Relationship to Later Coital and Reproductive Behavior: Evidence from Jamaican Women." *American Journal of Psychiatry* 133 (August 1976): 969-72.

Caldwell, J. C. "Education as a Factor in Mortality Decline: An Examination of Nigerian Data." *Population Studies* 33 (November 1979): 395-13.

———. "Fertility Attitudes in Three Economically Contrasting Rural Regions of Ghana." *Economic Development and Cultural Change* 15 (January 1967): 217-38.

Chaudhury, Rafiqul H. "Female Status and Fertility Behavior in a Metropolitan Urban Area of Bangladesh." *Population Studies* 32, no. 2 (July 1978): 261-73.

Chu, Cheng-ping. "A Study of the Effects of Maternal Employment for Pre-School Children in Taiwan." *Acta Psychologica Taiwanica,* no. 12 (1970), pp. 80-100.

Darabi, Katherine F. "Education and Fertility in Iran." *Community Development Journal* 11 (April 1976): 141-48.

Dixon, Ruth B. "Education and Employment: Keys to Smaller Families." *Journal of Family Welfare* 22 (December 1975): 38-49.

Encarnacion, Jose. "Family Income, Education, Labour Force Participation and Fertility." In *A Demographic Path to Modernity: Patterns of Early Transition in the Philippines,* edited by Wilhelm Flieger and Peter C. Smith. Quezon City: University of the Philippines Press, 1975.

Encarnacion, Jose, Jr., et al. "An Economic-Demographic Model of the Philippines." In *Studies in Philippine Economic Demographic Relations,* edited by Agustin Kintanar Jr., et al. Manila: Economic Research Associates, Inc., 1974.

394

Espenshade, T. "The Value and Cost of Children." *Population Bulletin*, vol. 32, no. 1 (1977).

Fernando, Dallas F. S. "Female Educational Attainment and Fertility." *Journal of Biosocial Science* 9 (July 1977): 339–51.

Goldstein, Sidney, et.al. "The Influence of Labour Force Participation and Education on Fertility in Thailand." *Population Studies* 26, no. 3, (1972): 419–36.

González, Cortés G. "Desarrollo, mujer y fecundidad." In *Chile: mujer y sociedad*, edited by P. Covarrubias and R. Franco. Santiago: Unicef, 1978.

Hass, Paula H. "Maternal Role Incompatibility and Fertility in Urban Latin America." *Journal of Social Issues* 28, no. 2 (1972) 111–27.

Hoffman, Lois. "The Employment of Women, Education and Fertility." *Merrill-Palmer Quarterly* 20, no. 2 (1974): 99–120.

Holsinger, Donald B. and Kasarda, John D. "Education and Human Fertility: Sociological Perspectives." In *Population and Development: The Search for Selective Interventions*, edited by Ronald G. Ridker. Baltimore: John Hopkins University Press, 1976.

Isi, al-, I.; Kanawati, A.; and McLaren, D. "Formal Education of Mothers and Their Nutritional Behaviour." *Journal of Nutritional Education* 7 (1975): 22–24.

Kaker, D. N. "Planning Culturally Relevant Nutrition Education Programmes: What Can Anthropologists Do?" *Journal of Family Welfare* 23 (September 1976): 45–53.

Kendall, Maurice. "The World Fertility Survey: Current Status and Finding." *Population Report* 7 (July 1979): M73–M103.

Ketkar, Suhas L. "Female Education and Fertility: Some evidence for Sierra Leone." *Journal of Developing Areas* 13 (October 1978): 23–34.

Khan, Mohammed Ali, and Sirageldin, Ismail. "Education, Income and Fertility in Pakistan." *Economic Development and Cultural Change* 27 (April 1979): 519–47.

Kim, S. Y., and Stinner, W. F. "Social Origins, Educational Attainment and the Timing of Marriage and First Birth among Korean Women." *Journal of Marriage and Family* 42 (August 1980): 671–9.

Kohli, K. L. "Regional Variations of Fertility in Iraq and Factors Affecting It." *Journal of Biosocial Science* 9 (April 1977): 175–82.

Kusuma, M. M. "Family Life Education in Indonesia." *ASPBAE Journal* 7 (August-November 1972): 15–18.

Lewis, Barbara C. "Economic Activity and Marriage among Ivorian Urban Women." In *Sexual Stratification*, edited by Alice Schlegel. New York: Columbia University Press, 1977.

Lloyd, Barbara. "Education and Family Life in the Development of Class Identification among the Yoruba." In *The New Elites of Tropical Africa*, edited by P. Lloyd. London: Oxford University Press, 1966.

Lötter, J. M. "The Effects of Urbanization and Education on the Fertility of Blacks in South Africa." *Humanitas* (Pretorial) 4, no. 1 (1977): 21–28.

Matheson, Alastair. "Teach a Mother—Save a Child." *UNICEF News*, no. 76 (July 1973): 12–14.

Minturn, L., et al. "Increased Maternal Power Status: Changes in Socialization in a Restudy of Rajput Mothers of Khalapur, India." *Journal of Cross-Cultural Psychology* 9 (December 1978): 483–98.

Mulay, Sumah. "Literacy and Family Planning Behavior of Rural Women." *Indian Journal of Adult Education* 37 (January 1976): 9–10.

Omari, T. Peter. "Changing Attitudes of Students in West African Society toward Marriage and Family Relationships." *British Journal of Sociology* 11, no. 3 (1960): 197–210.

Pascual, Elvira M. "Differential Fertility in the Philippines." *Philippine Sociological Review* 19 (July-October 1971): 209–29.

Pool, Janet E. "A Cross-comparative Study of Aspects of Conjugal Behavior of Three West-African Countries." *Canadian Journal of African Studies*, 6, no. 2 (1972): 232–60.

Salaff, Janet W. "The Status of Unmarried Hong Kong Women and the Social Factors Contributing to Their Delayed Marriage." *Population Studies* 30 (November 1976): 391–412.

Shah, Nasra M.; Green, Lawrence W.; and Sirageldin, Ismail. "Female Labour Force Participation and Fertility Desire in Pakistan: An Empirical Investigation." *Pakistan Development Review* 14 (Summer 1975): 185–206.

Sousa, Alfred de. "Women in India: Fertility and Occupational Pattern in A Sex-segregated Less Developed Society." *Social Action* 26 (January-March 1976): 66–79.

Stycos, J. Mayone. "Recent Trends in Latin American Fertility." *Population Studies* 32 (November 1978): 407–25.

Timur, Serim. "Demographic Correlates of Women's Education." In *International Population Conference*, Vol. 3. Belgium: International Union for the Scientific Study of Population, 1977.

Todaro, M. P. "Education, Migration and Fertility." In *Investment in Education: National Strategy Options for Developing Countries*, edited by J. Simmons. Washington, D.C.: World Bank, n.d.

"Turkish Program of Literacy and Family Life Planning." *World Education Reports* 2 (Summer 1973): 1–5.

Youssef, Nadia. "The Status and Fertility Patterns of Muslim Women." In *Women in the Muslim World*, edited by Lois Beck and Nikki Keddie. Cambridge: Harvard University Press, 1978.

Unpublished Materials

Achmad, Sulistinah Irawati. "A Study of the Relationship Between Educational Attainment and Fertility Behavior of Women in Java and Bali." Ph.D. Dissertation, Florida State University, 1980.

Anthony-Welch, Lillian Doloris. "A Comparative Analysis of the Black Woman as Transmitter of Black Values, Based on Case Studies of Families in Ghana and among Jamaicans and Afro-Americans in Hartford, Connecticut." Ed.D. dissertation, University of Massachusetts, 1976.

Arnold, Fred Sidney. "A Model Relating Education to Fertility in Taiwan." Ph.D. dissertation, University of Michigan, 1972.

Baldwin, Wendy Harmer. "The Influence of Selected Social Factors on Fertility in Columbia." Ph.D. dissertation, University of Kentucky, 1973.

Banguero, L., Harold Enrique. "The Social and Economic Determinants of Fertility in Colombia." Ph.D. dissertation, University of North Carolina, Chapel Hill, 1977.

Bhatnagar, Krishna Murari. "Education of Rural Women and Fertility Decline in India: An Education Policy Analysis." Ed.D. dissertation, University of South Dakota, 1980.

Cook, Frank Richardson. "Third World Population: The Effect of High School Enrollment on Fertility." Ph.D. dissertation, University of California, Irvine, 1980.

Harrision, David Selwyn. "Household Decisions about Fertility and Children's Education: The Case of Malaysia." Ph.D. dissertation, University of California, Los Angeles, 1980.

Khan, Mashal. "Socio-Economic Factors in the Reduction of Human Fertility in the Islamic World with a Case Study of Iran." Ph.D. dissertation, Stanford University, 1975.

Kim, Soung-Yee. "Social Origins, Educational Attainment and Family Formation among Korean Women." Ph.D. dissertation, Utah State University, 1979.

Makhija, Indira. "The Economic Contribution of Children and Its Effects on Fertility and Schooling." Ph.D. dissertation, University of Chicago, 1977.

Saulniers, Suzanne Margaret Smith. "Ecological and Social Factors Affecting Social Class Fertility Differentials in Peru." Ph.D. dissertation, University of Wisconsin, Madison, 1974.

Whittaker, Lurline Vernicia. "The Impact of Female Education and Other Selected Variables on Fertility in Jamaica." Ph.D. dissertation, Pennsylvania State University, 1980.

Contributors

C. ARNOLD ANDERSON is professor emeritus at the Comparative Education Center, University of Chicago. He has written extensively in the field of comparative education and was a founding member of the Comparative and International Education Society.

KAREN COFFYN BIRAIMAH received her Ph.D. from the Department of Social Foundations of Education at State University of New York at Buffalo. She has just returned from field work in Lome, Togo.

MARY JEAN BOWMAN is professor emeritus at the Comparative Education Center, University of Chicago. She has written extensively in the fields of economics of education and comparative education.

PAUL P. L. CHEUNG is on the staff of the Population Studies Center at the University of Michigan, Ann Arbor.

SUSAN COCHRANE is on the staff of the World Bank. She is author of *Education and Fertility: What Do We Know?* and numerous studies on women's education.

LORETTA DULBERG is currently coordinator of evaluation training on a grant to the School of Management, State University of New York at Buffalo. She received her Ph.D. in Educational Psychology at that university.

CAROLYN M. ELLIOTT is former director of the Center for Research on Women in Higher Education and the Professions, Wellesley College. She is currently a program officer for the Ford Foundation in India.

JOSEPH P. FARRELL is chairman of the Department of Educational Planning, the Ontario Institute for Studies in Education, Toronto. He is a past president of the Comparative and International Education Society.

JEREMY D. FINN is professor, Department of Educational Psychology, State University New York at Buffalo. He has written extensively on sex differences in educational attainment and on multivariate statistical techniques. He has been a research fellow with IEA in Stockholm.

MARION FREEDMAN has served as a community organizer and social service administrator for the past twelve years. She is currently a consultant on program development in human services.

MARIE THOURSON JONES is assistant professor, Comparative Education Center, University of Chicago.

NARENDRA NATH KALIA is associate professor, Department of Sociology, at the State University College at Buffalo. He has recently published a book on sexism in Indian school textbooks.

DAVID H. KELLY is a member of the Department of History, at D'Youville College. He is co-author of *American Students, International Bibliography of Comparative Education* and annotated bibliography on the Education of Women in the Third World published by the International Bureau of Education.

GAIL P. KELLY is associate professor at the Department of Social Foundations at the State University of New York at Buffalo. She is associate editor of the *Comparative Education Review* and has written extensively on the education of women and on colonialism.

ROBERT A. LE VINE is Roy E. Larsen Professor of Education and Human Development at the Harvard School of Education. He has done extensive field work in Kenya and Nigeria and has published extensively in the fields of child development and psychological anthropology.

CHITRA NAIK is the Honorary Director of the Indian Institute of Education where she is directing an experimental project on universalizing primary education. Formerly she was the State Education Director, Maharashtra, India.

BRENDA GAEL MCSWEENEY is currently a policy analysis officer in the Bureau for Programme Policy and Evaluation, United Nations Development Program. She served for seven years with the UNDP in the Republic of Upper Volta.

MAITHREYI KRISHNA RAJ is a Research Fellow at the Women's Research Unit of the S.N.D.T. Women's University in Bombay. She has conducted interview studies of women scientists and of women's cooperatives in the informal economic sector in Bombay.

RATI RAM is professor of economics at Oregon State University.

JANET REIS is research associate at the Center for Health Services and Policy Research at Northwestern University.

ERNESTO SCHIEFELBEIN is a researcher associated with the Centro de Investigaciones y Desarrollo de la Educacion and the Programa Interdisciplinario de Investigaciones en Educacion in Santiago, Chile.

PETER C. SMITH is on the staff of the East-West Population Institute of the East-West Center in Honolulu, Hawaii.

CATALINA H. WAINERMAN is a researcher at the Centro de Estudios de Poblacion, Buenos Aires, Argentina.

BEE-LAN CHAN WANG is assistant professor of sociology at Wheaton College, Wheaton, Illinois.

BARBARA YATES is professor, Department of Educational Policy Studies at the University of Illinois, Champaign/Urbana. She has written extensively about education in the Belgian Congo and is President-Elect of the Comparative and International Education Society.

400

Index

Madagascar
School enrollment rates, 19
Malaysia, 68-87, 334
Ethnic composition of, 70-71
Fertility and education, 315, 317,
320, 326, 327
Rates of return on women's educa-
tion, 221, 222
Secondary school students' educational
and career aspirations, 74-81
Urban/rural disparities, 70-71
Mali
School enrollment rates, 19
Maternal behavior and women's educa-
283-310, 340-41
Child development, 291-310
Child mortality, 288-91
Child's educational attainment, 23,
284-85
Child's nutrition, 284, 286
Mauretania
School enrollment rates, 19
Mexico
Fertility and education, 314, 317, 318
Labor force participation and women's
education, 213, 214-15, 217
Spatial diffusion models of girls'
education, 29
Middle East, 108
Literacy rates, 15
University enrollments, 47
Missionary Education, 23, 127-51
Morocco
Literacy rates, 14-15
Regional variation in school enroll-
ments, 23

Nepal
Fertility and education, 317, 319,
326, 327
Nigeria
Child development and mother's
education, 294-97
Child mortality and mother's educa-
tion, 288-91
Fertility and education, 315, 326

Labor force participation and
women's education, 213, 217
Muslims and school enrollments, 21,
108
Reading achievement in, 110
Yurobas, 288-91, 294-97
Non-formal education
Determinants of participation in
in India, 159-60
in Upper Volta, 88-103
Girls' expectations of, 170
Parents' expectations of, 170
Programs for women
in India, 152-72
in Upper Volta, 98-101
Texts for, 163-65
Wastage in, 168-69

Opportunity to Learn by Gender,
117-23

Pakistan (see also Bangladesh)
Fertility and education, 317, 319
Labor force participation and
women's education, 213, 216
Panama
Fertility and education, 314, 317
School survival rates, 17
Papua, New Guinea
Labor force participation and
women's education, 213, 216, 217
Parental status and girls' education, 26
Paraguay
Labor force participation and
women's education, 264-79, 339
Literacy rates, 266
School wastage rates, 266-67
Paternal education and child's schooling
in Senegal, 27
in Tunisia, 27
for daughters, 57-65
for sons, 57-65
Peru
Fertility and education, 314, 317
Labor force participation and women's
education, 213, 216

404

Labor force participation and women's
education, 217
Teachers
Attitudes toward girls' education, 25,
121–22, 191–93
Effect of teachers' gender on girls'
achievement, 110–11, 124–25
Selection for nonformal programs,
160–63
Teacher/student interactions, 121,
122–23, 191–96
Women as teachers, 20
Thailand
Fertility and education, 288, 314,
316, 317, 326, 327
Literacy rates, 14–15
Regional variation in school enroll-
ment, 23
Togo, 188–200, 336
Tunisia, 31–50, 333
Labor force participation and women's
education, 43–44
Parental status and girls' education,
26–27
School enrollments, 32–36, 332
Urban/rural disparities in, 36–41
School wastage rates, 34–35
Schooling and employment, 41–49
Turkey
Fertility and education, 288, 325
Labor force participation and women's
education, 216

United Kingdom. *See* England
United Nations Development Program
Project for Equal Access of
Women and Girls to Education,
88–103
United States, 110, 111, 112–13, 211
Child development and mother's
education, 293, 304–5
Child mortality and mother's educa-
tion, 260
Counseling practices, 119–20, 124
Curricula differentiation by gender,
117

Educational aspirations of girls, 82
Educational attainment of girls, 82
Fertility and education, 288
Higher education, 251
Labor force participation and women's
education, 213, 217, 218, 219
Mexican Americans, 304–5
Occupational segregation, 147
Peer tutoring, 125
USSR
Curricula differentiation, 119
Higher education, 251
Labor force participation and women's
education, 68
Peer tutoring, 125
Upper Volta, 88–103, 334
Enrollment rates, 19

Venezuela
Fertility and education, 314, 318
Labor force participation and women's
education, 213, 216

West Germany, 110
Fertility and education, 288
Higher education, 251
Women and the Professions
Career satisfaction, 252–58
in Chile, 230
in India, 249–63
Role conflicts, 253–58
Use of science in daily life, 259–61

Yugoslavia
Labor force participation and women's
education, 213, 215, 217, 218

Zaire
Curricula differentiation, 19, 132–138,
139–42, 335
Missionary education, 127–51
Post-colonial educational reforms,
139–40
School enrollments, 138, 143
Schooling and employment, 143–46